Michel Ulysse Maynard, Saint Louise de Marillac

Virtues and Spiritual Doctrine of St. Vincent de Paul

Michel Ulysse Maynard, Saint Louise de Marillac
Virtues and Spiritual Doctrine of St. Vincent de Paul
ISBN/EAN: 9783337424909
Printed in Europe, USA, Canada, Australia, Japan
Cover: Foto ©Lupo / pixelio.de

More available books at **www.hansebooks.com**

TRANSLATOR'S PREFACE.

The following translation has proved a labor indeed, but a labor of love. For long years the desire to see the "Virtues and Spiritual Doctrine of St. Vincent de Paul," clothed in an English dress has been constantly present to the translator. He had hoped, and waited, and longed for some able hand to undertake the task. He had prayed that some one, adequately fitted, might come across the work, and, charmed with its beauty and impressed with its suitableness for the present times, lovingly determine to make others sharers in his pleasure and profit. But expectation proved vain, hope withered, and longing died in delay. The thought arose, and would not away, that if he wished his desire fulfilled he must himself perform the work. Fully conscious of his limited powers he refused at first to listen; but, as the thought persisted, and suggested that love would compensate, in great measure, for what he might otherwise lack, he resolved, for the glory of God and the honor of his holy Patron, to make the attempt.

The result is now presented to the American public.

There were difficulties in the way. Among them was the existence of works of a similar nature, and apparently satisfying all that could be desired in relation to the life and doings of a particular saint. Of these it is a pleasure to mention and to recommend "The Spirit of St. Vincent de Paul," translated from the French of Mr. Ansart, by the Sisters of Charity, Mount St. Vincent, N. Y.

But, though St. Vincent be a particular saint, who lived in a certain locality, at a particular period, yet, since man's real life is in his works, it may be truly said that he has lived in every section of the known earth, and that to-day he labors with undiminished zeal in the busiest marts and centres of the civilized world as in the peaceful country villages and hamlets, amid peoples of the so-called civilized countries as among the semi-barbarous nations of the Orient; because suffering exists everywhere, and, wherever suffering and human misery are, there St. Vincent labors. Hence, it cannot be superfluous to multiply narrations of his life, or of his virtues; it cannot be esteemed out of place to recite to those who honor and revere him, who love him, other versions of his sayings and doings.

Moreover, the present work of all others, and there is no thought to derogate from their worth, presents most completely the virtue of the saint, and marks most fully and clearly his ideas and teachings in regard thereto. It specifically treats, as its title indicates, of the virtues of the saint and his spiritual doctrine. Other works exhibit his virtues in the history of his deeds. They are especially the work of the writers who narrate the circumstances of his life and draw their own conclusions. In the present the words of the saint himself are given. The entire book is scarcely other than the writings and discourses of the saint arranged and brought to bear on particular points. It is, as the author well remarks, a complete compendium of the writings of St. Vincent de Paul. The sum, the substance, both of all his conferences whether to the Missionaries and Daughters of Charity, or to the religious communities of which he had charge, or to the numerous societies of ecclesiastics, and of the laity of both sexes which sprung up at his word, and were willing, and actually did give their wealth and their time for the benefit of the poor and suffering whose father he was, and of the innumerable letters to individuals of all ranks, of all classes and of all countries, constitutes the book. The author has but little of his own. He never speaks but when to introduce the saint.

And this very feature has proved no little trial to the translator. Because, intent on fidelity to the sense, and even the very words of the saint, he has found it no easy task to transfer to ordinary intelligible English the complicated phrases and intricate sentences of the old style French of the sixteenth century. For, though Bossuet and Fenelon, Racine and Corneille, Boileau and La Fontaine were remodeling and immortalizing the language of the Frank, even while the poor and simple priest, Mr. Vincent, was providing the necessaries of life for entire provinces racked and ruined by war and famine, still the old fashion held sway, and but slowly and reluctantly gave way before the new.

To grasp the main idea, then, of the saint, and to pay attention to the accompanying and confirmatory clauses, and make them a united whole in English as they are in the French, was a serious obstacle. He presumes to think he has been faithful and exact in perceiving the meaning of the Saint and rendering it into running English. May be his hopes have overleaped his ability. His desire and effort, however, have been sincere and constant.

The author presupposes in his readers a general knowledge of the main facts in the life of the saint. Hence, frequent reference is made to the story of that life. This may prove to some an unsatisfactory feature of the work. Yet, everything in the book is complete and independent. True, for a more comprehensive understanding of the degree of virtue practised, for a deeper and more intimate feeling of the heroism of many of the acts narrated, an acquaintance with the history of the life of the Saint is requisite. For the work is a companion to the *Life*. It is presumed that the major portion of those who will read it are sufficiently familiar with the name and works of the Apostle of Charity, and, therefore, that a mere mention of certain circumstances is all that is required to recall the picture in all its vividness. Or, again, it is hoped that the reading of the work will create such interest as to beget in those, to whom the life of the Saint of suffering humanity is unknown, the desire to peruse it in all its details.

The general plan of the work is of the simplest. The author claims no credit therefor. He simply followed in the path of those preceding him, or rather, he says, in that mapped out by the Church both for them and him. For the Church, in her process of canonization, interrogates the memory of the one proposed for the honors of her altars, first in regard to the theological virtues of faith, hope, and charity, and then, their annexes. This plan, originated by the Church, has become that of all hagiographal writers, and any departure therefrom would only indicate temerity and over-weening self-love.

The particular method adopted in each of the chapters is

rather to hasten their ruin than promote their advancement. And this dependence ever kept him in humility, ever impelled him to seek by all the means in his power to learn the will of his Creator, and, once assured of the Divine pleasure, to boldly and with unbounded confidence set to work to accomplish it; never for an instant permitting anxiety for the result to trouble his mind or disturb the peace of his soul. God's work it was, and God would have it performed as it pleased Himself. This was sufficient.

Such was the guiding principle of Vincent's life, and such he taught all with whom he came in contact. For he ever strove to imitate Jesus Christ and to induce others to imitate Him. And what has been the life of the Savior if not absolute dependence on God, His Father, and faithful performance of all the Divine wills?

And this constitutes the charm in the virtues and teachings of St. Vincent. Though his instructions are given ordinarily to those who are called to the higher grades of piety, still the humblest, the simplest, can apply them and practise them. They may make them their own and yet outwardly go not out of their ordinary way. They can find in them the highest excellence of virtue, and by their practice become most holy servants of their God, without the slightest fear of illusion, without the accompanying vanity and deadly self-complacency of great works.

That the perusal of the virtues and spiritual instructions of St. Vincent de Paul may inspire some little effort to make them their own, and thus honor God and imitate the Saint, is what is most humbly and earnestly prayed for, and constitutes the highest praise and reward his readers can bestow upon the

TRANSLATOR.

PUBLISHER'S PREFACE.

In giving to the American public the following translation of Abbe Maynard's "Virtues and Spiritual Doctrines of St. Vincent de Paul," we feel that we are contributing, not a little, to the grand cause of Catholic literature. It does not befit us to say one word either in praise or in blame of the merits of the work. The high commendation which it has already received leads us, however, to indulge the hope that it is destined to fill to advantage its particular and peculiar sphere of usefullness.

The work is issued from the office of the NIAGARA INDEX, the organ of the Students of the Seminary of Our Lady of Angels. The typographical appearance is as perfect as we, with our limited facilities, could expect. Errors, indeed, may be found, but they are not of such importance as to demand the introduction of a department devoted to their correction. Any inaccuracies, then, that are discoverable throughout the translation will, we doubt not, be charitably laid to the credit of inexperience; and of anxiety, the never failing attendant of first endeavors.

The appendix, containing letters and heretofore unpublished selections from the discourses and writings of Mademoiselle Le Gras are presented almost literally. Even the title, "Letters and Unpublished Fragments of Mademoiselle Le Gras" indicates this. Both the "Virtues" and the "Letters" are now, for the first time, presented in an English dress, and that they may prove highly beneficial to their readers is the heartfelt wish of

THE PUBLISHER.

CONTENTS.

CHAP.	PAGE.
I—Faith	1
II—Hope and Confidence in God	6
III—Love of God	20
IV—Conformity to the Will of God—Resignation and Indifference	27
V—Presence of God	40
VI—Prayer	52
VII—Devotion and Piety towards God and the most Holy Sacrament—Imitation of Jesus Christ	70
VIII—Devotion to the Blessed Virgin and the Saints	81
IX—Zeal for the Glory of God and the Salvation of Souls	84
X—Charity	105
XI—Meekness	166
XII—Humility	180
XIII—Obedience	215
XIV—Simplicity	228
XV—Prudence	238
XVI—Justice and Gratitude	249
XVII—Detachment from Earthly Goods, and Love of Poverty	261
XVIII—Mortification	274
XIX—Chastity	294
XX—Composure of Spirit	301
XXI—Fortitude and Patience	305
XXII—Patience in Sickness	323
XXIII—Method of Direction	335

APPENDIX.

LETTERS.	PAGE.
I—Love of God	1
II—Little Practices of Devotion	3
III—While on a Pilgrimage	5

LETTERS.	PAGE.
IV—When Obedience calls to another House	5
V—Some Advices and Some Strength	6
VI—Advice in Regard to Recreation	6
VII—To the Sisters in Poland on the Occasion of sending other Sisters	8
VIII—On Christmas	9
IX—Mutual Affection	10
X—Against Division between Superior and Inferior	10
XI—Disunion among Sisters, and Discouragement in Contradictions	12
XII—Same Subject, to the Sisters at Nantes	13
XIII—To the Same	13
XIV—To the Same, on Mutual Support	14
XV—To the same in sending them a letter of St. Vincent	14
XVI—Patience in Trials	16
XVII—Same Subject—Danger of Office	17
XVIII—Some extracts of Letters	17
XIX—Advices to Sisters suggested by their names	18
XX—To a sick Sister	19
XXI—Petition for the Apostolic Benediction, 1652	20
XXII—Will of Mademoiselle Le Gras	20

APPROBATIONS.

The admirable work entitled: "The Virtues and Spiritual Doctrine of St. Vincent de Paul," by the Abbe Maynard, now for the first time appearing in an English dress, and published by the "Seminary of Our Lady of Angels," has been highly commended by his Eminence, Cardinal Marlot, Arch-bishop of Paris, and very favorably received by the Catholic people of France. The translation by a Priest of the Congregation of the Mission, now offered to the American public, has my fullest approbation, and I must also hope that the enterprise shown in contributing so valuable a work to our American Catholic literature, and publishing the same from the College press, will be appreciated and encouraged, as it deserves. The work itself cannot fail to be appreciated wheresoever known, and to do good wheresoever read. The spirit of St. Vincent is revealed in his virtues and spiritual doctrine, and the spirit of Vincent is the spirit and essence of genuine Christian charity, the very life and soul of Christianity. All classes will be benefitted by the perusal of this work. The simple faithful who seek to follow Christ and lead Christian lives, lives conformed to the maxims of the Gospel, will be edified and instructed and incited to imitation; the clergy will see the model Priest of modern times practising as well as teaching the virtues that adorn and sanctify the priestly character and calling; the religious of both sexes will find in its pages a practical illustration of that higher inner life and high religious perfection which they profess, and learn after Vincent how to sanctify themselves by the regular observances and ordinary every day duties of their community life. "The Virtues and Spiritual Doctrine of St. Vincent de Paul" will naturally become the favorite book of spiritual lecture in the conferences of St. Vincent, and the members of this wide-spread and admirable society will learn from it what true Christian charity means and what it imposes, will learn to kindle and keep alive in their own hearts love for the poor and disinterested zeal in promoting their temporal and spiritual welfare, and thus present to the world, in their every-day lives, an example of true charity that makes them love their neighbor for God's sake, and, by faith, see in the poor whom they succor only the needy and suffering members of Christ. May, then, this little work be widely circulated and fulfil its mission by teaching the principles and practices of the supernatural life, founded on faith and culminating in divine charity, which is the bond of perfection and the touchstone of all true religion! May it raise up in every state of life imitators of Vincent de Paul, true followers of our meek and humble and merciful Savior!

† STEPHEN VINCENT.
BISHOP OF BUFFALO.

Buffalo, May 5th, 1877,

The following letter of approbation, an honor to the author and to us a memorial of His Eminence, Cardidal Marlot, Arch-bishop of Paris is attached to the original work.

Paris, June 19th, 1864.

MY DEAR ABBE:—

I am grateful for your kind remembrance and touched by your thoughtfulness in sending me your book entitled: *Virtues and Spiritual Doctrine of St. Vincent de Paul.* These pages are most profound and edifying, and are, moreover, a fit and natural compliment of your history of the holy founder of the Mission. All those who are anxious to maintain themselves in the true spirit of Christianity, and to make new progress in virtue, will read them with interest. May their number increase from day to day, and may the posterity of the illustrious Priest, whose name serves as standard underneath which such generous devotedness is displayed, augment in like manner!

Accept, my dear Abbe, the assurance of my affectionate regard.

† G. ARCHBISHOP OF PARIS.

To THE ABBE MAYNARD, CANON OF POITIERS.

VIRTUES
AND
SPIRITUAL DOCTRINE
OF
ST. VINCENT DE PAUL.

CHAPTER I.

FAITH.

I

Faith is the first requisite to approach unto God (Heb. xi. 6,) and to engage in His service. It is the root of all Christian virtue, the foundation of the entire spiritual edifice. Such is the idea that St. Vincent had of faith, and he, therefore, regulated his conduct according to its dictates, and made it the corner-stone of all his holy undertakings.

Wonderful faith in St. Vincent! it partook of the simplicity of childhood and the vigor of age; it formed within him the principle of supernatural life, and he became the source whence sprang that charity which embraced the entire world.

His was a strong faith, and like unto those trees which take but the stronger root when tossed and beaten by the winds and storms, a faith that grew in strength when temptations assailed. At Tunis, this faith resists the blandishments and menaces of his masters; at the court of Queen Margaret it comes out victorious from the temptation of unbelief which, to free a friend, he had accepted; in the troubles of Jansenism it escapes all the snares of heresy and the seductions of sectaries. "I thank God," did he love frequently to say, "for having preserved me in the integrity of faith in the midst of an age that has brought forth so many heresies and scandalous opinions, and for the grace of never having held any opinion contrary to that of the Church. By a special protection of God, notwithstanding the many dangerous occasions wherein I might have been turned from the right path, I have always been on the side of truth"

His Faith, we see, was not only strong, but, moreover, pure and simple, that is, resting solely on the first truth, God and on the authority of the Church.

His was a faith at once expansive and communicative, as are all Christian virtues. It loved to diffuse itself by means of catechising and instructing, particularly among the poor peasants of the country; as the ocean, it sought to extend to all parts of the world, and being unable by its own direct efforts, it succeeded through the instrumentality of a company of Missionaries sent out to every infidel land.

An aggressive faith he had, ever on the alert against error, a faith armed with that *Credo* which the Saint wore as a breastplate; armed with prayer which he regarded as the best defense in combat, and as a source of all light and strength; armed with zeal and charity to preserve from the contagion of evil doctrines first his children, then the religious and secular communities of which he was Superior, and, finally, doctors of divinity and bishops of the Church whom he retained in the faith.

His faith was humble even in its victories. "Though," said the Saint, "God gave me the grace to discern the truth from error, even before the definition of the Holy See, still I have never had any feeling of complacency or vain joy because my judgment was formed in conformity with that of the Church fully recognizing that it was an effect of the pure mercy of God towards me, to Whom, therefore, I must render all the glory."

He possessed, finally, a full and active faith; a faith that enlightened his understanding, warmed his heart, animated his thoughts and affections, his words and acts, and guided him in everything, and everywhere, according to the truths and maxim of Jesus Christ; a faith that guided him not merely in things that referred directly to God, but which he introduced even into temporal and human affairs. He undertook nothing of which faith was not the principle, and which he did not refer to a supernatural end.

II

Such was the virtue of faith in St. Vincent; such likewise was the faith that he taught others. He reprehended those who, in explaining Christian truth, relied unduly on the light of science, or on the strength of human reason; and those who examined these truths with curiosity and temerity did not escape his censure. Against all he made use of this comparison: "As the more we fix the eye on the sun the less we see, so, in the truths of religion, the more we strain reason, the less we know by faith. It is enough that the Church proposes these truths; we certainly should not refuse to believe her and to submit." And he added: "The Church is the kingdom of God, and He inspires her rulers with principles of good government. His Holy Spirit presides over the councils; from Him have proceeded the light shed throughout the world which has enlightened the saints, dazzled the wicked, dispelled doubts, rendered truth evident, laid bare errors and disclosed the paths wherein the Church in general, and each of the faithful in particular, may walk in safety."

His charity and moderation had reached their limit, and yet he was requested to exercise both towards the people of Port Royal. He simply answered: "When a dispute has been decided there is no agreement possible, save in adhering to the judgment given. Before these gentlemen were condemned they did their utmost to have error triumph over the truth, and unwilling then to listen to any terms of agreement, they were so intemperate in their desire to obtain the upper hand that resistance hardly dared offer itself. Even since the Holy See has decided against them they have sought to give divers constructions to the Papal constitutions so that their effect might be evaded. And, though on the one hand they have made a semblance of sincerely submitting themselves to the common Father of the Faithful, and of receiving the constitutions in the real sense wherein the propositions of Jansenius were condemned, nevertheless their writers, who have maintained these propositions, and have written books and apologies in their defense, have, as yet, neither said nor written a word in disavowal. What union, then, can we have with them since they have no sincere intention of submitting? What moderation is possible in regard to what the Church has decided? They are matters of faith alike incapable of alteration or arrangement, and, by consequence, they cannot be adjustable to the sentiments of these gentlemen. Theirs it is to submit, and unite with us in the same belief, and in a true and sincere submission to the head of the Church. Without this we can only pray God for their conversion."

He blamed all hurry and anxiety even in the most holy works, for he saw therein a movement of nature and a hidden distrust of Providence. One day he wrote to Madamoiselle Le Gras: "I always see in you somewhat of human sentiment; you think all is lost when you see me unwell. Oh, woman of little faith! why have you not more confidence in the guidance and example of Jesus Christ? This Savior of the world confided in God, the Father, for the state of the entire Church, and you think He will fail you in regard to a handful of daughters whom His Providence has evidently gathered together! Go, Madamoiselle, humble yourself very much before God."

Little progress in virtue and in the things of God he attributed to the too great confidence placed in human reasons. "No, no," he said one day, "only eternal truth is capable of satisfying the heart, and conducting us safely. Believe me, we have but to lean firmly, strongly, on any one of the perfections of God, such as His Goodness, His Providence, His Truth, His Immensity,— we have but to ground ourselves well on these foundations to become perfect in a short time. Not that it is not well to convince by strong reasoning and solid argument; these always prove serviceable when subservient to the truths of faith. Experience teaches that he who preaches according to the light of faith effects more in souls than he whose discourse is filled with philosophical arguments and scientific reasoning. And the reason is that the lights derived from faith are always accompanied with a certain heavenly unction that secretly penetrates to the heart. Hence we may judge if it be not necessary, as well for our own perfection as for the salvation of souls, to follow always and in all things the light of faith.

He still further taught that things should not be looked upon as they externally appear, but were to be considered as they appeared in the eyes of God. And this he based on the word of the Apostle: "*For the things which are seen are temporal; but the things which are not seen are eternal.*" (2 Cor., ii., 2.) "I ought not," he said, "regard a poor peasant or a poor woman according to the exterior, nor according to the intellectual capacity, more especially as oftentimes so earthly and so stupid is he, that he seems to possess neither the figure nor mind of rational beings. But reverse the medal, and you will see in the light of faith that the Son of God, who has wished to be poor, is represented to us in these poor people; that, in His passion, He scarcely had the figure of man, and that the Gentiles considered Him a fool, and the Jews a rock of scandal; besides, He calls Himself the evangelist of the poor: "*To preach the Gospel to the poor He hath sent Me.*" (Luke ii., 18.) Oh, my God, how beautiful it is to look upon the poor, when we consider them in God, and in the esteem in which Jesus Christ held them! But to the flesh and to a worldly spirit they appear contemptible."

CHAPTER II.

HOPE AND CONFIDENCE IN GOD.

I.

Hope is begotten of faith and is proportional to it. He, who knows God and believes in Him can hope but in Him, can rely but on Him. What the view of Divine truth disengaged from all human reasoning is to faith, the goodness alone of God is to hope which, thenceforth, disdaining men and their earthly resources can no longer confide, no longer rest save in the Divine Providence.

Vincent so full of faith, carried his hope, after the example of the father of believers, so far as to hope even against hope. When everything seemed to fail him, then he hoped the more.

In the beginning of his motto this holy hope alone inspired him, alone directed him in their prosecution, alone sustained him in the midst of difficulties and obstacles, and alone assured him of success.

When there was question of undertaking anything for the service of God he commenced by having recourse to prayer to know the Divine Will. Assured of this, he began the work, and abandoned himself to the Divine mercy. Without doubt, according to the order of Providence itself, he made use of all the means that prudence suggested, but he did not place his reliance on them, he counted only on the assistance of Heaven. Even in the beginning he neglected human agencies. He first allowed Providence to act, delaying as long as possible from mixing his action with the Divine action, so convinced was he that the less of man there is in any affair the more there is of God. Once engaged, after this Christian manner, he feared nothing, either for himself or for his children. In vain the timorous or the worldly wise majority magnified the obstacles, or strove to demonstrate the impossibility of the undertaking.

"Let us allow our Lord to act" he answers, "it is His work and as it has pleased Him to begin it we may rest assured that He will perfect it in the manner most pleasing to Himself. Courage, then; let us trust in our Lord Who will be with us first and last in a work to the undertaking of which He has called us."

Then he would throw himself blindly into the greatest and most painful enterprises, redoubling his confidence in God in the midst of difficulties, as the soldier redoubles his ardor amid the dangers of battle. As the excessive expenses undergone by the order of God did not cause him any fear of exhausting the treasury of Providence, so neither did the wants and pressing necessities of his houses, though grieving his paternal heart, dim his hope, or alarm him in regard to the future of his Congregation.

Afflictions and disappointments, labors and perils, far from subduing him, only served as occasions to testify confidence in God, and to depend more entirely and absolutely on His will. The result, moreover, of any work mattered little to him; good or evil, he accepted it as coming from the hand of God and equally manifested gratitude for His mercy.

And he acted in this manner not only in things of secondary interest, but also in those that he had most at heart, as for instance, the birth, continuation and increase of that Congregation of Missionaries that was as dear to him as life. Whilst proceedings were going on at the Court of Rome for the erection of his band of Missionaries into a congregation, and whilst, at the same time, arrangements were being made for the transfer of the rich priory of St. Lazarus to Vincent, he said, not through presumption, but from Christian certainty of success: "I fear but my sins, and not for the success of our cause either in Rome or in Paris, neither for the bulls nor for the affair of St. Lazarus. Sooner or later all will be accomplished. *They that fear the Lord have hoped in the Lord: he is their helper and protector.*" (Ps. cxiii. 11.) And that the dependence on the designs of God which presided at the birth of his Congregation should still preside over its extension he never wished to make, nor would he allow to be made.

the least effort to obtain benefices, establishments, or subjects. Between two favorable propositions made him, he felt himself induced to prefer the less advantageous; between two subjects, to prefer him whose birth was the more humble, whose condition was the poorer, whose mind and knowledge were mediocre, lest in his choice there should be anything that savored of cupidity, of ambition, or of any other natural inspiration.

II.

To ground those under him in these maxims and in this manner of acting, he induced them to conceive a great diffidence in themselves, and to become thoroughly convinced that by their own efforts they could do nothing save spoil everything in the work and designs of God. He then dwelt on the greatness of the Divine mercy. "God, said he, "is a fountain wherefrom each draws according to his wants. He, who needs six, takes six pailsfull, he who requires three, only three, and the little bird that wants only to moisten its beak flies away immediately after; a traveller must drink from the hollow of his hand." Impressed with this idea of the mercy of God he desired entire abandonment to Providence, just as the child abandons itself to its nurse "If this nurse places the child on her right arm, the child is content; if she change it to the left, it does not mind, and, provided it has the breast it is content. Let us, then say to ourselves: God is my father. Let him put me on the right side, that is in peace and content, or on the left, which signifies the cross, it matters not; H will strengthen me and I will hope in Him." Confidence in God it was that he gave as a Viaticum to those he sent into the distant and difficult missions. "Go, Gentlemen, in the name of God." he said to them; "it is He who sends you; for His service and His glory you undertake this voyage and this mission; He, then, will be your guide, He will protect and aid you. This we hope for from His infinite Goodness. Keep yourselves always in a firm dependence on His faithful guidance; have recourse to Him in all places and in all circumstances; throw yourselves into His arms, for you should recognize Him as a tender father, with a firm confidence that He will assist you and bless your labors."

Did they grow weary and weak under the burden, it was confidence in God wherewith he renewed their courage. He wrote to their superior: "I sympathize with you in your labors; they are great, and they continue increasing whilst sickness is diminishing your forces It is our good Lord who does this, and certainly He will not leave so great a burden on your hands without aiding you to sustain it; He will, even Himself, be your strength as well as your recompense for the extraordinary services that, in this pressing need, you render Him. Believe me, when Our Lord gives a helping hand three can effect more than ten; and He always does when He deprives us of human means and places us in the necessity of doing what is above our strength; we will, however, beseech His Divine Goodness that it may be pleasing to Him to restore your sick to health, and to infuse into your community a great hope in His mercy."

He did not wish them to lose confidence, in times of want and scarcity. "You must not be surprised," he wrote them on these occasions, "nor frightened because the year is bad, no, never, if many be bad. God abounds in riches. Nothing has been wanting to you up to the present; why, then, fear for the future? You would like to have all provision made so as to be assured of having all you desire. I say you wish so according to nature, for I think, that according to the spirit, you are glad to have an opportunity of relying on God alone, and, like a real poor man, of depending on the liberality of this Lord, who is infinitely rich. May God help the poor people; they are to be pitied in times of distress because they do not know how to turn this time to their advantage, nor do they seek first the kingdom of God and His justice that they may be made worthy to receive the things necessary for this, over and above the succor required for eternal life."

Losses the most ruinous were not to shake their confidence "All that God does He does for the best; and therefore we must hope that this loss, since it comes from God, will be profitable to us. All things are of benefit to the just; and we are assured that the adversities we receive from the hand of God will become a joy and a blessing. I pray for them, gentlemen and my dear brethren; let us thank God for this affair, for the derivation of this property, and for the disposition He has given us to accept this loss for His love. The loss is great, but His adorable wisdom will know how to turn it to our good, and that in a way that to us is, at present, unknown, but one day we will see ; yes, we will see. And I trust that the manner after which you all have borne yourselves in the accident, so little foreseen, will serve as a foundation to the grace God will give you, of making in future a perfect use of all the afflictions it will please Him to send us."

Nor should intrigues and persecutions trouble them any the more. He wrote: "As regards the intrigues that are being carried on against us, let us pray God to guard us from this spirit; since we blame it in others it is all the more reasonable that we keep it far from ourselves. It is a fault against Divine Providence which renders those who commit it unworthy the care God takes of everything. Let us establish ourselves in entire dependence on His holy leading, and on the assurance that in so doing all that men will do or say against us will turn to our good. Yes, my dear sir, even were the entire world to rise up to destroy us it could do nothing but what is pleasing to God in whom we have placed our hope. I beg you to enter into these sentiments, and to dwell firmly therein so that hereafter your mind will not be troubled with useless apprehensions."

The sense of their own imperfections and miseries should not, according to him, militate against their trust in God. "We have within us," he said to them, "the germ of the omnipotence of God and this ought to be a great motive to hope and to place all our confidence in Him, nothwithstanding all our poverty. No, we must not be astonished when we see miseries among us, for each has his own good share. It is well to know them, but not to be immoderately troubled by them; it is even good to turn away the thought of them when it leads to discouragement, and redouble our confidence in God and our abandonment into his tender arms." Still further he wrote: "I know the fidelity and care you have for the work of God: what remains for you, then, but to rest in peace? God only demands this with an humble acquiescence in the success which he gives, and which, I am sure, will be complete in your soul. Why, then, become discouraged? You point out to me your miseries. Alas! and who is there that is not full of them! The only thing is to know them and to love the humiliation arising from them, as you do, without stopping save to lay a strong foundation of confidence in God; for then the house is built upon a rock and when the storm comes it remains firm. Do not be afraid, then. This is your case, I know; for these feelings of distrust and discouragement are but from nature, and not from your heart, which is far too generous for anything like that. Let God, then, do with us and our works as he chooses. Though our pains and troubles for men be in vain, and though they show only ingratitude and contempt for us, still we will not neglect, on that account, to continue, knowing that in this way we fulfill the law which is to love God with our whole heart and our neighbor as ourselves."

He frequently taught them this maxim: "When God begins to do good to a creature, He continues to do so to the end unless the creature become unworthy." And he said again: "When God once takes a soul into his affections, no matter what that soul does, He supports it. Have you never seen a father who has a little child that he loves very much? He bears with all the little one pleases to do; he even at times calls upon it. "Bite me, my child." And why thus? Because he loves that little child. God acts the same with us." And in conjunction, he cited the example of their own Congregation. "Let us have confidence in God, gentlemen and my brethren, but let it be entire and perfect, holding it for certain that having once begun His work in us He will finish it. For, I ask you, who is it that has established the Congregation? who has appointed us to the missions, to the ordinations, to the conferences, to the retreats, and other works in which we are engaged? Is it I? By no means. Is it Mr. Portail whom God united to me in the very beginning? Not at all; for we did not think of them, had no design of them. And who then, is the author of all this? It is God, it is His paternal Providence, and His pure Goodness. For we are all pitiable workers and poor ignorant persons; and among us there are few, if any at all, who are of noble birth, powerful, learned, or capable of anything. It is God, then, who has done all this, and who in doing it, made use of persons according to His own pleasure so that all the glory should redound to Him; for if we place it in men, or if we lean on any advantage of nature, or fortune, God will withdraw from us. But, some one will say, we must make friends both for ourselves as individuals, and for the community—Oh! my brethren, let us beware of listening to such a thought for we will be deceived. Let us seek solely God; he will provide us with friends and with all else, in such a way that we will want for nothing. Do you wish to know why we do not succeed in such, or such an employment? It is because we lean too much upon ourselves This preacher, that superior, this confessor trusts too much in his prudence, in his learning, in himself. What does God do? He withdraws from him; He leaves him there; and though he works, all that he does produces no fruit, that thus, he may recognize his own uselessness, and learn from his own experience that, no matter how talented, he can do nothing without God."

We must let God act, then; we must intrigue for no favor, not be sollicitous, we should fear nothing. On this subject he wrote to one of his priests in Rome. "Every day you give me reason to praise God for your affection for the congregation and your care for its affairs; and I do with all my heart: but I must likewise say to you, as our Lord said to Martha, there is a little too much sollicitude in your action, and that only one thing is necessary, namely to allow more to God and His direction than you do. Foresight is good when it is subject to Him; but it goes to excess when we become anxious to avoid anything we fear: we hope more from our own care than from His Providence, and we imagine we do a great deal in anticipating His orders by our disorder which causes us to trust rather in human prudence than in His word. This divine Savior assures us in His Gospel, that neither the little sparrow, nor even a single hair of our head will fall without His permission; and you fear our congregation will not be able to maintain itself if we do not use such and such precautions, and if we do not do this thing and that; so that should we defer doing it others will come and establish themselves upon our ruins. So soon as a design against us appears we must oppose it; should anyone wish to profit by our moderation we must be beforehand with him, else all is lost. This is nearly the sense of your letters; and, what is worse, your quick, lively disposition urges you to act as you speak, and in your enthusiasm you think you possess sufficient light without having need to receive any from others. Oh! my dear sir, how little this proceeding becomes a missionary."

He took delight in frequently citing the example of Abraham as one of perfect confidence. "You remember this grand old patriarch whose son, God had promised, was to people the entire earth? And yet He commands him to sacrifice this son. Whereupon any person might have said: If Abraham put his son to death how is God to fulfill His promise? This holy man, however, who had accustomed his mind to submit to all the wishes of God, disposes himself to execute the order without putting himself in pain about anything else. It is the affair of God, might he have said, to think of everything; if I execute His command He will fulfill His promise—But how?—I do not know; it is enough to know that He is All-Powerful; I am going to offer Him what I hold most dear in the world since He wishes it—But it is my only son—No matter—But, in taking the life of this child, I will deprive God of the means of keeping His word?—It is all the same; He desires it; it must be done.—But if I preserve him my race will be blessed. God has said—Yes, but He has also said I should put him to death; He has manifested it to me; I will obey Him, no matter what happens, and I will hope in His promises—Admire this confidence; he is in no trouble about what will happen. And yet the affair concerned him very nearly; but he hopes all will go well since God takes part in it. Why should not we, gentlemen, have a like confidence if we leave to God the care of all that concerns us, and if we prefer that which He commands?

"In this connection, too, will we not admire the fidelity of the children of Jonadab, son of Rachel? He was a good man who received an inspiration from God to live in a manner different from other men, to dwell in a tent and not in a house. He abandons, therefore, the one that he has. Behold him now in the country; here the idea strikes him to plant no vine so as not to drink wine; and in fact he plants none and never after drank wine. He forbade his children to sow wheat or other grains, to plant trees, or to cultivate gardens. See, then, they are all without bread, without grain, without fruit. What, then, will you do, my poor Jonadab?"

"Do you imagine that either you, or your family, can subsist without eating? 'We will eat,' he says within himself, 'whatever God will send.' This seems very hard; even the poorest religious orders do not carry the spirit of renunciation to such a degree. However, be that as it may, the confidence of this man was such that he deprived himself of all the commodities of this life to depend absolutely, he and his children, on the care of Divine Providence. And they continued in this way for three hundred and fifty years ; that is he, his children, and his children's children. This was so agreeable to God that, complaining to Jeremias of the hardness of his people abandoned to their pleasures, he tells him : " *Go to those obdurates, and tell them there is a man who does this, &c.*"

"Jeremias, then, to verify the extreme abstemiousness of the father and his children causes the Rechabites to be brought to him. He sets a table, and places thereon bread, and wine, and glasses. When they are come he says to them: 'I am commissioned by God to bid you drink wine'—' And we,' answered the Rechabites, 'have a command not to drink ; for so long a time we have not drunk, our father having forbidden it.' Now, if this father had so great a confidence that God would provide for the subsistence of his family that he gave himself no trouble, and if the children were so careful in faithfully carrying out the intentions of their father, oh, gentlemen, what confidence should not we have, that, no matter in what state God may place us, He will provide us with all that is necessary ! What is our fidelity to rule in comparison with that of these children who, otherwise, were not obliged to abstain from the comforts of this life, and yet practised such poverty ? Oh, my God! gentlemen, Oh my God! my Brethren, let us ask of His Divine Goodness a great confidence in Him no matter what happens in our regard. Provided we be faithful to H m nothing will be wanting to us ; He will Himself live in us. He will conduct us, defend and love us ; all that we say, all that we do, all will be acceptable to him."

" Look at the birds. They neither sow, nor reap ; yet God sets a table for them everywhere; He gives them clothing and nourishment, He extends His Providence to the flowers of the field, to the lilies whose ornaments are so magnificent that Solomon in all his glory had nothing similar. Now, if God thus cares for the birds and plants why will you not trust in a God so good and so provident ? What ! will you trust rather in yourselves than in Him ? And yet, you well know that He can do all, and you nothing; notwithstanding this, you dare confide in your own endeavors rather than in His goodness, in your poverty rather than in His wealth! Oh misery of man!"

"I will say here, however, that Superiors are obliged to look after the wants of each individual and provide all that is necessary; and as God takes care to furnish all His creatures, even the little midge, with what is necessary, He wishes that superiors and officers, as instruments of His Providence, would see that nothing be wanting, either to the priests, clerics, or to the brothers; either to a hundred persons, two hundred, three hundred, or more, were they in the house; either to the little or to the great. But my Brethren, you in your turn should quietly rest in the loving care of the same Divine Providence for your maintenance, and content yourselves with what it gives without seeking to know whether the community has it or not; nor should you trouble yourselves about anything except to seek first the kingdom of God, for His infinite Wisdom will supply all the rest."

"Not long ago, I asked a Carthusian, who is prior of a house, if, for the government of their temporal matters, they called a council of the religious? 'We summon,' he answered me, 'the officers, such as the superior and the procurator; the others have no concern; they occupy themselves only in chanting the praises of God and in doing what obedience and the rule prescribe.' With us, thanks be to God, the same practice holds. Let us continue firm in it; we, too, are obliged to possess property and to care for it in order to meet all demands. There was a time when the Son of God sent his disciples without money or provisions; afterwards He judged it proper to have wherewith to maintain his company and to assist the poor. The Apostles continued in the same way; and St. Paul says of himself that he labored with his own hands, and that he collected for Christians who were in want. It belongs, then, to superiors to watch over the management of the house; but let them care, also, that this vigilance over temporal things do not lessen that which regards virtue; and let them manage so that the spiritual life will be vigorous in their houses, and that God will there reign over everything. This should be their first object."

He gave the same advice, and prescribed the same conduct

for persons from without, who came to consult him. "Put away from your mind whatever causes you pain," he told them, "God will take care of it. You cannot allow yourself any anxiety in regard to this matter without, so to speak, saddening the heart of God, because He sees you do not honor Him sufficiently with holy confidence. Trust in Him, I beseech you, and you will obtain the accomplishment of all that your heart desires. I say again, cast aside all those thoughts of mistrust which you sometimes entertain. And why should not your soul be full of confidence since by His mercy it is the dear daughter of our Lord?... Oh! how great are the treasures hidden in holy Providence, and how sovereignly do they who follow, but do not crowd it, honor our God. I recently heard a noble, high in power, say that he had thoroughly learned this truth from his own experience, for he had never undertaken by himself but four things, and these instead of advantage brought him injury. Is it not true that you wish, as is but reasonable, your servant should never undertake anything without you, or your order? And if this be reasonable in man with his fellow man, how much more so is it in the Creator, with His creature?"

He did not believe there could be excess of confidence in God. Said he: "Just as you cannot believe too firmly in the truths of faith, so, too, it is impossible to hope too much in God. It is true, we may be deceived either in hoping for that which God has not promised, or in hoping for what he has promised only under condition, when we are unwilling to fulfill the condition: as for instance—a sinner hopes for pardon and yet does not wish to forgive his brother; he asks for mercy and will not change his life; he hopes to overcome temptations and yet neither combats nor resists them. All such hopes are false and illusory; but true hope founded on the goodness of God and on the merits of Jesus Christ can never be too great."

With such principles, both in heart and mind, the Saint naturally combated in others, as in himself, all temptation to despair. He wrote, on this point, to an ecclesiastic who confided to him his troubles. "I hope, then since you wrote your letter, God has dissipated the clouds that overshadowed you; hence, I will say but a word in passing. It seems to me you have some doubt whether you are of the number of the elect. To which I will answer that, though it be true that no person, without a special revelation from God, possesses infallible marks of his predestination yet, according to the testimony of St. Paul, there are marks whereby to know the true children of God so probably that there is scarcely room for doubt. And these marks, my dear Sir, I see in you, by the grace of God; the very letter wherein you tell me you do not see them discloses a number of them, and my long acquaintance with you points out the others. Believe me, Sir, I do not know a soul more given to God, nor a heart more free from evil and more ardent for good than your own— But, you tell me, it does not appear so to you. And I answer that God does not always allow his chosen ones to discern, amid the movements of corrupt nature, the purity of their interior, so that they may have occasion to humble themselves without ceasing, and that their treasure, being hidden, may be in greater security—The holy Apostle had seen the wonders of Heaven; but he did not for this reason consider himself justified, for he perceived within himself too much darkness, too many struggles. Still he had such confidence in God that he thought nothing in the world capable of separating him from the charity of Jesus Christ. This example, Sir, ought to suffice to keep you in peace amidst your doubts, and to give you an entire and perfect confidence in the infinite goodness of Our Lord, Who, desirous of completing the work of your sanctification, urges you to cast yourself into the hands of His Providence. Let His paternal love conduct you, then, for He loves you; and so far from rejecting a man of virtue, as you are, on the contrary He never abandons a sinner that hopes in His mercy."

But it was to his Missionaries and to his Daughters of Charity that he took pleasure in recommending Confidence in God. To the Missionaries he said: "The true Missionary ought never be in trouble about the goods of this world, but should throw all his cares on the Providence of the Lord, holding it for certain that, while he is well established in Charity, and well grounded in this confidence, he will always be under the protection of God, and consequently, no evil can come to him, and no good can fail him, even when he imagines, according to appearances, that all is going to ruin. I do not say this of myself; it is the Sacred Scriptures that teach it, and that declare: '*He that dwelleth in the aid of the Most High shall abide under the protection of the God of Heaven.*' (Ps. xc. I.) He who abides in the confidence of God will ever be favored with a special protection, and in this state he should deem it certain that no evil will befall him, because for him all things work to his benefit, and no good will be wanting since God, giving Himself to him, brings all necessary goods, both for body and soul. And hence, my Brethren, you should hope that, whilst you remain constant in this confidence, not only will you be preserved from all evil, and all sad accidents, but also that you will abound in all kinds of good."

This same confidence he counselled to the Daughters of Charity by citing the instances of special protection with which God favored them in perilous circumstances. One of them came forth unhurt from the ruins of a falling house. He said to them: "Can God show you better how acceptable to Him is the service you render Him in the persons of the poor? Is there anything more evident? A new house falls, thirty five or forty persons are found crushed beneath its ruins, and this Daughter, who with her soup was in the same house, on a corner of the steps that Providence, it seems, supported expressly to sustain her, escapes all harm; she comes out of this danger safe and sound. We must believe that the angels drew her thence; for what probability is there that men did it? They, indeed, lent their aid, but the angels were necessary to sustain her. Oh, what protection! Do you think, my Daughters, that it was without a purpose God permitted this house, entirely new, to fall? Do you think it was but by chance it fell just when our Sister was within? Do you think it was by good luck she escaped without injury? Oh, no, not at all. All that is miraculous; God had pre-ordained all that to prove to your company the care he takes of it." Another time it was a floor that gave away in the house of the Sisters, just at the moment that there was no person either on, or under it. "Ah My Daughters" said the Saint on this occasion "what reason have not we to trust in God? We read in history of a man being killed in the open fields by a turtle, dropped on his head by an eagle, and we see to-day houses entirely overturned, and Daughters of Charity coming from under the ruins without the slightest injury. What is this if not a mark and a testimony, whereby God wishes to show them that they are as dear to Him as the apple of His eye? Oh My Daughters, rest assured that. provided you keep within your hearts this holy confidence, God will preserve you, no matter where you be."

CHAPTER III.

LOVE FOR GOD.

I

Love is all interior, and the eye of Him above that penetrates to the depth of hearts sees its ardor and its flame. However, from this inner hearth, as from a subterranean fire, dart forth sparks which reveal it to the eyes of men.

Vincent's love for God manifested itself, in the first place, by a perfect obedience to His holy law. It is the Apostle of charity himself who has said: "*Whosoever keepeth His word, the charity of God is truly perfect in him;*" (I John ii., 3), and again, "*For this is the charity of God that we keep His commandments.*" (I John vi., 3). Vincent was the l'ving law of God; everything in his body, as in his soul, all his thoughts, all his affections, all his words and all his actions were regulated by the law of God, and his life was a continual holocaust consumed by the fire of Divine Love.

Again, this love manifested itself by his ardent, continuous and efficacious desire to have God known more and more, to have Him adored, served, obeyed, loved and glorified at all times, in all places and by all creatures; a desire that frequently escaped him in such like ardent aspirations: "O, my Lord! O, my Savior! O, Divine Goodness! O, my God! When wilt Thou grant us the grace to be entirely Thine, and to love but Thee alone."

It manifested itself in his words which, coming from his heart, testified by their burning accent how bright was the fire within. Of Vincent, as of Charity incarnate itself, his hearers said: "Were not our hearts burning within us whilst he discoursed with us?" This, the wife of the President, De Lamoignon, addressing the

Dutchess of Mantua, expressed one day in a meeting of the Ladies of Charity, exclaiming: "Well, Madam, might we not say, with the disciples of Emmaus, that our hearts glowed with the ardor of Divine Love while Mr. Vincent was speaking to us? For my part, though little sensible to the things of God, I assure you my heart is all aflame with what the holy man has just said." "It is not astonishing," replied Mary De Gonzaga, "he is an angel of the Lord bearing on his lips the ardent coals of that Divine love which burns in his heart." "That is very true," added a third, "and it depends only upon ourselves to participate in the ardor of that same love." In the ecclesiastical conferences he produced the same impression. "As we eagerly listened to his words," Bossuet has related, "there was not one who did not feel the accomplishment of the words of the Apostle, St. Peter: *If any one speak, let him speak as the words of God,*" (1 Peter iv., 11). It was at the conclusion of one of these conferences that Tronson, Superior of the Seminary of St. Sulpice, in a transport, cried out: "Behold, there is a man all filled with the spirit and the love of God." Many came to the conferences only to hear him, and they went away saddened whenever his modesty had forbidden him speech. Bishops of the highest renown were often present. When through humility and respect, Vincent yielded to them the conclusion of the exercises, which, in the quality of director, by the regulations and by usage, belonged to him, they refused in order not to be deprived of the happiness of hearing him. One day, the most venerable of them said to him: "Mr Vincent you must not deprive the company by your humility of the good thoughts with which God has inspired you on the subject in question. There is a certain indescribable unction of the Holy Ghost in your words that touches every one; moreover, these gentlemen pray you to impart your views, for one word from you will have more effect than all that we can say." And, on leaving the conference after having heard him, they used to say to the missionaries: "You are, indeed, happy in seeing and hearing daily a man so filled with the love of God."

This love manifested itself, finally, in the rectitude and purity of his intentions which tended, in the least as in the greatest things, solely and incessantly to the glory of God.

II.

And purity of intention was precisely the means he employed to form in his disciples a love for God. He said to them: "God does not look so much to the exterior of our actions as to the degree of love and purity of intention with which we perform them. Little actions are not so subject to vain glory as are more brilliant ones, which often end in a puff of smoke. We must accustom ourselves to please God in little things if we wish to be acceptable to Him in all our actions."

From this we may judge of his horror of anything done through human respect. One of his missionaries in Rome, thinking to impress the Cardinals favorably, wished to commence with their provinces in giving the missions. Vincent, to whom he had communicated his thoughts answered: "O, my Jesus! my dear Sir, may God preserve us from ever doing anything with such base views! His divine Goodness demands that we should never do any good work, anywhere, in order to be esteemed, but that, on the contrary, in all our actions we regard Him directly, immediately, and solely. I take this opportunity, prostrate in spirit at your feet, and for the love of Our Lord Jesus Christ to ask of you two things: the first is that you avoid as much as possible all desire of appearing; and the second, that you never do anything out of human respect. In accordance with this request it is but entirely proper that you honor for some time the hidden life of Our Lord. There must be something precious in the hidden life, since the Son of God, before making Himself known lived for thirty years as a poor artisan And on humble beginnings He always bestows more grace than on those that are surrounded with pomp and magnificence. You will ask me, perhaps; what will they think of us at this court, and what will they say of us in Paris?—Permit them, my dear sir, to say and think of us as they please, and do rest assured that the maxims of Jesus Christ and the examples of His life are not unavailing; that they will bear their fruit in proper season; that what is not conformable to them is vain and that he who is animated with contrary maxims will fail in all that he undertakes. This is my belief, and it is my experience. In the name of God then, sir, regard it as infallible and cherish retirement."

"It would be better," he said again, "to be bound hand and foot and cast into a burning fire than to do anything to please men." And then the better to show the injustice, and folly of those who act through human motives, he contrasted the perfections of the Creator with the miseries of creatures and added: "Let us always honor the perfections of God, let us take for models of what we have to do, those that are most opposed to our imperfections; as His Meekness and Clemency directly opposed to our wrath and anger, His Knowledge, so contrary to our ignorance, His grandeur and infinite Majesty, so far above our lowness and vileness, His Infinite Goodness ever opposed to our malice. Let us strive to perform actions in honor of that perfection that is directly contrary to our defects." The value and worth of what we do depend according to him on the intention and end we have in view. "For," he said, "just as garments are, ordinarily, not so much prized for the material from which they are made, as for the laces of gold and rich embroideries, the pearls and precious stones with which they are adorned, so we must not be content with doing good works, we must also elevate and enrich them with the merit of a noble and holy intention, doing them solely to please and glorify God." He concluded with the words of the Gospel, "*Seek first the Kingdom of God,*" commenting as follows: "Our Lord, in these words, recommends us to make God reign within us, and then to co-operate with Him in extending and enlarging His Kingdom by the conquest of souls. Is it not a great honor to be called to aid in so immense and so important a design? Is it not doing as the angels, who labor incessantly, and only for the extension of the Kingdom of God? What, then, My Brethren, will hinder us from corresponding worthily with so holy and sanctifying a vocation?"

His practical good sense, always keeping in the just middle, would have no excess, even in the love of God. He has left us a beautiful conference on this subject. At the conclusion of a repetition of prayer, in August, 1655, he expressed himself in these terms: "It is certain that Charity, when it dwells in a soul, takes complete possession of all its powers. There is no rest, it is an ever devouring fire. The person who is once touched by it is continually in movement, always in action. O, My Saviour! the memory wishes to remember only God, it loathes other thoughts, and considers them a torment; it must;. by every possible means, render His presence familiar. Such a means is not good, others must be tried. If I could only practice this devotion, I would succeed. It must be done. But I have still that other devotion; how harmonize both? No matter; I will perform both. And when this new devotion is taken up, others are sought after, and still others. The poor soul embraces all, and yet is not content. It surpasses its strength, it becomes overburdened, and believes it can never do enough. O, My Sweet Saviour, what will become of it? The will continues all inflamed and is called upon to produce such frequent acts that it can no longer comply; there are acts upon acts redoubled at every moment, and in every place, in the refectory, even in conversation and in company. In a word, here, there, everywhere; there is nothing but ardor, but fire and flames, but incessant acts. The soul is almost beside itself. O! but how dangerous and imprudent are these exercises, this eagerness, this zeal!—But what! Can there be imprudence in loving God? Can we love Him too much? or can we even love enough a God who is infinitely amiable?—No, indeed. O, My Saviour, My God! Who can ascend to that astonishing love you bear us—a love that shed for us, miserable creatures, all Your blood, a single drop of which is of infinite price. Still, though God commands us to love Him with our whole heart and with all our strength, we must remember that His Goodness does not wish this love, by its multitude of acts, to impair and ruin our health. For, in this state, the blood warms, and burning with those ardors it sends hot vapors to the brain which in turn is soon afire. Then follow dizziness, dullness, heaviness, as if a weight were oppressing the brain: the organs grow weak, and the person becomes powerless, helpless, until death, which is very much hastened, intervenes. It seems this ought to be decried. To die after this manner is to die a most beautiful death, it is to die of love; it is the happy lot of a martyr, a martyr of love. It seems that these blessed souls can apply to themselves the words of the Spouse, and say with her: "*Thou hast wounded my heart; it is Thou, O loving God, Who hast wounded me; it is Thou Who hast pierced and burned my heart with Thy fiery darts!"* Oh, be forever blessed, O! My Saviour! Among the sacrifices that were offered to God under the Old Law, the Holocaust was the most excellent, because the victim, in acknowledgement of the sovereignty of God, was burnt, was entirely consumed on the altar, no portion being reserved. In like manner these souls seem to be holocausts entirely consumed by the fire of Divine Love. And yet is it much better not to become so strongly affected, not to turn the head in order to make this virtue so sensible, and, as it were, a part of nature. For, at last, after all these vain efforts, we must relax, we must let go our hold; and then beware, beware that we fall not into a state worse than the one in which we were, into a condition, from which St. Paul tells us it is impossible, that is, extremely difficult, to rise. Yes. here is what often results from these excesses: a disgust for all species of devotion, a distaste for virtue, a distaste for the most holy things. This excess takes place in beginnings. When we commence to taste the sweetness of devotion we can never satiate ourselves, we think it impossible ever to have enough, we plunge too far ahead. Oh, this is too much, this is too much! Very often the Devil turns this into temptation for us. When he cannot induce us directly to commit evil, he inspires us to undertake more practices of piety than we can regulate, and overburdens us continually until we break down under too great a weight. My Brethren, virtues are always in a just middle, and each virtue has two equally vicious extremes, between which, deflecting neither to the right nor to the left, we must walk, if we wish our actions to be worthy of praise. Be neither carried away, nor cowardly; mortify nature but do not destroy it. Such is the will of God. He is so good and so just that He requires nothing more. He well knows our wretchedness, He takes pity on us and supplies, by His mercy, for our defects. We must act with Him in entire simplicity, and not give ourselves too much uneasiness. I remember a word of the Bishop of Geneva on this subject, and one every way worthy of so great a man: 'Oh, I would not want to go to God, if God would not come to me.' Remarkable utterance, and coming from one thoroughly enlightened in the science of the love of God! According to this, then, a soul truly affected with charity, understanding what it is to love God, would not desire to go to God if God did not anticipate it and attract it by His grace. This is very far removed from wishing to seize Him and draw Him by force of arms and strength of machinery. No, no, nothing is gained, in such cases, by force. When God wishes to communicate himself, He does so without effort, after a sensible, sweet, quiet and loving manner."

CHAPTER III.

CONFORMITY TO THE WILL OF GOD.
RESIGNATION AND HOLY INDIFFERENCE.

I.

Love unites hearts; but it unites especially wills. Hence the greatest proof of true love for God is submission and conformity to His most Holy Will.

As was the love, so, consequently, was the submission of St. Vincent de Paul. No one, before acting, ever asked with more simplicity: "*Lord what will Thou have me to do?*"—(ACTS ix, 6). None ever separated with more care, in all his thoughts, in all his affections, all that came from man from that which came from God, in order to cast aside the one, and adhere to the other. None, during the course of an action, or enterprise, ever regulated himself more constantly according to the plan traced out by the Divine Will. He practiced this conformity to the will of God, not only in regard to his own personal conduct, but also in all his good works for his neighbor, and in all that related to his congregation. Lest he might anticipate God he never took the initiative in any project or foundation, and before commencing to act he awaited an external impulse which he looked upon as the invitation and approbation of Providence. If there were question of subjects, or of an establishment, or of a temporal advantage for his community, he accepted it only as from the hand of God which he perceived both in the nature and circumstances of the proposition made; and if he, afterward, labored to preserve the goods he had received it was simply because God so wished it; for respect, gratitude and love for the giver require that we prize and utilize his gifts. His invariable law was to await the Divine Will and never to forestall it, when known to render obedience to it as to a sovereign, to follow it, no matter at what cost, be it of labor, or of property, or of honor, or, even if necessary, of life itself. When once he knew this will, either by interior inspiration or by an external command or counsel, he straightway conformed his own to it and directed all his intentions, which he was careful to renew from time to time, lest anything foreign should glide in. He submitted with patience and resignation, nay more, with joy and affection, sacrificing all his natural repugnances, to this will as revealed to him in events that are absolutely of its own domain, such as sickness, losses, afflictions, and all the other accidents of this life.

Resignation to the good pleasure of God, no matter how painful, is, in truth, a sign of submission to His Adorable Will. In the most distressing events but a single word, "God be blessed, God be blessed," the perfect expression of his acquiescence in the dispositions of Providence, came from the lips, or rather from the heart of St. Vincent.

But above and beyond resignation there is still something that subdues, but does not destroy, nature; and this is holy indifference. Vincent went to such a degree of obedience to the will of God that he accomplished it both in his person and in his works. Health or sickness, life or death, all was equal. He took, with indifference, nourishment, remedies, even those for which he had the greatest repugnance, or those he knew to be unsuitable for him, being no less content with the evil effects than with the happiest results.

Indifferent in regard to himself, he was none the less so in regard to the growth and progress of his congregation. He was told that to obtain good subjects he should establish his congregation in large cities. He answered: "We can take no steps towards establishing ourselves in any locality whatever if we desire to follow the ways of God and the usages of the congregation; for, up to the present time, His Providence has called us to those places where we now are, without our having sought them either directly or indirectly. Now, it is impossible that this resignation to God which keeps us in dependence on His direction be not very agreeable to Him, more particularly since it destroys the promptings of nature, which under pretext of zeal for the glory of God, often urge us to undertake projects that He neither inspires nor blesses. He knows what is suitable for us, and if, like true children, we abandon ourselves to so good a Father, He will give it to us at the proper moment. Certainly were we persuaded of our unprofitableness, we would be far from meddling in the work of another, unless invited, and would use no means to have ourselves preferred to other laborers whom, perhaps, God has destined for the work."

A proposal very advantageous to his community was made him, and he answered, on the 30th of January, 1656: " I think we will do well to let that affair rest for awhile in order to blunt the impetuosity of nature which wants profitable things done immediately, as also to exercise ourselves in holy indifference, and allow Our Lord to make known His will, whilst, in the meantime, we will recommend the matter to Him in prayer. If He will the thing to be done, the delay will hurt nothing, and the less we appear in it the more will He be present."

The death of his best missionaries, of his dearest children, could not remove him from his beloved indifference. He recommended them, whilst sick, to the prayers of the community, in this wise: " We will pray God that it may be pleasing to Him to preserve this good missionary, submitting ourselves, however, entirely to His Divine Will. For we must believe, and it is true, that not only this sickness but also the maladies of others, and in a word, all that happens to the congregation is done but by His holy direction and for the good of the congregation. Hence in praying to God for health for the sick, and for relief in other necessities, let it be always with the condition, if such be his good pleasure and for his greater glory." His invariable formula in announcing their death's was: "It has pleased God to deprive us of such a missionary." And he added: "I have no doubt but that the death of this person, who was dear to us, has affected us deeply; but, God be praised, you have also told Our Lord He has done well to take him from us and that you would not wish Him to have done otherwise. since such was His good pleasure."

II

St. Vincent reduced this conduct, so admirable in submission and holy indifference, to theory in his maxims, in the letters he wrote and in the instructions which he addressed to his community. "To conform," said he, "in all things to the will of God, and to take pleasure only in it, is to lead the life of an angel on earth, it is even to live the life of Jesus Christ. . . . . Our Lord is in continual communion with those virtuous souls who hold themselves faithfully and constantly united to His Holy Will, who have no other will but His."

This doctrine came from his distrust in men and his confidence in God. "He said: "In regard to Divine things I place no more reliance in human means than I would in the assistance of the Devil. The things of God are done by themselves, and true wisdom consists in following Providence step by step. And let us convince ourselves of the truth of a maxim that appears paradoxical: 'That he, who hurries in the things of God, recedes." (To Codoing, 15th of May, 1643, and 6th of Aug. 1644.) Again: "A weathercock is no more subject to the movement of the air than is the spirit of man to external agitation. . . . God be praised for having willed that all earthly things be uncertain and perishable, in order that in Him alone we would seek stability for our projects and our works, for, then, all that happens will turn to our profit." (26th and 31st of Aug. 1657.) "May it be pleasing, then, to the goodness of God to give us part in the eternal thought which he Has of Himself whilst perpetually governing this world and providing for the needs of all His creatures even to the smallest insect. Oh! how we must labor to acquire a participation in this spirit." (To Portail, 25th of Aug. 1638.) And he explained further this government of God to which we must submit, and subordinate our conduct: "God is not governed in His works according to our views and desires. We should content ourselves to turn to best account the little talents that He has placed in our hands, without desiring to have greater. If we be faithful in small things He will place us over more important; but that is His concern, not ours. Let Him act, and let us withdraw ourselves still further into our own shell. The congregation was begun without any intention on our part, it has been multiplied by the hand of God alone, and has been called everywhere by superior orders, without our contributing in anything save obedience. For more than twenty years I did not dare ask of God the extension and propagation of the congregation, considering that, if it be His work, to His Providence alone should be left the care of its conservation and increase. But by dint of thinking of the recommendation which is given us in the Gospel, to ask Him to send laborers into His harvest, I have become satisfied of the importance and utility of this devotion. Let us continue it. God will receive this abandonment as very agreeable, and we will be in peace. The spirit of the world is very restless, and desires to do everything. Let us leave it there; we do not wish to choose our path, but to walk in that which it is pleasing to God to point out to us. Let us esteem ourselves unworthy to be employed or that men should think of us; we will be happy. Let us offer ourselves to Him to do and to suffer everything for His glory and for the edification of His Church; He wants nothing more. If He desires results, they are in His power, not in ours. In His presence let our wills and our hearts expand, ready for anything without determining on any till He shall have spoken. In the meantime, let us beg Him to give us the grace to labor in the exercise of the virtues that Our Lord practised in His hidden life." (To the ladies, 25th of Aug. 1659.)

He condemned alike confidence and natural eagerness in action, as discouragement and sadness in misfortune, all appearing to him to be derived from want of a submission to Providence. He wrote: "I will tell you two things in regard to the inquietude and melancholy you say you have when things do not go right with you. The first is, that it is God, and not men, who makes things go well, and He, sometimes, either to show us we can do nothing ourselves, or to exercise our patience, permits that they turn out otherwise than we wish. And the second is, that you trust too much in your own power of direction, being of the opinion that as you love good order it depends on you to preserve it; and hence it is that, not being able to succeed you grieve excessively, whereas were you firmly convinced that all you can do is to spoil, you would be astonished that things were not far worse, and you would remain as tranquil in events that appear to you contrary and disagreeable, as in success, knowing that it is God who thus orders things. I beg of you, then, to regard all things in the light of His Providence, doing humbly and carefully all that depends on you to contribute to their success, and for the result, submit to the good pleasure of God." (To M. Pernelle, in Geneva, 22d of Nov. 1658.)

Obstacles and misfortunes seemed to him forerunners of success; and to show this he made use of the following ingenious comparison: "There is reason to hope that, as with fruit-trees, so will it be with you; for the more a long and severe winter checks and retards them, the deeper root they take and the more fruit they bear." (To M. Des Dames, in Poland, 20th of June, 1659.)

We see that he varied the application of the same doctrine according to the circumstances and the needs of each one. To a pastor who desired to exchange his parish he said: "Pray and take counsel, for the question is to know whether God wishes you to leave the spouse He has give you;" to superiors of houses who made known to him their fears of loss, or persecution: "Nothing will happen but what is pleasing to God; He is master not only of what we posses, but also of our lives, and it is but proper that He dispose of all according to His Divine Will;" to those who complained of their physical infirmities, or their spiritual dryness: "Remain subject to the good pleasure of God; rest content in every condition in which it will please Him to place you, and, as long so you know it to be agreeable to Him, never desire to leave it. This is the most excellent and the most sublime exercise that a Christian, or even a priest, can practice on earth." To Mademoiselle Le Gras, who was very uneasy on account of the sickness of Mr. Portail, the then director of the Daughters of Charity, he said: "We must fight against that which gives pain, we must rend our hearts, or soften them so as to prepare them for everything.

It appears that Our Lord wishes to take away His part of the little congregation; it belongs entirely to Him, as I trust, and He has a right to do with it as He pleases; for myself, my greatest wish is to desire only the accomplishment of His holy will. I cannot express to you here how far advanced our dear sick one is in this practice, and it is for this reason, it seems, that our dear Lord desires to place him where he can continue it more happily for all eternity. Oh! who will give us this grace of submission of our senses and of our reason to this Adorable Will? It will be the author of both the senses and reason, provided we use them only in Him and for Him. Let us pray that both you and I have only the same will with Him and in Him, for this is Paradise on earth." He said to her again, when anxiety in regard to the conduct and the future of her son caused her torments: "Give both son and mother to our Lord, and He will render good account of both; only permit Him to do His will in you and in him; seek this same will in all your exercises and desire no other practice, for this alone is sufficient to make you entirely God's. Oh! but it requires little to be a saint! The most sovereign, and almost only, means is to accustom yourself to do in all things the will of God." On another occasion, when she begged him to point out the evil of her soul, which she thought was the cause of her bodily ailment, he said: "I can indicate no other cause of your sickness than the good pleasure of God. Adore, then, this good pleasure without inquiring whence it is that God rejoices in seeing you suffering. He is glorified greatly by our abandonment to His direction without discussing the reason of His will, unless it be that His will is the reason, and His reason, His will. Let us, therefore, abandon ourselves to it as Isaac did to the will of Abraham, and as Jesus Christ to the will of His Father."

And his joy was great when he perceived that his children walked in this holy practice. He wrote to one of them: "God be praised that you are ready to do, in everything and everywhere, His most holy will, and to go live and die wherever it may be agreeable to Him to call you! This is the disposition of good servants of God and of really apostolic men who are attached to nothing; it is the mark of the true children of God who are always prepared to correspond to the designs of so good a Father. With lively sentiments of tenderness and gratitude I thank Him for you, not doubting but that your heart, thus prepared, will abundantly receive the graces of heaven so that you may do a great deal of good on earth; and such is my prayer to His Divine Goodness."

In one or two of his conferences he condensed, and thoroughly expounded, this doctrine which is found scattered in hundreds of his letters, and given in fragments in his numerous familiar discourses. "The perfection of love," he says, "does not consist in ecstasies but in properly doing the will of God; and He, whose will is most conformable to that of God, will be, among men, the most perfect. Hence our perfection consists. in so uniting our will to the will of God that His and ours may be but one and the same will; and he who will excel more in this point will be the more perfect. When our Lord wished to teach the young man, mentioned in the Gospel, the means to arrive at perfection, He said to him: '*If anyone will come after me, let him renounce himself, take up his cross, and follow Me.*' But, I ask you, who renounces himself more, or bears the cross of mortification better, and follows Jesus Christ more perfectly than he who studies never to do his own will, but always the will of God? The Scripture also tells us in some other place that he who adheres to God has but one mind with him. Now, I ask you, who adheres more perfectly to God than he who does only the will of God and never his own, who wishes and desires only what God wishes? Oh, but this is a short and easy way to acquire in this life a great treasure of graces."

Oh, then what happiness for the Christian! "See in what holy dispositions He possesses his life, and the blessings that accompany all that He does. He holds to God alone, and God conducts Him in every thing and in every place; so that he can say to Him as did the prophet: '*Thou hast held me by my right hand, and by thy will thou hast conducted me.*' (Ps. LXVII, 24.) God leads Him, as it were, by the right hand, and he, in turn, keeping Himself in entire submission to this

Divine guidance, can be seen to-morrow, after to-morrow, the entire week, the entire year, in fine, all his life, in peace and tranquillity, in fervor continually advancing towards God and constantly infusing into the souls of those around him the sweet and salutary effects of the spirit that animates him. If you compare him with those who follow their own inclinations you will see that his actions shed a brilliant light and bear rich fruits; a notable progress is remarked in his person; a force and energy in all his words; God gives a special blessing to all his works, and accompanies with his grace the designs he undertakes for Him and the counsels he gives others; and his every action gives great edification. But, on the other hand, we see that persons attached to their own inclinations have thoughts only of earth; their language is the language of slaves; and their works are lifeless. The difference arises from this, that they attach themselves to creatures while the former separates himself from them. Nature acts in base souls, and grace in those that elevate themselves to God, and breathe but His will."

But it is in the conference of the 7th of March, 1659, that we find this doctrine of submission to the will of God fully explained, in its motives, means and practice, according to the usual manner which the Saint styled the LITTLE METHOD:

"Motives.—1. The exercise that consists in always doing the will of God is the most excellent, for it embraces indifference, pure intention, and all the practices and exercises of perfection. Who is there more indifferent than he who does the will of God in everything, who seeks himself in none, and who wishes what he may lawfully wish only because God so desires? Can there be any person more free, of purer and more perfect intention?

"2. It is certain that actions, done after a human manner, mechanically, unless they have a worthy end, such as to accomplish the will of God, are dead. Meditation, preaching, working without discretion, assisting at office, are but so many inanimate actions; they are a money that has no value, not having the stamp, for God does not regard our works save inasmuch as He sees Himself in them, and inasmuch as they are performed for His sake.

"Our father, Adam in the Garden of Paradise was a tree that naturally bore fruit agreeable in the eyes of its Lord; but sin in severing his will from that of God rendered him incapable of doing anything that might be pleasing to Him; and we who spring from this tainted source have, humanly speaking, the same inability.

"There are theologians who think that all that is not done for God is sin; but if it be not sin, it is at least useless.

"3. It was the maxim and practice of our Lord to do the will of His Father in everything. Oh, My Saviour, what prominence and what brilliancy thou givest to the exercise of your virtues! Thou art the King of Glory, and yet Thou camest into the world to do but the will of Him who sent Thee! This sacred disposition was most dear to Him: '*My will,*' He said, '*is to do the will of Him who sent Me.*' (John IV. 34.) O, My Saviour, that was Thy practice! St. John had that of penance, he was full of the desire to practice it and to persuade others to do it. For it was for that He came into the world. And Thou, O Lamb of God, Thou who takest away the sins of the world, Thou camest full of ardor to do, and to inculcate the will of Thy Father. Elias had a burning zeal for the glory of God; he put everything to fire and flames in order to imprint on the hearts of men fear and respect. And Thou, My Saviour, Thou wert animated with that sweet and incomparable desire that the will of God be done by all His creatures. It is for that reason Thou hast placed in the Lord's Prayer: '*Thy will be done.*' Thou hast wished that all men would do, and would demand, what? the will of the Heavenly Father; where? on earth and in Heaven; and how? as the angels and saints do, promptly, completely, constantly, lovingly. I am sure there is not one here present who has not, to-day, endeavored to perform some actions that of themselves are good and holy; and yet it may be that God has rejected them, because 'they were done through your own will. Is it not this that the prophet declared when he said, on the part of God: '*I do not want your fasts, by which in thinking to honor me you do me the contrary; because, when you fast you do your own will, and by this will you spoil and vitiate your fast.'* Now, the same may be said of all other works of piety. The presence of our own will taints our devotions, our labors, and our penetential works. For twenty years, I have never read in the Holy Mass the Epistle, taken from the 58th Chapter of Isaias, without being greatly troubled.

"What, then, must be done, not to lose our time and our labor? This, that we never act through motives of self-interest, from inclination, humor, or fancy; but accustom ourselves to do the will of God in all things — I say in all, and not in part, for this is the peculiar effect of grace, to render the person and action agreeable to God. Jesus Christ said that many will call out: *'Lord, Lord, have we not prophesied, and in Thy name cast out devils, and done many wonderful works in Thy name?'* 'I never knew you,' He will answer, 'I never knew you; depart from Me, you that work iniquity.' 'But, Lord, dost Thou call works of iniquity the prophesies and miracles we have performed in Thy name?' 'Retire from Me, ye wicked,' He will say to them; 'I never knew you.' Who then are they that will enter the Kingdom of Heaven? Those who will perform the will of God. O, My Saviour! give us the grace to be filled with the desire not to bear wild fruit, but that all we produce be for, and by Thee, so that all may be pleasing in the eyes of Thy Father.

"But now, how shall we do the will of God? The things to to be done are either forbidden, or commanded, or indifferent. In regard to works commanded or forbidden, it is the Will of God that we do the first and abstain from the second. How does a child do the will of his father, or a subject that of his king? In performing what they ordain, and in refraining from what they forbid; the child does so, to honor its father, and the subject, in obedience to his king. In like manner will we do the will of God if, in doing what is commanded, and not doing what is prohibited, we have the intention of glorifying this admirable father, and of lovingly obeying this king of love. We must obey when He commands directly or indirectly, that is to say, by Himself, or by the Church, for the Church is His spouse and He is the father of the family, and He desires His children to obey their mother as Himself.

"There are actions that are indifferent, some of which are agreeable to nature, others disagreeable, and still others that are neither the one nor the other.

"Between two indifferent actions, one agreeable, and the other disagreeable to nature, I should, in order not to live according to the flesh, choose the latter. If, for instance, I have my choice to visit either of two persons, one of whom I know will be pleasing, whilst the other will be less so, or not at all, I should, according to the rule, prefer the second to the first. I except the case wherein there is no choice, as when there is an obligation to go where my inclination leads; for then the will of God being made manifest by the command, we should seek therein His pleasure, and not ours. With regard to actions that are neither agreeable, nor disagreeable, as to be seated, or to remain standing, to go by one way, or another, I do them fortuitously; and in so doing there would seem to be no merit. Yet, by offering them to God and in doing them in the name of our Lord, as St. Paul teaches, they may be made meritorious.

"There is a fourth manner wherein we may know the will of God, and that is by inspiration: for God often enlightens the understanding and moves the heart. But in order not to be deceived, we must use the salt of discretion. Amid a number of thoughts and sentiments there are found many apparently good, which, however, do not come from God, and are not according to His good pleasure. We must, therefore, examine them carefully in prayer, considering their motives and their object, propose them to the learned, take advice in relation to them with our directors, who are for us the depositories of Divine Wisdom; and in doing what they direct we will do the will of God.

"We will perform it, again, in doing what is reasonable, according to this prayer of the Church: '*Grant, we beseech Thee, O God, that always thinking rightly, we may accomplish in word and act those things which are pleasing to Thee.*' To do a thing which appears reasonable is, then, to do the will of God. This, it must always be understood, is to be taken with the grain of salt of Christian prudence, and with the advice of those who direct us, for it may happen that the thing to be done may be reasonable in itself, but not in its circumstances of time, place, or manner.

"To do the will of God in the ways we have said is to do it actively. It is done passively when we acquiesce in what God does in us, as in unforeseen events. A motive for consolation surprises us; we receive news, what will I say? of the conversion of some important personage or of an entire country; or that God is fervently served by persons whom we love; or that peace is re-established between two princes whose dissensions gave great scandal to the Church. We must receive this as coming from the hand of God, and rejoice in spirit as did our Lord when He returned thanks to His Father for having revealed His secrets to the simple. On the other hand, some cause for sorrow overtakes us, such as sickness, loss, calumny. This, too, we must accept as coming from the hand of God, because it is His pleasure to try us in that way, and because He it is who sends all afflictions. '*Shall there be evil in the city, which the Lord hath not done?*' (Amos 3G.) Our Lord in the Garden of Olives, meditating on the torments that He was about to suffer, regarded them as willed by His Father, and we should say with Him: '*Let not my will be done, O Lord, but Thine!*'

"Means: The first is taught us in the Lord's Prayer: '*Thy will be done;*' for our Lord, having placed these words in our daily prayer, desires that, every day, we ask of Him the grace to do His will as it is done in Heaven, perfectly and without ceasing, with a simple and unvaried conformity of our own. 2d. Let us accustom ourselves to say this prayer not only with our lips, but also to practice it. Let us begin to-morrow, this very hour, and say to God: Lord, in order to glorify Thee, I wish to obey and to do all that will be made manifest to me in Thy name. In this manner let us enliven our will and frequently renew our particular intention. But, you will tell me, I do not remember, I am for hours, for entire half days, without thinking to offer to Him what I do. We must humble ourselves very much for this, and be sorry for the loss of merit in so many actions, or, at least, of the pleasure that God otherwise would have received had they been offered to Him. And to supply for this defect let each one, on rising in the morning, make God a general oblation of all the actions of the day, and afterward renew the offering once or twice during the course of the morning, and as often during the afternoon, saying to Him: My God, be pleased to accept all the motions of my heart and of my body; draw them to Thee; I offer them with all my labors and my suffering! The more we do this, the easier will it become and the more advantage will we find in it. By this means, we will acquire new motives for loving, and love will cause us to persevere and grow in this holy practice. Alas! how many there are, even in the world, who do not lose sight of God. I lately met a person who made it a matter of conscience for having failed three times in one day in the recollection of the presence of God. These people will be our judges and will, one day, condemn us before the Divine Majesty for our neglect—we who have nothing else to do but to love God, and to testify our love by our services, and by our every movement. Let us beg of our Lord, then, to grant us the grace to say with Him: '*My meat is to do the will of Him that sent me.*' (John iv, 34.) Thy delight, O Savior of the world, Thy ambrosia and thy nectar was to do the will of Thy Father. We are Thy children, and we throw ourselves into Thy arms, in order to imitate Thy practices. Give us this grace; for, as of ourselves we are powerless, we ask it of Thee, and from Thee we hope for it; but with a confidence and with a strong desire to follow Thee."

Absolute submission to the Will of God produces resignation and holy indifference, one act of which, said St. Vincent, " is worth more than a hundred thousand temporal successes." Whether events happened by the express will of God, or were come to pass simply by His permission, the saint still wished resignation to God's good pleasure " in order to suffer all that may be pleasing to Him, and as much, and for as long a time as He may please. This is the great lesson taught by the Son of God; and those who are docile, and imprint it deeply in their hearts are in the first class in the school of this Divine Master. And, for my part, I know of nothing more holy, or of greater perfection than this resignation when it leads to complete renunciation of self, and to holy indifference for all classes of conditions, sin excepted, no matter how we may have been placed in them. Let us hold to this idea, and let us pray to God to bestow on us the grace to remain constantly in this indifference."

Here, again, the saint multiplied and diversified his instructions according to the necessities of each one. "O, sir," said he to one, "how beautiful an ornament is holy indifference in a missionary, since it makes him so pleasing to God that he who possesses it will always be preferred by Him to all other workers in whom He will not see this disposition of indifference in regard to the accomplishment of His designs. If we ever were once divested of all self-will, we would then be in a condition to perform with assurance the will of God —a will in which the angels find all their felicity and men all their happiness." To another, he wrote: "I give God infinite thanks for the disposition that He has given you to go to foreign countries, or not to go, but to remain where you are, according as you may, or may not be sent. Holy indifference for all things is the state of the perfect; and yours gives me hope that God will be glorified in and by you: such is my heartfelt prayer. And I beg of you, my dear sir, to ask of Him, for us all, the grace to abandon ourselves entirely to his holy conduct. We should serve Him according to His good pleasure, and we should renounce our own choice, both as regards locality and employment. That we belong to God is enough to induce us to wish to belong to Him in the most perfect manner, and, like His best children, be honored with the title of servants of the Gospel, by which our Lord desires to be made known and served. And what matters it to us, how, or in what place, provided it be done? And most assuredly will it be if we allow Him to act."

In his conference to the Daughters of Charity, as also in those to his missionaries, he gave fully his ideas and views on holy indifference. He said to the Daughters of Charity, (14th of December, 1659): "The state of indifference is the state of the angels who, at the least sign, are ever prepared to accomplish willingly, both in heaven and on earth, the wishes of God, desiring to do only what He commands them. Thus acts the indifferent soul. Again, it resembles the angels in this, that they, no matter what may be their employment, never lose sight of God, but contemplate Him everywhere and in all things. It regards the will of God in whatever it is given to do, and is equally content wherever sent, just as the angels, who, since their only enjoyment is to accomplish the will of God, are as happy in being the guardians of a wicked man as of a man of virtue. The soul that is possessed of indifference resembles the angels, then, in three ways: 1st, in as much as it always walks in the presence of God; 2d, since it is always prepared to do His holy will without solicitude as to the manner; and 3d, in this that it is as much, and more content, in occupations that are lowly than in those that are elevated. On the other hand, a soul that is wanting in indifference, and that desires to be in such an employment, or in such a place, in preference to another, may be styled a demon. Never to wish to do the will of God, but ever to do one's own, is the spirit of the demon. It is true that he does the will of God in hell, as he did when, at the command of Our Lord, he entered the swine, but it is by constraint and in spite of himself. And as the demon carries his hell with him everywhere, and is devoured by flames even when in the bodies of the possessed, so, too, a soul that is filled with a thousand desires, and at one time wishes this, and at another, that employment, never has any true peace. This unrest is its hell."

But, to have the instructions of the saint on this subject in their entirety, we must listen to his conference to his missionaries, on the 16th of May, 1659. "Indifference," he says, "is a state of virtue in which man detaches himself from creatures to unite himself to the Creator. It is not a virtue, but a state, wherein virtue acts, wherein the heart detaches itself from those things that hold it captive. Where is the loving heart? In the thing that it loves; consequently, where our love is, there is our heart, captive. It cannot leave, it cannot rise, it cannot go either to the right or to the left; it remains fixed. Wherever the treasure of the avaricious is, there, too, is his heart, and where our heart is, there is our treasure. And what is deplorable, the objects that hold us in slavery are, ordinarily speaking, the most unworthy. What! a nothing, an imagination, a short word that is addressed to us, an absence of kindly greeting, a little refusal, the thought merely that enough ado is not made about us, all this so wounds and sores us that we cannot be cured, we do not know how to escape, we are always affected and held captive by it. The peculiar property of indifference is to take away from us all feeling and all desire, to detach us from ourselves and from every creature. This is its office, this the happiness to which it leads, provided it be active, provided it labors. And how? To know ourselves we must study ourselves, we must say to to ourselves: 'Now, my soul, where are thy affections? What do we hold dear? What is it that captivates us? Do we possess the liberty of the children of God, or are we bound to worldly goods, to our own ease, to honors? We must examine to discover our bonds in order to break them.

"God, having sent His Son into the world to redeem us, made us His children, and the cowardly man, who allows himself to be overcome by creatures, is a slave; and, losing the liberty of the children of God, he seems to utter an eternal blasphemy, as if he said that God is not His Father, or that God is less lovable than that which he loves, or the pleasures that captivate him.

"To what did the Son of God attach Himself? You know how He was subject to the Will of His Father. By the mouth of the Prophet-King, He compares Himself to an animal subject to the will of its master. His perfect resignation readily suggests that of the animal that has neither choice nor desire. With it you do as you please; it is always ready to go out, to receive a saddle or a pack-saddle, to be attached to a plow, or to stand still. To it everything is indifferent; it permits any treatment, it has no preference for its stable, nor inclination to go this way rather than that; it has no attachment. Have you not, in passing, often seen mules drawn up before a gate? Sometimes five and six together, all await the coming of the person who has charge, and when he has come they start off. They turn to the right, or to the left, as he chooses, and they stop as soon as he says the word. They are totally indifferent. '*I am become as a beast before thee.*' (Ps. xxii, 23) 'This is how I am,' says our Lord, in order to show us that He was ever ready to do whatever God wished. Oh, what tractableness! Oh, what abandonment! And what was the result: '*And I am always with thee.*' He was always with God.

"What does he who is perfectly submitted to the orders of Divine Providence? He acts as the dumb beast, which is ready for whatever is demanded, whenever, and however it may be demanded. And what do I, when I thus abandon myself? I attract God, because I have no will. '*Thou hast led me by my right hand, and by Thy Will Thou hast conducted me.*' (Ps. xxii. 24.) If I have done any good it is Thou who hast guided me; the least sign of Thy Will was sufficient for me, I am become as a beast of burden before Thee; I have submitted to contempt, to suffering and to all the dispositions of Thy good pleasure; and hence it is, O Lord that my occupations are pleasing in Thy sight.

"Do you not see the happy success of those that are in this disposition of indifference? They adhere to God alone, and God is their guide. You can find them to-morrow, the entire week, all the year, all their life-time, in peace, in favor and in continual love for God, and always diffusing around them the sweet and salutary effects of the workings of God within them. And compare the indifferent with those who are not so, and you will see, on the one side, actions all resplendent with light and rich in fruit; advancement in the entire person, force in words, enterprises blessed, grace attending counsels given, and the good odor of sanctity accompanying every action: '*And by Thy Will Thou hast conducted me.*' (Ps. xxii. 24) But, on the part of those given up to their own satisfaction, you can find only thoughts of earth, speech of slaves, and works that are dead. The difference, then, between them is, that these unite themselves to creatures, whilst those separate themselves from them; that nature animates low souls, whilst grace vivifies those that raise themselves to God, and breathe but His Will. Therefore is it that the latter may say, after a manner, with Our Lord: '*Thou hast received me with glory.*'

(Ps. xxii. 24) Thou hast given me power both in heaven and on earth.

"Oh, My God, I know that is beautiful, and I have a strong desire to act in that way, and I see only too plainly that I am held captive. I find difficulty in detaching myself from things that I like; I suffer because I do not preach, because I am not employed, because I am not suited, because I am not in good repute. I will have a great deal of trouble in bearing with persons of every sort of disposition, but with Thy help, my God, I will do all. I do not ask to be an angel, nor like an apostle; what I desire is simply the submissive disposition you give to animals, the strength of endurance you give to soldiers, and a firmness similar to the steady adherence they manifest for the military order. Oh, my brethren, we should blush for shame to see ourselves surpassed by simple, common soldiers, and even by the poor beasts of the field, in things that are so agreeable to God that His Son Himself has wished to perform them.

"Ah! great St. Peter, you said well that you had abandoned all, and you proved it clearly when, having recognized your Master on the shore, and having heard His well-beloved disciple say to you: '*It is the Lord,*' (John xxi. 7), you cast yourself into the water to go to Him. You did not think of the vessel, nor of your clothing, no, nor of your life itself, but only of your Divine Savior, who was your all. And you, O, St. Paul, great apostle, who, endowed with a most special grace from the moment of your conversion, practiced so perfectly this virtue of indifference in saying: '*Lord what will Thou have me to do.*' (Acts ix, 6).

"This language marked a wonderful change and a detachment that could only be the sudden effect of grace, St. Paul having been, in an instant, rendered indifferent to his law, his commission, his pretentions, and his sentiments, and placed in a state so perfect that he was unsolicitous, and ready for all that God might demand of him. If, then, these great saints so cherished and practiced this virtue of indifference we should imitate them, and follow after them; for the missionaries do not belong to themselves, but to Jesus

Christ, Who wishes to so dispose of them that they do as He has done, and suffer after His example. 'As the Father has sent me,' said He to His apostles and disciples, 'so do I send you, and as they have persecuted Me so will they persecute you.'

"After all these considerations, should we not empty our hearts of all desire, save that of rendering ourselves conformable to Jesus Christ, and of all will, but that of obedience? I think you all are in this disposition, and I trust that God will give us this grace. Yes, my God, I hope it for myself the very first, for I have so much need of it by reason of my many miseries and my many attachments from which I see myself almost powerless to withdraw, and which cause me, in my old age, to cry out with David: "Lord have pity on me." But you will be edified, my brethren, when I tell you that we have amongst us weak and infirm old men who have asked to be sent to the Indies, and have asked even whilst suffering from their infirmities, which were not slight. Whence comes such courage? It is because their hearts are free; they go willingly and joyfully wheresoever God wishes to be known and adored, and nothing but His holy will keeps them here. And we others, my brethren, all of us, were we not entangled in some wretched briers, should we not, each one of us, say in his heart: 'My God, I give myself to Thee to be sent any place on this earth to which my superiors will judge proper I should go to announce Thy Holy Name, and even should I die, then I will still dispose myself to go, knowing well that my salvation is in obedience, and obedience is Thy Holy Will.' Those who are not in this disposition of mind should strive to know what it is that draws them one direction more than another, so that, by means of continual mortification, both interior and exterior, they may attain, with the help of God, to the liberty of the children of God, which is holy indifference."

With the intention of teaching the lesson more vividly, and of rendering it more effective, the saint would take occasion from some severe loss that happened to befall the congregation, to excite it to the practice of an indifference, pushed even to heroism. Thus, in 1657, when the plague had snatched away nearly all his missionaries in Genoa, he interrupts himself in the course of a conference on confidence in God, and exclaims: "O, but is it not very true, gentlemen and my brethren, that we should have great confidence in God, and place ourselves entirely in His hands, being convinced that His Providence will direct to our advantage all that it wishes, or permits to happen to us? Yes, whatever God gives, and whatever He takes away, is all for our good, because such is His good pleasure, and His good pleasure is our aim and our happiness. In this view, I make known to you the affliction which has come upon us, and I can say, my brethren, in all truth, one of the greatest that could fall upon us; it is that we have lost the main stay and principal support of our house in Genoa. Mr. Blatiron, the superior of that house, who was a great servant of God, is dead; he is gone. But that is not all: the good Mr. Dupont, who labored so joyfully in the service of those stricken with the plague, who had so great a love for his neighbor, such fervor and zeal in procuring the salvation of souls, has also been taken away by the distemper. One of our Italian priests, Mr. Dominic Bocconi, a very virtuous and good missionary, as I have been informed, died in a pest-house in which he shut himself so as to assist the poor plague-stricken people of the country. Mr. Tratebas, who was likewise a true servant of God, an excellent missionary, and great in every virtue, is also dead. Mr. Francis Vincent, whom you knew, and who did not yield in anything to the others, is dead. Mr. Ennery, a prudent, pious, and exemplary man, is dead. It is all over with them, gentlemen and my brothers; the plague has taken from us these stout workers; God has taken them to Himself. Out of eight, but one remains, Mr. Le Juge, who, having been stricken down, recovered and is now assisting the other sick. Oh, My Savior, Jesus, what a loss and how great an affliction! Now it is that we have great need to resign ourselves thoroughly to the will of God; for, otherwise, what can we do but uselessly weep and lament the loss of these great servants of God who were so inflamed with zeal for His glory? By resignation, however, after having accorded a few tears to our grief for the separation, we can elevate ourselves to God, and praise and bless Him for all these losses, since it is by the disposition of His Divine Will that they are come upon us. Yet, gentlemen and my brothers, can we say we lose those whom God takes? No, we do not lose them, and we should believe that the ashes of these good missionaries will prove to be the seed whence others will spring. Rest assured that God will not withdraw from this congregation the graces that he bestowed upon them, but will give them to those who shall have the zeal to go take their places."

CHAPTER V.

PRESENCE OF GOD.

I

Love, uniting hearts and wills, annihilates space, and is happy only in the presence or in the continual sight of the object beloved. Vincent, full of love for God, took great care not to lose, for a single instant, the thought of His holy and amiable presence. Alone, or in public, in quiet or immersed in duty, in joy as in sorrow, in the silence of his room, or in the noise and distraction of the street, of the court, and of meetings, he was constantly with God, always united to Him in thought and in heart. No matter at what moment, or in what place you met him, it was readily seen from his recollected manner, from his evenness of temper, from the nature and accent of his words, that God was ever present with him. When asked a question, he invariably paused before answering, in order to reflect, and to consult God, and it was in the name of God, "In the name of the Lord," his ordinary formula, that he gave a decision or an advice. He thought of God's presence at least four times an hour; whenever the clock struck he immediately uncovered himself, made the sign of the cross, and raised his eyes to Heaven. Ordinarily, he kept them cast down, and even closed, whenever he rode in a carriage, and he opened them only to look upon the Crucifix of his rosary which he always carried attached to his cincture. That he might not see, nor be seen, and that he might the more easily entertain himself with God he almost always closed the curtains of the carriage. For that matter, however, the sight of creatures, far from distracting him, only served to elevate him to their

Creator. Fields covered with grain, trees laden with fruit afforded him an occasion to bless the goodness of God and to adore His paternal Providence: flowers, birds, or any other agreeable object would occasion the exclamation: "What is comparable to the beauty of God, Who is the source of all the beauty and perfection of His creatures? Is it not He who lends them their lustre and their brilliancy?" Most frequently, however, he honored God, and kept himself united to Him in depriving himself of the view of pleasing objects, and in mortifying his senses.

If he went on foot through the streets he preserved the same recollection, and observed the same practice. In passing before a church he would enter and prostrate himself with his face to the earth. When the *Angelus* rang, whether he was in the midst of a crowd, or at court, he uncovered, and fell on his knees to recite it. Though all looked at him in admiration he saw no one. The little children in the streets pointed him out to each other, saying: "See, the Saint is passing."

II

He counselled others to adopt what proved in his own case a means to maintain the presence of God. Being one day at Court, in one of the grand *salons* which was all lined with mirrors so that even the smallest insect or grain of dust was reflected, he was struck with a thought which he hastened to communicate to his Community. "If men" he said, "have been able to represent, in this manner, all that passes in a place, even the least movement of the smallest thing, have we not greater reason to believe that they are all represented in the grand mirror of the Divinity that fills all space, and contains all in its immensity, and in which the Blessed see all things, and particularly the good works of faithful souls, and consequently all their acts of patience, of humility, of conformity to the will of God, and of other virtues?"

He placed in different parts of the house of St. Lazarus the words, "God sees me," written in large characters, in order to familiarize his children with the thought of the presence of God; and he desired that these tablets would be considered as the eye of God looking on those passing, and visible to their hearts. Of the exercise of the presence of God he said: "Whosoever is faithful to it, whosoever acquires an affection for it, will soon attain to a very high degree of sanctity." And he said again: "The thought of the presence of God will render us familiar with the practice of constantly doing His will; the remembrance of the Divine presence will establish itself, little by little, in the mind, and, by His Grace, it will become a habit, so that we will, at last, be animated by this Divine presence."

CHAPTER VI.

PRAYER.

I

Love is not content with the presence alone, it likewise demands converse with the object loved. He, then, who loves God, is, necessarily, a man of prayer. Vincent de Paul had a most religious and profound esteem for prayer; he had the greatest relish for it, and it possessed for him the sweetest attraction. Every morning he devoted one hour to it; and in the midst of the greatest multiplicity of affairs, and though he were obliged to be bled, or to take medicine, he would not permit the consequent fatigue, no matter how severe, to prevent him from being present on the morrow. He made his prayer on his knees, in the church with his entire community. Not content to consecrate to God the first fruits of the day he also gave himself up to prayer during his long nights of sleeplessness, and devoted to it every leisure moment that his duty or his labor for the poor left him. Every year, be his engagements what they might, he retired eight entire days to give himself up to prayer, and in the meanwhile he interrupted the most holy occupations, that he might the better entertain himself with God alone.

At all times his prayer was fervent. Sighs of a love that he could not control were heard escaping him, and he alone was unconscious. What passed between God and him? Did his prayer follow the ordinary way of considerations in the understanding, and affections in the heart, or did it proceed solely, without labor and without any effort of nature, from the operation of the Divine Spirit? His humility carefully concealed all. But when descending from the holy mountain, his countenance at times appeared all resplendent, like unto that of Moses, and the ardor of his soul, illuminating his entire person, entered into his words and actions. His discourse at the conclusion of prayer more than ordinarily burned with faith and with charity; his humility, his mortification, his patience, all his virtues shone with new lustre in his conduct.

11

He induced all those over whom he exercised any influence to make this morning mental prayer, or meditation. He desired that those preparing for the reception of orders and those performing the exercises of retreat should be instructed in it, that they might take away with them, as the most precious fruit of their retreat, the habit of it, and the resolution to continue it. He himself led the ecclesiastics of his Conference, and even the ladies of his Assembly, to practice it.

He recommended it particularly to preachers, to catechists, and to directors of souls. "Mental prayer," he said, "is a great book for a preacher; it is there that he will draw from the Eternal Word the Divine truths of which He is the source, in order to diffuse them afterwards among the people; prayer will fit him to touch the heart and to convert souls."

But it was his own missionaries, both in their own interest and in behalf of the people, that he especially exhorted to the practice of mental prayer. He said to them: "Give me a man of prayer, and he will be capable of everything; he can say with the Apostle: 'I can do all things in Him who strengthens and comforts me.'" And he said: "The Congregation of the Mission will subsist as long as the exercise of mental prayer is faithfully maintained in it, because prayer is like an impregnable rampart that will protect the missionaries from every assault; it is a mystic arsenal, or like the Tower of David, which will furnish all sorts of arms, not only for defence, but also to attack and rout all the enemies of God's glory and of the salvation of souls."

He required that meditation be made as well in sickness as in health, on days of repose as on those of labor. "My Lord, the Prince of Conti" he said in this connection, "will one day be our judge, at least he will be mine. He is admirable in His fidelity to the exercise of prayer; he devotes two hours to it every day, one in the morning and the other in the evening. Be his occupations ever so great, no matter what company he has, in it he never fails. It is true he is not so bound to the precise hour that he cannot advance or delay it according to necessity. May God grant us this attraction for union with Him in prayer."

It was in the morning, at the conclusion of his own prayer, that Vincent gave his counsel and instructions to his missionaries. He called upon them, at least twice a week, to give an account of the good thoughts that God had given them during meditation. This *repetition of prayer* had for him an especial charm. Even when away from his Community, in travelling, he made use of it. When he journeyed, even with seculars, he succeeded in gaining them over not only to employ a certain time each day in meditation, but also to interchange the communications which the Spirit of God had made to each. The domestics were invited to speak in their turn, and one of them once related: "Having considered that our Lord has recommended assistance to the poor, I thought I ought to do something for them; but being poor myself, and not able to give anything, I took the resolution of at least rendering them some little honor, to speak kindly to them when they speak to me, and even to take off my hat in saluting them."

These words impressed Vincent; he thanked God who loves to communicate Himself to the simple, he induced pious ladies to establish the custom, of repetition of prayer among their servants, and he was confirmed in his own practice of interrogating the least of his brothers, at St. Lazarus, as well as the most learned of the missionaries.

In fact, at each repetition of prayer, he always invited three or four to speak, and, no matter how pressing were the calls elsewhere, he listened to them with kindness and with joy, for entire hours. It afforded mutual edification; it was a school, a practical lesson from which the new-comers and the inexperienced might form themselves in the great art of mental prayer.

Our Saint set himself to explain to the Daughters of Charity, in the conferences of the 1st and 31st of May, 1648, the nature and the excellence of this prayer. He said: "There is nothing which Our Lord has so much recommended to His Apostles, since he exhorted them to ask the Father anything in His Name and promised them at the same time that it would be granted. But these words were not addressed merely to the Apostles; they were also intended for all Christians. There are certain persons, naturally timid and fearful, who dare say nothing through fear of being repulsed, who dare propose nothing out of fear of being ill-received, and who dare ask nothing through fear of being refused. Now, Jesus Christ gives us complete assurance that the Eternal Father will be well pleased to have us ask Him, in the Name of His Son, what we desire, and that He is ready to grant it to us; and He is not content to assure us of this, but that we may pray with more confidence, He promises it with a kind oath, of using the words: 'Amen, I say to you.'

"He Himself has given us the example. Jesus was a man of prayer. From His most tender age, He, at times, escaped from the presence of the Blessed Virgin and St. Joseph, that He might, with more liberty, address His prayers to God, His Father. When about thirty years of age, He withdrew into the desert where He remained forty days in order to prepare Himself, by prayer and fasting, for the preaching of His Gospel; and during the entire course of His laborious life He was ever punctual to prayer, going from time to time to Jerusalem, and often separating Himself from His Apostles in order to pray. The night before His passion, He prayed at different intervals with such fervor that for three hours He was in a bloody sweat and suffered mortal agony.

Learn, therefore, well, the nature of prayer. What nourishment is to the body, prayer is to the soul; and as a person who takes his repast only every two, or three, or four days would directly become faint and unable to perform his duties, having neither strength nor vigor, so a soul that does not devote a certain specified time to prayer, or does it but rarely, will become entirely tepid, will languish, will be without strength or virtue, will be troublesome to others and insupportable to itself, and will become disgusted with its state and its vocation.

"Prayer is, as it were, the irrigation of our souls. Florists and gardeners are careful to take their time in watering their plants twice a day, during the heats and dryness of summer, and they do so with intelligence, for otherwise their plants would perish. But with this care the roots receive nourishment from the earth, and a certain humidity, coming from the watering, runs up the stock, and gives life to the branches and to the leaves, and taste to the fruit. So, too, dryness coming upon the garden of our souls, all plants therein would perish if the care and labor of the gardener were wanting, that is, if they be without prayer which, like a gentle dew, every morning softens our souls by the grace which it draws down upon them. Are we wearied from the incidents and annoyances with which, during the day, we meet, we have, again, in the evening, this sweet and refreshing means to give vigor to our actions. Oh, what great fruit the soul would bear in a short time were it careful to refresh itself with this sacred moisture! It would be seen to advance every day from virtue to virtue, just as the gardener perceives his plants growing in proportion as he waters them: as a beautiful aurora that rises in the morning and constantly increases till noon, so, too, that soul makes uninterrupted progress until it reaches the Sun of Justice, Who is the true light of the world, and is lost in Him, as the aurora is, in some measure, lost in the midday sun.

"Prayer is, as it were, as the soul of our soul. The soul it is that gives life to the body, that gives motion to it, that enables it to speak and to act, and as the body without the soul is but an unsightly corpse with neither movement nor action, so a soul without prayer is devoid of feeling and movement for the service of God, having no longer any but low and grovelling thoughts for the things of earth.

"Prayer is a mirror in which the soul sees all its stains, its ugliness, and all that which makes it disagreeable to God. People in the world never leave their houses without precisely attiring themselves neatly, and consulting their mirror to see if there be anything about them that might shock propriety, and some are so vain as to bear a mirror attached to their girdle so as to be able to look at themselves from time to time. Now, if people of the world employ such means to please men, is it not far more just that persons consecrated to God would adorn themselves in the mirror of prayer, by means of aspirations and little reviews, and when they discover anything displeasing to the Divine Majesty, to ask pardon in order to enter again into His favor.

"It is chiefly in prayer that God makes known to us what He wishes us to do, or to avoid. The holy fathers are exultant when they speak of prayer, and declare, among other things, that it is a fountain of Juventas wherein the soul grows young again. It is in prayer that a blinded soul recovers its sight, that a soul, deaf to the voice of God, becomes attentive to His holy inspirations, that the soul which was heavy and sluggish in the things of salvation, on account of its evil habits, becomes strong, full of courage and of fervor. Whence comes it that we see persons stupid, ignorant, without education, and without knowledge of the mysteries of our religion change, in so short a time, if it be not through prayer, the fountain of Juventas, in which they grow young and are renewed?

"Prayer is an elevation of the mind to God. In prayer the soul goes out of itself, as it were, to seek God in Himself. Prayer is an interview of the soul with God; it is a mutual communication wherein God tells the soul interiorly what He wishes it to know, and to do; wherein the soul tells God the demands which He Himself has made known to it.

"Prayer is a sermon which we preach to ourselves to convince ourselves of the necessity of having recourse to God and of co-operating with His grace to extirpate vice from our souls and to implant virtue in them. We must occupy ourselves in prayer particularly in combatting that passion or vicious inclination that predominates in us, and strive to continually mortify it; because, when we overcome that, all the rest is easy. But we must be firm in the combat. It is also important to act quietly in prayer and not strain the mind by force of application and through a desire for fine and subtle thoughts; we must raise the mind to God and listen to Him, for one word from Him will effect more than a thousand reasonings, and more than all the speculations of our understanding. I would we had this manner of prayer, of elevating ourselves from time to time to God, keeping ourselves in humble recognition of our own nothingness, waiting until it pleases Him to speak to our hearts and to give us some word of eternal life. Only that which God inspires and comes from Him can profit us. We must, also, receive from God what we are to communicate to our neighbors, according to the example of Jesus, who, speaking of Himself, said He taught others only what He had heard and had learned from His Father.

'It is natural to pray. We see little children do it with joy, and God takes a singular pleasure in their little prayers. Mr. de Berulle held their prayers in so great esteem that when he met children he took them by the hand that they might give him their blessing.

"There are two kinds of prayer; the one, vocal, which consists in the sole use of words, and the other, mental, which is made by the mind and heart, without words. The example of Moses shows us clearly what virtue, what efficacy there is in mental prayer; for the people of God, engaged in battle, gained advantage according as the holy prophet, without making use of a word, raised his hands towards heaven, or lost ground, as he lowered them. At another time, when Moses was in mental prayer, God spoke to him: 'Why do you prevent me from destroying this ungrateful people?' The Holy Law-giver only wished the more in prayer, and obtained mercy for his people. What, then, must be the efficacy of prayer, since it can tie the hands of God?

"Mental prayer is made in two ways: either by the understanding or by the will. The prayer of the understanding is when we strive to recollect ourselves, and to place ourselves in the presence of God in order the better to seek to understand the mystery or the truths proposed, so as to draw from them suitable instruction, to excite affections proper to the subject, and to take strong resolutions to fly evil and to embrace the good which God gives us the grace to know. Though the resolutions and affections are acts of the will, yet the prayer is called of the understanding, because it consists principally in the search of truth. It is named, more frequently, meditation.

"The other, which is principally in the will, and is called affective, is not suitable for every one. God gives it to whom He pleases, and when He pleases. Men cannot teach it; they can attain to it neither by their own industry, nor by their own effort. In this prayer, a soul, without contributing anything of its own, finds itself suddenly filled with lights and holy affections. The understanding is at times enlightened in certain truths incomprehensible to all others, and the will is aflame with all species of good desires."

Thus we see that the prayer which the saint counselled and taught was particularly positive and practical, following the character of his mind and of his virtue. He respected that extraordinary and sublime prayer to which God elevates certain favored souls by a particular operation of His spirit rather than by their own industry and the efforts of their faculties; he recognized that God's conduct in regard to privileged souls is admirable and His ways incomprehensible; still, he held to the maxim of the apostle, not to easily believe in all spirits, and to prove them well to discover if they be from God; he knew further, from St. Paul, that Satan often transforms himself into an angel of light, and that he leads astray as well by the appearance of good as by the suggestion of evil; he knew, too, from his own experience that there are kinds of prayer elevated and perfect in appearance which, nevertheless, lead in the wrong way. He, therefore, advised all to follow the humblest and commonest way, as being the more secure and within the reach of all, until God, but God Himself and God alone, would take hold of the hand and lead unto another.

Moreover, recalling to mind the predilection of God for the lowly and simple, he said further to the Daughters of Charity: "Although persons of learning have great facilities to make their prayer well on account of the lights and the knowledge which they possess, yet God's intercourse with the simple is far different from that which He holds with the learned, as our Lord assures us in these words: 'I give Thee thanks, O Father, Lord of Heaven and earth, because Thou hast hidden these things from the wise and prudent, and hast revealed them to the little,'

On those souls God delights to shed His most glorious lights, and His greatest graces; He lays open before them what the schools have been unable to discover, and He develops for them mysteries in which the most learned see but darkness. A theologian, it is true, discourses of God, as science has taught him, but a person of prayer speaks of Him in a totally different manner; the theologian speaks from an acquired science, and the person of prayer, penetrated with cha..y, from an infused science; and in this case the theologian is the more learned, and he must maintain silence in the presence of a man of prayer because the latter treats of God far differently.

"Let us, therefore, persevere in prayer without being discouraged by dryness or difficulties. During twenty years, St. Teresa was unable to make mental prayer, and did not understand it. She, however, persevered, and God imparted to her an eminent gift of prayer. In faithfully striving to make our prayer, we, at least, practice every kind of virtue; obedience, humility, faith, hope, charity, and, above all, mortification, which, like an inseparable companion, should always accompany prayer." All these instructions, and others still, we find admirably developed in a conference to the missionaries, on the 10th of August, 1657. The saint explained, successively, what is to be avoided, and what must be practiced in order to pray properly and well.

Carelessness first must be avoided. "Prayer is not thought of; we come to prayer I know not why, through custom, because others come; we think of everything, we do not at all dispose ourselves for prayer. Prayer is an elevation of the mind to God, wherein we represent to Him our necessities, and implore His Divine assistance; we should, then, beforehand prepare ourselves well for it. What are we about to do? What should we hope for in treating with so great a Majesty? Of what have we the most need? What grace should we ask of Him?

"Let us place a guard over the levity and inconstancy of our poor minds, that we may retain our thoughts in the presence of God, that we may enchain that flighty imagination that runs everywhere, and yet, let us do so without too great an effort, without strain, for that is always hurtful, and never good.

"Finally, let us avoid curiosity. We must not come to prayer to hear what will be said, to learn, to study, to enter deeply into the most hidden mysteries in order afterwards to discourse well on them. You will say: 'I will be asked an account of my prayer. I must have something good to say.' In such case, we invent, we subtilize, we arrange in order in our mind, and all this is done for the purpose of display in repetition, to have something beautiful to say, and to be able to say it in a way other than common. No, gentlemen, this is not to pray but to study, and God grant it may be nothing more.

"But here, now, is what we must do. We must first place ourselves in the presence of God, in considering Him either as He is in the heavens, seated upon His throne of Majesty, whence He turns His eyes upon us, and contemplates all things; or in His immensity, everywhere present, here and elsewhere, in the highest heavens and in the lowest depth of the abyss, seeing our hearts and penetrating the most secret folds of our conscience; or in His presence in the most holy sacrament of the altar. Oh! my Savior, behold me, a poor and miserable sinner, behold me at the feet of Thy Divine Majesty, behold me at the foot of the altar when Thou reposest. Grant, oh, my Savior! that I may do nothing unworthy this holy presence. Or, finally, we may consider Him as within us, penetrating our inmost nature and resting in the depth of our heart. And, do not question if He be there. Who doubts it? The Pagans themselves have said: 'God is among us, and we have within us communings with Heaven; that spirit comes from above.' This truth is not questioned. 'But Thou, O Lord, art among us.' (Jere. 14-9). Nothing is more certain. And this point, this placing ourselves in the presence of God, is very important, for upon it depends the body of the prayer; that well done, the rest follows of itself.

"Then, let us beg God to give us His grace, that we may properly converse with His Divine Majesty, recognizing that of ourselves we can do nothing, conjuring Him by His great love for us, by His infinite merits, through the intercession of the Blessed Virgin and the saints."

"We, then, propose to ourselves the subject of prayer. This subject is either sensible, or insensible: if it be sensible, as for instance a mystery, we must represent it to ourselves and pay attention to all its parts and all its circumstances; if it be imperceptible by the senses, as a virtue, we must consider in what it consists, what are its chief qualities, as also its signs, its effects, and especially its acts and the means to put it in practice. It is good, also, to seek after reasons that will induce us to embrace the virtue upon which we meditate, and to pause at those motives that touch us most. They may be drawn from the Sacred Scriptures, or else from the holy Fathers; and when memory recalls certain passages from their writings, appropriate to the subject of prayer, it is well to digest them in our mind; but we should not search for them in time of prayer, nor even apply our mind to the consideration of many of them; for, to what purpose delay the thought on a collection of passages, and reason, unless, perchance, to enlighten and render subtle our understanding? And this is to apply ourselves to study rather than to prayer.

"When fire is wanted, flint is used, it is struck, and, as soon as the fire catches the substance prepared for it, the candle is lighted; and he, who having lighted the candle would still continue to strike the flint, would make himself ridiculous. In the same way, when a soul is sufficiently enlightened by considerations, what need is there to seek after more and to hammer and rehammer our thoughts in order to multiply reasons and thoughts? Do you not see that it is a loss of time, and that then we must apply ourselves to move the will, and to excite its affections by the beauty of the virtue and the deformity of the contrary vice? This is not difficult, for the will follows the light of the understanding, and inclines to what is proposed to it as good and desirable. But this is not yet enough. It is not sufficient to have good affections, we must go further and take resolutions to work earnestly, further to acquire the virtue, proposing to ourselves to put it into practice, by producing its acts. And this is the important point, and the fruit that we should derive from prayer; hence it is that we must not pass lightly over our resolutions, but reiterate them and imprint them well on our hearts; and it is good to foresee the obstacles that way arise, and the means that will aid to put our resolutions into practice, and to resolve to avoid one and to adopt the other.

"Now, for this, it is not necessary, nor often expedient, to have grand thoughts on the virtue that we wish to acquire; no, nor even to desire to have these high thoughts; for the effort to render virtues present to the senses whilst they are purely spiritual qualities may often injure and trouble the mind, and the two great application of the understanding heats the brain and occasions pains in the head; as also acts of the will too often repeated, or too much forced, dry and weaken the heart. We must use moderation in everything; excess in no matter what, and particularly in prayer, is never praiseworthy. We should act moderately and calmly, and preserve, above all, peace of mind and of heart.

"In finishing our prayer, we should thank God for the lights and graces that He accorded us during it, and for the resolutions with which He inspired us, and beg His assistance to put into execution, as soon as possible, what we proposed to ourselves to do.

"God be praised! this is what we do in prayer. And now let us devote ourselves to this practice of prayer, since through it all good comes to us. If we persevere in our vocation, it is on account of prayer; if we succeed in our labors, it is on account of prayer; if we avoid falling into sin, it is on account of prayer; if we continue in charity, if we be saved, it is to God and to prayer we owe it. As God refuses nothing to prayer, so also does He grant scarcely anything without it: *Pray ye therefore the Lord of the harvest.* (Mat. ix, 38); no, nothing, not even the diffusion of His gospel and what interests most His glory: *Pray ye therefore the Lord of the harvest.* But, O Lord, that concerns Thee, and is Thy affair. No matter: *Pray ye therefore the Lord of the harvest.* Let us all, then, humbly ask of God that He will cause us to adopt the practice of prayer."

To ascertain if he were well understood, if his method were well followed, or to give each one some special advice he interrogated in turn the brothers and the priests: "Brother, what method do you always follow in your prayers?" "Father, I always divide the subject into certain points." "You do well, brother. Yet when we take a mystery as a subject for meditation it is not necessary, nor expedient, to delay on a particular virtue and to make our ordinary division of the subject in regard to that virtue; it is better to consider the history of the mystery and pay attention to all the circumstances, there being none, be they ever so little, or so common, in which great treasures of grace are not hidden, if we only knew how to search. This I recognized lately, at a conference of these gentlemen who assemble here. They had, as the subject of their entertainment, what was necessary to be done to spend well the time of Lent. It was a very common subject, one they were accustomed to treat every year, and yet such good things were said that all present were greatly moved, and I, myself, particularly; and I can say in all truth, I never saw the members of the congregation more devout, nor heard discourses that made a greater impresssion on the mind; for, though they had previously spoken several times on the same subject, yet it seemed as if they were not the same persons who spoke, God having inspired them in prayer with a totally different language. See, my brethren, how God conceals treasures in things that appear so common, and in the least circumstances of the truths and mysteries of our holy religion. They are as the little grains of mustard-seed which become large trees when it pleases our Lord to extend His blessings to them. Our subjects of meditation resemble the stores of merchants; and as there are stores in which you can find only one class of goods, and others in which you can obtain anything you desire, so, too, are there subjects of meditation which instruct in one virtue only, whilst others contain the riches of every virtue; such, for instance, are the mysteries of the birth, of the life, and of the death and resurrection of our Lord Jesus Christ. To draw fruit from them we must adore our Lord in the condition in which the mystery represents Him, praise Him, and return thanks for the graces that He has merited for us, humbly represent to Him our miseries and our wants, and ask of Him the succor and the graces necessary to imitate and practice the virtues that He there teaches."

"Brother," he asked of another, "do you derive any profit from prayer? 'But little, Father.' 'How does this come,' rejoined the Saint, "during the repetition of prayer I was thinking within myself how it was that some made so little progress in this holy exercise. There is reason to fear lest the evil be that they do not sufficiently practice mortification and that they give too much liberty to the senses. If we read what the most expert masters of the spiritual life have left us in their writings, we can see that they unanimously held that the practice of mortification is absolutely necessary in order to pray well, and that, to dispose ourselves properly for prayer, we must mortify not only the eyes, the tongue, the ears and all the exterior senses, but we must also mortify the faculties of the soul, the understanding, the memory and the will. In this way, mortification will be a good preparation for prayer, and reciprocally, prayer will help to properly practice mortification.

"Another cause of this little progress is that some have fine thoughts and good sentiments, but do not apply them to themselves, and do not reflect on their own conditions. And yet has been very often recommended that, when God communicates in prayer any light or any good sentiment, we make use of it for our own particular wants. We must reflect on our own defects, confess and acknowledge them before God, and at times even accuse ourselves of them before the congregation for the sake of humbling ourselves and to experience greater confusion, and take strong resolutions to correct ourselves. This is never done without profit."

Thereupon, a brother fell upon his knees and asked pardon for having done nothing in prayer for some time back, and for not being able even to apply himself to it. "May God bless you, brother," said the Saint, "He sometimes permits that we lose the liking that we felt for prayer, and the attraction prayer had for us, and even that we grow weary in it. But this is, ordinarily, to exercise and to try us, and we must not become down-hearted, nor give way to discouragement. There are many good souls who are treated in that manner, and so have been many of the saints. Yes, I know several very virtuous persons who feel only repugnance and dryness in prayer; but as they are faithful to God, they make good use of them, and this contributes, not a little, to their advancement in virtue. It is true that when this aversion and dryness happen to those who begin to give themselves to prayer, there is sometimes reason to fear that this comes from negligence on their part, and it is to this, my brother, that you must pay attention. But, perhaps, it is not your fault. 'Do you not experience a pain in your head?' 'Yes. Father; and it comes from having wished, in the last retreat, to make everything in prayer present to the senses.' 'You should not act in that manner, brother, nor strive, in prayer, to perceive by the senses that which by its nature is imperceptible, for this is self-love, which in this way seeks itself. In prayer we should act in a spirit of faith, and in a spirit of faith consider the mysteries and the virtues upon which we meditate, sweetly, humbly, without making any effort with our imagination, employing the will in producing affections and resolutions rather than the understanding to obtain knowledge. And, meanwhile, we should persevere courageously, in imitation of our Lord, who '*being in an agony prayed the longer.*' (Luke xxii., 43.) Prayer is a gift of God which we must demand of Him with importunity, saying with the apostles: '*Lord, teach us to pray,*' (Luke xi., 1); and we must, in patience and humility, await this grace from His Goodness.'"

Another brother speaks in his turn: "I cannot make my prayer well because I have no mind. Of my faculties I am able to use but one, and that is the will. It begins, from the moment the subject is proposed, and without any reasoning, to produce affections, at one time thanking God, again asking pardon and exciting confusion and regret for sin; or else supplicating Him to grant the grace to imitate our Lord in some of His virtues, and then in taking resolutions."

"Continue that way, brother," interrupted the saint, "and do not trouble yourself about the employment of the understanding which is used only to excite the will. Since yours, without considerations, goes thus to the affections and to the resolutions of practicing the virtue, may God grant you the grace to keep on in that way and become more and more faithful to His holy will! The soul resembles a galley that moves on the water by means of oars and sails. As the oars are not used unless when the wind fails, and as the sailing is more pleasant and faster when it is favorable, so we, in like manner, must use considerations in prayer when the movement of the Holy Ghost is not felt, but when this heavenly wind blows in upon our hearts we must abandon ourselves to its actions."

Vincent then applied himself to show the difference between the thoughts that are inspired by God and those that come from ourselves. "Remark," said he. "the difference between the light of the fire and that of the sun. At night, our fire gives us light and we see things by means of its flame, but we see them only imperfectly, we perceive but the surface, and the brightness can go no further; but the sun fills and vivifies everything with its light; it not only discloses the exterior of things, but by an inherent force penetrates the interior. Now, the thoughts and considerations which spring from our understanding are but as little fires which show, only slightly, the outside of things, and effect nothing more; but the lights of grace, which the Sun of Justice sheds upon our souls, disclose and enter into the depths of our hearts. and excite and stimulate them to produce wonderful effects. We must, consequently, ask of God that He Himself enlighten us and inspire us with what is pleasing to Him. All these lofty and far-fetched considerations are not prayer; they are often rather the outcome of pride. And of those who content themselves with such thoughts. and who find their pleasure in them, it may be said. as of the preacher who would show off his fine language, whose entire delight and complacency would be to see his auditory satisfied with what he utters; in this, it is evident, it would not be the Holy Ghost, but rather the spirit of pride that would enlighten the understanding and give expression to all those fine thoughts; to speak more properly, it would be the demon that would influence him and cause him to speak in that fashion. It is the same in prayer when we strain after beautiful considerations, when we entertain ourselves with extraordinary thoughts, and especially when this is done for the purpose of giving them out in repetition that others may admire. There is in this a species of blasphemy; it is, after a manner, to be idolatrous of our own minds. For, whilst treating with God in prayer. you meditate on what satisfies your pride, you employ this holy time in seeking your own gratification, and, in taking delight in the beauty of your thoughts, you sacrifice to this idol of vanity.

"Ah! my brothers, let us guard against this folly; let us acknowledge that we are laden down with misery; let us seek only after that which will lead us to the solid practice of virtue. Let us, in prayer, abase ourselves even to nothingness, and in our repetitions humbly tell our thoughts; and should any that seem to us beautiful present themselves let us greatly distrust and fear lest it be the spirit of pride that produces, or the Devil that suggests them. For this reason we ought always profoundly humble ourselves when these fine thoughts come to us, either whilst in prayer, or in preaching, or in conversation with others. Alas! The Son of God could have charmed all men by His all-Divine eloquence and yet He did not wish to do so; but, on the contrary, in teaching the truths of His Gospel, He made use of common and familiar expressions and words; He loved always to be despised and contemned rather than to be praised and esteemed. Let us, then, my brethren, see how we may be able to imitate Him best, and for this purpose let us suppress, in prayer, as elsewhere, all thoughts of pride; let us follow in everything the traces of the humility of Jesus; let our words be simple, common and familiar; and, when God permits it, let us be glad that what we say obtains no consideration, that we are despised, that we are laughed at, holding it for certain that without a true and sincere humility, it is impossible for us to be of profit, either to ourselves or to others."

His practical sense always preferred in prayer affections to thoughts, and, again, resolutions to affections. "I am in doubt," said a missionary in repeating his prayer, "whether I should hereafter take any more resolutions, so unfaithful am I in putting them into practice." "My dear sir," Vincent immediately rejoined, "that is not a sufficient reason; for, as in taking nourishment, though we do not appear to derive any benefit, still we do not, for that reason, abstain from eating. To take good resolutions is one of the most important parts, nay, the most important part of prayer. It is to this we must devote ourselves, and not so much to reasoning or to language. The principal fruit of prayer consists in forming good and strong resolutions, in being penetrated with them, in being well convinced of their necessity, and in taking the proper means to put them into practice, foreseeing and overcoming all difficulties.

Yet this is not enough, for, after all, our resolutions are in themselves but physical and moral actions, and, though we do well in forming them in our hearts and in being steadfast in them, we ought, nevertheless, recognize that whatever good they possess, that their practice and their effects depend absolutely on God. And why is it, think you, that we most frequently fail in our resolutions? It is because we trust too much in them, we confide in our good desires, we lean on our own strength, and this is the reason we derive no fruit. Hence, after taking resolutions in prayer, we must pray to God, and, with a distrust in ourselves, ask for His grace that it may please Him to communicate all that is necessary to fructify these resolutions. And, although, after this, we again fail in them, not only once or twice, but in many instances, and even during a length of time, then, notwithstanding that we did not practice a single one of them, nevertheless we should not neglect to renew them and to have recourse to the mercy of God and ask for the aid of His grace. Past faults, should, indeed, be a subject of humiliation, but not a reason why we should lose courage; and no matter into what fault we fall we should not, on that account, diminish in anything the confidence that God wishes we should have in Him; but, on the contrary, we should take a new resolution to rise, and, with His grace, which we should ask, be careful not to fall again. Although physicians see no effect produced by the remedies they prescribe to a sick person, yet they do not, on that account, cease to continue and renew them until they perceive some ground for hope. If, then, in sickness of body, though long and dangerous, remedies are constantly applied, even when no improvement is visible, how much greater reason is there to do the same in regard to the infirmities of our souls in which, when it pleases God, grace works wonders?"

CHAPTER VII.

DEVOTION AND PIETY TOWARDS GOD AND THE BLESSED SACRAMENT—IMITATION OF JESUS CHRIST.

I

Devotion, such as we understand it here, is a virtue whereby we manifest respect and affection for all that relates to Divine honor and worship.

The devotion of St. Vincent de Paul took its rise in the exalted and profound idea that he entertained of the infinite grandeur of God.

This devotion filled his heart, animated all his words, manifested itself in every action of the day, in his entire conduct. In the morning, at the first sound of the bell, he arose from his bed, made the sign of the cross, prostrated, and kissed the floor. He adored the Majesty of God, gave Him thanks for His glory, for that which he gave His Son, the Blessed Virgin, the Holy Angels, his Guardian Angel, St. John the Baptist, the Apostles, St. Joseph and all the other Saints in Paradise. He again thanked Him for the graces bestowed upon the Church, for those that he received himself, and particularly, for having preserved him during the night. He offered Him his thoughts, his words and actions, in unison with those of Jesus Christ; he asked of Him to keep him from all sin and to aid him in faithfully accomplishing all that would be most agreeable to Him.

After these first acts of religion he repaired to the Church, where, notwithstanding his age and the swelling in his limbs, he arrived before the youngest and the most healthy. The sight of his family assembled before our Lord rejoiced and consoled his soul.

Having finished his prayer, he recited the litanies of the Holy Name of Jesus, and, among the glorious epithets the Church applies, he dwelt with an especial delight on the one: "Jesus, Father of the poor." After prayer, he went almost every day to confession, because he could not bear in himself even the appearance of sin. Scarcely ever could his confessor find matter for absolution. "Ah! sir," the humble Saint would say, "if you could see me as God makes me see myself, you would judge otherwise."

He then prepared himself for mass, and, though but just come from prayer, he spent a considerable period in this preparation. He finally vested and celebrated mass. He appeared at the altar as another Jesus Christ, victim and sacrificer; as victim, he abased and humbled himself; as a criminal, as one condemned to death, he recited the *Confiteor*, pronounced the *Domine, non sum dignus*, and all the words of the liturgy that express humility and compunction, especially the *Nobis quoque peccatoribus*, concerning which he wrote: "When you come to the *Nobis quoque* of the mass think of me as of the greatest sinner in the world;" as sacrificer, he was grave and majestic as the Savior, and at the same time full of sweetness, of serenity, of mercy; it was with these sentiments expressed on his countenance and in his attitude that he turned towards the people, and, by the sound of his voice, by the manner in which he extended his arms, it was perceived that his heart expanded and that he desired to embrace them all, as on another Calvary, in the charity of Jesus Christ. He recited the prayers of the mass and performed the ceremonies with neither slowness nor precipitation, occupying, but not going beyond, the half-hour. He pronounced all the words in a tone moderate and agreeable, distinct and devout, and with evident unison between the lips and the heart. At the reading of the Gospel, he redoubled his respect and his attention, and, when he met with some word of our Lord, he recited it in a more tender tone of voice, and with more affection. At the double affirmation of the God of Truth: "Amen, amen, I say to you," he recollected himself more especially, so as to pay greater attention to the words that followed, wherein he suspected something important, or some mystery; and he read them slowly, with faith and submission, in order to impress them deeply on his heart. All who assisted at his mass were greatly edified. "My God," they said, "behold a priest that says mass well!"—"That must be a holy man," added one; another said: "He is rather an angel at the altar."

And thus he said mass every day, except on the first three days of his annual retreat, on which, according to the usage of the Congregation, he omitted it. These days of penance and greater purification excepted, in the city or country, at home, or in traveling, sick or well, he never, up to the last weeks of his life, when his limbs refused longer to support him, omitted the daily sacrifice.

Having said mass, he assisted at, and often served, a second. He was overburdened with work, he was old,—eighty years of age,—he could not walk without a support nor could he kneel without the greatest difficulty; no matter, the venerable superior, with the simplicity of a young cleric, and with more respect and greater devotion, served the least of his priests at the altar. He did it in faith and in love; he also wished to give an example to his clerics, that they should never permit, while they were present, a lay person to serve mass. "It is a shame for an ecclesiastic, one who is set apart for the service of the altar," he said to them, with Bourdoise, "to allow, in his presence, others to fill his office."

On festivals and at solemn offices his piety shone with new lustre. He foresaw and carefully informed himself in regard to all the ceremonies. No rubric, consequently, was violated by him, nor did he permit a departure from any. He humbled himself greatly before God, and before his brethren, for his inability to make the genuflexion in the manner prescribed by the Church, and whenever he thought that he failed in any other of the ceremonies, he, immediately after the service, on his knees asked pardon of the whole Community. And faults committed by others he imputed to himself, which, however, did not hinder him, notwithstanding his great weakness, from severely reprimanding them. Moreover, he gave such example and such edification that the services at St. Lazarus were known throughout all Paris for the religion, the dignity and the modesty that accompanied them. Vincent himself, when he sang, or recited the psalms in choir, resembled less a man than an angel from Heaven chanting the praises of God. His priests and his clerics imitated his respect and his piety. With eyes cast down and fixed on their books, in a modest immobility, they gave no signs of life save by the pious sound of their voice and the emotions emanating from the Divine love within them.

Such as Vincent showed himself in the public offices, such was he in the private recitation of the breviary under the eye of God alone. He always recited it with uncovered head, on his knees, except during the last two or three years of his life when his infirmities, forbidding him that humble and respectful posture, forced him to remain seated. And on his knees, too, and with uncovered head, he daily read a portion of the Sacred Scripture, and particularly of the New Testament.

His devotion extended to all the mysteries of our holy religion, and, in particular, to that of the Most Holy Trinity, the first of all; then to the Incarnation which, for us, is the most touching manifestation of the Trinity, and to the Holy Eucharist which perpetuates, on earth, the Incarnation.

If his devotion to the Holy Eucharist, considered as sacrifice, were great, it was none the less so towards this same mystery considered as Sacrament.

When before the Holy Tabernacle, he always maintained himself on both knees, and in a posture so humble that he seemed, the more to testify his respect, to wish to abase himself to the centre of the earth, and with such faith manifested in his countenance, one would say that he saw Jesus with his eyes; with such devotion, he would have inspired the most incredulous with faith and the most insensible with piety; in such modesty and silence, that he had not a single glance for the greatest magnificence, nor a word for the most august personages.

There he loved to remain all the time that his duties left at his disposal, and there he forgot himself for hours together. There he went, like Moses of old, to consult the Divine oracle in all his difficulties. It was there, back of the high altar of St. Lazarus, or in whatever other place he found himself, that kneeling and with bare head, he opened and read the letters which he saw were important. One day, in the court of the Palace in Paris, a letter was handed to him, in which was announced the success of some very important affair. Though suffering greatly in his limbs, he ascended to the high chapel of the Palace, and, finding it closed, he at least knelt at the door and in this position informed himself of the contents of the letter.

Before going out he visited our Lord in the Blessed Sacrament, whom he called the master of the house, to salute Him, to take leave of Him and to receive His blessing; on re-entering he returned to render, as it were, an account of his mission, and also to thank Him for the graces that he received whilst away, and to humble himself for the faults he believed he had committed.

In passing through the streets if he met the Blessed Sacrament, he immediately, in whatever place he was, threw himself on his knees and remained so until it had passed out of sight, and often, even, he, with bare head, followed it, striving to be as near as his old and infirm members would permit.

On his journeys, as he passed through a village he would dismount, or leave the carriage, to go visit the Church and salute our Lord in the Blessed Sacrament, or, should it happen to be closed, to kiss the doorstep; and when come to the end of his journey his first visit was again to the church.

In his sickness, being unable to celebrate mass, he wished at least, to receive Holy Communion, which he did to the eve of his death, and with such a respect and such a rapture, that it is as useless, as it is impossible, to attempt to describe.

Profanations, committed by heretics, or by the military, grieved him mortally. Tears, extraordinary penances, fervent prayers, all were offered in reparation and atonement He went himself or sent some of his community in pilgrimage to the profaned churches; the priests said mass and the others received Holy Communion there in reparation. He made good the material loss caused by sacrilegious thefts of sacred vessels and ornaments; and by means of missions he repaired the injury done the honor of God and souls by impiety and heresy.

He adored, in the Incarnation and Eucharist, his God abasing himself to our level, and becoming like unto us, and his grateful love for Jesus inspired him with the desire to render himself, in his turn, similar to Him. He formed himself upon and he lived according to this Divine model. In imitation of Jesus he hid, under cover of a lowly and apparently common life, the most heroic virtues; under the exterior of a poor peasant, the most excellent gifts of both grace and nature; under a constant profession of stupidity and ignorance, a judgment the most perfect, and a knowledge most extensive. He breathed but Jesus, and in his words, in his thoughts and in his actions, he repeated but His language, he acted only with Jesus before him as a model. Jesus always, Jesus everywhere, Jesus in all persons and in all things; such was his doctrine, such his morality and such his policy, and this he loved to express in one word: "Nothing pleases me but in Jesus Christ."

This constant and universal keeping in view of Jesus enlightened, elevated, and spurred on his charity. He saw Jesus as Supreme Pontiff in the person of the Pope, as bishop and prince of pastors in the bishops, as high priest in the priests, as master and sole doctor in the doctors of divinity, as king of kings and as judge of judges in princes and magistrates, as great and noble in men of birth, and as little in the lowly, as workman in the person of artisans, as a divine merchant in men of traffic, as poor in the poor, as prisoner in prisoners, as infirm and agonizing in the sick and dying. Hence, his respect and his tenderness for all classes of men, and especially for all those whose lowliness and whose suffering presented a greater resemblance to the God annihilated and to the man of sorrows.

II

So faithful an imitation himself of Jesus Christ, he could, in turn, serve as a model to his brethren, and transform into rules and lessons for them his own practices. And, first of all, he endeavored to imbue them with a very high idea of God. He said to them one day: "Let us strive, my brethren, to conceive a great, a very great idea of the majesty and sanctity of God.

If our mind were sufficiently strong to penetrate a little into the immensity of His sovereign excellence, O my Jesus, what high sentiments of it would we not conceive! We could then well say with St. Paul that eye hath not seen, nor ear heard, nor hath it entered into the heart of man to conceive anything comparable to Him. He is an abyss of perfections, an Eternal Being, most holy, most pure, most perfect and infinitely glorious, an infinite good, comprising all goods, and Himself incomprehensible. Now this knowledge, which we have, that God is infinitely above all knowledge and all created understanding, ought to be a sufficient motive for us to esteem Him infinitely, to annihilate ourselves in His presence, and to cause us to speak of His Supreme Majesty with the greatest reverence and submission; and in proportion as we esteem Him, so will we love, and this love will beget in us an insatiable desire to acknowledge His benefits, and to procure Him true adorers."

Devotion to the mysteries of the Most Holy Trinity and the Incarnation he made an express rule for his community, and the Holy See especially approved it in the bull of erection of his congregation. "We will endeavor to acquit ourselves of this duty with very great care, and if possible in every manner, but principally in doing these three things: First, in eliciting from our inmost heart acts of faith and religion in regard to these mysteries; second, in offering every day in their honor some good works, and in celebrating their festivals with as much solemnity and devotion as possible; third, in laboring strenuously, both by instruction and example, that the people know and honor and worship them." He said to them with regard to the celebration of mass: "It is not enough to celebrate mass, we must, moreover, offer this sacrifice with the greatest possible devotion, according to the will of God Himself; conforming ourselves, with His grace, as much as we can, to Jesus offering Himself, when on earth, to His eternal Father. Let us use all endeavor, then, gentlemen, to offer our sacrifices to God in the same spirit, in which our Lord offered His, and as perfectly as our poor and miserable nature will permit."

He prescribed the greatest respect in the church and in the ceremonies. Precipitation, genuflexions half-made, the least negligences in the Divine service were a torment to his exalted idea of religion, and an alarm to his soul ever trembling before the possibility of scandal. Hence, he took care to correct in private, and, if necessary, in public, all the faults that he observed. If one of his members passed before the altar, making a genuflexion carelessly and thoughtlessly, he immediately called him back, and showed him in what manner and how far he should bend before God. On these occasions he would say: "We should never conduct ourselves as mere puppets, which are made to move quickly, and the salutations of which are without reverence or soul." And, after his humble habit of accounting himself responsible for all faults he added: "Who is guilty, my brethren! It is this miserable person who is speaking to you, and who would cast himself on his knees if he could. Excuse my infirmities." And in fact, it was a cruel privation to him, and one that he attributed to his sins, when he could no longer kneel, and he publicly asked pardon for it, and besought them not to be scandalized. "Nevertheless," he added, "if I see the congregation relax I will force myself on my knees, cost what it will, and rise as best I may, with the aid of some of you, or in making use of my hands, so that I may thus give the example that I ought to give. For, the faults committed in a community are imputed to the superior, and the faults of the congregation in this point are always serious, as much because there is question of a duty of religion and of an exterior reverence that marks the interior respect we show God, as because, if we be the first to fail, those preparing for ordination, and the clergy who come here, will believe themselves under no obligation to do better; and those who will succeed us in the congregation and who will model themselves after us, will do still less, and thus everything will tend to decay; for if the original be defective what will the copies be? I beg you, then, gentlemen and my brothers, to pay great attention to this, and to comport yourselves in this action in such a manner that interior reverence may suggest and always accompany the exterior. God desires to be adored in spirit and in truth, and all good Christians should do so in imitation of the Son of God, who, prostrate on the earth in the Garden of Olives, united to this devout posture a profound interior humility, out of respect for the Sovereign Majesty of His Father."

What he said of the genuflexion he applied to all the ceremonies. "They are, in truth, only the shadow, but the shadow of the greatest things, and this is the reason we should perform them with all possible attention, in a religious silence, and with great modesty and gravity. How will these gentlemen who come here carry them out if we ourselves do not perform them well? The singing must be grave, without being hurried, the psalms recited with an air of devotion. Alas! if these ceremonies are not properly performed, how will we answer when God will demand an account."

The holy ardor which he drew from Holy Communion burned in his words. "Do you not, my brethren," he said, "do you not feel a Divine fire burning within your heart every time you receive the adorable body of Jesus Christ!" He would not have any remain away easily on account of interior trials or troubles. "You have done somewhat wrong." he wrote to a person, "in abstaining from holy communion to day on account of the interior trouble harassing you. Do you not see that it is a temptation, and by this means you give a hold to the enemy of this most Adorable Sacrament? Do you imagine that, by remaining away, you will become more fit and better disposed to unite yourself to our Lord? O, surely, if such were your thought you have deceived yourself very much, and all this is but pure illusion!"

It is well known how grieved he was when he perceived among Christians the falling off from the frequent use of Holy Communion, and with what eagerness and earnestness he condemned the book of Arnauld and the Jansenist doctrines which were calculated to detach both faithful and clergy from the "frequent use of the Sacraments."

He urged especially the imitation of Jesus Christ. "Let us honor the unknown state of the Son of God. There is our centre, that is what He desires of us for the present, and for the future, and always, until His Divine Majesty will make known, in a way that cannot lead astray, that he wishes something else of us. Let us honor, I say, the simple, common life our Lord led upon the earth, His humility, His abasement, and all the excellent virtues He practiced in this manner of life. But, let us honor this Divine Master particularly in his moderation in action. No, he did not wish always to do all that he could do, in order to teach us to be content whenever it is not expedient to do all that we may be able, but only that which charity demands, and which is in conformity with the orders of the Divine Will.

"Oh! how I esteem that generous resolution you have taken to imitate the hidden life of our Lord! It is evident that this thought comes from God, since it is so removed from the sentiments of flesh and blood. Consider it as certain, that that is properly the disposition of the children of God, and consequently, be firm in it, and resist with courage any and all contrary ideas that may suggest themselves. Rest assured that by this means, you will be in the state God wishes, and that, thus you will constantly do His holy will, which, after all, is the end to which we should tend, and to which all the saints have tended."

We have seen how he wanted his missionaries to conform to the example of Jesus in their sermons and in all the other functions of their ministry. "He who says missionary, says a man called by God to save souls; for, our object is to labor for their salvation in imitation of our Lord Jesus Christ, Who, alone, is the true Redeemer, and who has completely verified the lovely name of Jesus, which signifies Savior. He came from Heaven to earth to exercise the office of Savior. To save was the object of His life and of His death, and He still continues to manifest this quality of Savior by the communication of the merits of the blood which He shed. Whilst He lived upon earth all His thoughts were directed to the salvation of men, and He continues in the same sentiments, because He sees that such is the will of His Father. He is come, and He comes, to us every day for this purpose, and by His example He has taught us all the virtues peculiar to the office of Savior. Let us, then, give ourselves to Him that He may continue to exercise this same quality in us and by us."

Finally, he said in general of the rules of the mission: "These rules are almost all drawn from the Gospel, as each one may see.

and they all tend to conform our life to that which Jesus led upon earth. For it is said that this Divine Savior came, and was sent by His Father to preach the Gospel to the poor: *'To preach the Gospel to the poor He hath sent Me.'* (Luke iv, 18.), as, by the grace of God, the little congregation tries to do, and it has great cause for humility and confusion in this, that, as far as I know, there is, as yet, none other which has for its particular and principal end the announcing of the Gospel to the poor, and to the poor the most neglected; *to preach the Gospel to the poor He hath sent Me.* that is our end. Yes, gentlemen and my brothers, the poor are our portion. What a happiness to do the very same thing which, our Lord has said, He came from Heaven to earth to do, and by means of which we hope to go from earth to Heaven. To do this is to continue the work of the Son of God Who willingly went into the country places in search of the poor. Behold to what we are obliged by our constitution, to serve and aid the poor, upon whom we must look as our lords and masters. O, poor but blessed rules, which oblige us to go into the villages, to the exclusion of cities, to do as Jesus has done! Reflect, I beseech you, on the happiness of those who observe them, in thus conforming their lives, and all their actions to those of the Son of God. O, my Lord, what a motive we have in this to observe well our rules—rules that will conduct us to so holy and so desirable an end!"

CHAPTER VIII.

DEVOTION TO THE BLESSED VIRGIN AND THE SAINTS.

I

The Blessed Virgin was, in a certain manner, the first instructress of St. Vincent de Paul, and she received the first fruits of his piety. Among the ruins of the chapel of Our Lady of Buglos he passed his childhood; from his most tender age, when he had scarcely left his mother's arms, he loved to go to pray at the foot of a little statue which he himself had placed in the hollow of an oak. He grew up amid the traditions of the pilgrimage to the holy chapel and of the miracles wrought by Mary, and it was in a chapel dedicated to her honor that he said his first Mass. Such was the origin of that tender devotion to the Blessed Virgin for which he was distinguished even to extreme old age.

He made it a law to prepare himself for her festivals by fasting and good works, to celebrate on those days with solemnity, to offer the holy sacrifice in chapels or on altars dedicated to her honor, to terminate his conferences and his meetings with one of her anthems, to recite the rosary every day, and to wear it constantly at his girdle, as the livery of a holy vassalage, and to salute her at the sound of the Angelus bell.

He frequently visited her churches, and in times of danger, for religion and the state, he went on a pilgrimage to Chartres.

In each mission he pronounced, at least, one discourse in her honor, and two hundred years before the definition of the Church he proclaimed the privilege of her Immaculate Conception.

Finally, he placed under her protection all the confraternities of charity, and all the works that he established for the good of the Church, or of the poor.

Founder of a congregation of evangelical laborers, he naturally had a great devotion to the holy Apostles, those first and greatest missionaries, and among all, particularly to St. Peter, the first vicar, and, in his successors, the continuator of Jesus Christ, and to St. Paul, the first master, the first doctor of those Gentiles among whom he, too, wished to spread the glad tidings of the Gospel.

On entering, and before leaving, his room he saluted his guardian angel. He did not forget St. Vincent Martyr, his patron saint, the traditions of whose life and doings, in Spain, he had collected; nor St. Vincent Ferrer whose name he bore, though not under his special patronage ; nor St. Joseph whom he gave as a patron to his internal seminaries, and whose devotion he introduced into all his houses, and whose intercession he besought in his important undertakings, with vows, masses, and pilgrimages; nor the blessed Bishop of Geneva whose canonization he, more than any other, brought about. He honored the saints in heaven in their glory, and on earth in their relics. He honored in them particularly the gifts of God, and to God, the Author of all sanctity, he always referred the worship he rendered them.

He still honored the saints in his devotion to the souls in Purgatory, for in them he recognized the living members of Jesus Christ, animated by His grace and assured of partaking, one day, in His glory. And this is why he prayed in their intention, and often offered for them the holy sacrifice of the Mass.

II.

He embodied all these devotions in the rules that he gave his community. He recommended to his brethren to pray for the dead, to say Mass for the least prayed for, to fly to the succor of the most miserable and the least provided for, and to recite before each meal the *De Profundis* for the benefactors of the Congregation.

This is what he says in his rule in regard to the devotion of the Blessed Mother: "We will strive, each and every one of us, to render, in the most perfect manner, with the help of God, the especial worship we owe to the Most Blessed Virgin Mary, Mother of God; 1st, in honoring every day, with an especial devotion, this most worthy Mother of Christ, and our Mother; 2nd, in imitating her virtues, as far as in us lies, but particularly her humility and her purity; 3rd, in earnestly exhorting others, as often as the opportunity offers and the power is given, to always render her great honor and worthy service." During the troubles of the Fronde he induced the ecclesiastics of his conferences and his ladies of charity to make several pilgrimages to shrines consecrated to Mary, in order to obtain, through the intercession of this Mother of Mercy, peace and prosperity for the kingdom. He required his missionaries to preach devotion to her, and to inspire the people with a great confidence in her protection. When, in its annual procession, the Chapter of Notre Dame would bring the principal relics of the Cathedral to St. Lazarus, he said to his community: "We will so dispose ourselves to receive these precious relics as though it were the saints themselves, whose relics they are, that were to do us the honor to pay us a visit; and thus we will honor God in his saints, and we will supplicate Him to make us partakers in the graces with which He endowed their souls."

CHAPTER IX.

ZEAL FOR THE GLORY OF GOD AND THE SALVATION OF SOULS.

I

That Vincent was devoured by zeal for the house of God his entire life testifies, because that life was employed in combating evil and in extending the reign of good; and in this consists true zeal. So many works, undertaken for the renovation and sanctification of the clergy, so many confraternities, so many assemblies, so many institutions, so many missions given in France and in other countries of Europe and in lands beyond the seas, all these, what are they if not so many living and speaking proofs of a zeal that burned to prevent all outrage against God, and to procure, in every place, His glory and the salvation of souls?

His zeal was enlightened, since it followed in the light of the Gospel and the decisions of the Church: it was wise, equally free from weakness and excessive rigor, prudent and discreet, devoid of bitterness and caprice, always tempered with respect or tenderness, according to the manner of person with whom he dealt; his zeal was invincible, never yielding to storms or persecutions, not even to death itself; disinterested detached at one and the same time from material interests as well as from those of self-love; indefatigable and persevering, believing never to have done enough whilst anything yet remained to be done, a zeal which neither old age nor infirmity could conquer or condemn to rest. He was already old when he said: "I remember, that formerly, when I returned from a mission, it seemed to me, on approaching Paris, that the gates of the city should fall upon and crush me; and, rarely did I return from the mission without being filled with this thought. The reason of that was that I reflected within myself just as if some one had said to me : ' You go away and behold, there are other villages that expect from you the same succor which you have just given to this and to that one. Had you not gone there, in all likelihood, such and such persons, dying in the state in which you found them, would have been doomed and lost forever. Now, if you found such and such sins in that parish, have you not reason to think that like abominations exist in the neighboring parish where these poor people expect a mission? And you depart! You leave them as they are! If, meanwhile, they die, and die in their sins, you will, in some manner, be the cause of their destruction, and you ought to fear lest God should punish you.' Thus was my mind agitated." And later still, at the age of seventy-eight, he envied the labors of his children. He wrote, in 1654 : " Oh how ashamed I feel when I see how useless I am, in this world, in comparison with you! . . . . In truth, my dear sir, I can scarcely contain myself; I must tell you, in all simplicity, that what you write gives me such new and ardent desires to be able, with my little infirmities, to go and finish my life under a bush in laboring in some town, that it seems to me I would be very happy did God grant me that grace."

II

"Is there anything" said the Saint, "more beautiful than zeal? If the love of God is a fire, zeal is its flame; if love be a sun, zeal is its ray."

This zeal inflamed his discourses and his letters, and enkindled the same fire in the hearts of his missionaries.

He wrote : "Oh! how happy are they who worthily give themselves to God, to do what Jesus Christ has done, and to practice, in imitation of Him, the virtues that He practiced, poverty, humility, patience, zeal for the glory of God, and the salvation of souls. For in this way they become true disciples of such a Master; they live purely in His spirit, and diffuse, with the odor of His life, the merit of His actions for the sanctification of souls for whom He was pleased to die.

"Are we not truly happy, my brethren, to be able to manifest in truth the vocation of Jesus Christ? For, who express better the manner of life that Jesus led upon earth than the missionaries? I do not say it of ourselves alone; I understand it also of those great apostolic laborers of different orders who give missions, both within and without the kingdom. They, indeed, are great missionaries whose shadows only we are. See how they betake themselves to India, to Japan, to Canada, in order to continue the work Jesus Christ began, and which He has not abandoned since the first moment He was appointed to it by the Will of His Father! Let us imagine that He says to us interiorly: Depart, missionaries; go where I send you! See the poor souls awaiting you, whose salvation depends upon your sermons and your catechetical instructions. This, my brethren, is what we should seriously consider; for God has destined us to labor at such a time, in such places, and in behalf of such persons. It is thus He appointed for His prophets certain places and certain persons, and did not wish them to go elsewhere. But what could we answer to God if it should happen that, through our fault, any one of these poor souls died, and was lost? Would not that soul have the right to reproach us with being the cause, in some manner, of its damnation, because we had not succored it as we should have done? And should we not fear that at the hour of death we will be asked an account of it? On the contrary, if we faithfully correspond to the obligations of our vocation, will we not have great reason to hope that God will augment in us His grace from day to day, that He will multiply, more and more, the congregation, that He will draw to it men who will possess the dispositions that are proper to act in His spirit, and that He will bless all our works? And, finally, all those souls who will have obtained their eternal salvation by means of our ministry will render testimony to God of our fidelity to our functions.

"How happy will be they, who, at the hour of death will see accomplished in them these beautiful words of our Lord: *'To preach the gospel to the poor He hath sent Me.'* (Luke iv., 18.)

But woe to us if we become relax in serving and in aiding the poor! For, after having been called by God, and having given ourselves to Him for that purpose, He, in some sort, depends upon us. Bear in mind these words of one of the Fathers: '*If thou hast not nourished, thou hast killed,*' words indeed, taken in reference to corporal refection, but which may, with as much truth and more reason, be understood of spiritual nourishment. Judge, then, if we have not cause to tremble should we fail in this point, and if, on account of age, under pretext of some infirmity or indisposition, we should relent and fall away from our first fervor. As regards myself, notwithstanding my age, I do not hold myself excused from the obligation of laboring in the service of the poor; for what can prevent me? If I be unable to preach every day, I will preach twice a week; and if I have not sufficient strength to make myself heard in large churches I will speak in small ones; and again, if I have not voice enough for that, what will prevent me from speaking simply and familiarly to those good people, as I do at present, gathering them around me as you are? I know aged men who at the day of Judgment can rise up against us, and among others, a good Jesuit Father, a man of holy life, who, having preached many years at Court, was seized, at the age of sixty, with a sickness that brought him to the verge of Death, during which sickness God showed him how vain and how useless, for the most part, were these studied and polished discourses of which he made use in his preaching. And this produced in him such great remorse of conscience that, having regained his health, he asked and obtained from his superiors permission to go teach catechism and give familiar instruction to the poor in the country. He labored for twenty years in this charitable employment, and persevered till death. On seeing himself about to expire he asked one favor, which was that the wand which he used in teaching catechism might be buried with him, so that, he said, it might bear witness that he had abandoned the service of the Court to serve our Lord in the persons of the poor country people.

"Some of those who seek to live a long time might fear that the labor of the missions would shorten their days and advance the hour of death, and for this reason they might, as far as possible, strive to avoid it as an evil that was to be dreaded; but I would ask of him who would entertain such a sentiment: Is it a misfortune for him who is journeying in a foreign land to make progress in his journey and to near his own country? Is it a misfortune for those who are on the sea to approach the port? Is it an evil for a faithful soul to go see and enjoy its God? Is it, finally, a misfortune for missionaries to quickly go to possess the glory which their Divine Master merited for them by His sufferings and death? What! Do we fear that that should happen, which we cannot sufficiently desire, and which happens only too late?

"But what I say to the priests, I say also to those who are not priests, to all our brothers. No, my brothers, you must not think because you are not employed in preaching that therefore you are exempted from the obligations which we all have to labor for the salvation of the poor. For you can labor in your own manner, and perhaps with just as much fruit as the preacher himself, and certainly with less danger for yourselves. You are obliged thereto, being members of the same body with us, just as all the members of the sacred body of Jesus Christ contributed, each in its way, to the work of our redemption. For if the head was crowned with thorns, the feet were pierced with nails whereby they were fastened to the cross; and if, after the resurrection, the sacred head was recompensed, so, too, were the feet, and they participated in the glory wherewith it was crowned."

He sustained their courage in their labors and sufferings. "Oh, sir, what consolation I have in thinking of you who are entirely God's, and of your vocation which is truly apostolic! Love, then, this blessed lot that has fallen to you and which ought to bring down upon you an infinity of graces, provided you are faithful to the first. You will, doubtless, have much to struggle against, for the malign spirit and corrupt nature will league together to oppose the good you wish to do; they will represent to you the difficulties as greater than they really are, and in order to sadden and depress you they will use every effort to persuade you that, in your need, grace will fail you; they will raise up men who will contradict and persecute you, and, perhaps, among those upon whom you looked as your best friends, who should sustain and console you. Should such happen, my dear sir, you must look upon it as a good sign; for, then, by this means, you will have closer relations with our Lord who, being overwhelmed with sorrow, saw Himself abandoned, denied, and betrayed by His own, and rejected, as it were, by His own Father. Oh! how truly happy are they who lovingly carry their cross in following such a Master! Remember, sir, and firmly believe that whatever befalls you, you will never be tempted beyond your strength, and that God Himself will be your stay and your force, and so much the more completely as you will have neither refuge nor confidence in any but in Him alone."

He upheld them in their missions when these were apparently unfruitful, and he wrote: "Blessed be the Father of our Lord Jesus Christ, who has so sweetly and firmly inspired you with the thought of the mission which you have undertaken for the propagation of the faith! And blessed be the same Lord who has come into the world, not only to redeem the souls you go to instruct, but also to merit for you the graces that are needful to procure their salvation and your own! Since, then, these graces are all prepared for you, and since our Lord God, who bestows them, desires nothing so much as to grant them to those who wish to make good use of them, on what does it depend that you be not filled with them, and that by their virtue the remains of the old man be not destroyed within you, and the darkness of ignorance and of sin dispelled from this people? I will hope that, on your part, you will spare neither labor, nor health, nor life; you have given yourself to God for this purpose, and exposed yourself to the perils of a long voyage, and, therefore, it only remains for you to take a strong resolution to put your hand to the work in all earnestness. Yet, to begin well, and to succeed, you must remember to act in the spirit of our Lord, unite your actions with His, and give them a noble and all Divine end by dedicating them to His greater glory. By this means, God will shower down upon you and upon your works every sort of blessing. Still, it may possibly happen that you do not see them, in this, at least, to the full extent; for God sometimes, for very just reasons, conceals from His servants the fruits of their labors, but He does not fail to make their success very great. It is a long time before a farmer sees the results of his work, and sometimes he does not perceive at all the abundant harvest that his sowing has produced. This is what happened to St. Francis Xavier, who, during life, did not see the wonderful fruits his holy labors were to produce after his death, nor the wonderful progress of the missions which he began. This consideration should keep your heart free, and elevated to God, being confident that all will be well though the contrary may seem probable."

He turned persecution itself into a motive of zeal. "Who knows but that God has sent this misfortune to test our faithfulness? Do the dangers which they encounter deter merchants from travelling over the seas, or do soldiers refuse to go to war on account of the wounds, or even of the death, to which they are exposed? And should we fail to do our duty in succoring and in saving souls, on account of the worry of mind and the persecutions with which we meet?"

When he learned that any of his missionaries were a prey to the ravages of war, of pestilence, or of any other scourge, he esteemed them happy and took occasion to excite in those at home the desire of martyrdom. He said: "They suffer, by the grace of God, in the proper spirit, and they are happy in suffering, first because they render a service to God, and secondly, because they procure the salvation of souls. Now, we, too, gentlemen, ought to have a like disposition, and a similar desire to work for God and our neighbor, and be willing to wear ourselves out for this purpose. Yes, gentlemen, and my brothers, we must belong to God and to the service of our neighbor without reserve; we should be ready to go naked to clothe him, to give our lives to procure his salvation, to hold ourselves in readiness to do all and to suffer all for charity's sake, to be disposed to go wheresoever it may please God to send us for this purpose, be it to India, or to places still more distant, and, in fine, to be willing to expose our lives to procure the spirtual good of our dear neighbor and to extend the empire of Jesus Christ over souls. And I, myself, though old and worn, should not neglect to keep myself in this disposition, and be ready to go to the Indies, there to gain souls to God, even though I should die on the way. For do not think that God demands of us strength and healthy disposition of body; no, He only requires good will, and a true and sincere disposition to embrace all opportunities, to serve Him even at the peril of our lives, which our hearts should desire to sacrifice for God, and, should He so will, suffer martyrdom. And this desire is sometimes as agreeable to the Divine Majesty as the reality itself; the Church herself has a similar idea of this disposition, for she honors as martyrs many saints who were only exiled for the faith and died in exile a natural death. O, how our brothers, who labor in foreign lands, are learned in this science of suffering! Some are exposed to the dangers of pestilence in attending those who are stricken down; others are amid all the dangers of war; others are suffering all the pangs of hunger; and all in inconveniences, in labors, and in sufferings. Yet, notwithstanding all this, they remain firm and unshaken in the good work which they have undertaken. Let us acknowledge, and be grateful, gentlemen, for the grace God has given to this poor and pitiable Congregation, to see itself composed of such persons and such members so faithful and so constant in suffering for the service and love of His Divine Majesty. Courage, then, gentlemen, and my brothers; let us hope that our Lord will strengthen us in the crosses that will come upon us, how great soever they may be, provided He perceives in us a love for them and a confidence in Him. Let us say to sickness, when it presents itself, or to persecution, should it come, to interior and exterior pains, to temptations, and to death itself, when He sends it: ' Welcome, ye heavenly favors, graces from God, holy trials, which come from a paternal and all loving hand for my good; I receive you with a heart full of respect, of submission, and of confidence in Him who sends you; I abandon myself to you that I may give myself to Him.'"

Let us hear the Saint further in one or two of those discourses wherein he excited in his children a desire to die for Jesus, and for the salvation of souls. One of his missionaries, sent to Scotland, was imprisoned by Cromwell, that is, was on the threshold of martyrdom. The Saint said: "I do not know whether we should rejoice or be sorrowful for this. On the one side, God is honored in the state in which our brother is detained, since it is for His love; and the Congregation would be blessed should God find it worthy to offer Him a martyr, whilst he himself would be happy in suffering for God's name and in offering himself, as he has done, for whatever it may please Him to ordain in regard to his person or his life. What acts of virtue does he not, at present, practice; acts of faith, of hope, of love of God, of resignation and of oblation, whereby he prepares himself more and more to merit such a crown? All this excites us, in God, to great joy and gratitude. But, on the other hand, it is our brother who suffers; should we not suffer with him? As for me, I confess that, according to nature, I am greatly afflicted, and my grief is very sensible; but, according to the spirit, I judge we should bless God as for a very special grace. See how God acts! After a person has rendered Him some remarkable service He loads him with crosses and afflictions and opprobrium. O, gentlemen, and my brothers, there must be something very great in crosses and in suffering which the understanding cannot fathom, since, ordinarily, God causes the service done Him to be followed by afflictions, persecutions, prisons, and martyrdom, in order to elevate to a high degree of perfection and glory those who devote themselves perfectly to His service. Whosoever wishes to be a disciple of Jesus Christ must expect that; but he should also hope, that in case the occasion offers, God will give him the strength to support the afflictions, and to overcome the torments."

Two missionaries of Poland were in the midst of the ravages of war and pestilence. Vincent took the occasion to say to his Community: "Others would become discouraged in seeing themselves in such a condition, three or four hundred leagues away from their own country. They would say: 'Why were we sent so far away? The others are in France in comfort, and we are left to die in a strange land.' This is what carnal men would say, men who would cling to their natural feelings and who would not enter into the sentiments of our suffering Lord by placing all their happiness in suffering. Oh! how beautiful a lesson these His servants give us, from which we may learn to love all the conditions in which it may please Divine Providence to place us. They are indifferent both to life and death, and are humbly resigned to whatever God will ordain. They manifest no sign of impatience, nor of murmuring; on the contrary, they seem disposed to suffer still more. Are we in this condition, gentlemen, and brothers? Are we ready to undergo the trials that God will send, and to smother the movements of nature so as to live but the life of Jesus Christ? Are we prepared to go to Poland, to Barbary, to the Indies, to sacrifice to Him our gratifications and our lives? If such be the case, let us thank God; but if, on the contrary, there be those who fear to forego their care and comforts, who are so tender that they complain if the least thing be wanting to them, and so delicate that they want to change house and occupations because the air is not good, the food poor, or because they have not sufficient liberty to go and come as they would like, in a word, gentlemen, if some of us be still slaves of nature, addicted to the pleasures of the senses, as is the miserable sinner speaking to you, and who, at the age of seventy, is entirely worldly, let them consider themselves unworthy the apostolic state to which God has called them, and let them be ashamed in seeing their *Confreres* so worthily fulfilling their obligations whilst they are so far devoid of their spirit and their courage.

"But what have they suffered in that country? Famine? It is there. The plague? Both have been seized by it, and once a second time. War? They are in the midst of armies, and have fallen into the hands of the enemy's soldiers. In a word, God has tried them by every sort of scourge. And we, here, will be as if tied to home comforts, without heart, without zeal! We will look on at others exposing themselves to danger for the service of God, and we will remain as timid as wet hens!

Oh, misery! Oh, meanness! See, there are twenty thousand soldiers who go to war, there to suffer every kind of pain, where one will lose an arm, another a leg, and many their lives, and all for a little vain-glory, for hopes extremely uncertain; and yet they have no fear, they hasten there as if after a treasure. But to gain Heaven, gentlemen, there is scarcely one who stirs, and often, those, who have undertaken to conquer it, lead lives so soft and sensual that they are unworthy not only of a priest and a Christian, but even of a reasonable man. If there be such among us, they are but carcasses of missionaries.

"But, oh, my God! be forever praised and glorified for the graces Thou hast given those who abandon themselves to Thee; be Thou; Thyself, Thy praise for having given to this little Congregation these two men of grace.

"Let us give ourselves to God, gentlemen, to go to carry His holy Gospel over the entire earth and into whatever part He may lead us; there, let us maintain our part, and continue our duties until such time as His good pleasure will withdraw us. Let no difficulties move us; the glory of the eternal Father and the efficacy of the word and of the passion of His Son are at stake. The salvation of men and our own are so great a good that they merit to be obtained at any price. And it matters not that we die the sooner, provided we die with arms in our hands; we will be only the happier, and the congregation will not be any the poorer; for *the blood of martyrs is the seed of Christians.* For one missionary who shall have given his life for charity's sake, the goodness of God will raise up several who will take up the good where he will have left it. Let each one, then, determine within himself to combat the world and its maxims, to mortify His flesh and His passions, to submit to the orders of God and to give Himself entirely to the practices of His state, and in the accomplishment of the Divine Will, in whatever part of the world it may please God to place him. Let us, now, altogether take this resolution, but let us take it in the spirit of our Lord, with perfect confidence that He will assist us in our necessities. Do you not freely wish to do so, my brothers of the seminary? Do you not freely wish to do so, my brothers, the students? I do not ask the priests, for, without doubt, they are all so disposed. Yes, my God we all wish to correspond with the designs which Thou hast upon us. This is what all propose in general, and each in particular, with the help of Thy grace. We will, no longer, have any affection either for life or health, for our comforts or joys, or for one place or another, or for anything in the world that can hinder Thee, Oh Good God, from showing this mercy which we all, each for the other, ask of Thee."

Seeking to enlarge their zeal in proportion to the vast provinces that Providence opened to them, he added: "See the beautiful field that God opens up for us as well in Madagascar as in the British Isles and elsewhere. Let us pray that God will inflame our hearts with the desire to serve Him, and let us give ourselves to Him to do with us as He pleases. St. Vincent Ferrer encouraged himself with the thought that there would rise priests who, by the fervor of their zeal, would embrace the entire earth. If we do not deserve that God would give us the grace to be of those priests let us beg Him to make us, at least, their representatives and precursors. But be that as it may, we must be convinced that we will not be true Christians until we are ready to lose all, and give even our life for the love and glory of Jesus Christ, resolving, with the apostle, to choose torments and death itself rather than to be separated from the love of this Divine Savior."

In thus presenting to the holy ardor of his children vast spheres of labor, he influenced their zeal for the good works in which, in France, they were engaged, and especially for the spiritual retreats which, perhaps, after his death, they might be tempted to abandon. "Oh, gentlemen," he said, "how we should properly esteem the grace that God shows us in leading to us so many persons in order to aid them to work out their salvation! Among those who come are many soldiers, and, some days ago, one of them said to me: 'Sir, I must soon go to the war, and I desire, beforehand, to put myself in a good state. My conscience troubles me, and, uncertain of what will happen to me, I come to dispose myself for whatever

God may ordain in my regard.' We have now in the house a goodly number of persons on retreat. Oh, gentlemen, what immense good may not this produce if we only work faithfully in it! But what a misfortune if this house should tire of this practice. I tell you, gentlemen, and my brothers, I fear lest the time should come, when it no longer will have the zeal that up to the present has induced it to receive so many persons in retreat. And then, what will happen? It should be feared lest God take away from the congregation not only the grace of this work, but also lest He deprive it of all the others likewise. I was told, the day before yesterday, that the parliament had on that day degraded a councillor, that having brought him, clothed in his red robe, into the great chamber, where all the others were assembled, the president called the court-officers and commanded them to take from him that robe and his cap, since he was unworthy of these marks of honor, and unfit for the office that he held. The same thing will happen us, gentlemen, if we abuse the graces of God in neglecting our first functions. God will take them from us as being unworthy of the position in which He has placed us, and as unfit for the works to which He has appointed us. My God, what a subject of grief! But, in order to be thoroughly convinced how great an evil this would be should God deprive us of the honor of rendering Him this service, we should consider that many come here to make this retreat in order to know the will of God in the inspiration they have received to quit the world, and I recommend to your prayers one who has just finished his retreat, who goes, on leaving here, to the Capuchins, to take the habit. There are some communities that direct to us many of those who wish to enter among them, and send them here to perform the exercises of the retreat in order, before receiving them, the better to try their vocation. Others come expressly, ten, twenty, fifty leagues distant, not only that they may here recollect themselves and make a good general confession, but also to determine upon a state of life in the world, and to take the means to save themselves in it. We also see so many parish priests, and so many ecclesiastics who come here from all quarters to renew themselves in their calling, and to advance in spiritual life. They all come without troubling themselves about money, knowing that they will be well received without that. And, on this point, a person told me lately that it was a great consolation for those who had no money to know that there was a place in Paris always ready to receive them through charity whenever they would present themselves with the real design of making themselves right with God.

"This house, gentlemen, formerly served as a retreat for lepers; they were received, and not one recovered; and now it serves as a refuge for sinners, who are covered with a spiritual leprosy, but who, by the grace of God, recover; we go further, and say they are the dead who rise again to life. What a happiness that the house of St. Lazarus should be a place of resurrection! St. Lazarus, after being dead three days, and in the tomb, rises from it alive; and our Lord, who resuscitated him, does the same favor to many who, having remained some days here, as in the sepulchre of Lazarus, depart with new life. Who would not rejoice at so great a blessing, and entertain sentiments of love and gratitude for the goodness of God in conferring so great a favor! What a shame if we become unworthy of such a grace! What humiliation, gentlemen, and what regrets will we not have one day, if, by our fault we are degraded in this, to see ourselves in ignominy before God and man! What a subject of affliction to a poor brother of the Congregation who now sees so many people of the world coming from all parts to seclude themselves for awhile with us, in order to change their lives, and who, then, will see this great good neglected? He will see that none are any longer received; in a word, he will then no longer see what he had seen, for it may come to this, gentlemen, not perhaps, immediately, but in time. And what will be the cause? If a poor missionary who has become lax is asked: Sir, will you please direct this person in his retreat?—this request will be a torment, and if he do not excuse himself he will only, as the saying is, drag himself along; his desire to satisfy himself will be so great, and he will have such disinclination to curtail his ordinary recreation for a half-hour, or thereabouts, after dinner and after supper, that this hour will become unsupportable, though given to the salvation of a soul, and the most holily employed of the entire day. Others will murmur at this employment under pretext that it is very burdensome and very expensive; and in this manner the Priests of the Mission, who formerly gave life to the dead, will have no longer but the name and the appearance of what they had been; they will be but dead bodies and not true missionaries; they will be as the carcass of St. Lazarus and not as St. Lazarus' resuscitated, still less, men who raise the dead to life. This house, which now is a salutary pool in which so many come to wash themselves, will no longer be but a foul, corrupt cistern, through the laxity and idleness of those who inhabit it. Let us pray God, gentlemen and my brothers, that this evil fall not upon us, let us have recourse to the Blessed Virgin that she may, by her intercession and her desire for the conversion of sinners, turn it away. Let us pray to the great St. Lazarus that he may be pleased to be always the protector of this house, and that he may obtain for it the grace of perseverance in the good which it has begun."

He required, however, that their zeal should be discreet. "Zeal," he wrote, "is not good unless it be discreet. It seems you undertake too much at the beginning. By going too fast we often spoil good works, for then we act according to our inclinations which carry away with them judgment and reason, and make us think that the good, which is to be done, can be accomplished, and is proper at that time, when it is not so, and this the evil success afterwards verifies. The good that God wishes is done, as it were, by itself without being thought of. . . . . Oh, how I would like you to moderate your ardor, and weigh things well in the scales of the sanctuary before coming to any resolution. Be passive rather than active, and then God will alone do, by you, that which all men together could not do without Him."

He wished their zeal to be meek as well as discreet and moderate. Writing to one of his missionaries at Annecy, whose zeal was too severe and harsh, he said: "It seems to me that the zeal you have for the advancement of the congregation is always accompanied with some harshness, and even goes to bitterness.

What you tell me, and what you term laxness and sensuality in some prove this, and particularly the manner in which you tell it. Oh my God! My dear sir, great care must be taken in regard to this. It is easy to pass from a lack to an excess of virtue, it is easy from being just to become a reprobate, and all through inconsiderate zeal. They say good wine easily becomes vinegar, and that complete health is a sign of approaching sickness. It is true that zeal is the soul of virtue; but then, sir, it must, as St. Paul says, be according to knowledge; that is, understood of knowledge from experience. And because young people, generally speaking, have not this knowledge their zeal tends to excess, and notably those who are naturally harsh. Oh, my dear sir, we ought to guard against this, and distrust the majority of the movements and impulses of our mind, whilst we are young and of such a disposition. Martha murmured against the holy idleness and holy sensuality of her dear sister Magdalene, and considered her as doing wrong because she was not all anxiety, as herself, to wait upon our Lord. You and I, perhaps, were we present, would feel the same. And yet, '*O the depth of the riches, of the wisdom and of the knowledge of God! How incomprehensible are his judgments*' (Rom. ii., 33.) See how our Lord declares the idleness and sensuality of Magdalene more pleasing to Him than the less discreet zeal of St. Martha! In the name of God, my dear sir, let us enter into these true sentiments and these practices, and fear, lest the evil spirit design, through our excess of zeal, to induce us to fail in respect towards our superiors, and in the charity we owe our equals. That, sir, is where our less prudent zeal terminates, that, the advantage which the evil spirit reaps. Therefore, I beg of you, in the name of our Lord, let us labor to rid ourselves of all zeal opposed to respect, esteem, and charity; and, because, as it seems to me, the evil spirit aims at that in your and in my case, let us study to humble our understanding, to interpret favorably, in our neighbor, his manner of acting and bear with him in his little infirmities."

He recommended to them, above all, a disinterested, or rather, a gratuitous zeal. He wrote: "Do you not know, then, that a missionary, who labors on the strength of another's purse, is not less culpable than the Capuchin who receives money? I pray you, once for all, never give a mission but at the expense of your house."

He desired that they should be no more jealous than himself of the monopoly of good works, that they, every day, demand of God to send laborers into His vineyard, that they repeat, with a desire as ardent as his own, the *would that all could prophesy* of Scripture, that they experience no egotistical grief at the labors of others, but rather consider them far superior to their own, whilst, at the same time, they thanked God for the fruitfulness granted, as he said, to the little functions of the congregation. He wrote, in this sense: "It would be preferable to have a hundred missions established by others than to hinder a single one. Let us have more confidence in God. Leave to Him the care of guiding our little bark; if it be useful to Him, He will protect it from shipwreck. And so far from the number and size of other vessels causing it to sink, it will, on the contrary, sail among them with greater security, provided it go straight to its destination and do not amuse itself in crossing them."

Again, he wrote on the occasion of a mission given by Father Eudes: "Some priests from Normandy, directed by Father Eudes, came to Paris to give a mission, and with a special blessing. The court of *Quinze-Vingts* is very large, but it was too small to contain all that came to hear the sermons At the same time, a great number of ecclesiastics left Paris to go labor in other cities, and it is impossible to describe what wonderful fruits all have produced. And in all this we have had no share because our portion is the poor of the country. We have only the consolation to see that our little functions have appeared so beautiful and so useful that they have aroused the emulation of others, who apply themselves as we, and with more grace from God than we, not only in the function of missions but also in that of seminaries which are becoming numerous in France. There is cause to thank God for the zeal He excites in many for the advancement of His glory and for the salvation of souls."

And, with a humility still more disinterested, he said one day: "Let us, my brethren, be as the country-man, who carried the luggage of St. Ignatius and his companions weary in the journey. When he saw them fall upon their knees whenever they arrived at any stopping place, he did the same; when he saw them pray, he, too, prayed; and when these holy persons once asked him what he was doing, he answered: 'I pray to God that He may grant you what you demand. I am as a poor beast, that does not know how to pray. I pray Him to hear you. I would like to be able to pray to Him as you do, but I do not know how; hence I offer Him your prayers.' Oh, gentlemen and my brothers, we should look upon ourselves as the luggage-bearers of these worthy laborers, as poor simpletons who know not how to say anything, who are the refuse of others, and as poor little gleaners coming in the wake of these great harvesters. Let us thank God that in this He has been pleased to accept our little services. Let us offer Him, together with our little handfuls, the rich harvests of others, and be ever ready to do what is in our power for the service of God, and the assistance of our neighbor. If God gave such a beautiful light and so great a grace to this poor country-man as to merit a mention in history, let us hope that in doing our best, as he did, to contribute to His honor and service, His Divine Goodness will favorably receive our offering and bless our works."

In the same spirit of disinterested zeal he made for himself an inviolable rule, and imposed it upon his members, never to induce any to enter his community, either by promises, or by favors rendered, or by pious counsels. "Ah, gentlemen," he said, "be careful, when you serve and direct those who come here to make their spiritual retreat, never to say anything that may attract them to the congregation. It belongs to God to call them and to give them the first inspiration. Still more, even should they disclose to you that they had such a thought, and should they show such an inclination, be careful to avoid deciding them either by exhortation or advice, to become missionaries. Simply tell them that, as this is a very important thing, they should think on it, and recommend it more and more to God. Even represent to them the difficulties with which, according to nature, they are likely to meet, and that they must be prepared, should they embrace this state, to suffer much and to labor hard for God. But if, after this, they take their resolution, very well; then they may be brought to the superior to confer more fully in regard to their vocation. Let us allow God to act, gentlemen, and keep ourselves humbly in expectation and dependence on the orders of His Providence. By His mercy, such has been the custom in the congregation up to the present, and we can say, there is nothing in it that God has not placed there, and that we have sought neither men, nor goods, nor establishments. In the name of God, let us continue in this practice, and let God act. Let us follow His orders, I beg you, and not anticipate them. Believe me, if the congregation do this God, will bless it."

For a still greater reason he would not have those, who had the intention of entering another order, or those whom superiors had sent to try their vocation, retained at St. Lazarus: "Should we perceive that they have an idea of retiring elsewhere, to serve God in some holy order or community, oh, my God, do not let us hinder them; otherwise we ought to fear the indignation of God falling upon the Congregation for coveting what He did not wish it to possess. And tell me, if the Congregation had not been, up to the present, in this mind, not to desire other subjects, no matter how excellent, than those whom it pleased God to send, and who previously had, for long, the desire to enter, would the Carthusian Fathers and other religious communities send us, as they do, to make their retreat here, a number of young men who wish to join them? Indeed, they would be very careful not to do so. What! here is a subject who has the notion of becoming a Carthusian; he is sent here to confer with our Lord by means of a retreat, and you will try to persuade him to remain here! And what is this, gentlemen, if not to wish to retain that which does not belong to us, and to desire a man to enter a congregation to which God has not called him, and of which he has not even thought? And in what can such a mode of acting result, if not in bringing the entire congregation into disgrace with God? O, poor little Congregation of Missionaries, into how wretched a plight you would fall did you come to that! But, through the mercy of God, you have always been, and still are, far removed from such a practice. Pray to God, gentlemen, pray to God that He may confirm this Congregation in the grace He has given it of not desiring to have anything but that which He is pleased it should have."

He answered one of the priests who wished they would abandon the ruinous mission of Barbary. 'If the salvation of one soul is of such importance that we ought to risk our life to procure it, how can we abandon so great a number through fear of expense? And if no other good should result from these stations than to show this accursed land the beauty of our holy religion, which sends these men who have traversed seas, who have voluntarily given up their country and ease, and who expose themselves to a thousand dangers in order to bring consolation to their afflicted brethren, I think both men and money well employed."

Even the death of the missionaries in Madagascar, in Poland, in Genoa, in the British Isles, everywhere, should not affright their zeal nor diminish, in aught, their resolution to succor these poor people. And how he inveighed against the cowardly! "It is impossible," he said, "for a priest of the mission who leads a weakly, cowardly, tepid life to succeed in his state, or to meet with a happy end; for, what injury, think you, do these timid, weak souls effect in a community? And what prejudice do the slothful not do both to themselves and to others whom they discourage by their example and by their impertinent language? What good are all these employments, they say, all these missions, these seminaries, conferences, retreats, assemblies, and voyages for the poor? When Mr. Vincent is dead, all these will soon be abandoned; for how keep up all these undertakings? Where will you find missionaries to send to Madagascar, to the British Isles, to Barbary, to Poland and elsewhere, and where money to defray the expenses of missions so distant and so burdensome? To which we must answer: if the Congregation at its birth, and in its cradle, has had the courage to embrace these opportunities to serve God, and if the first that have been sent to these countries have manifested such fervor, is there not every reason to hope that it will become strengthened and augmented in time? No, no, gentlemen, if God presented to the Congregation still new occasions to serve Him, we should not fail, with the help of His grace, to undertake them. Those cowardly spirits are only capable of discouraging the others. For this reason you should beware of such persons; and when you hear them utter such language, say boldly with the Apostle: ' *Even now there are become many Anti-Christs in the world.*' (1 John, 2-18), anti-missionaries who oppose the designs of God. Ah, gentlemen, as yet we experience but the first graces of our vocation flowing in upon us, which graces, however, are very abundant; and we ought to fear lest, by our cowardice, we become unworthy of the many blessings which God has, up to the present, poured down upon the Congregation, and of the many holy employments His Providence has confided to it; we should tremble lest we fall into the state in which we see some communities,—an evil that would be the greatest that could come upon us."

CHAPTER X.

CHARITY.

I

The name of St. Vincent de Paul is a synonym for charity. Charity was the first exercise of his childhood and the last of his old age. Charity inaugurated his priesthood. His life was one uniform and uninterrupted act of charity. This chapter, therefore, would be as long as his life if it were to recount all the acts of charity performed by St. Vincent, who, like the Savior, went about the earth doing good. Hence, in order to avoid repetition, it will suffice to refer to his life which forms, in some manner, the first part of this work.

Charity was his soul; it exhaled from his person the good odor of Jesus Christ, it inspired all his words, it directed all his actions.

His charity was universal, embracing all creatures capable of receiving its effects, extending to all the necessities of body and soul; having a mouthful of bread for all hunger, a covering for all nakedness, an instruction for all ignorance, a consoling word for all sorrow, a heart and arms for the abandoned.

He carried his charity to the heroic ideal of the Gospel, to contempt and sacrifice of life. How often, in his journeys of charity, did not the Saint descend from his carriage and throw himself, at the risk of his life, between the drawn swords, and succeed, by his courage and his pious entreaties, in disarming adversaries! We cannot forget his voluntary captivity among the galley slaves, nor his substitution of himself for a doctor of divinity, who was troubled with a cruel temptation against faith.

His charity was well regulated. It ascended to the Sovereign Pontiff, the vicar, on earth, of Jesus Christ, in order to descend to the poorest and most lowly without neglecting any one in the interval. How many prayers he himself said, and begged of others, during the vacancies in the Holy See! What respect, what filial affection, he immediately professed for the elect of the Holy Ghost!

Bishops had in Vincent the most religious and the most devoted of servants. His correspondence with them is admirable for its humility and charity. He felicitated them in their successes and united with them in thanking Heaven. He moderated them in their labors. "It is true, my Lord, that I desired you would use moderation, but it is, that your work may endure, and that the excesses to which you continually go may not so soon deprive your diocese, and the entire church, of the incomparable good you do. If this desire accord not with what zeal inspires, I will not be astonished, because the human sentiments, which bind me, remove me too far from the eminent state to which the love of God has elevated you. I am, as yet, all sensual, and you are above nature: and I have no less cause to humble myself for my defects, than to thank God, as I do, for the holy dispositions which He gives you. I very humbly supplicate you, my Lord, to ask of Him for me, not, indeed, equal dispositions, but a little portion, or only the crumbs that fall from your table."

For like motives he did not wish them, unless in case of necessity, to expose themselves in time of contagion, and he traced out for them this beautiful line of conduct: "I know not, my Lord, how to express my affliction on account of the contagion with which your city is threatened, nor the confusion, on account of the confidence with which you are pleased to honor me. I pray God, with all my heart, to turn away this scourge from the people of your diocese, and that He will make me worthy to respond in His spirit to your command. My little thought, then, my Lord, is that a prelate, in such cases, should keep himself in readiness to provide for all the spiritual and temporal wants of his entire diocese during the general distress, and not shut himself up in any one place, nor engage in any occupation that will deprive him of the means of providing for others; and so much the more so, as he is not the bishop of any one place alone, but of his entire diocese, in the government of which he should so divide his care as not to confine it to any one particular locality, unless in case that he cannot provide for the souls of that place by means of parish priests or other ecclesiastics. In such a case, I think, that he is obliged to risk his life for their salvation, and commit the rest to the care of the Adorable Providence of God. It is thus, my Lord, that one of the greatest prelates of this kingdom acts. He has disposed his priests to run any risk for the salvation of their parishioners; and when the disease breaks out in any place, he hastens thither to see if the priest is firm in his part, to encourage him in his resolution, and to give suitable advice and the means to assist his people. He, without exposing himself among the sick, makes his visit, and then returns home prepared to incur the risk himself if he cannot supply, by others, the wants of any parish. If St. Charles Borromeo acted differently, it was, in all probability, through some special inspiration from God, or because the city of Milan alone was infected with the contagion.

"But, since it is difficult to do in an extensive diocese what can easily be done in one less great, it seems, my Lord, that in order to encourage your priests, it would be well for you, if agreeable, to visit the infected districts; or, if any indisposition, or the danger of being taken prisoner in these times of war, prevent you, you should send the archdeacons, or in their default, some other ecclesiastics to these localities, for the same object; and when you learn that the evil has broken out in some new place you should, in order to encourage the pastor and to give corporal assistance to the infected, send thither some ecclesiastic.

"The poor people, in country places, who are stricken with the contagion, are, ordinarily, abandoned and in great need of food. It would be an object worthy of your piety, my Lord, to provide for that by sending to all such places alms which might be put into the hands of good pastors who should procure bread, wine, and a little meat, for which the poor people could go to the place and at the time appointed. If the integrity of the pastor be doubted, it would be necessary to give the order to some other pastor or vicar in the neighborhood, or to some good lay persons of the parish who would undertake it. There is always, generally speaking, some one to be found who is capable of this charity, especially when there is no question of any intercourse with the plague-stricken. I hope, my Lord, if it please God to bless this good work, that to Him will accrue great glory, to you, my Lord, consolation in life and at the hour of death, and to your diocese great edification. But a necessary condition is not to shut yourself up in any one place."

He labored to find worthy successors to those who believed it their duty to resign their dignity. Sometimes he prevailed on them to remain at their posts. "You have not, my Lord, more difficulty in your episcopacy, than St. Paul found in his; and yet he sustained the weight until death, and not one of the apostles laid aside his apostleship, or its labor, or fatigue, unless to go receive his crown in Heaven. It would be rashness on my part, my Lord, to propose their example to you, did not God, who has promoted you to their supreme dignity, invite you Himself to follow them, and did not the liberty I take proceed from the great respect and inexpressible affection our Lord has given me for your sacred person."

He consoled them in their troubles and when they were accused before the king. He spared them, as far as possible, all pain and all humiliation, even to the detriment of his congregation. "It is preferable," he was accustomed to say on these occasions, "that suffering and confusion should fall upon us rather than that we should do anything to injure this good prelate."

During the public troubles he prevailed upon them, in the interest of the king and of the people, to remain in their dioceses, in order to suppress all factions, to alleviate existing misery and to preside over the pious exercises undertaken in supplication of the Divine Mercy. To those who had an idea of coming to Paris to complain of the injury done by the army, and to seek redress, he answered that all efforts for particular cases would prove useless in a calamity that extended over almost all France; that by remaining in their dioceses they could help their people more effectually, and that by keeping them in submission and fidelity they might open a way to royal gratitude.

He knew, also, how to give them firm advice, but with what wise and affectionate precautions! One of them was at law with his clergy. Vincent desired nothing better than to assist him, but he would have wished to do it by way of accommodation, and he wrote to him: "In the name of God, my Lord, pardon me, if I, from this place, intermeddle in these affairs, and not knowing that the overtures that I make will be acceptable to you. It may be that you will be dissatisfied. But I cannot help it, since what I do is through excess of affection, to see you delivered from the cares and distractions which this troublesome affair may occasion, so that you may occupy yourself, with greater tranquility of mind, in the government and sanctification of your diocese. For this object I frequently offer to God my miserable prayers. . . . . . "But, my Lord, there is one thing that grieves me greatly, namely that you have been represented to the council as a prelate who has a great facility in going to law; so much so that this impression has taken firm hold of the minds of the members. As for me, personally, I admire our Lord Jesus Christ, Who has diapproved of lawsuits, and yet, has graciously willed to have had one and to lose it. I doubt not, my Lord, that if you enter into some, it is for the sole purpose of maintaining and defending His cause. And, because you consider God alone and not the world, you preserve a great interior place amid all the contradictions from outside; you seek solely to please His Divine Majesty, without troubling yourself with what men will say. For this I thank the Divine Goodness; for it is a grace found only in souls intimately united with God. But I must tell you, my Lord, that this unfortunate opinion of the council can injure you in the present case, and prevent you from obtaining what you desire."

The Bishop, having refused any accommodation, the Saint insisted in these terms: "I humbly beseech you, my Lord, to bear with me this once, if I presume to make a proposal for an accommodation. I am sure you do not doubt that it is the affection of my poor heart for your service that makes me desire it; still, you might take it ill that one, so little intelligent as I am, and knowing that you have not found my first proposition agreeable, should presume to offer a second. Nor do I propose it of myself, but by the order of your agent who advises a friendly termination of these disputes. He gave several reasons, and, among others, that it is but propriety in so great a prelate to terminate the affair in a friendly way; particularly, since the difference is with your clergy among whom there are spirits who are disposed to rebel, and capable of harassing you all your life-time. And, judging from the temper of the council, he fears for the result of the proceedings; because many of those who compose it, not knowing your saintly life, nor the upright intentions which induce you to act in this manner, might think that there is something contrary to the patience and mildness suitable to your dignity. I humbly beseech you, my Lord, to excuse my boldness and not to consider what I represent to you as coming from me, but from your agent who is one of the wisest men of his age and one of the best judges in the world. I pray God to restore peace to your church and quiet to your mind. You know the power you possess over me and the singular love God has given me for your service; if, then, you judge me worthy of doing anything to serve you, His Divine Goodness knows that I will devote myself to it with all my heart."

He overwhelmed himself in excuses when he found it impossible to serve the bishops as they wanted. "I blush with shame, my Lord, as often as I read the last letter you have done me the honor to address to me, and, even when I think of it, considering how far your greatness has humbled itself before one born a poor swine-herd, and a miserable old man full of sin. At the same time, I experience great grief to have given you the occasion of coming to that, when I had taken the liberty to represent to your Greatness that we were unable to give the men desired. Your Greatness may well think that it has been through no want of respect or submission to all its wishes, but simply from pure inability to obey on this occasion.

In the name of God, my Lord, deign to pardon our poverty. You well know, my Lord, that there are none in the world more disposed to receive your commands than we, and in particular, myself, over whom God has given you a sovereign power."

When they consulted him, his humility knew no bounds: " Alas, my Lord, what are you doing in communicating so many important affairs to a poor, ignorant man such as I am, abominable in the sight of God and man for the innumerable sins of my past life, and so many present miseries, which make me unworthy of the honor your humility does me, and which, truly, should enforce silence on me did you not command me to speak! Here, then, are my miserable thoughts which I propose with all the respect I owe you, and in the simplicity of my heart."

Or again : " I have read and re-read your letter, my Lord, not to examine the question you propose, but to admire the judgment you arrive at, wherein there appears something more than the spirit of man; for, only the spirit of God, residing in your sacred person, could unite justice and charity in the degree you purpose in this affair. I have, then, but to return thanks to God, as I do, for the holy lights that He has given you, and for the confidence with which you deign to honor your useless servant. What you propose is so far above me that I cannot, without great confusion, think of the opinions you require of me. I will not, however, fail to obey you . . . . ."

Justice and mercy were the virtues with which the saint was ever inspired. Hence, it was only in extreme necessity that he would have ecclesiastical censures employed. Consulted on this head in regard to some religious who were unfaithful, particularly in the vow of poverty, he answered: " Alas! sir, how you confound the son of a poor peasant, one who has herded sheep and swine, who is still in ignorance and vice, in asking him for counsel; I will, however, obey, in the spirit of that poor ass that formerly spoke by virtue of the obedience he owed to him who commanded, and on condition, that, as no consideration is given to what fools say, my Lord, the bishop, as well as yourself, will pay no attention to what I may say, save in as much as it conforms with the best judgments of my Lord, and with your own."

After this usual beginning, he opens his opinions: "In general, we must treat unruly religious as Jesus Christ, in His time, treated sinners. A bishop and a priest, as such obliged to be more perfect than a religious, considered purely as a religious, should act for a considerable time, only by good example, and should bear in mind that the Son of God followed no other way during thirty years. After this, it is necessary to speak with charity and sweetness, then with earnestness and firmness, without, however, as yet making use of either interdict, or suspension, or excommunication, terrible censures which the Savior never employed. I well believe, sir, that what I say surprises you a little; but what will you have? This sentiment is the effect of what I feel touching the truths our Savior has taught by word and example. I have always remarked that what is done according to this rule succeeds admirably well. In following it, the blessed bishop of Geneva, and, after his example, the late Mgr. de Comminges, sanctified themselves, and were the cause of the sanctification of so many thousands of souls. You will, doubtless, tell me that a prelate who acts in this way will be despised. That will be true, for a time, and it is even necessary it should be so, in order that we may honor in our persons the life of the Son of God in all its conditions, as we honor Him in the condition of our ministry. But it is also true, that after having suffered for a time, and just as long as it pleases our Lord, He will give us the grace to do more good, in three years, than we, of ourselves, could do in thirty. Indeed, sir, I do not think success can be obtained otherwise. Fine regulations may be made, censures employed, and powers withdrawn; but will reformation result? There is scarcely a probability. Those means will neither extend nor preserve the empire of Jesus Christ in hearts. God formerly armed Heaven and earth against man; did He thereby convert him? Alas! it was necessary for Him to abase and humble Himself, in order to induce man to accept His yoke and His government. How can a prelate effect by his power that which God has not done by His Omnipotence?"

The charity of the Saint for the religious orders is well-known. No one, in truth, in the seventeenth century, rendered them more service. Minims, the order of Malta, the Congregations of St. Genevieve, of Premontre, of Grand-Mont, of St. Anthony, of St. Bernard, of St. Benedict, all had reason to be thankful for his charitable intervention in their behalf, and they rendered, by the voice of their superiors, or of bishops, ample testimony to his memory at the time of the process of his canonization. He treated all religious with an affectionate respect, throwing himself at their fee', and remaining prostrate until he received their blessing. "I have remarked," he used to say, "that everything succeeded with me on those days on which some one of these servants of God was pleased to bless me."

Humble and charitable as was his zeal for religious communities, it was also disinterested. He loved to make others the recipients of the honors and the advantages that were offered to himself. An ecclesiastic of Anjou, wishing to install a community of priests in one of his benefices, asked him for some missionaries for this object. He referred him to either the priests of St. Sulpicius or of St. Nicholas du Chardonnet. "They are," he answered him, "two holy communities which do great good in the Church, and which extend very much the fruits of their labors. They are better suited, and more capable, than we, to commence and perfect the good work you have so much at heart."

Into the hands of the priests of St. Sulpicius again he advised a lady to place the revenue of a foundation made by her ancestors for the formation of good ecclesiastics: "If, Madame, you make this disposition you can rest assured that the intentions of the donors in regard to the advancement of the ecclesiastical state will be faithfully executed. And if, for this purpose, you are pleased to inform yourself of the good that is done at St. Sulpicius, you may hope for like results when this community is established in your place, since it is everywhere animated with the same spirit, and since it has but one pretension, the glory of God."

From this we may judge of his esteem and affection for St Sulpicius, and of which, at this period, he gave an heroic proof. The enemies of Olier had stirred up against him a vile populace. Informed of the tumult, St. Vincent came on the spot in all haste, resolved to defend the life of his friend at the peril of his own. In effect, the fury of the crowd turned itself upon him. Without respect for the age of the holy old man, without consideration for his character and virtues, without gratitude for the immense services of this father of the people, they loaded him with reproaches, they even went so far as to strike him. Vincent uttered no complaint, but contented himself with repeating: "Strike St Lazarus, without fear, but spare St. Sulpicius." He rejoiced to thus serve as a protection for his friend; he was happy, he triumphed when he saw some friends of Olier, who, profiting by the turn in the popular fury, snatch him from the tumult and carry him off to the palace of the Luxembourg. Amid the jeers and scoffs of the multitude, Vincent then withdrew, thanking God for having braved persecution for justice and friendship. But he was not at the end of his role of substituting himself for others. The affair was brought before the council of state. There, all the blame of the sedition was thrown on St. Vincent. The title of Missionaries, which the Sulpicians, at that time, assumed, the frequent confounding of the Priests of the Conference with the Priests of the Mission, all gave occasion to many to regard Vincent as the Superior of Olier, and the disciples of the latter as members of Vincent's congregation. In consequence, the first time he went to the Council of Conscience he was received with an almost universal murmur of disapprobation. Courtiers, ministers of state, and even the princes, warmly censured his conduct. To turn away all this blame he had but to say one word: "The priests of St. Sulpicius are entire strangers to my conduct and my congregation." With what eagerness would he have said this if they had attributed to him the good done by Olier and his priests! But, there was question of sharing in a persecution; he carefully avoided declining the mutual responsibility that was thrust on him. He, therefore, took up the cause of Olier and his priests as his own, and defended it with more warmth than he would have shown in the interest of his own congregation. The truth was soon known. Then astonishment and admiration took the place of blame. And when he was asked, why he had, against all the rules of prudence, incurred the danger of compromising, for the sake of others, his own person and the members of his community, he simply answered: "I have only done my duty. Every Christian who follows the maxims of the gospel should do the same." The holy enterprises of a good priest appeared to him not as a private work, but as a public good which all were bound to preserve and defend.

This is why he was faithful until death to Mr. Olier. He closed his eyes, consoled his children, presided at the election of his successor and labored to perpetuate his work.

What the Saint did for religious men he did at the same time for religious women. The orders of the Visitation, of Magdalene of Providence, of the Orphan Sisters, of the Sisters of St. Genevieve, of those of the Cross, were indebted to him for good direction, or for their reformation, for their establishment or for their preservation.

And what did he not do for the secular clergy? The exercises of the ordinands, the ecclesiastical conferences, the spiritual retreats, the erection of seminaries, so many institutions established for their reformation and sanctification, sufficiently testify. And to complete this work in favor of the clergy, how great a charity, fearing neither expense nor ingratitude, did he exercise in receiving at St. Lazarus, the priests who flocked to Paris from every province.

In the so loving heart of Vincent de Paul, his children, even according to the order of the Gospel, should have a privileged place. From his *Life*, we learn how great was his tenderness for them, but especially when in persecution and sickness. This tenderness assumed a most touching character whenever any believed they had reason to complain of him. Immediately rising from his chair and throwing himself on the neck of him who avowed his aversion and discontent, he would say: "Ah, sir, had I not already given you my heart, I would now give it to you wholly." He used his utmost efforts to retain those who were tempted to leave the congregation. If, in spite of him, any left he still pursued them with his charity. In 1655, one of his young seminarists, contemning his advice, departed and enrolled himself in a company of Swiss guards which, too, he soon deserted. But this second desertion had like to cost him far more than the first. For, being captured and put in prison, he was condemned to death. In this extremity he remembered the father whom he had abandoned, and he had recourse to him. Vincent, full of pardon and charity for that prodigal son, interceded in his favor, and obtained his life.

To those whom he could not induce to remain, he gave the expenses of their journey, and recommended them to the superiors of his houses in the province. "I trust" he would write "that God will always give the congregation grace to exercise its kindness towards all the world, and especially towards those who may separate themselves from it; not only that they may have no cause of complaining, but also that, by heaping burning coals upon their head, they may recognize, even to the end, the charity of their good mother."

He listened to the complaints of the least of his brothers: "You have done well to inform me of it; I will attend to it. Always come to me, my brother, when you have any trouble, for you know how I love you." He reassured them when fearful of importuning him: "No, my brother, do not fear in any manner, that you will annoy, or importune me by your demands, and know now, once for all, that a person whom God has appointed to aid others, is no more overburdened with the assistance and instruction that is required of him, than would be a father with his child."

His charity followed his children in their travels, and everywhere prepared for them a like kindness. "I recommend such a one to your care," he always wrote to the Superiors of his houses, "I trust he will have great confidence in you, when he sees the patience, the charity which Our Lord has given you for those whom He commits to your direction." He responded to all their demands and provided for all their wants when on the mission. One of them wrote to him once to request, among other things, a skull cap. As he found none at hand, he took off his own and handed it to the brother. "But Sir," said the brother, "we can buy one in town and send it on some other occasion."—"No, my brother, we must not make him wait for it, he may need it right away. Send him ours, I pray you, along with the other things he asked."

His charity included the entire family of each of his confreres. "We will pray to God for this afflicted family," was he accustomed to say. "I request the priests, who have no special obligation, to say mass, and our brothers to receive holy communion for its intention; and I, first of all, will offer up to God for it, with a good heart, the mass I am about to celebrate."

With the lever of a like affection he moved all hearts and stimulated them to the most difficult sacrifices. The soldiers of Turenne exposed themselves to the fire of the enemy and braved all dangers at the least of his orders, because they saw in him, besides the renowned captain, the most attentive and compassionate of fathers. In like manner, the sons of Vincent, on a word from their superior, whose charity was to them as the image of that God, who was to be their recompense, were ready to fly to the most barbarous nations, there to brave pestilence the sword, death. And so much the more so as his charity still sustained them in the midst of their laborious work in distant missions. On their departure he fell at their knees and kissed the feet of the evangelists of peace; he, afterwards, watched over their wants, and sent them, at the extremity of the earth, these words of tenderness : "After the true and extraordinary marks which God has placed in you, of your vocation for the salvation of that people, I embrace you in spirit; with all the feeling of joy and tenderness merited by that soul which God has chosen, among so many others upon the earth, to lead to Heaven so great a number of souls, as yours, which has left all all for this purpose. And, truly, who would not love this dear soul, so detached from creatures, from its own interests, and even from its own body which it animates solely for the purpose of serving the designs of God who is its end and sole ambition? But yet, who would not take care to husband the strength of that body which has certainly given sight to the blind, and life to the dead? This is what induces me, Sir, to beg you to regard it as an instrument of God for the salvation of many, and, in this view, to preserve it."

But what will we say of his charity to the poor? Here, far more than in the presence of the glory of the Prince de Condé, one feels himself equally embarrassed, both by the greatness of the subject, and by the uselessness of the attempt. For, to continue with Bossuet: "What part of the habitable world has not heard of the charitable institutions of Vincent and the marvels of his charitable life? The Sisters of Charity, the Assemblies of Ladies, and of Lords, the work of the Galley Slaves, and of Barbary, the hospitals for foundlings, of the Name of Jesus, of the Holy Queen, and the general hospital—is not the mere list of these institutions, founded by Vincent, sufficient to impress the mind with an idea of the immense charity of the Saint for the miserable? I will not mention the Congregation of the Mission, established for the sole purpose of aiding the poor in their salvation, and in reference to which Vincent often repeated: "We are the ministers of the poor; God has chosen us for them. That is our principal object; all else is but accessory."

Vincent was, in truth, wrapped up in the poor; they were the object of all his thoughts and of all his affections, the subject of his grief and of his sorrow. "I am in trouble about the congregation," he sometimes said. "but, to tell the truth, it does not effect me as do the poor. We have but to go and ask what we want from our other houses, if they have it, or serve as curates in parishes; but the poor, what will they do, or where can they go? I confess that that is my burden and my grief. I am told that, in the country, the poor people say that while the fruit lasts they can live, but after that they have nothing left but to dig their graves and bury themselves alive! O, my God, what extreme misery! And the means to remedy it?"

The history of his life, shows how he did so. There, too, will be found how he saved Lorraine, Picardy, Champagne, and so many other provinces, and how he snatched from starvation and death the environs and faubourgs of Paris; how his action in this was direct and personal, how immense were his alms, and how he was proclaimed by the voice of public gratitude the general almoner of France, the savior and father of his country.

In this present work, we have but to gather a few particular facts, some anecdotes, a few ears gleaned after the harvest.

And first, some facts relative to the famous carriage which the charity of the Saint soon turned into a public conveyance. If he met any poor person in the streets of Paris or in the country he immediately made him or her enter the carriage. He did this one day in the case of a poor woman whom he, some leagues from Paris, met doubly tired, both by the walk and from the weight of the child she carried in her arms. Another time he again met a woman, and the disgusting ulcers which covered her were a new title to admission to his carriage. Not content with receiving her into his carriage, he wished to convey her to her destination. It was then, only, that he directed his carriage and that charity disarmed humility. It is true, that when he did not have his carriage, or when important business called him in another direction, he endeavored to procure a chair to transport the poor and the sick either to their homes, or to the Hôtel Dieu.

But he loved far better to conduct them himself. One day, in the faubourg St. Denis he saw a poor woman prostrate on the ground. Priests, levites, and people of the world all passed by without stopping, as in the case of the wounded man in the Gospel; or answered her moans with barren pity only. But, see! The good Samaritan comes. Vincent leaves his carriage, approaches, and, seeing that it was impossible for the poor woman to walk, he caused her to be put into his carriage, and, though his business called him to a far different and far distant section, he gave orders to drive to the *Hôtel Dieu.* After a few minutes' driving, the poor woman became sick and it was necessary to take her from the carriage, the motion of which she could not bear. Vincent ordered some wine to be brought, to strengthen her, and when she had somewhat recovered he paid the porters, and, with their burden, he gave them a letter of recommendation to the sister superior of the *Hôtel Dieu.*

Similar traits are innumerable in the life of this holy priest. Thus again, stopped one day in the streets of Paris, by the distressing cries of a little child, he immediately got out of his carriage, questioned the child and it, having shown a sore it had on its hand, he conducted it to a surgeon, had the sore dressed in his presence, paid the one his charge, consoled and returned the other to its parents. Such was the daily use of the famous carriage.

Here are other instances of his charity. A journeyman tailor, who had worked at St. Lazarus, wrote him from his home to please send him an hundred needles from Paris. The Saint, at that time, pressed with the most serious occupations both at court and in the city, found the request quite natural and hastened to comply.

He visited the prisons of the Chatelet and the Conciergerie to instruct and assist the prisoners. By procuring dowries for girls in danger, he secured them honorable marriage, or he obtained for them an entrance into a religious house. He settled the disputes of the entire district of St. Lazarus, restored peace among families, and even among the soldiers. When fire, sickness, or any other misfortune, ruined a family, he went to console it, he furnished what was immediately wanted, and finished by re-establishing it in its previous condition, procuring furniture, and material, and implements for work.

A poor carman lost his horses. He begged Vincent to help him to repair the loss, and immediately he received one hundred livres. Another died, leaving his seven sons stricken down with sickness. Having seen to their recovery, the Saint gave them a horse and a cart, and thus relieved their misery. A poor laborer died, leaving, to his wife and two little children, a hopeless lawsuit and want for an inheritance; Vincent supported the wife, and took the boys and maintained them till they were able to gain their own livelihood.

And how many poor, who will never be known, were indebted for their very existence to Vincent? Many regularly received a monthly sum. During his last illness, one of those, failing to receive his allowance, came to St. Lazarus, to demand, as if due him, the two crowns he had been receiving for the last seventeen years.

For many years he supported a poor blind man, and, before dying, Vincent recommended the continuance of that charity.

A woman, having told him of her distress, received a half-crown. "This is indeed very little in my extreme want" she sent him word, and instantly she obtained another half-crown.

A farmer, ruined by three consecutive inundations, was deprived of his farm by the landlord, who likewise seized his farm implements and his horses. Vincent gave him a piece of land belonging to St. Lazarus, already in seed, and furnished him with what was necessary to cultivate it. And as he could no longer keep his son at school, Vincent sent the boy to his house at Richelieu, obtained for him an ecclesiastical title and succeeded in making him a good priest.

An old soldier, the number of whose wounds procured him the nickname, *Riddled*, came one day to St. Lazarus, and called for the superior: "Sir," said he without any other introduction, in the rough freedom of his profession. "I have heard it said that you are a charitable man. Would you be kind enough to receive me into your house for some time?" "Willingly, my friend," replied Vincent and he ordered a room to be given him. Two days after, the soldier took sick. He was immediately placed in a warm, comfortable room, a brother was expressly appointed to wait on him, medicine and proper nourishment were supplied, and he was retained until he had fully recovered.

On one occasion, in coming home from the city, Vincent found at the gate of St. Lazarus some poor women, who asked him for some alms. He promised. But, having scarcely entered, serious and pressing duties occupied his whole attention and drove away all thoughts of the poor women. Some time after, the porter came and reminded him. He quickly went and brought the alms himself, at the same time throwing himself on his knees to ask pardon for having forgotten them.

Nothing had the power to discourage him; not even the insults of the poor. He did not wish vengeance for his brethren any more than he did for himself, on account of the ill-treatment with which their charity so often met. Two of his clerics, sent to visit the sick in the domain of St. Lazarus, were met by soldiers, and deprived of their cloaks. Two of the thieves were taken by the people of the neighborhood and brought to the prison of the Bailiwick. To punish them, Vincent had but to allow his officers of justice to act. But, far from this, he caused them to be visited and supplied with food, persuaded them, for their punishment, to make a good confession, and, on their promise to rob no more, ordered them to be set at liberty.

On another occasion it was the death of one his brothers he had to arrange in a Christian manner. Poor women, admitted to glean in the great enclosure of St. Lazarus were, by a brother, surprised in the act of stealing from the harvest. One of them took up a stone, and struck the brother dead. Vincent, immediately informed, sees this blood crying for vengeance. But the thought of the blood of Jesus Christ recalls mercy. He sent for the husband and advised him to quickly take his wife away, and, as they were both poor, he supplied them with money for the journey.

For greater reason did he pardon them, when they shot the pigeons of St. Lazarus. He used simply to say to the poachers: "Why do you kill the parent birds? If you want pigeons, why do you not come and ask me for the young ones?".

In general, he would never consent to punish any thefts committed on the property of St. Lazarus. "They are poor people, and I pity them." It was thus he excused them, and often he invited them to his table, and dismissed them with some little money.

His charity, then, in accordance with the counsel of the Gospel, extended even to the love of his enemies. Sometimes, wretches, aroused by political passion, or by suffering, outraged and maltreated him, either because they took him for a royalist, or because they looked upon him as the author of the very evils he worked so hard to prevent and alleviate. Thus, one day, when returning from St. Germain where he had been called by order of the queen, the gate-keepers, as he entered Paris, fell upon him, loaded him with insult, tore his clothes, and even struck him. The most brutal of them forced him off his horse and threatened him with death. The magistrates, shortly after informed of the affair, desired to bring the perpetrators of so dastardly an act to justice. But Vincent went himself to solicit the judges in favor of the guilty; moreover, to place an obstacle in the way of investigation, and prevent it from reaching any termination, he refused to tell the hour in which it happened, and so they could not know who were on duty at the time. Yet, to avoid the repetition of like outrages, he called for a passport to leave and enter Paris at will, which the Duke of Orleans immediately forwarded.

But in Paris itself he often had to suffer from a mutinous populace. From among many occasions we select this. Once, when but a few steps from St. Lazarus, an infuriated man, pretending that the Saint, in passing, had brushed against him gave him a slap in the face, and called out to the indignant crowd gathering around: " He is the author of all our evils, of the subsidies and the taxes with which the people are burdened " Instead of punishing his insolence with prison, by virtue of the different judicial powers that St. Lazarus at that time enjoyed, Vincent, following the maxim of the Gospel, threw himself at the knees of the man, presented the other cheek, and said: "I am not, my friend, the author of the subsidies, the imposition of which never was of my province; but I am a great sinner, and I ask pardon of God and of you for the cause I may have given you to treat me in this way." At this sight, and by these words, the fury of the man was disarmed.

On the following morning he came to St. Lazarus and in his turn made the most sincere apologies to the humble priest. Vincent welcomed him as a friend, kept him in the house six or seven days, and, inducing him to make the spiritual exercises, gained him to God.

His great means for revenging himself on all those who had insulted him was the spiritual retreat. A man requested him to speak in his favor to the chief justice, de Lamoignon. Some days after, he met the Saint in the street, and, imagining himself badly served, poured out a torrent of abuse which even the humility of the saint, prostrate at his feet, asking pardon, could not arrest. But the next day he gained his suit and learned that it was owing to the intervention of Vincent. He thereupon hastened to St. Lazarus to apologize, and the Saint, in answer, proposed the exercises of retreat.

His charity towards his enemies is fully shown in the history of the Orsigny law suit, and in the details of his conduct while a member of the Council of Conscience. An instance at random. The Queen had just exiled a lord in punishment for an insult offered to Vincent. "No, Madame, it must not be," said the holy priest, "I will not put my foot in this council until this good noble be restored to your favor."

He showed himself full of charity and forbearance for his tenants, and the debtors of his community. He was far from adding, by seizures and costs, to the losses caused by mortality among the cattle, or arising from unpropitious seasons. Not only did he in such cases remit their debts and their rents, but he advanced assistance to help them in reestablishing their affairs. And he prescribed this mode of action to his priests: "It would be a sad thing," he wrote to one of them, "were you obliged to seize the granary of the farmer of Chausee; for the poor people are sorely enough pressed without adding to their distress." And to another: "If you could pay your domestic for the four months he was sick, and defray, also, his expenses for doctor and for medicines, I think you would do well, since he is a poor man."

Again, and what is perhaps far more difficult, the Saint showed himself charitable towards the ungrateful. He had already aided the Irish priests thrown into France by the revolutions in their own country. And more, he had commissioned one of his Missionaries to assemble them on certain days of the week for the purpose of instructing them in what pertained to their sacred calling, and afterwards to obtain for them some ecclesiastical employment. "By assembling them together in this manner we might be able," he said, "to find a way to assist them; for their good will to render themselves more useful and exemplary will thus become evident I beg you, sir, to work for that object." "Sir," objected the missionary, "you know that by your orders these meetings have already been begun and have been continued for some time. But, as the exiles are difficult to manage, and as divided among themselves as the provinces of their country, this good work has been discontinued. They became distrustful and jealous of each other, and, though you have shown them many kindnesses and obtained for them many favors, they have lost confidence in you yourself, sir; they have complained of you, and have been so inconsiderate as to tell you to your face to have nothing more to do with them or their affairs, and they have written to Rome in the same sense.

Now, sir, it seems that this ingratitude merits no further kindnesses on your part." "Oh, sir, what do you say?" answered Vincent, "that is just why we should be kind to them." And, like Jesus Christ, finding in ingratitude even a new motive for charity he continued to assist these poor priests with all his power.

Even when faith and the religious honor of his house had to suffer from ingratitude, his charity did not weaken. A young German Lutheran, who had abjured his Protestantism, in Paris, was directed to him by a superioress of a community, who up to that time had provided for the false neophyte.

The nun recommended the young man as a subject of bright promise and as one who, as a member of the congregation, might render great service to the Church. The saint received him, gave him a room, and, according to custom, put him on retreat. The new novice, after having studied the different parts of the house better than his vocation, stealthily entered one of the rooms and appropriated a soutane, a long cloak and some small objects. He, then, without being seen, made off through the door of the church. Thence, in the garb of a missionary, he went to the Protestant pastor at Charenton, and afterwards to the Faubourg, St. Germain, to the Protestant minister, Drelincourt. To whom he said: "I belong to the Congregation of the Mission, but God having opened my eyes, I come to you to make profession of the reformed religion." Drelincourt, to whom every cast-away, even the most dubious, but particularly one from the ecclesiastical ranks, was a godsend, received this one and marched him in triumph from street to street, and from house to house of those of his sect—an operation which admirably suited both the one and the other. The one received forced congratulations, the other forced alms. During one of these promenades they were met by the Lord Des Isles, a man very zealous for the faith, and of some success in controversy. At the sight of the clerical costume of the companion of Drelincourt, Des Isles divined all. To make himself certain he followed them to the first house, entered with them, and letting Drelincourt ascend, he asked the German what was his object with the minister. Thinking that he was speaking to a Huguenot, the young man again said he had left St. Lazarus and had the intention of embracing Calvinism. Without waiting another moment, or any further answer, Des Isles went to find de Bretonvilliers, pastor of St. Sulpicius, and had this young man, who had found means to dishonor, at one and the same time, the Church and the Mission, arrested and conducted to the prison Chatelet. Immediately informed of all by Des Isles, Vincent was far less sensible to the outrage done his house than to that done to God. Importuned by his friends to punish, in prosecuting the guilty, both the theft and the scandal, he thanked them for their advice, and promised to consider it. He then sent to the judges to ask not justice, but mercy. He himself, went to the king's advocate and the public prosecutor, and declared, in the name of his community, that he demanded nothing either for the robbery or for the outrage He added: "As for myself, I humbly supplicate you to free the young man. To show mercy is the attribute of God. His Divine Majesty will receive it as very acceptible if you send away, without punishment, a poor stranger, guilty, at most, of youthful levity." Though the result of this singular request be unknown, yet, it is to be presumed that the magistrates did not refuse. It was a precedent that would not embarrass through frequent repetition.

II.

Let us now listen to the Saint speaking to us, from the abundance of his heart, of that charity with which he was filled, of that charity which emanated from him as the figure from its substance, and transformed into itself all who heard him. "For," he said, "each thing produces, as it were, a species and image of itself, as we see in the case of the mirror which represents objects as they are. Ugly features are there represented as ugly, and beautiful, as beautiful. In the same way, good and bad qualities diffuse themselves externally. Charity, especially, which is of itself communicative, produces charity. A heart really inflamed and animated by this virtue causes its ardor to be felt, and everything in a charitable man breathes and preaches charity."

He first gave the general doctrine of Charity. "The precept

of charity sums up the whole law, especially when it includes our neighbor as well as God. There is not a congregation more obliged to the practice of perfect charity than is ours. For our vocation is to go, not to one parish alone, nor to one single diocese, but all over the earth in order to inflame the hearts of men, and to do as did the Son of God, who Himself said that He was come to bring fire upon the earth in order to enkindle his love in the hearts of men. It is, therefore, true that we are sent, not only to love God, but, moreover, to make others love Him. It is not enough for us to love God if our neighbor, too, do not love Him; and we cannot love our neighbor as ourselves if we do not procure for him the good we are bound to wish for ourselves, namely, the Divine love which unites us to Him who is our Sovereign Lord. We should love our neighbor as being the image of God and the object of His love, and so labor that men may in turn love their most Amiable Creator, and mutually love one another, for the love of God, who has so loved them as to give, for their sake, His own Son to death. But, gentlemen, we must look upon this Divine Saviour as the perfect model of the charity that we owe our neighbor. Oh, my Jesus, tell us if it please Thee, what induced Thee to descend from Heaven to share in the malediction of earth? What excess of love forced Thee to lower Thyself to our level, and to suffer the infamous death of the cross? What excess of charity has made Thee expose Thyself to all our miseries, take upon Thyself the form of a sinner, lead a life of suffering, and undergo so shameful a death? Where else can charity so admirable, so excessive be found? None but the Son of God is capable of it, and none but Him has had such a love for His creatures as to leave His throne of glory to come and assume a body subject to the infirmities and miseries of this life, and carry out the strange and wonderful measures he adopted to establish, between us and among us, both by word and example, love for God and charity towards our neighbor. Yes, it is this love that crucified Him, and that produced the marvellous work of our redemption.

"O, gentlemen, had we but a spark of the sacred fire that consumed the heart of Jesus Christ, would we remain with our arms crossed, and abandon those whom we could assist? No, indeed, for true charity knows not idleness, nor does it permit us to look upon our friends and brethren in want without manifesting our solicitude ; and, ordinarily, exterior action testifies to interior feeling. Those who have true charity within show it externally. It is the property of fire to give heat and light, and it is characteristic of love to be communicative. We should love God with all our strength and in the sweat of our brow. We ought to serve our neighbor with our wealth and our life. O, how happy to become poor in charity to others ! But, we should not fear such a result, unless we doubt the goodness of our Lord, and the truth of His Word. But if, notwithstanding, God permitted us to be reduced to the necessity of serving as curates in villages, in order to obtain a subsistance, or even to go and beg our bread, or overcome and penetrated by cold to seek a resting-place in some corner of a hedge, and, if, in that condition, some one would ask us : 'Poor Priest of the Mission what has reduced you to such an extremity,' what happiness, gentlemen, would ours be in being able to answer : 'Charity it is that has done this!' O, how this poor priest would be esteemed by God and by His angels!

"And, now, what are the acts of charity ? The first act is to do unto everyone as we rationally wish should be done unto us. This first act is, of itself, so beautiful and so luminous that it carries light into the understanding; this light produces esteem, esteem moves the will to love, and convinces the person who loves of the duties of charity which he owes his neighbor. It is the property of fire to give light and heat, and it is the property of love to illumine and give rise to sentiments of respect and affection for the person loved. Yes, if we possess the divine virtue which is a participation in the Sun of Justice, it will dissipate the vapors of disdain and aversion, and will show us what is good and beautiful in our neighbor that we may esteem and cherish him.

Second. Act: "Not to contradict. I do not gain my brother by contradicting him, but by taking kindly, in our Lord, what He advances. He may be right, and I, possibly, may be wrong ; he does his part in contributing to an honest and becoming conversation, and I turn it into a dispute ; what he says may be taken in a sense I would approve did I but know it. Far from us be all contradiction that divides hearts! Let us avoid it as a fever that dries up, as a pestilence that desolates, as a demon that carries ruin into the most holy consciences. Let us banish this evil spirit by our prayers. Far from combating, let us enter into the sentiments of others; they say simply what they think, let us take in like simplicity what they say. If some should give way to detraction and raillery, oh, my Savior, do not permit it; but should it happen, we should not reprehend them publicly, for that is neither according to our rules, nor to theology, nor to the maxims of the Gospel; correct them secretly and in private. I was just thinking whether our Lord had ever contradicted any of His disciples in the presence of others, and only two instances came to my mind. One was when He contradicted St. Peter, saying to him: 'O, Satan!' and the other when, wishing to reprehend him for his presumption, He said to him: 'This night thou wilt deny me thrice.' Be that as it may, we see that our Lord was very reserved in contradicting; why, then, should we not be the same? He had the right to publicly reprimand His disciples, for He was the way and the truth; but we who are subject to err, should be extremely guarded in opposing any one, lest we bring shame upon our brother, excite a struggle, or go against truth.

Third Act: "Mutual support. Who is perfect? No man on earth. But who is not called imperfect? Since, then, all men have their faults, all have need of support. He who studies himself well will discover in himself a number of weaknesses and failings and will even recognize that he cannot prevent them, nor consequently help being a trial to others. Let us examine ourselves in relation to our bodily condition and mental dispositions: at times we experience an extreme distaste for the most holy things; often, we discover within ourselves a strange opposition to some one who is no more imperfect than ourselves, and yet, everything in connection with him displeases us. Let this person merely look, or listen, let him speak or act, everything, no matter what, by reason of our evil disposition, will appear blameworthy in him.

Another may use pure language, may speak according to the rules of grammar, and we, through an involuntary antipathy, will consider his thoughts obscure, his words pointless. But, should we become conscious of this on our part, we would feel very much pleased, should he manifest no displeasure but rather excuse us. Why, then, should not we, too, excuse him when he is gruff with us, or when he criticises our actions? For the antipathy may be reciprocal. We are, at times, gay and cheerful, and, at other times, we are sad and depressed; yesterday, we were thought too joyful, to-day, we are too melancholic. Since, then, we wish our neighbor to bear with us in the excesses of our extravagant humors, is it not just that we do the same by him in similar cases? Let us put ourselves to the question, let each examine carefully all his miseries, all the infirmities of his body, the disorders of his passions, his proneness to evil, his infidelity and ingratitude towards God, and his injustices towards his neighbor, and he will discover in himself more malice, and greater cause for confusion than in any other person in the world; and then, let him say sincerely: 'I am the greatest sinner and the most insupportable of men.' Yes, indeed, if we studied ourselves properly we would find that we are a great burden to those with whom we live; and whoever has succeeded in thoroughly knowing his own wretchedness, (and this is an effect of the grace of God), may rest assured that he is come to the necessary point to perceive his obligation to bear with others. He will see no faults in them, or if he do, they will appear very trivial in comparison with his own; and thus, in the midst of his own weaknesses, he will bear with his neighbor, particularly when he considers the need he has of being borne with by Almighty God. O, admirable forbearance of our Lord! You see that beam sustaining all the weight of the ceiling which, without it, would immediately fall. He, in like manner, has sustained us in our languors, in our blindnesses, and in our falls. We were all, at one time, as if crushed beneath the weight of our iniquity and our miseries both of body and soul, and this gracious and gentle Saviour took them upon Himself in order to suffer the pain and the opprobrium. If we give our attention to this we will readily see how much we deserve to be punished and despised, especially we who are guilty, and, above all others, I, myself.

Fourth Act. "To sympathize with the sufferings of our neighbor, and to weep with him. Love unites hearts, and makes one heart feel whatever the other feels. They compassionate each other. Such hearts are not found in those who experience no grief for the afflicted, nor for the sufferings of the poor. Ah, how great was the tenderness of the Son of God! I cannot help always contemplating that prototype of charity. He is called to see Lazarus, and He goes; Magdalene rises and weeping goes to meet Him, the Jews follow Him, and likewise weep, every one begins to weep: what does our Lord do? He weeps with them. It is this loving tenderness that brought him down from Heaven. He saw man deprived of his glory, and He was touched at that misfortune. We should, ourselves, be moved to pity at the sight of our afflicted neighbor, and share in his suffering. O, St. Paul, how sensitive were you in this respect! O my Savior, Thou Who hast filled this apostle with Thy spirit and Thy sentiments, make us say with him: 'Who is weak and I am not weak?'

"But how can I feel within me his sickness and his afflictions? Through the union we all have in Jesus Christ, Who is our head. All men form a mystic body; we are all members of each other. Now, it has never been heard, not even in animals, that one member was insensible to the pain of another; that one part of man was bruised, injured, or strained and the others did not feel it. That cannot be; all our members have such sympathy, and are so connected together that the evil of one is the evil of the other. By far greater reason should Christians, being members of the same body and members of one another, commiserate with each other. Yes, to be a Christian and to see a brother in affliction, and not weep with him, not feel for his sickness, is to be devoid of charity, is to be a Christian in appearance only, is to be without humility, is to be worse than the beasts of the fields. Let us, then, strive to have sentiments of grief and of sorrow for our neighbor. Let us do, through virtue, what people of the world frequently do through human respect when they visit a distressed person who has lost father, or wife, or relative. What do they do? Generally, they put on mourning; when they are come to the house sadness is depicted on their countenance and they say to the bereaved person; 'Alas! I cannot express my sorrow for the loss I suffer in common with you; I am inconsolable! I come to mingle my tears with yours'; and other fine words that testify to the share they take in the affliction. This custom comes from the practice of the first Christians. Originally, all these were actions inspired by charity; and the evil is that they have been separated from their source and are rendered wrong in being done through hypocrisy, for fashion's sake, through interest, or natural affection, and not from that unity of mind and heart, which the Son of God came to establish in His Church — a unity that causes all the faithful, having one and the same spirit in Jesus Christ, as his members, to be afflicted and saddened at the misfortunes of their brethren. According to this we should regard whatever befals our neighbor as happening to ourselves, and this, as well in joy as in sorrow, for it is also an act of charity to rejoice with those who rejoice. Let us, then, rejoice at the good success of our neighbor, and be glad that he surpasses us in honor, in name, in talent, in grace and in virtue.

Fifth Act: "To anticipate each other in honor. And why? Because, otherwise, it might seem as if one acts the gentleman, the great, or the haughty, all which contracts the heart, whilst the contrary opens and expands it. Humility is a product of charity, and it impels us, when we meet our neighbor, to make the first advances in the honor and respect we owe him, and in this way it conciliates his affections. Who does not love an humble person? A ferocious lion, ready to devour the animal that would resist, is immediately appeased when he sees it trembling, and, as it were, humbled at his feet. What else can we do but love a person who humbles himself? He is like a valley that receives the moisture of the mountains; he draws down upon himself the blessings and the good will of all.

Sixth Act: "To manifest the affection we bear each other, we should, each one, show that we love each other cordially. This is done in offering our services, provided we offer them with a good will and sincerely, saying for example: 'How I would like to afford you pleasure! To do you a good turn in order to prove how I cherish you!' And after having said it with the lips, to confirm it by action in effectively striving to serve every one, and to make ourselves all to all. For, it is not sufficient to have charity in the heart and in word; it should pass into action, even to the extent of giving, if required, our life, as did our Lord. Then it is perfect and becomes pregnant: it engenders love in the hearts of those in whose favor it is exercised."

It was charity, also, that he preached to the communities of which he was director, and notably to the Nuns of the Visitation. He said: "Each one of you must burn with charity, and charity must be practiced among you in every possible manner. Any want of mutual esteem, or any words or speech injurious to our neighbor is, in communities, insufferable. I fear very much that ruin will fall upon those communities, the members of which are not closely united to each other. And this never happens but through lack of esteem, of forbearance and of charity. Nuns must look upon each other as the spouses of Jesus Christ, the temples of the Holy Ghost, and the living images of God, and in this light, they must reciprocally bear for one another a great love and respect. For this purpose we must employ two means. The first is to have recourse to the goodness of God, who is all love and charity, in order to beg a portion of the lights and the Divine fervor of His spirit; the second is to conceive a great desire for our amendment, and to labor in earnest to correct the faults which we commit against charity; making our particular examen on this carefully so as to rectify, and take from our hearts, whatever may in any manner impair the union we ought to have with God and among ourselves."

To particular individuals, as well as to communities, he loved to render services. He dissuaded religious, who consulted him, from entering lax communities. "It is a disorder and not an order," he would say; "a phantom of religion where there is no safety for conscience."

Rarely, and then only in the case of disorder in a community, did he permit any one to change his order. From the following letter we may judge of all the others, and also perceive the humble and charitable precautions under cover of which Vincent administered severe reproaches and gave difficult counsels: "I have read your letter, Reverend Father, with respect, and, indeed, with confusion, seeing that you address yourself to the most worldly-minded and least spiritual of men, and one that is by all recognized as such. Yet, notwithstanding all this, I will not neglect to give you my little thoughts on what you propose to me, not through any desire to give advice, but simply through that courtesy that our Lord wishes we should show towards our neighbor. I was consoled in seeing the attraction you have for a perfect union with our Lord; your faithful correspondence with grace for this purpose and the caresses with which His Divine Goodness so often favored you, the great difficulties and contradictions you have met with in the different states through which you have passed, and, finally, in noticing the singular love you have for that great mistress of spiritual life, St. Theresa.

"But, though all this be so, I yet think, Reverend Father, that there is more security for you to remain in the common life of your holy order and to submit yourself entirely to the direction of your superior, than to change and enter another, though holy. And first, because it is a maxim, that a religious should aspire to animate himself with the spirit of his order, otherwise, he will have but the costume; and as your order is recognized as one of the most perfect in the Church you have a still greater obligation to persevere in it, and to labor to put on its spirit by the practice of those virtues by which you were induced to enter it. In the second place, it is another maxim that the spirit of our Lord acts quietly and sweetly, whereas that of nature and the malign spirit act harshly and morosely. But, it would seem from what you tell me that your manner of acting is harsh and morose, and makes you hold with too much obstinacy and attachment to your own opinions in opposition to those of your superiors and to this even your natural disposition carries you. Consequently, Reverend Father, I think you ought to give yourself anew to God in order to renounce your own judgment and to accomplish His most holy will in the state to which His Providence has called you."

He made his sentiments and his conduct in regard to religious communities the rule for his priests and his Daughters of Charity: "Entertain esteem and respect for all," he said to them, "and never allow any envy, jealousy, or any other feeling contrary to the humility and charity of Jesus Christ to enter your minds. Always speak of them in terms of esteem and affection. Never find fault with their conduct; make open profession of considering as good whatever they do."

He wrote again: "You ask me how you should comport yourself towards members of religious orders. You should endeavor to serve them, and, on occasion, prove to them that you have such a disposition; visit them at times; never take sides against them, nor interest yourself in their affairs save to charitably defend them; speak of them in good part; say nothing either in public or private that might wound them, even though they do not the same by you. I would like that we all would do this; for they are religious and in a state of perfection, and, therefore, we ought to honor and serve them."

When there was rivalry or conflict between members of his own and other orders, as it happened in Poland, he wrote: "I adore in this the hand of God, without whose order nothing is done, and we would do better to look, in the light of His good pleasure, on all the evils and disappointments that happen us, than to lay the blame on any one. And even were it true that those of whom you were informed bore us envy and worked their worst against us, still, I would never tire in esteeming, in loving, and in serving them as much as possible, whether here or elsewhere."

And two years after: "In regard to the attacks you fear from a certain community, I hope, in the mercy of God, that they will not take place, and I beg you to take all possible measures to avoid them by anticipating these good Fathers in your respect, your offers of service and your deference. This is what we strive to do here, and we do not find much trouble in it. I am firmly resolved, even were they to throw dirt into my face, never to manifest the least resentment, in order not to break with them, nor depart from the esteem and honor I owe them. I do this for the sake of God. Should they chance to say or do anything injurious to your little bark, even with the intention of submerging it, suffer it for the love of God who knows well how to preserve you from shipwreck, and how to make the calm succeed the tempest. Do not complain, say not a single word about it, and do not cease to manifest affection for them when you meet them just as if nothing were the matter. You must not be astonished at things of this nature, but rather dispose yourself to receive them properly. For, as oppositions existed among the apostles, and even among the angels, without, however, any offence against God, each acting according to his lights, so God permits sometimes His servants to contradict and oppose each other, and allows one congregation to persecute another. There is far more evil in this than is imagined, though all have an upright intention, but for those who humble themselves, and do not resist, there is always a great gain."

The missionaries, having reiterated their complaints, he, with still greater persistence, repeated his counsels. "Is it possible, my dear sir, that these good fathers treat us in the manner you describe? I have great difficulty in believing it. But granting it to be so, I beg of you and the community with you two things: the first, not to mention it, nor to complain to any person. This would be far worse; and secondly, you should *overcome evil with good*, which means that you should visit them as formerly, and speak favorably and respectfully of them on every occasion, and also, should it please God to give you the opportunity, do them a good turn. These practices are according to God, and to true wisdom, whilst the contrary produce a thousand unfortunate results."

A reconciliation having been effected, he exclaimed:

"Blessed be God that the congregation lives in peace and respect with these very reverend fathers, and pray our Lord to give us the grace to do the same with all the others!"

He addressed to Rome similar answers during an opposition, on the part of the Oratorians, to his members: "It is true that they wish to embroil us. . . . All that would not astonish me, did not my sins make me tremble. . . . Yet, I cannot express how all these artifices surprise me. Nevertheless, you will act in the most Christian manner possible with those who cause us embarrassment. Here, I see them as often and as cordially, thanks be to God, as before; and it seems to me that, by the grace of God, I not only bear them no aversion, but that I honor and cherish them the more." In the meantime, the Oratorians asked of him some of his priests, in order, by their lessons and example, to form themselves in the method of giving missions, and he complied: "For," he said, "I would not believe myself a Christian did I not endeavor to participate in the *O would that all could prophesy* of St. Paul. Alas! my dear sir, the field is so vast! There are thousands who fill hell: all the ecclesiastics with all the religious orders would not suffice to remedy the evil! Would you have us so wretched as to be jealous of those persons applying themselves to succor these poor souls who are going in the way of destruction! Oh! surely, this would be to hinder the accomplishment of the mission of Jesus Christ on earth! If, on the other hand, people try to prevent us from working, we must pray, we must humble ourselves, and do penance for the sins we have committed in this holy ministry." And, three years after, the opposition still continuing, he again wrote to Rome, on the 9th of July, 1655: "That will not hinder me, even though they take out my eyes, from esteeming them, and cherishing them as children do their parents. *They think they do a service to God.* I desire and I pray our Lord that each one of the congregation do the same."

Providence, having called upon the Congregation of the Mission to serve the clergy by means of the spiritual exercises for those about to be ordained, and by the direction of seminaries, almost at the same time that they were called to labor for the salvation of the poor people, the Saint strove, in the first instance, to impress his children with the divine greatness and the necessity of this new ministry: "To be employed in training good priests and to contribute thereto, as a second efficient instrumental cause, is to perform the work of Jesus Christ, Who, during His mortal life, seems to have assumed the task of making twelve good priests, who were the apostles; having deigned to live with them for years in order to instruct and form them in the Divine Ministry. . . . We are, then, all called by God to the state we have embraced, to labor in this eminent work; for, to help to make good priests is a preeminent work, than which nothing greater or more important in this world can be thought. What is there in the world so grand as the ecclesiastical state? Principalities and kingdoms bear no comparison to it. Kings cannot, like the priests, change bread into the body of our Lord, forgive sins, or do the other wonders whereby priests surpass all temporal greatness,"

If such be the greatness of the priest, judge of his action whether beneficent or fatal according as he is faithful or otherwise to his vocation. "As is the pastor, so will be the people. To the officers of the army is attributed the good or evil success of the war. In like manner we can say that if the ministers of the Church are good, if they perform their duty, all will be well; but if, on the contrary, they are unfaithful, they are the cause of all disorders. . . . Yes, we are the cause of the desolation that at present ravages the Church, of the deplorable diminution it has suffered in so many places; being almost entirely destroyed in Asia, in Africa, and even in a great portion of Europe, as in Sweden, in Denmark, in England, Scotland, Ireland, Holland and the United Provinces, and in a great part of Germany. And how many heretics do we not see in France! . . . Yes, O Lord, we, it is, who have provoked Thy wrath; our sins have drawn down these calamities. Yes, it is the clerics and those who aspire to the ecclesiastical state, it is the subdeacons, the deacons, the priests, it is we, who are priests, who have been the cause of this desolation in the Church." And entering more particularly into details he passed in review the different classes of ecclesiastics of his time. Some are useless. "They read their breviary, celebrate mass, but very negligently, a few administer the sacraments so so, and that is all." But a great number of others are in disorder and vice. And he mentioned the priests of an entire province, who were so given up to intemperance that it was necessary to hold a council of bishops in order to devise a means to stay so ignoble a vice, and none could be found. Yet, to console himself and his confreres, he added: "But you must not imagine that all are disorderly. No, O my Savior! O, how many holy ecclesiastics there are! A great many, both pastors and others, come here to make their retreat, and they come from a distance expressly to place their interior in good order. And how many holy priests there are in Paris! There is a very great number; and of these gentlemen of the conference, who assemble here, there is not one who is not exemplary; they all labor with wonderful fruit. If, then, there are in the world bad ecclesiastics — and I am the worst, the most unworthy and the greatest sinner of them all — there are, also, on the contrary, those who openly praise God by the holiness of their lives."

But our vocation is to correct the bad and perfect the good. And who are we for such a ministry? "We are but wretched men, sons of farmers and peasants; and what proportion is there between us, miserable as we are, and an employment so holy, so eminent, and so heavenly? . . . Yet, it is to us that God has confided so great a grace as is that of contributing to the reform of the ecclesiastical order. God did not, for this purpose, apply to the doctors in theology, or to the many communities and religious orders so full of learning and sanctity; but He has addressed Himself to this wretched, poor, and miserable congregation, the last and most unworthy of all. What has God found in us to merit so great an occupation? Where are our wonderful exploits? Where are the brilliant and illustrious actions we have done? Where, that great capacity? There is nothing of all this. God, simply of His will, has addressed Himself to poor miserable idiots to try to repair the ruins in the kingdom of His Son, and in the ecclesiastical state. Oh, gentlemen, let us carefully watch over this grace which God has given us in preference to so many learned and holy persons who merited it far better than we: for if, through our neglect, we permit it to lie idle, God will withdraw it from us and to punish our unfaithfulness He will give it to others.

"Alas! who among us will be the cause of so great an evil, and who will deprive the Church of so great a good? Will I, miserable, be the one? Let each one put his hand on his conscience and ask of himself: Will I be the unfortunate one? Alas! it requires but one miserable person, such as I am, who, by his abominations, turns away the favor of Heaven from an entire house, and brings upon it the curse of God. O, my Lord, Thou who seest me all covered and filled with sins that bear me down, do not, on this account, deprive this little congregation of Thy grace. Grant that it may continue to serve Thee in humility and with fidelity, and that it may co-operate with the design, it seems Thou hast, of making, through its ministry, a last effort to contribute in re-establishing the honor and glory of Thy Church!"

Thus Vincent always delighted in his lowliness, thus he took pleasure in plunging into it, and strove to instil into his disciples the same sentiments. But, far from finding in it despair, he drew from it fresh confidence. "God," he said, "has always made use of weak instruments for His greatest designs. In instituting His Church, did He not choose twelve poor, ignorant, and rustic men? And yet, by their means, our Lord overturned idolatry, subjected to the Church the princes and the powerful of the earth, and extended our holy religion throughout the entire world. He can also make use of us, pitiable as we are, to aid in the advancement in virtue of the ecclesiastical state. In the name of our Lord, gentlemen and my brothers, let us give ourselves to Him, in order that we may contribute to this object by all the means in our power, by good example, by prayer, and by mortification."

In these last words he summed up the means he was accustomed to advise for the success of the holy work. First, last, and at all times, prayer. "In view of our want of ability we must pray much. My Savior, nothing will avail if Thou dost not lend a helping hand. Thy grace must work all in us, and must give us that spirit without which we can do nothing. What do we know how to do, we, who are miserable persons? O, Lord, give us the spirit of Thy priesthood, such as had the Apostles and the first priests who succeeded them. Give us the true spirit of that sacred character which Thou hast impressed on poor fishermen, on artisans, on poor persons of that period to whom Thou didst, by Thy grace, communicate that great and divine spirit." Then, at the time of the ordinations, he asked of all, in order to obtain good priests, to offer to God their communions, their prayers and all their good works. He asked this of his own community, he asked it of the religious communities, and of the Ladies of Charity, whom he sent to the altar of the Blessed Virgin in the Church of Notre Dame. And, to encourage them in their prayers, he said: "St. Theresa, who in her time saw the need the Church had of good workmen, asked of God that he be pleased to send good priests, and she wished that the sisters of her order would pray for that object. And, perhaps, the change for the better which is now discernible in the clergy is owing, in part, to the piety of this great saint.' He was assured that these prayers would obtain their object, in proportion as they were offered by the humble. For this reason, he begged them of the most humble brother in his community. "It may be," he added, "that, should it please God, any fruit should come, it will come from the prayers of some brother who will not even see the ordinands. He, whilst occupied with his ordinary duty, and whilst working, will often elevate his mind to God to pray Him to be pleased to bless the ordination; and, perhaps, without his thinking it, God will grant the grace he desires, on account of the good dispositions of his heart. There is a verse in the Psalms: *The Lord hath heard the desires of the poor.*" . . . Here Vincent stopped suddenly, not remembering the rest of the verse, and, according to his humble, familiar and dramatic manner, turned towards his assistants, and asked: 'Who will tell me the rest?' Some one finished the verse: "*Thy ear hath heard the preparation of their heart."* (Ps. ix., 17.) "God bless you, sir," said the saint. That was his ordinary thanks. And, charmed with the beauty of the passage he repeated it several times with feelings of joy and devotion, and continued: "Wonderful manner of speech, worthy of the Holy Ghost! 'The Lord hath heard the desire of the poor, He hath heard the preparation of their heart,' to show us that God hears souls well disposed even before they pray. This is a great consolation, and we ought to take courage in the service of God though we perceive in ourselves nothing but misery and poverty."

To prayer he recommended them to join humility. "These ought to be the arms of a missionary. By means of humility, which causes us to seek for ourselves only confusion, all will succeed. For, believe me, gentlemen and my brothers, believe me, it is an infallible maxim of Jesus Christ, and one I have often announced to you on His part, that as soon as a heart is void of itself, God fills it; it is He who dwells and acts within it. And it is the desire of confusion that empties us of ourselves; it is humility, holy humility. Then we will no longer act, God will act in us, and all will go well. Oh, you, then, who labor directly in this holy work, you should possess the spirit of the priesthood and infuse it into those who have it not, you, to whom God has entrusted these souls to dispose them to receive this holy and sanctifying spirit, aim not at anything but the glory of God. Have simplicity of heart with Him, and respect for these gentlemen. Know that thus you will succeed; everything else will be of but very little use. Humility alone and a pure intention of pleasing God have, up to the present, caused this work to prosper."

To prayer he recommended them to join humility. These ought to be the arms of a missionary. By means of humility, which causes us to seek for ourselves only confusion, all will succeed. For, believe me, gentlemen and my brothers, believe me it is an infallible maxim of Jesus Christ, and one I have often announced to you on His part, that as soon as a heart is void of itself God fills it; it is He who dwells and acts within it. And it is the desire of confusion that empties us of ourselves; it is humility, holy humility. Then we will no longer act, but

God will act in us, and all will go well. Oh you, then, who labor directly in this holy work, you should possess the spirit of the priesthood and infuse it with those who have it not you to whom God has entrusted these souls to dispose them to receive this holy and sanctifying spirit, aim not at anything but the glory of God. Have simplicity of heart with Him, and respect for these gentlemen; know that thus you will succeed; everything else will be of little use Humility alone and a pure intention of pleasing God have, up to the present, caused this work to prosper."

Humility is devoted and obliging. " Let us show these gentlemen, the ordinands, every mark of respect and deference, not appearing proud and reserved, but waiting on them humbly. . . . being particularly vigilant in seeing, in going after, and bringing without delay whatever may please them; being prompt in meeting their wants; designing even, if possible, their inclinations and desires, and anticipating them in order to satisfy them as far as is reasonable."

But, for the success of the exercises, he counted especially on the preaching by good example, of all preaching the most eloquent and efficacious: " What the eye sees." he said, "touches us far more than what the ear hears, and we believe rather in the good we see than in that which we hear. And though faith enters by the ear, *Faith then cometh by hearing,* yet the virtues we see put into practice have more effect on us than those we are taught. Physical things have all their different properties whereby they are distinguished. Every animal, even man himself, has its qualities which make it known as it is and distinguish it from every other of a like kind. So, too, the servants of God have their peculiar qualities that distinguish them from carnal men. It is a certain external composure, humble, recollected, and devout, proceeding from the grace within them, and carrying its operations into the souls of those who beheld them. There are some here, in the house, so filled with God that I cannot look upon them without being moved. Painters, in their pictures of the saints, represent them to us as surrounded with rays: it is because the just who live holily on this earth shed about them a certain light which is peculiar to them alone. Such grace and modesty appeared in the Blessed Virgin that all who had the happiness of beholding her were impressed with reverence and devotion; and, in our Lord, these appeared to a far greater extent, and it is the same, in proportion, with all the saints. All this proves, gentlemen, and my brothers, that, if you labor in the acquisition of virtue, if you abound in divine things, if each one, in his own particular, tends continually to perfection, even when you possess no external talent to direct these gentlemen, the ordinands, God will so work that your presence alone will shed a light on their understanding and will excite their will to become better."

He thus concluded this chapter on the edification of the ordinands: "How blessed you are, gentlemen, in pouring into these souls the spirit of God by your piety, your meekness, your affability, your modesty and humility, and in serving God in the persons of His greatest servants! How happy are you who give them good example at the conferences, in ceremonies, in choir, in the refectory, and everywhere. Oh, how happy we all will be, if, by our silence, our discretion, and charity, we correspond with the intention of God in sending them to us."

In those who preached the retreats to the ordinands Vincent required simplicity in style and purity in intention. But, for this, self must be forgotten, God must be invoked, and all inspiration demanded of Him: " For God is an inexhaustible source of wisdom, of light, and of love. In Him we should drink in what we say to others. We should reject our own understanding and our particular sentiments in order to give place to the operations of grace which alone illumines and warms the heart. We must go out of ourselves and enter into God. We must consult Him to learn His language, and beg Him, Himself, to speak in us and by us. He, then, will do His work and we will spoil nothing. Our Lord, when conversing among men, did not speak as of Himself: " My doctrine," said He "is not of Myself, but of My Father: the words which I speak to you are not Mine, but are of God." This shows us the great necessity of having recourse to God, that He, and not we, may speak and act."

When the Congregation saw the number of seminaries which

it directed increasing the Saint likewise redoubled his encouragement, in order to strengthen the charity of his members against the weight of their employments and against the fear that the work of the clergy would injure that of the Mission. He said: "The Missionaries are particularly sent by God to labor for the sanctification of ecclesiastics, and one of their ends is to instruct ecclesiastics not only in human knowledge, but also in the practice of virtue; for, to show them the one without the other is to do little and almost nothing. Talent and a good life are necessary; without the latter, the former is useless and dangerous. We should lead them equally to both, and this is what God requires of us. In the beginning, we did not think at all of serving the clergy, we simply thought of ourselves and of the poor. How did the Son of God begin? He hid Himself, He seemed to think only of Himself, He prayed to God, and performed only those things which pertained to Himself; this is all that He seemed to do. Afterwards, He announced His Gospel to the poor. And then, after that, He called His apostles. He took the pains to instruct them, to admonish them and to train them, and finally, He animated them with His spirit not for themselves alone, but for all the peoples of the earth. He also taught them all that was necessary for priests to administer the sacraments and to acquit themselves of their ministry. In the same way, our little Congregation, in the commencement, only busied itself with its own spiritual advancement and in evangelizing the poor. At certain periods, it retired into its own privacy, and, at others, it went out to instruct the country people; God permitted that alone to appear in our beginnings. But in the fullness of time He called us to contribute our share in forming good priests, in giving good pastors to parishes, and in pointing out to them what they out to know, and what they ought to practice. Oh, but this employment is eminent! It is sublime! Oh, how far above us it is! Who among us ever dreamt of the exercises for the ordinands, or of the seminaries? Never did that undertaking come into our minds until God signified that it was His pleasure that we should devote ourselves to it. He has, then, led the Congregation to these duties without any choice on our part, and therefore, He requires that we apply ourselves to them; but our application must be serious, humble, devout, constant, and in accordance with the excellence of the work. Some, perhaps, will say that they entered the Congregation only to labor in the country, and not to enclose themselves in a city in teaching in a seminary; but each and all of us know full well that the occupations in which we are engaged in the house in regard to ecclesiastics, and particularly, the work of the seminaries, are not to be neglected under pretext of giving missions. We must do the latter, and not neglect the former, since we are almost equally obliged by our institute to acquit ourselves of the one as well as of the other, and because long experience has proved that it is extremely difficult for the fruits of the missions to endure for long without the aid of the pastors to whose advancement in virtue the other works of the Congregation seem to contribute not a little. Therefore, each one will give himself to God, with a good heart, in order to perform his duty well and faithfully. To labor for the instruction of the poor is a great work, it is true, but it is still more important to instruct the ecclesiastics, for, if they be ignorant, the people they conduct must, by necessity, be ignorant likewise. The Son of God might have been asked: 'Why art Thou come? Is it not to preach the Gospel to the poor in obedience to the order of Thy Eternal Father? Why, then, dost Thou train up priests? Why take so much care in teaching, and in forming them?' To which Our Lord could have answered that He came not only to teach the truths necessary for salvation, but also to ordain good priests, and better than those of the Old Law. You know that, of old, God rejected those priests who were polluted, or who had profaned the sacred things, that He held their sacrifices in abomination, and that He said He would raise up other priests who, from the rising to the setting of the sun, from the South to the North, would make their voices and their words resound ' *Their sound hath gone forth into all the earth.*' And by whom has he accomplished this promise? By His Son, Our Lord, who has instituted a priesthood, who has instructed and fashioned His priests, and through whom He has given power to His Church to ordain others: '*As the Father hath sent me so do I send you.*' And this for the purpose of continuing, by their ministry, throughout all ages, what He Himself did towards the close of His life, in order that all nations may be saved by their instructions, and by the administration of the sacraments. It would, then, be an illusion, and a great illusion, in a missionary not to wish to apply himself to the work of contributing to form good priests, and all the more so, as there is nothing greater than a good priest. Think as long as we may, we will find that we can co-operate in nothing greater than in forming a good priest, to whom Our Lord gives a power over His natural body which is the amazement of angels, and over His mystic body the power of remitting sin which for them is a subject of wonder and of gratitude. Oh, my God, what a power! Oh, what a dignity! Is there anything greater or more admirable? Oh, gentlemen, how great a thing is a good priest! What can a good ecclesiastic not do? What conversions can he not procure? Upon the priests depends the happiness of Christendom. This consideration, then, obliges us to serve the ecclesiastical state which is so holy and so elevated, and still more the need the Church has of good priests to remedy the immense ignorance and the innumerable vices with which the earth is covered, and for which pious souls ought to shed tears of blood.

"There is question whether all the disorders we witness be not attributable to the priests. This may scandalize some, but the subject requires that by the magnitude of the evil the importance of the remedy be shown. For sometime back, this question has been the subject of several conferences, and it has been thoroughly treated, in order to discover the sources of so many evils; and the conclusion arrived at was that the Church had no greater enemies than bad priests. Heresies sprang from them We have the instance of the last heresies in those two great heresiarchs. Luther and Calvin. They were priests. It is by priests that heresy has prevailed, vice has reigned, and ignorance established its throne among the poor people; and this, because of their own disorders and their neglect to oppose with all their strength, as was their bounden duty, these three torrents that inundated the earth. What sacrifice, then, gentlemen, will you not make to God, in order to labor for their reformation so that they may live conformably to the sanctity of their state, and that the Church may rise from out her shame and desolation?"

But the privileged object of that charity which he so recommended to his children was the poor. He said: "God loves the poor, and, by consequence, He loves those who love the poor. For when we have a great love for anyone we have also an affection for his friends and servants. Now, the little Congregation of the Mission strives to devote itself with affection to the service of the poor, who are the well beloved of God, and hence, we have reason to hope that, out of love for them, He will love us. All who, during life, love the poor, need have no fear of death. Courage, then, my brethren, and let us devote ourselves with renewed love to serving the poor. Let us even seek out the most wretched and the most abandoned. Let us acknowledge before God that they are our lords and masters, and that we are unworthy to render them our little services. . . . . When we visit them let us enter into their feelings and suffer with them; let us inspire ourselves with the sentiments of the Great Apostle, who said: *I became all things to all men,* that thus we may not fall under the complaint formerly made by our Lord through one of His prophets: *And I looked for one that would grieve together with me, but there was none.*

"For this we must try to move our hearts to pity and to make them susceptible of the sufferings and misfortunes of our neighbor, and pray to God to give us the true spirit of mercy, which is the spirit of God Himself, that when a missionary is seen it can be said: There goes a man filled with compassion and mercy. We should abound in mercy far more than other priests; for we are obliged, by our state and our vocation, to serve the most miserable, the most abandoned, and those most burdened with corporal and spiritual miseries Let us have this compassion in our hearts; let us manifest it in our exterior and on our countenance, after the example of our Lord who wept over the City of Jerusalem on account of the calamities that were about to overtake it. Let us use words of sympathy, proving to our neighbor that we take an interest in him and in his sufferings; finally, let us aid and assist him in his necessities and misfortunes as well as we can, and endeavor to relieve him entirely or in part, for the hand ought to be as far as possible conformed to the heart."

The insane and the young libertines detained at St. Lazarus

also formed the subject as well of his recommendations as of his charity. In frequent conferences he sustained the courage of those who gave themselves to so ungrateful and so repugnant a task: "It is," he said to them, "all the more meritorious because nature finds in it no satisfaction, and because it is a good work done in secret, and in favor of those who will return no sign of gratitude. These are sick in body, those in mind; these are stupid, those light; these are crazy, those vicious. In a word, all are estranged in mind, the former by infirmity, the latter through malice. What a spirit of direction we priests need to guide them! What grace, what strength, what patience our poor brothers require to bear with so much trouble and endure such labor." And he animated their courage by the memory of some of the Sovereign Pontiffs whom the Pagan Emperors condemned to guard the beasts of the circus "The men of whom you have charge are not beasts; yet are they, by their disorders and debaucheries, in some ways, worse than animals." He proposed to them especially the example of our Lord who wished to experience in his person every species of misery, and he exclaimed: "Oh, my Savior, Thou who art uncreated wisdom, Thou who hast suffered Thyself to be a rock of scandal to the Jews and foolishness to the Gentiles, Thou hast been willing to pass for a fool!" It was again by the example of Jesus Christ that he answered those who said to him: "We have no rule which obliges us to receive at St. Lazarus either crazy people or young demons." He replied: "Our rule in this is Jesus Christ, who has wished to be surrounded by the insane, by the obsessed, by idiots, by those tempted and by those possessed by the devil. From all sides they brought them to Him to be freed, and this He did with great kindness. Why, then, blame us, or find fault, because we endeavor to imitate Him in a thing which He has shown to be so agreeable to Him?

"If He received the estranged in mind and those possessed by demons, why should not we also? We do not go to seek them, they are brought to us. And how do we know that His Providence, which so ordains, does not wish to make use of us to heal the infirmities of these poor people with whom our gentle Savior wished to sympathize to such a degree as to seem to have Himself assumed their weakness? Oh, my Savior and my God, grant us the grace to look upon these things with the same eye with which Thou hast regarded them!"

There was another motive which he urged for assisting these unfortunates; it was thus that St. Lazarus became a grand school of experience wherein they could learn to compassionate with all classes of evils, and exercise themselves in all their charitable functions. "Bless God, gentlemen and my brothers," he said, "and thank Him, because He gives us the care of these poor people deprived of sense, and of the power of governing themselves; for, in serving them, we see and we experience how great and how varied human miseries are, and by this knowledge we become the better fitted to labor successfully for our neighbor. We will acquit ourselves of our functions with so much the more fidelity as we the better know from our own experience what it is to suffer. For this reason I beg of those who tend these persons to take good care of them, and I ask the Congregation to frequently recommend them to God, and to prize this opportunity of exercising charity and patience towards those poor people. Otherwise, God will punish us. Yes, be prepared to see a curse fall upon the house of St. Lazarus, if the proper and just care of them be neglected. I recommend, especially, that they be properly nourished, and, at least, as well as the community. I would prefer that it would be taken away from me, and given to them."

With what indignant charity he reproved those who closed their hearts in the presence of the miserable! One of his priests, having condemned his great liberality in favor of the foundlings, and having complained of the straits to which thereby the house of St. Lazarus was reduced, and the ruin that threatened, the Saint returned this beautiful answer: "May God pardon him this weakness which so removes him from the sentiments of the Gospel! Oh, what meanness of faith to believe that, in doing and procuring good for poor and abandoned children as these, our Lord will have less bounty for us, He who promises to recompense a hundredfold whatever may be given for His sake! Since this gentle Savior said to His disciples: 'Permit little children to come unto Me,' can we, without going contrary to Him, neglect or abandon them when they come to us? What tenderness has He not shown for little children, embracing them and laying His hands upon them! Did they not furnish Him the occasion for establishing for us a rule of salvation, ordaining us to become like unto them if we wished to enter the kingdom of Heaven? But to have charity for children and to take care of them is, in some measure, to become a child. And to provide for the necessities of foundlings is to take the place of their fathers and mothers, or rather it is to take the place of God, Who has said that, if the mother forgot her offspring, He Himself would take charge and not forget it. Were our Lord still living on earth among men, and did He see children abandoned, would He, too, think you, wish to abandon them? Such a thought would, surely, do injustice to His infinite goodness. And we, too, in our turn, would be unfaithful to His grace, if, after having been chosen by His Providence to provide for the preservation of their bodies, and to procure spiritual good for the poor foundlings, we became wearied, and abandoned them on account of the trouble we experienced."

The service of the poor was his favorite theme with the Sisters of Charity. ". . . . Oh, how happy you are, my daughters, to have been destined by God for so great and so holy a work. The great ones of the world consider themselves happy when they can devote to it a portion of their time, and you are witnesses, you, particularly, our Sisters at St. Sulpicius, with what zeal and what fervor the good princesses and the great ladies who accompany you tend the poor. Oh, my daughters, how you should esteem your state wherein you have, every day, and every hour of the day, an occasion of doing works of charity, which are the means God makes use of to sanctify many souls! Did not a St. Louis, my daughters, with a holy and an exemplary humility serve the poor in the *Hotel Dieu,* an exercise that greatly contributed to his holiness? Have not all the saints looked upon it as a good work, and sought to tend the poor? Humble yourselves, therefore, whenever you practice this charity, and often reflect, my daughters, that God has given you a grace far above your deserts. . . . . Your principal care, after the love of God and the desire to make yourselves more agreeable to His Divine Majesty, should be to serve the sick poor with sweetness and cordiality, compassionating their sickness and listening to their little complaints as a good mother ought to do, for they look upon you as persons sent to assist them, as mothers who nurse them. In this way, you are destined to represent in regard to the sick poor the goodness of God. But this goodness acts towards the afflicted in a sweet and charitable way; hence, you, too, must treat the sick poor with gentleness, with pity and love, for they are your lords and masters as well as mine. Oh, what great lords they are in the eyes of Heaven! It will be their duty, as it is said in the Gospel, to open the gate. Now you perceive what obliges you to serve them with respect, because they are your masters, and with piety, because they represent the person of our Lord. You ought not forget to suggest to them some good thoughts, something, for example, like this: 'Well, my brother, how do you think of making the journey to the other world?' Then to another: 'Well, my child, do you not wish to go see our Lord?' You must not, however, say much at a time to them, but little by little give whatever instruction is necessary, just as to children at the breast they give but little to drink at a time. So, too, should you do when your sick are great personages in the world, for, notwithstanding, they are but children in piety, and a word coming from the heart and uttered in the proper spirit suffices to lead them to God.

"You see, my sisters, though it be something to assist the poor in their bodies, it never was the design of God in establishing your congregation that you should care for the body only, because there will not be wanting those who will do that; but the intention of our Lord was that you should assist the soul of the sick poor. That is your beautiful vocation. What! leave all we have in the world, father, mother, brothers, sisters, relations, friends, possessions, if we have any, and even our country? And why? To serve the poor, to aid and instruct them how to go to Heaven. Is there anything more beautiful or more worthy of esteem? Could we see a daughter thus formed we would see her soul resplendent as the sun; we could not gaze upon its beauty without being dazzled. Give yourselves, then, to God for the salvation of the poor you serve."

The service of the poor is so essentially the principal vocation of this congregation, that the Saint would have, if necessary, all things else subordinated to it, every point of the rule, even mental prayer and mass; for, as he unceasingly repeated: "It is to leave God for God." He said: "Would you think God less reasonable than a master who, having commanded his servant to do a certain thing, and before the order was fulfilled, bade him do something which must be done done instantly! Oh, this master would not certainly blame his servant for neglecting his first order; on the contrary, he ought to be better pleased. It is the same with God. He has called you to the congregation to serve the poor, and that this service might be the more agreeable He has caused rules to be given you; but if, at the time of the exercises, He calls you elsewhere, go on the instant and do not once doubt but that you do His most holy will. Oh, what a source of consolation for a good Daughter of Charity to be able to think and to say to herself: 'Instead of making my prayer, or my reading, I will go and tend my poor sick who are waiting for me, and I know God will look upon my action as agreeable.' Oh, with such a thought, a sister goes gladly wherever God calls."

But he also exhorted his confreres to love one another, taking as his text these words of St. John: *Little children, love one another*. He told them: "The congregation will last as long as the virtue of charity abides in it." He then pronounced a thousand maledictions on those who, in destroying charity, would be the cause of the ruin of the congregation, and added: "Charity is the soul of all virtues, and the paradise of communities. Yes, the house wherein charity reigns is a paradise, for, where charity is, there God dwells. A great personage has said that charity is the cloister of God, it is there He lodges, there He makes His sojourn, there is His palace of predilection. Let us be charitable, meek, let us bear with each other, and then God will take up His residence with us, we will be His cloisters, He will lodge with us and we will have Him in our hearts."

Whoever, in a community, has neither charity nor forbearance, resembles, amid so many dissimilar dispositions and different methods of action, a vessel, with neither anchor nor rudder, sailing among rocks at the pleasure of wind and wave, and which soon becomes shattered into a thousand fragments.

He wrote: "How I pray God from my heart for you and all yours that it may please His Infinite Goodness to give you one heart and one soul! Charity is the cement that binds Christians to God, and individuals among themselves; so that he who contributes to the union of hearts in a congregation binds it indissolubly to God. May it please His infinite bounty to animate us all with His love for it." And when he learned of an act of charity, he exclaimed: "Oh, goodness of God, unite thus all the hearts of the little Congregation of the Mission, and then command what Thou pleasest. All pain will be sweet, all work easy, the strong will assist the weak, the weak will cherish the strong and obtain for them from God an increase of strength, and then, O God, Thy work will be according to Thy pleasure and to the edification of the Church, and Thy laborers will multiply, drawn by the good odor of such charity." (To Gennes, 13 Nov. 1647).

Union was his parting word to the missionaries who went to labor together. He said to them: "Be united, and God will bless you; but let it be by the charity of Jesus Christ, for all union not cemented by the blood of this Divine Savior cannot subsist. It is, then, in Jesus Christ, by Jesus Christ and for Jesus Christ, that you should be united to one another. The spirit of Jesus is a spirit of union and peace; how, then, can you attract souls to Jesus Christ if you be not united among yourselves and with Him? It cannot be done. Have, then, but one mind and one will; otherwise you will resemble horses attached to the same plough, each one pulling in opposite directions, and thus destroying and breaking everything God calls you to labor in His vineyard. Go, having in Him but one and the same heart, one and the same intention, and then you will reap abundant fruit."

He sought an example of this union in the most Holy Trinity itself. He said to the Daughters of Charity: "I have been desiring and wishing for a long time, that our sisters had attained to that degree of respect for each other that the world outside could never know which one was the sister servant. For, see, my Daughters, though God be one in Himself, yet there are in Him three persons, and the Father is not greater than the Son, nor the Son greater than the Holy Ghost. In like manner, the Daughters of Charity, who ought to be the image of the most Holy Trinity, though numerous should yet have but one heart and one mind. And as, again, in the sacred persons of the most Holy Trinity the operations, though diverse and attributed to each one in particular, have such a relation between themselves that when we attribute Wisdom to the Son and Goodness to the Holy Ghost, we do not intend to say that the Father is deprived of these two attributes, nor that the Third Person possesses not the power of the Father nor the wisdom of the Son; so, too, among the Daughters of Charity, she who serves the poor must have a relation with the one who tends the children, and she who has the care of the children should have a relation with her who has charge of the poor. And I would still further wish that our sisters would conform themselves to the Holy Trinity, in this, that as the Father communicates Himself entirely to the Son, and the Son entirely to the Father, from which union the Holy Spirit proceeds, so they, too, would be all in all to each other that they may thus produce the works of charity that are attributed to the Holy Ghost, and, in this way, have a relation with the Most Holy Trinity. For you see, my Daughters, he who says charity says God. You are the daughters of charity; therefore, you ought, as far as possible, conform yourself to the image of God. To this tend all communities that aspire to perfection. And what is there in God? There are, my Daughters, equality of persons and unity of essence. Well, what does this teach you if not that you all, every one of you, should be but one and equal? But if there must be a superioress, a sister servant? Oh, this ought to be but to give an example of virtue and humility to the others by being the first to do everything; the first to humble herself at the feet of her sister, the first to beg pardon, and the first to renounce her own opinion to follow that of another."

He recommended, especially, mutual forbearance. "It is," he said, "the stay of a Congregation, just as in a house the parts below sustain those placed above." The defects of others should not discourage us. "Let us look upon defects whether of body or of mind as a special mercy from God, and always show a particular reverence for those who are afflicted with these failings, regarding their persons as strokes of a great master though the piece be not finished (Conference, 21st. of Oct. 1043). "We should not be astonished when, at times, we see faults in certain persons, because God permits this for ends of which we know nothing; but what do I say? God even makes use of sins for the justification of a person; yes, sin itself enters, in a certain sense, into the order of predestination, and by means of it, God produces in us acts of penance, of humility, of humility, yes, gentlemen, of humility which is Our Lord Jesus Christ's own virtue. And, tell, me have not roses their thorns? There is no rose without thorns. The defects then, which God permits in certain persons, in some more, in some less, serve as ashes to cover up the virtues that are in them, so that seeing their faults they may maintain themselves in humility and abjection. And who is there not subject to some fault, when even the saints had their failings, and none but the Son of God and His Blessed Mother were exempt? The Apostles were taught in the school of Jesus Christ and from His own lips, and yet, you know what passed between them! Petty rivalries, want of faith, so that at the very time the Son of God was ascending into Heaven He reproached them with their incredulity. . . . What you should fear are the sins of the understanding, for they are very rarely, scarcely ever, corrected; they are the most dangerous faults." (Conference, 27th of April, 1657).

Having thus preached forbearance and mutual support, the humble old man, throwing himself on his knees, said: "And because I have greater need than any other that the Congregation bear with me, on account of the many miseries I perceive within myself, the many causes of disedification I give my brethren and, particularly those who assist me in my little infirmities, I therefore, pray you, my brothers, to kindly please to continue your charity and forgive the past. Old men, as

David said, have great need of support; bear with me, then, my brothers. I beg of you, and pray to God that I may improve." He then kissed the floor, as was customary, all the others doing the same. (Conference, 25th of July, 1658.)

He afterwards cautioned them against whatever could trouble charity, against scandal, of which he said: "The malice of scandal may be compared to the malice of a person who would dig a deep and wide ditch in the middle of a great thoroughfare that the passers-by might fall into it, and the better to prevent them from being on their guard, would cover the ditch so as to hide it from their view. Scandal is something still worse, because the malice of that person tends to precipitate only bodies into the ditch, whereas the malice of scandal tends to precipitate souls into hell. (Conference to Sisters of Charity, 15th. of Nov. 1654).

He likewise combated detraction, of which he said: "The darts first pierced the heart of Our Lord before striking those for whom they were meant." He condemned those who lent a willing ear, no less than those who slandered: " As they say that there would be no thieves were there none who received stolen goods, so, too, can it be said none would dare to detract were none willing to listen." (Conference, Sisters, 28th. of Oct. 1646.) He added: " Detraction is like a ravenous wolf that desolates and ruins the sheepfold that it enters. One of the greatest evils that can befall a Congregation is to have within it persons who detract, who murmur, and who, never content, always find fault."

Finally, he branded envy: "To envy is to find fault with the order of God; for if we become displeased because another is better off than we, we attack not so much him who has the advantage over us as Him Who gives it, and God can say to us: *Is thy eye evil because I am good?* It is to grieve because the blood of Jesus Christ is not useless, for to this blood are due all graces as well natural as spiritual, whilst we, by our sins have merited but hell. It is to place ourself in opposition to the communion of saints, for in the Church there is a communication of good works. Now, would a merchant, who formed a partnership with another, be angry because his partner made great gains, seeing that he is to share in them? Will one part of the body rise up in anger, because another is sound and healthy." (Repetition of Prayer, 1656.) In a word, envy has caused the death of Jesus Christ—the envy of the devil and the envy of the Jews. Envy is the gate through which sin entered Heaven and came upon the earth. Envy ruined Lucifer, and from being an angel of light it changed him into an angel of darkness. Then the demon, seeing that man was made to occupy the place whence he had fallen by his rebellion against God, envied him and resolved to destroy him by inducing him to fall into sin. He succeeded, and thus, in causing the fall of Eve and Adam, he introduced sin into the world. And hence, then, it may be said, no evil happens in a congregation but through envy, which is thus the first source of all the sins committed.

"It is said that they who commit sin experience a certain satisfaction, but it is not so in the sin of envy. This vice is an executioner who instantly punishes those who are given to it. Look at the envious person; everything gives him pain; the good he sees in others and the good he hears of others wither him immediately. He has a serpent in his soul. You know the torments those suffer who are afflicted with the tape worm, and how they can rest neither by day nor by night. The Holy Ghost declares that envy dries up even the marrow in the bones; in fine, the envious are in a condition far more deplorable than those afflicted with tape worm. Let us take the resolution never to envy the good of others, nor the esteem of men, nor occupations, but choose for ourselves that which is least, the employment which is the most painful, the worst garments, and look upon ourselves as the least and last of all." (Conference to Sisters of Charity, 24th of June, 1654.)

Let us further hear the Saint giving us both the precept and example of charity, in the efforts he made to retain in their vocation those of his members who were tempted to abandon it. He wrote, in November 1656: "If you understood the gift of God you would not prefer a change to the happiness of serving our Lord in the state to which He has called you, a grace so great that it ought to be dearer to you than life. When I contrast your present dispositions with those in which I formerly saw you, you seem to me no longer the same man. Where, now, is that gratitude that so often forced you to thank God for having withdrawn you from the world, that you might find in the congregation so many means of sanctifying yourself, and so many exercises of charity to aid others in procuring their salvation? Where, now, is that holy indifference to riches and employments that caused you so frequently to say that you were ready to go, or to stay. in order to follow our Lord? Where is that great fervor you had to do in all things the will of God, and, according as it might be made known to you by holy obedience." He wrote similarly to a brother, on the 5th of September, 1649: "Do you not remember the lights God so often gave you in prayer, lights that made you resolve before His Divine Majesty to publicly declare before the whole community that you would rather die than leave it? And, behold, on the slightest occasion, when there is question neither of death, nor of shedding blood, nor of menaces, you surrender without the resistence which a promise made to God demands, for God is a firm and jealous God and requires to be served according to His pleasure! Will you now contradict that promise, and abuse His grace. make light of His goodness and afterwards endure the regrets that others experienced through like disorders? I have not seen any one, to whom God gave the graces which you have received from His kindness leave any community, without feeling in his conscience the reproach of God, and in his daily life a thousand vexations. But, you will say, I have the intention of always pleasing God. Alas! there is no lack of good pretexts; and if you examine you will find that your action is not prompted by the desire of rendering yourself better, of becoming more submissive, more detached from the world and from your own ease, more humble, more mortified, and more united to your neighbor by charity, as is necessary in order to become more pleasing to God. You think, however, my dear brother, to render Him service and work out your salvation in removing yourself from the way of perfection: this is an illusion. Had you not already entered upon the way of the perfect, ah! very well; but St. Paul says that those who have once been enlightened and have tasted the word of God, and fall, can, with difficulty, be renewed in penance. How can you persuade yourself that you will be able to preserve yourself, in returning to the world, when even now, being out of it, you find so much trouble in overcoming yourself? If you believe the contrary, at least do not leave but by the same door through which you have entered the congregation: this door is the spiritual retreat which I beg you to make before determining on a separation of such importance."

We find all these reasons, all the efforts of his charity, united in the following letter to a missionary, (2d Jan., 1656): "Reflect on these reasons: First, reflect on the graces of your vocation in which God puts into your hands so many means of perfecting your own soul and of saving others, '*Thou hast not chosen me but I have chosen you,*' says our Lord. But He will not be obliged to give you those graces in another condition to which He will not have called you. Secondly, reflect on the blessings it has pleased God, up to the present, to give to all your labors, whereby you have done much good both within and without, and which, besides your merit before God, has made you esteemed, and endeared to every one. Third, reflect on the promise you have made to God to serve Him in the little Congregation; if you fail in your word with God, with whom will you keep it? Fourth, reflect on these words of our Lord: 'He who does not leave father and mother for my love is not worthy of me.' Thank God, you have left yours to give yourself entirely to Him. What pretext, then, have you, at this hour, for abandoning Him in order to return to your parents? Fifth, think of the remorse you will have at the hour of death, and for what you will have to answer at the judgment seat of God, if, through human respect, or for a temporal gain, or to live more at your ease, or for all these together, though hidden under other pretexts, you should become guilty of the infidelity of which we have spoken and lose the opportunities you now have of advancing the glory of Our Master God forbid, sir, that this evil should ever happen! They will tell you, perhaps, as you already have been told, that you can work out your salvation anywhere. I admit; but I add, it is extremely difficult, not to say impossible, to save your soul in a place and in a state wherein God does not wish you,

especially after having left, without cause, a true vocation such
as you have recognized yours to be. You cannot say that you are
wanting in the strength required for the functions of the Congregation, since you know, sir, these are varied, that the labors
of each are regulated according to his talents, and that even
those who labor the most have less anxiety than a parish priest
in the country who strives to do his duty well. If it be
objected to you that you owe more to the souls of your relatives
than to those of strangers, answer, without fear of contradiction,
that one mission, lasting for a month or three weeks, which you
will procure for the parish in which they live, will be of more
advantage to them than all that you, living among them, could
do during your entire life. And the reason of this is, that
familiarity diminishes esteem and often destroys it altogether;
and then one is no longer capable of producing any fruit. This
is why a person is rarely a prophet in his own country. Hence
it is, that Our Lord returned only once to Nazareth, and then
the inhabitants wished to precipitate Him from the summit of
a rock, a treatment, He, perhaps, permitted to teach evangelical laborers the danger they incur, in returning to their homes,
of losing the high esteem their labors have won for them, and
of falling into shameful disorders. For this reason, further,
He did not wish to allow two of His disciples to return to their
parents when they asked permission, the one desiring to go
bury his father, the other to sell his property and distribute it
to the poor. "If you say you are obliged to assist your mother,
that is true in only one case, which is, when she is in need of
the necessaries of life, and when, without your aid, she would
be in danger of death from hunger. But, thanks be to God,
she is well enough off in the goods of this world, and can do
without you in the future as in the past. For all these reasons
I will hope, sir, that you will give yourself anew to God to
serve Him in the congregation according to His eternal designs,
without further thinking of your relations, save the more to
detach yourself from them, and to recommend them to His
mercy; for, by this means, His Divine bounty will continue to
bless you, and will bless, on account of you, the souls of those
that are dear to you. I hope and pray for this from the bottom
of my heart."

But if Vincent would not permit his children to leave the congregation and go out into the world, he willingly exhorted them, when on the point of death, to depart from the world and the congregation to go to Heaven. Here is, almost entire, one of his exhortations before death, admirable alike for its sweetness, and its sublime faith: "Well, my brother, how are you at present? So you believe, then, that our great general, the first of all missionaries, our Lord, really wants you in the mission of Heaven? You see He wishes that we all, each in his turn, go there, and this is one of the principal rules and constitutions He made while on earth. *I will that where I am there also may my minister be.* My God! What consolation you should feel thus to be chosen among the first to go to the eternal mission where all the exercises consist in loving God! Is it not true that our great superior is graciously willing to give you the grace of being of the number of these happy missionaries? Oh, without a doubt, you should hope for it from His mercy and goodness, and, animated with this confidence, say to Him in all humility: 'Oh my Lord! whence comes this happiness? Alas! it is not because I have merited it, for what proportion is there between the toil of missions given on earth and the joy and recompense of the missionaries who are with Thee? It is, then, from Thy bounty and liberality alone, O, my Master, that I hope for it. And what! Besides the inequality between the labors of missions here below and the reward Thou givest above, I have been guilty of a number of sins, of infidelities, and of cowardice which render me unworthy of the recompense. Still, I hope in Thy infinite goodness and generosity that this great debt will be remitted, as was done to the poor debtor in the Gospel: *And He forgive him all the debt,* because Thy mercy and benevolence are infinitely greater than my unworthiness and my malice. It is certain that the greatest glory you are capable of rendering Him at present is to hope with all your heart in His goodness and His infinite merits, for the magnitude of the faults to be pardoned will only manifest the better the greatness of His mercy. He expects that confidence from you, so as to be forced to say to you, with all the affection of a father: *This day thou wilt be with Me in Paradise.* Now, too, is the time to make frequent and ardent acts of love for your dear and good master. And all those beautiful acts of hope, so agreeable to God, which you may have made should lead you to love, for if He is so magnificent, so liberal, so good, as you hope, is it not true that you have great reason to cry out and say: 'Oh, God of my heart! Thy infinite goodness does not permit me to divide my affections. Oh! do Thou alone take possession of my heart and my liberty! How can I desire aught else but Thee! How attach myself to anything not Thee! Would it, perhaps, be to myself? Alas! Thou bearest me infinitely more love than I can have for myself. Thou art infinitely more desirous of my good and hast the power of doing it, than I who have nothing and hope for nothing but in Thee. Oh, my only God! Oh, Infinite Goodness! Why have I not for Thee the love of all the Seraphims together! Alas! it is very late to imitate them! *Oh, ancient Bounty, I have loved Thee too late.* But, at least, I offer Thee with all the strength of my affection the love of the most holy Queen of Angels, and, in general, the love of all the blessed. Oh my God! in the presence of Heaven and earth I give Thee my heart such as it is. I adore, out of love for Thee, the secrets of Thy paternal Providence in regard to Thy wretched servant. I detest, in Thy presence, and before the entire heavenly court, all that can separate me from Thee. O Sovereign Goodness, Thou, Who wished to be loved by sinners, give me Thy love, and then command what Thou wilt. '*Give what Thou commandest and command what Thou wilt.*' Yes, my very dear brother, it is true, and you must in no way doubt it, that it always has been the good pleasure of God that you love Him and especially that you love Him at this time. It is that we might love Him that He created us to His own image and likeness, since we only love what bears a resemblance to us, if not entirely, at least in part. This lover of our hearts, seeing that, unfortunately, sin had spoiled this likeness, has wished to break through all the laws of nature in order to repair the damage, but so wonderfully, that He has not contented Himself in restoring in us His image and the character of His dignity, but He has been pleased to make Himself like us in clothing Himself with our humanity. And more, as love is infinitely inventive, after being nailed to the infamous gibbet of the cross, in order to gain the souls of those by whom He wished to be loved, foreseeing that this absence might bring forgetfulness and coolness to our hearts, He instituted the most august Sacrament of the altar, in which He is as really and substantially present as in Heaven above. In this sacrament, He has wished to abase and annihilate Himself still more than in His Incarnation, and in some measure to make Himself more like us by being our meat and drink, intending, by this means, that the union and resemblance, produced between our bodies and nutritious substance, be effected between Him and men, for love can do all, and wills all. Thus has He willed, and fearing that men, not comprehending rightly this ineffable mystery and stratagem of love, would neglect to approach this divine sacrament He laid upon them the obligation of so doing under pain of incurring His eternal displeasure: '*Unless you eat the flesh of the Son of Man you will not have life in you.*' Excite yourself, then, to love Him. Remember that the greatest gift you can give Him is your heart; He asks nothing more: '*Son, give me thy heart.*' If your thoughts suggest that it is temerity for a poor debtor and a miserable slave to aspire to caresses and marks of affection from the Supreme Master, answer that it is God Who commands you and Who desires it. If any difficulty you may have felt in making acts of faith cause you pain or scruple, have recourse to acts of love which will please God better, and will, moreover, contain acts of all other interior virtues. If you have difficulty in forming acts of contrition, make them by way of love; for they are nothing else. Do you not wish that the will of God be accomplished in you? Do you not desire that He should take infinite delight in you? Are you not willing that He should receive all the glory He expects from the sufferings He permits you to endure at present? Were it in your power to procure Him all the glory that He expects from all creatures, would you not willingly do it? And are you not very glad of all the glory and perfection that God has in Himself? Do you not detest, from the bottom of your heart, all that is in you contrary to the good pleasure of God? Do you not wish you had loved Him all your lifetime, as did the Blessed Virgin? Well, now, entertain yourself frequently with these beautiful sentiments and look upon them as the lighted lamps of the wise virgins who were admitted, for that reason, to eternal nuptials with the spouse. Oh, but that is a beautiful disposition in which to enter with Him! And will you not leave us the hope that you will not forget us when you will be in Heaven among the little troop of missionaries who are already there? Grant us the favor to kindly tell them of the confidence we have in their holy prayers, so that they may obtain for us the grace to perform our mission here below faithfully, that thus we may belong again to the mission in Heaven — a mission of love that will endure eternally."

CHAPTER XI.

MEEKNESS.

I

Meekness is the flower and the odor of charity. Wonderful flower! With Vincent it sprang up and shed all its beauty upon an ungrateful earth. He was naturally choleric, being of a splenetic temperament, and of an active nature. Yet, by efforts of virtue, and with the aid of grace, he succeeded in repressing even the least appearance of anger, and conquered in himself its most secret movements. The struggle was long and obstinate. Whilst yet in the house of Gondi the wife of the general of the galleys was distressed at his fits of melancholy, and it was in 1621 that he was able to say: "I addressed myself to God and earnestly prayed Him to change in me this dry and repulsive humor and give me a meek and benign spirit; and, by the grace of our Lord, with a little attention to sallies of nature, I have rid myself somewhat of my gloomy disposition."

Once in possession of the virtue of meekness, he guarded it carefully, cultivated it, and faithfully practiced all its acts After the example of the blessed Bishop of Geneva whom he, himself, took as a model and recommended to others, he ever after presented an open address and an amiable affability which tinctured all his conversations with kind and obliging words without, however, any shade of false flattery: he never praised any in their presence unless actuated by motives of the most elevated interest.

His meekness excelled in reprimand and correction. On these occasions, he threw into his manner and his words, such moderation and such sweetness that he softened the hardest hearts and triumphed over all resistance.

His meekness became all the more compassionate and more tender towards sinners whose faults he loved to hide, and, as it were, to bury. Never a word of complaint did he use against those who had abandoned him, no retaliation for their murmurs. Far from revealing the motives of their departure, he said of them all the good possible that truth would permit, and avenged himself on their petty spites by all kinds of good offices.

In the exercise of his duty as Superior, he had worn the air of one who had asked a favor rather than of a superior who gave his orders. Were his commands neglected, he contented himself with saying: "Perhaps, had you done that in the manner I asked you to do it, God would have blessed it." Often, even when the disobedience was without thought, indirect, or of little import, he said nothing, his silence and patience being the only correction.

He showed himself particularly mild towards the infirm, either of body, or of mind. With regard to them he never complained, never used a word that in the slightest degree conveyed the idea that they were a burden. He sometimes admitted to the congregation, on trial, notwithstanding all representations to the contrary, certain subjects who appeared as if they never could become suitable members; and more than once by his gentle care he merited that God should deliver them from all their ailments, and should make of them efficient missionaries. With still greater reason did he treat with meekness and patience those who already belonged to the congregation, how great soever their infirmities. "Have no fear," he said to them, "of being a charge to the congregation; on the contrary, it is a blessing for it to possess infirm members, for they, by their sufferings, merit more than do the others by their labors."

The least among the members of his congregation, the brothers, and, among the brothers, the most uncouth and the least useful, were the privileged objects of his mildness and benignity. He called upon them in conference, no matter what their roughness, listened to them with gentle patience, never interrupted them, but to help them, and by mingling excuses and praises he corrected them of any errors which they might have advanced.

His meekness, so tolerant with natural defects of body, or of mind, was not disconcerted even by vices of the will. He bore with intractable subjects that they might have an opportunity for repentance and conversion: and when there was hardly any hope of amendment he still bore with them in order to exercise himself in meekness.

Even when overwhelmed with pressing duties his mildness opened, to all, his room, his ear, and his heart. He was at all times ready to listen to the least of his subjects, before mass, during the recitation of his breviary, and even at night. Those troubled with scruples could apply to him several times during the day or hour, even when he was engaged with persons of distinction, and he would ever receive them with kindness. He would rise from his chair, go to meet them, take them into a corner listen to them, repeat his advice, even write it down for them and make them read it to him so as to be assured they understood; nothing wearied his sweet and gentle charity.

And this is why Tronson, Superior General of St. Sulpicius, could say that Vincent possessed the virtue of meekness in so eminent a degree, that in seeing him you imagined you saw St. Paul conjuring the Corinthians by the meekness and modesty of Jesus Christ.

II.

And yet the humble Saint believed himself to be without this meekness—his reward for so many combats. And so, in exhorting his children to acquire it on the same conditions, he said: "We sometimes see persons who seem gifted with remarkable meekness, and yet it is but an effect of their quiet disposition; they have not Christian meekness the special duty of which is to repress and stifle all the sallies of the contrary vice. He is not chaste simply because he feels no unchaste movements, but because when he feels them he resists. We have in the house an example of true meekness; I mention it because the person is not present, and because you can all perceive that naturally he is of a sharp and arid disposition.

It is Mr. N. And you may judge if there be, in the world, two men as rough and forbidding as he and I. And yet we see this man overcome himself to such a degree that we can truly say he is no longer what he was; and what has done this? It is the virtue of meekness in the acquisition of which he is struggling, whereas, I, miserable, remain as sharp as a briar. I pray you, gentlemen, not to fix your eyes on the bad example I give you, but rather, I exhort you, to use the words of the Apostle, ' to walk worthily and with all meekness and gentleness in the state to which God has called you.''

He would not have this meekness soft, nor weak and indulgent, but rather, full of force and firmness on account of that close union existing between all real virtues. For, he said, '' there are none more constant, or more firm in good than the meek and gentle; whilst, on the contrary, those who allow themselves to be carried away by anger and by passions of the irascible appetite, are ordinarily very inconstant, because they act only in fits and starts. They are similar to torrents which have force and impetuosity only in their irruptions, and are exhausted as soon as these subside, whereas rivers, which represent the meek, flow on without noise, tranquilly, and never become dry. Therefore, let us be firm in regard to the end we propose to ourselves in our good works, but let us employ meekness in the means we make use of, imitating in this the action of the wisdom of God which *reacheth its ends mightily and yet ordereth the means sweetly*. Let us, again, imitate the blessed Bishop of Geneva, the most mild and gentle man that I ever knew. The first time I ever saw him I recognized in his address, in the serenity of his countenance, in his manner of speech and in his conversation, a well-marked image of the meekness of our Lord Jesus Christ, and my heart was gained.''

Meekness is particularly necessary for persons living in a community, and for those who labor for the salvation of souls. The Saint said: ''We have all the greater need of affability as we are, by our vocation, more obliged to frequently converse with one another and with our neighbor. This intercourse is the more difficult whether among ourselves, because we are either from different countries, or are of different temperaments and natural dispositions, or whether with our neighbor because often we have much to bear with in him. It is the virtue of affability which overcomes all these difficulties, and which, being the soul of good conversation, makes it not only useful but also agreeable; it makes us, in conversation, comport ourselves with propriety and with condescension for each other. And, as it is charity that unites us as members of one body, it is affability that perfects the union.

"Let us practice the virtue of meekness, especially with the poor people in the country; otherwise, they will be discouraged and not dare to approach us, thinking us too severe, or too grand for them. But when we treat them with affability and cordiality they conceive different sentiments for us and become better disposed to profit by the good we wish to do them. Since God has destined us to serve them we ought to do it in the manner the most profitable to them, and, consequently, act towards them with great kindness, and take, as if addressed to each of us in particular, the admonition of the Wise Man: 'Make thyself affable to the congregation of the poor.'

"Be affable, but never flatter; for nothing is so despicable and unworthy a Christian soul as flattery. A man truly virtuous abhors nothing so much as this vice.

"On the other hand, do not contend with any, not even with the vicious whom it may be necessary to reprehend; but ever use in their regard sweet and courteous speech, according as charity and prudence will dictate. In our discussions with heretics let us not enter into altercation, or employ harshness; they are far more readily won by a sweet and amiable remonstrance. This is how the angels act towards us. They inspire good thoughts, but do not force us to follow them. Experience has shown me that more is gained over minds in this way than in urging them to enter into our sentiments, and in wishing to triumph over them. It is usual with the malign spirit to be eager, and his custom is to disquiet souls. In a journey I made to Beauvais I had, on one occasion, the happiness of converting three heretics, and I must say that the kindness and mildness I exercised with them contributed more to their conversion than all the rest of the discussion. When we argue with any one, the manner of conduct of the dispute easily shows that we want to gain the upperhand; hence, our adversary prepares for resistance rather than to learn the truth; so that the debate, instead of shedding any light on his mind, ordinarily closes the door of his heart; whilst, on the contrary, sweetness and affability would open it. We have a beautiful example of this in the person of the blessed Francis de Sales who, though very expert in controversy, nevertheless converted heretics rather by his meekness than by his learning. And, on this point, His Eminence, Cardinal De Perron, used to say that he could, indeed, convince heretics but it belonged to the Bishop of Geneva to convert them. Bear well in mind the words of St. Paul to that great missionary, St. Timothy: 'But the servant of the Lord must not wrangle.' And, I can assure you, I have never seen or heard of any heretic who was converted by the power of a dispute, or by subtlety of argument; but, indeed, yes, by means of meekness, so true is it that that possesses a secret charm for gaining men to God."

The Saint seemed to take a pleasure, so tireless were his exhortations, in reverting to the mildness and affability which should be exercised towards the poor; he attributed to this all the success he heard of the missions given by the Congregation. And he would take occasion, both in his instructions and in his letters, to recommend more than ever the practice of this virtue. He wrote in this sense to one of his priests accused of treating, in his sermons, the people with too much asperity: "If God, in some degree, blessed our first missions, it was remarked that the reason of it was that the missionaries acted amiably, humbly, and sincerely towards all classes of persons; and if it has pleased God to make use of the most miserable of all in the conversion of some heretics these have themselves acknowledged that it was the patience and cordiality he exhibited that gained them. The galley slaves even, with whom I have been, are gained in no other way. Whenever I happened to speak with severity I spoiled all. On the contrary, when I praised them for their resignation, when I pitied them in their sufferings, when I told them they were happy to have their purgatory in this life, when I kissed their chains, condoled with them in their grief and manifested sorrow for their disgrace, then they listened to me, then they gave glory to God and became reconciled to Him. I beg you, sir, to unite with me in giving thanks to God for this and ask Him to be pleased to inspire all the missionaries to treat their neighbors, both in public and in private, kindly, humbly, and charitably, and even sinners, and the most obdurate, never employing against any invective, or reproach, or harshness. I have no doubt, sir, but that you try to avoid this unfortunate manner of serving souls which, instead of attracting, embitters and alienates. Our Lord Jesus Christ is the Eternal Meekness both of angels and of men, and, by this virtue, we should, in conducting others, go to Him."

He recommended meekness towards the poor, and also towards sinners. "We must not be astonished," said the Saint, "to see others commit faults, because, as it is natural for briars and thistles to bear thorns, so, in the state of corrupt nature, it is natural for man to fall, since he is conceived and born in sin, and since the just man, according to Solomon, falls seven, that is, several times a day. The spirit of man has its inequalities and maladies as well as the body; instead, then, of being troubled and discouraged, we should, in view of its miserable condition, be humbled, and say with David, after his fall: 'It is good for me that Thou hast humbled me, that I may learn Thy justifications.' We must bear with ourselves in our weaknesses and, in the meanwhile, labor to surmount them. We must, moreover, bear with others, and charitably cover their defects; for if it be forbidden to judge ill of another, it is still less lawful to speak ill of him, the peculiarity of charity being, as the Apostle says, to cover a multitude of sins. Hear the Wise Man, once more: 'Hast thou heard a word against thy neighbor? Let it die within thee."

He would have meekness exercised even with those who seemed the most unworthy of it, for example, the priest and religious, who, enslaved in Tunis and Algiers, fell into the most shameful license. He wrote to one of his priests who performed the duties of grand vicar: "You should never allow yourself to become incensed against abuses since you foresee only that a greater evil will follow. Draw what good you can out of the priests and religious who are slaves . . . . by mild and easy ways, and employ severe measures only in extremity, for fear the evils they endure, by reason of their captivity, joined to the rigor which you, in your authority, would wish to exercise, might lead them to despair. It is impossible to fulfill the duties of your charge in all the rigor of full justice without augmenting the trials of these poor people and exhausting their patience, and injuring yourself. You should not, especially, undertake to immediately abolish certain customs in vogue among them, even though they be bad. Somebody brought, the other day, to my attention a beautiful passage from St. Augustine, wherein he says, one should be particularly careful in attacking an abuse that reigns in a place, because he will not only not succeed, but, on the contrary, will alienate those in whom the custom is, as it were, ingrained, so that he will thus deprive himself of the power of doing other good which he might have done, had he taken them differently. I beg you, then, to condescend to human infirmity as much as you can. You will gain, in compassionating them, the ecclesiastics who are slaves, far sooner than by reproof and correction. They are not wanting in light, but in fortitude, which is insinuated by the external unction of word and example. I do not say you should authorize or permit their disorders, but I do say that the remedy should be mild and kind and applied with great precaution."

Again, meekness should accompany conviction, which the Saint has recommended in so many of his letters. When complaint was made of another, he invariably answered: "If he did not have these faults he would, in all probability, have others, and had you nothing to suffer, your charity would have but little exercise, and your life not sufficient relation with that of Jesus Christ, Who has been pleased to have for disciples men who were coarse and vulgar, and subject to different failings, simply in order to have the opportunity, by practicing meekness and forbearance, to show us, by His example, how those who have charge of others should act. I pray you, sir, regulate yourself according to this Holy Model; He will teach you not only how to bear with your *confreres*, but also how to aid them to become rid of their imperfections. You must not, through a too weak toleration, neglect the evil, but you must likewise use meekness in remedying it."

To a second superior, engaged with another priest of the Congregation, in a distant mission, he wrote: "If you only have cordiality and forbearance between you two I have hopes in the goodness of God that He will bless your works; and I beg of you sir, in the name of God, let that be your constant practice. And, because you are at the same time the older and the superior, bear with all, in the spirit of meekness, from him who is with you; I say all, so that laying aside within yourself all authority, you may, in the spirit of charity, accommodate yourself to him. This is the means by which our Lord gained and perfected His apostles, and it is the only means whereby you can succeed with this good priest. Therefore, give a little play to his humor, never contradict just at the moment you think there is occasion, but wait, till sometime after, to remonstrate with him, and then do so humbly and cordially. Particularly, so conduct yourself that no division between you and him will ever become apparent; for you are there as on a stage exposed to the eyes of all classes, and with whom one single act of bitterness, noticed in you, would spoil all. I hope you will receive and make use of this advice I give you, and that God will make the million acts of virtue you will perform the base and foundation of the good He wishes you to do."

Here, again, the Saint collects, in his particular conferences, all these scattered teachings on the nature, the excellence, and the practice of meekness: "Meekness and humility," he said one day, "are twin sisters that agree admirably. We have a rule that requires us to study them very carefully in Jesus Christ, who says to us: 'Learn of Me because I am meek and humble of heart.'

"Meekness has several acts which may be reduced to three principal ones. The first of these acts has two branches one of which is to repress all movements of anger, all the flashes of that fire which mounts to the face, which troubles the soul, which transforms one so as to be no longer capable of recognition, and changes the calm and serene countenance into one dark and lowering, or glowing and inflamed. And what does meekness do? It arrests this change; it hinders him, who is affected, from manifesting these evil effects. It does not, however, prevent the movements of the passion, but it sets itself as a barrier, so that the passion cannot carry all before it. Some commotion may show itself in the countenance, but it soon subsides. Besides, we should not be surprised to see ourselves combated: the movements of nature are quicker than those of grace, but the latter vanquish. We must not be astonished at assaults, but we should rather demand grace to overcome them, being certain that, though we feel within us a certain revolt against it, yet meekness has the power to suppress it. This, then, is the first duty of the first act, and it is marvellously beautiful, so beautiful, in fact, that it restrains the ugliness of the opposite vice from manifesting itself; it is a certain activity in the mind and soul that not only moderates the ardor of anger, but even extinguishes its least sparks.

"The second duty of this first act consists in this, that, it being, at times, expedient to manifest displeasure, to reprehend, to punish, it governs those in whom the virtue of meekness resides so that they do these, not from an impulse of nature, but from duty, just as the Son of God who called St. Peter, *Satan*, and Who said to the Jews, not once, but several times: *Go, hypocrites!* this word being found ten or twelve times in a single chapter. Again, He drove the sellers from the temple, overturned their tables, and exhibited other signs of displeasure. Were these the transports of anger? No. He possessed meekness in a supreme degree. In us this virtue renders us masters of our passion, but in our Lord, Who had only propassions, it merely, according as it was expedient, advanced or retarded any manifestation of anger. If then, He, Who was mild and kind, showed Himself severe on certain occasions it was to correct those to whom He spoke, it was to drive out sin, to take away scandal; it was to edify souls, and to give us a lesson Oh, what great fruit a superior would produce did he act after this manner! His admonitions and corrections would be well received, because reason, and not caprice or humor, would govern them. While reprimanding strongly, he would not allow his passion to overmaster him, but would look to the good of the person admonished. As our Lord should be our model in every condition of life, those who govern others ought to consider how He acted and order themselves accordingly. Now He governed through love; and if He, at times, promised recompense, at others, He threatened chastisements: we must do in like manner, but always be actuated by the principle of love. We, then, will be in the disposition in which the prophet desired God to be when he said: 'Oh, Lord, rebuke me not in Thy indignation.' It seemed to this poor king that God was in anger with him, and, therefore, he prays Him not to punish him in His fury. All men are, in this, of like mind; none wish to to be corrected in anger. It is a favor accorded to but few not to feel the first emotions, as I have said; but the meek man soon recovers, he masters his anger and his vengeance. so that nothing follows save what is influenced by love. This, then, is the first act of meekness, to repress the contrary emotions as soon as they are felt, by either subduing anger altogether, or, in the necessity, so using it that meekness may still govern. Therefore. gentlemen, now that we are speaking of meekness, let us all resolve that, in all provocations to anger, we will cut short our inclinations, recollect ourselves, and raise our minds to God, saying to Him:' 'Oh Thou, Who, seest me assailed by this temptation, deliver me from the evil it suggests.'

"The second act of meekness is to show ourselves affable, cordial, and calm of countenance, so as to reassure and please those who accost us. This is why some with a cheerful and agreeable manner of address please everybody, God having endowed them with this grace whereby they seem to offer you their heart, and to request yours in return. Whereas, there are others, just as I am, who are rough, that present themselves with forbidding mien and contracted brow, who are gloomy and repelling; all this is opposed to meekness. Hence, a true missionary would do well to make himself affable, and study to acquire a cordial and amiable manner that he may, by these external marks of the kindness within, inspire confidence and assurance. You know, according to the word of our Lord, how this sweet insinuation gains and attracts all hearts: *For the meek shall possess the land;* and, on the contrary, how it has been remarked of persons of condition who are in office, that when they are too grave and reserved every one fears and avoids them

"And as our duties bring us in contact with the poor people of the country, with those preparing for orders, with those making the exercises of spiritual retreat, and with all classes of people, it is impossible for us to do any good if we be as barren soil producing nothing but thistles. We must possess some attraction, and have a pleasant countenance so as not to discourage or embarrass any one.

"I was consoled, three or four days ago, in witnessing the joy a certain person who was leaving manifested. He was delighted, he remarked, because he found here a pleasing manner, an openness of heart, and a certain charming simplicity (these are his words) that had deeply touched him.

"O, my Savior, how happy were those who approached Thee! What a countenance! What mildness! With what cordiality didst Thou not draw them! With what confidence didst Thou not inspire them to come to Thee! Oh, what marks of love! St. Andrew was the first captivated, and through him, St. Peter, and then all the others. Oh, my Savior! he who has this loving manner, this charming benignity, oh, what fruit will he not produce in Thy Church! Sinners and the just will crowd to him, the first to become reconciled to God, the second to be encouraged in good. Isaias said of our Lord that His nourishment would be butter and honey, to show us the meekness that would be given Him in order to know good and evil. Those souls only, that possess meekness, can discern things; for anger being a passion that troubles the reason, it must follow that the opposite virtue gives discernment. Oh, mild Savior, give us this virtue!

"The third act of meekness consists in not dwelling on any displeasure we may have received from any one, and in manifesting no resentment, saying in excuse: 'He did not think, he acted hastily, or impulse carried him away;' and, finally, in averting our thoughts from the imagined injury When disagreeable things are said to a meek man in order to exasperate him, he never opens his mouth in answer, he pretends not to hear.

"Meekness not only excuses the affronts and injustices done us, but it moreover acts mildly towards those who are guilty and has a kind word for them; even should the outrage go as far as blows, it suffers it for God's sake. Oh! if the Son of God appeared so kind in His conversation, how much more striking was His meekness in His passion! It went to such a degree that it did not permit a single hasty word to escape His lips against the deicides who covered Him with insult and spat in His face, and who mocked at His sorrow. 'My friend,' He says to Judas, who delivers Him to His enemies. Oh! what a friend! He meets him with that endearing title 'my friend.' He acts towards all the others with similar kindness 'Whom seek ye,' he says to them, 'behold I am He.' Let us meditate on these prodigious acts of meekness—acts that surpass human understanding. Consider how He maintains that mildness amid the most terrible tortures of His crucifixion. Oh, my Jesus! what an example for us who have undertaken to imitate Thee!

"After all this, ought we not to love this virtue of meekness, by which God not only gives us the graces to repress all movements of anger, to act kindly with our neighbor and return good for evil, but also the grace to suffer peaceably all the afflictions, all the injuries, all the torments, and even death itself, that men can inflict. Grant us, O, my Savior, the grace to profit by the pains Thou hast endured with so much love and meekness! Many, through Thy mercy, have profited, and perhaps I am the only one here who has not yet begun to be both meek and patient."

In another conference, St. Vincent de Paul, with that positive sense which he carried into the highest spirituality, reduced to still more precise counsels the practice of this virtue of meekness.

"In the first place," he said, "in order not to be surprised by the occasions wherein we may fail in meekness we should foresee these occasions, and represent to ourselves whatever may, probably, excite our anger, and then form, in advance, in our own minds, the acts of meekness we propose to practice on all occasions.

"Secondly, we must detest the vice of anger, in as much as

it displeases God, without, however, becoming indignant or provoked with ourselves, because we perceive ourselves still subject to it; for we must hate this vice, and love its contrary virtue, not because we have aversion for the one, and take delight in the other, but solely out of love for God whom the virtue pleases and the vice offends. If we do this the sorrow we conceive for faults committed against this virtue will be calm and sweet.

"Thirdly, when we perceive ourselves being moved to anger we should strive to refrain from acting, or even speaking, and especially we should come to no determination, until the emotion is quieted, because actions done in such agitation, not being fully directed by reason which is troubled and obscured by passion, though otherwise they appear good, yet can never be perfect.

"In the fourth place, during this emotion we should make an effort to prevent any sign of it appearing in the countenance which is the mirror of the soul, but we should restrain it and reform it by Christian meekness. This is not contrary to simplicity, because we do it, not to appear different from what we are, but from a sincere desire that the virtue of meekness, which is in the superior part of the soul, may show itself in our features, in our language, and in our exterior actions, in order to please God, and our neighbor for the love of God.

"In the fifth place, finally, we must, during these movements, endeavor to restrain our tongues, and notwithstanding all the transports of anger and the ardor of zeal we may imagine we have, not utter any but kind and pleasant words that thus we may gain others to God. Oftentimes, it requires but one kind word to convert the most obdurate, whereas, on the contrary, a rough and hasty word may grieve a soul and occasion a bitterness extremely dangerous. I employed, but three times in my life, words of harshness in reprimanding and correcting others, thinking I had just cause for so doing, and I have ever since repented of it, because I did not succeed, and because I perceived, on the contrary, that I always obtained by means of meekness whatever I desired."

CHAPTER XII.

HUMILITY.

I

We now come to the fundamental virtue of St. Vincent de Paul, the virtue of humility,—a virtue which no saint, after Him to whom nothing is comparable, after Him, who, being in the form of God, has annihilated Himself and taken upon Himself the form of a slave, after her who has extracted from her lowliness the principle of her greatness,—a virtue, I say, which no saint has possessed in the same degree as St. Vincent. His was a prodigious humility which astounds not only our pride, but even our intelligence, when we see this admirable man lower himself beneath earth and hell; when we see him prefer to himself the most perverse, the galley-slave, those condemned to death, and even the demons! And yet a humility that alone explains St. Vincent de Paul, which alone, by the incessant self-sacrifice of himself it impressed upon him, explains his charity, as prodigious as itself. He was the most charitable of men only because he was the most humble. Some have said it was an excessive humility. But no, if the Saint exceeded in the good opinion he had of others and exaggerated their praises he did not do so from the low esteem he had of himself. In comparison with the demon and with the greatest sinners, beneath whom he loved to debase himself, he did not, surely, put himself in their place; but what, in comparison with God, with His grandeur, and with His sanctity are the greatest and most holy on earth but baseness and imperfection? It is this truer and more profound sentiment in regard to God that has made the saints, though relatively greater, more humble than other men, and hence more charitable and more devoted.

It has been said: "Were clemency to be exiled from earth it ought to find a refuge in the hearts of kings." This is the word the Cardinal de la Rochefoucauld applied to the humility of St Vincent de Paul. It is not enough to say that humility was his virtue, it was in some sort his very passion. Never did ambition thirst for honor, voluptuousness for pleasure, as did Vincent for contempt and humiliation.

Not only did he never say anything of himself, but he tried his utmost to destroy all the honorable recollections of his life. How he worked to destroy the letter that has remained as a monument of his captivity in Tunis! That letter, in 1658, had been found among family papers and transmitted to the canon Saint-Martin. The latter thinking to give him pleasure in leading back his old age to youthful years immediately sent a copy of the letter to St. Vincent. But Saint-Martin, himself, notwithstanding his long intercourse with Vincent, had not yet sounded the depths of a humility that only sought in these recollections of the past new humiliations, only sought a means to draw down upon him the contempt of men. At the sight of that witness to his glorious slavery Vincent blushed, and hastened to commit it to the flames. But it was only a copy, and the orignal still remained in stronger hands, and might be adduced against him should he, according to his custom, publish and exaggerate his miseries and his nothingness. He, therefore, wrote to Saint-Martin imploring him to send the original letter. But the Canon was on the alert, and penetrating the thought of his humble friend, he was in no hurry to obey his request. For more than a year Vincent continued his entreaties, and on March 15th, 1660, six months before his death, he wrote to Saint Martin employing these strong and pressing terms: "I conjure you, by all the graces it has pleased God to bestow upon you, to do me the favor of sending me that wretched letter which makes mention of Turkey. I beseech you, moreover, by the bowels of our Lord Jesus Christ, to grant my request as soon as possible."

Never was more sacred language used in imploring life.

For Vincent there was question of far more; there was question of not leaving behind him an authentic testimony, written and signed by his own hand, that was a title of honor. And time pressed, for he felt himself dying; hence, his urgent prayer.

Still more; during the entire course of his life, he spoke but once of his slavery, and that only when it was still fresh in his memory, and, moreover in confidence to a single priest whom, perhaps, he had need to prepare for the holy ministry in those barbarous regions. Further than this he maintained an absolute silence on this subject. Twenty times in meetings for charitable purposes had he the opportunity to entertain his audience with its story; twenty times did he remain silent. And yet, what motives would any humility, but his, have found to excuse, to justify the recital! For instance, the need to arouse pity in behalf of the unfortunate slaves by relating, not the sufferings of hearsay, but personal sufferings, tortures endured by himself, placing himself on the scene in a dramatic picture, and even showing, after the manner of ancient eloquence, the trace of the iron still imprinted on his members. He alone did not believe that the most exacting charity could require such a sacrifice from humility. And more astonishing still; his captivity at Tunis, despite all his efforts, was known, but not the details, and the subject was often broached in his presence. A secretary of the king, particularly, named John Baptist Danlier, who had been a slave at Tunis, strove many a time by the recital of his own adventures to entice Vincent to recount his. Vain efforts! Vincent listened to the description of the cities of Barbary, as if the country were entirely new to him, heard all the recitals of sufferings in slavery without rejoining that he had endured them all, and never yielded to the temptations to speak of himself so natural to travelers, and especially to those who have encountered strange adventures.

A worker of the greatest things he considered himself incapable of the least, looked upon himself as more apt to destroy than to build up in the Church of God. Hence, his contempt and his diffidence of himself; his fear of intruding himself into any undertaking unless he was, as it were, thrust into it by the hand of God. He would have preferred that good were done by others rather than by himself. Obliged to act, he, at least, awaited some external impulse wherein he saw the will of Heaven, to which, from that time forth, he referred all the honor and glory of the work. He would say: "It is God Who has done all without my having even thought of it; I count in the work only by my sins which have fettered the action of God."

For he strove to hide all special graces that God gave him, and all personal action in his enterprises. Charity alone could do violence to his humility and induce him to disclose what was of a nature to turn to his credit. Moreover, he invariably guided himself by this maxim: "If when doing a public action I find I can enhance it, I will refrain from doing so, but, on the contrary, will retrench whatever may give it any renown or myself any reputation. Of two thoughts that arise, when speaking on any subject, when charity does not otherwise demand, I will give expression to the less fine for the sake of humility, and retain the more beautiful to sacrifice it to God in the secret of my heart. For our Lord is pleased only with humility of heart and simplicity in word and action."

Even when obliged to speak of the works which God did by his means, or of the blessings that attended his action, he found means to disengage and withdraw his personality. He attributed all to the congregation, or united himself with it in the plural in regard to everything honorable; but he did not forget to speak in the first person in all humiliating formulas and when reciting ill success—jealous to reserve for himself alone whatever could occasion any abasement or mortification. To God and to others he attributed the praise for all the good done in the congregation; to himself alone, to his coarseness, to his sins, the responsibility for all the evil that might happen.

For, if he were silent concerning his merits, if he carefully concealed his gifts, he revealed with eagerness his smallest imperfections which his humility magnified into abominable crimes, and he spoke with holy intemperance of all that, either in his birth, his person or his conduct could bring upon him disregard and contempt. Hardly arrived in Paris, and avoiding publicity with the same ardor others seek it, and dreading to be considered of noble, as others fear to be accounted of plebeian, birth, he retained, after the manner of servants, only his baptismal name and caused himself to be called simply Mr. Vincent. And when in public and in legal documents he was obliged to sign his name in full he took care to write the two parts for fear the separation would give rise to a suspicion of nobility.

He took pleasure in relating on all occasions his lowly extraction and the humble duties of his childhood. The bishop of Saint-Pons during a visit he made to St. Lazarus accidentally spoke of the Castle of Montgaillard from which his family took its name: "Oh, I know it well," interrupted Vincent, "in my youth I often led my animals in that direction." "I have the honor of being a relation of yours," a young man of good family wrote him from Dax, in asking his influence— "I will do for you what I would do for my brother," wrote the humble priest in answer, "but do not claim a relationship with a man whose father was but a poor peasant and whose own first occupation was tending swine." He used the same language with the little as with the great. One day a poor woman who thought to obtain his favor, said: "My lord, an alms"—"Oh, my poor good woman" rejoined the Saint, "you know me very little, for I am only the son of a poor villager." "You make a mistake, my good woman," he said to another who pretended she had been the servant of Madam his mother, "my mother, having to do her own work, never had a servant for she was the wife, as I am the son, of a poor peasant." Not content with thus publishing his low origin, at the court and in the city, in public and in private, he proclaimed it in other lands and sought in it a new motive for gratitude for favors rendered either himself or his congregation, or found in it a refuge against the praise his virtue called forth. "What, I ask, can you find praiseworthy in one in whom everything is wanting and whose father was but a poor farmer?" Thus he wrote to Count Obidos who had befriended one of his priests cast on the coast of Portugal, and who, in one of his letters, had testified a profound respect for his own person. To all, to the rich and the poor, he loved to make known his lowly birth; to the poor particularly, that they might look upon him as having been once in their conditions. Thus, one day, a villager having come to St. Lazarus to speak with him and the porter answering that he was just then engaged with some lords, the man broke out: "He is, then, no longer Mr. Vincent, for he himself told me that he was like myself only the son of a simple peasant."

In these humble avowals none will see that hypocritical calculation that recalls with complacency humble beginnings so as to force a comparison with present eminence and laud the merit that attained to it. With Vincent it was simply a craving and a passion for humiliation. And, at times, he felt a scruple when that passion satisfied filled his soul with joy. In 1633, he wrote to one of his priests: "I experienced a consolation a few days back when preaching to a community in declaring that I was the son of a poor peasant; and in a worthy community, that I once guarded swine. Would you really believe, sir, that I fear entertaining a vain satisfaction in witnessing the pain nature suffers in this?" Admirable remorse for being happy in humiliation and suffering—the delights of the *Love to be unknown and accounted for nothing!*

In 1623, when he still resided in the College Bons-Enfants his humility was put to a test from which it came out gloriously victorious. He was in his room when the porter came to announce to him that there was a young peasant, not over well-dressed and claiming to be his nephew, who wished to speak with him. Fatal fermentation of pride even in the most humble! Vincent, himself, at first turned red and begged one of the priests to go and receive the young man. But he soon blushed for having blushed, and going down himself he went as far as the street where his nephew had remained, embraced him tenderly, took him by the hand and brought him into the college yard. Then he summoned all the priests of his congregation, and presenting them the confused peasant, said: "Gentlemen, this young man is the most creditable of my family." "Nephew," he added turning to the young man, "salute these gentlemen." And during the entire day he presented him in his provincial costume as an important person to all the visitors of rank that came to see him. But remorse for the movement of false shame rankled in his heart. It was a necessity for him to discharge it at the first retreat he made in common with his children. "Gentlemen and my brothers," he said publicly, "pray for a proud individual who wished to receive his nephew secretly in his room, because he was a peasant and poorly clad."

This visit of his nephew recalls an incident of his childhood which he related in his old age to the wife of the President de Lamoignon. One day, when on a pilgrimage, in her company, to St. Fiacre, in the environs of Meaux and about eight leagues from Paris, the conversation turned on the saint they were going to venerate. Said Vincent: "He was a very humble man and I am full of pride and sin. I remember that, whilst at college, I was told one day, that my father, who was a poor countryman, had come to see me; I refused to go to speak to him and in doing so I committed a great sin." "It is the greatest I believe," added the lady in relating it. "that he committed in all his life." Wonderful virtue of this old man who, at that period, was renowned for his reputation for holiness and for his position; it found means to perform a double act of humility at the same time, in confessing a fault of his youth and in recalling his low birth!

Moreover, his humility would never permit him to make any effort to raise any of his relations from their poor and mean condition. "They are happy in their condition as peasants one of the most innocent, and safest for salvation." Such was his invariable answer to all requests. Still less would he consent to introduce any of his nephews into the Church, to give them a share in the riches of the sanctuary. Such sacrilegious intrusion was particularly distasteful to his virtue. "Peasants in preference to beneficiaries," he answered to the solicitations of all, even of the pious and of bishops. In relation to this he wrote to the Abbé St. Martin, one of his oldest friends: "I thank you for the care you take of my little nephew. I must tell you, though, that I never desired that he be a priest and still less did I have the thought of educating him for this object — the priesthood being the most sublime state on earth, and the one our Lord has wished to assume and exercise. As for me, had I known, when I had the temerity of entering it, what it is, as afterwards I knew, I would have much preferred to till the earth than to engage in so formidable a state. I have said the same more than a hundred times to the poor people in the country, when, wishing to encourage them to remain content with their state in life I told them I considered them happy in their condition."

This admirable letter explained the formula adopted by him in his correspondence. Preserving his title of superior for all public acts, his qualification in all else was but *unworthy priest*.

Notwithstanding his long theological studies, his diplomas of Bachelor in Theology and Licentiate in Canon Law, notwithstanding his extensive learning, his penetrating intellect, his infallible good sense, he spoke only of his stupidity, of his ignorance, calling himself but a poor scholar of the fourth form, signifying thereby that he had finished because unable to complete his studies. "You are but an ignorant person," the proud St. Cyran told him one day, "and far from deserving to be at the head of your congregation you merit to be driven from it, and what surprises me is that you are suffered to remain in it." "Ah, sir," answered the humble saint, "I am still more surprised than you, for I am far more ignorant than you can imagine, and, were justice done, I would be immediately sent away from St. Lazarus."

One day, after repeated consolation and counsels to a young student assailed with a temptation to despair, he added: "Should the devil still suggest that evil thought, answer as I have directed, and tell the miserable tempter that it is Vincent, an ignorant man, only of the fourth form, who has told you that."

On another occasion, in reference to a superior whose manner, it was claimed, was not sufficiently urbane for his position, he answered among other things: "And I, how am I made? And how is it I have, up to the present, been suffered in my office. I who am the most rude, the most ridiculous, and the most stupid of all when in the company of persons of rank, where I do not know how to answer six consecutive words without manifesting my want of intelligence and judgment; and what is still worse I have none of the virtues of the person named."

We see he delighted to belittle himself in his virtue as in his birth and natural qualities. Answering Marie Henrietta de Rochechouart, Superioress of one of the houses of the Visitation in Paris, who had recommended herself to his prayers, he said: "I will offer you to God since you request it, but I, more than any person in the world, have need of the aid of good souls, on account of the immense miseries that weigh me down, and which force me to look upon the good opinion others have of me as a punishment for my hypocrisy—a hypocrisy that makes me other than I am."

To a prelate that had called him a perfect Christian, he replied: "Oh, what are you saying? I, a perfect Christian! I should be looked upon as one already damned, as one of the greatest sinners in the world."

To a young missionary, lately received into the community, who accused himself of having so little profited by the good example and the wonders of his life, he said: "Sir, we have among us a practice of never praising any one in his presence. It is true I am a wonder, but a wonder of malice more wicked than the demon who has not so justly deserved hell as I: I say this not through exaggeration but according to my real sentiments."

An author wished to dedicate a book to him. He answered: "What do you tell me, sir! Had you only reflected that I am the son of a poor peasant you would never have given me this cause for confusion nor done such injury to your book as to place on its title page the name of a poor priest whose only claims to publicity are his wretchedness and his sins.

To another author, with similar intent, he said: "You will extremely disoblige me should you really do as you say,

A dedication is made in praise of those to whom it is addressed, and I am altogether unworthy of praise. To speak of me properly you must say that I am the son of a peasant, that I herded swine and cattle in my youth, and to this you must add that that bears no comparison with my ignorance and wickedness. Judge from this, sir, if so pitiable a person as I am should be publicly named in the way you propose. It would be to me the greatest possible annoyance. Yes, sir, I would feel it so much that I know not whether I could ever forget it."

All his letters are full of like professions of humility. "I am confused," he wrote to the Baroness de Renty, "that you should address a poor priest like me, since you are unaware either of my shallowness of mind or my wretchedness."

He wrote to the Superioress of the Visitation in Warsaw: "For more than thirty years I have had the honor of serving your houses in Paris. But, alas! my dear Mother, I am none the better for that, though, at the sight of those incomparably holy souls I should have made great progress in virtue. I humbly beseech you to aid me in asking pardon of God for the bad use I have made of all His graces."

And he wrote again: "The flattering way in which you speak of me afflicts me very much. I see myself far removed from the state in which you suppose me to be. On the contrary, unless God take pity on me, I see myself on the path that leads to the abyss beneath; for I am most useless, most wretched, and I require all the mercy of God, I beg you to ask it for me."

In the assemblies of piety, the meetings of the Ladies of Charity as in the ecclesiastical conferences, humility often enforced silence on him, or made him abandon the idea he had already begun to develop to take up that of others.

A lady, one day, remarked this and mildly reproached him with it. "Why," said she, "do you not maintain your opinion more strongly since it always is the best?" "May God forbid, madam," he rejoined, "that my poor thoughts should prevail over those of others! I am indeed well pleased that God do His work without me—I who am but a wretch."

But it is in the council of conscience, that is to say, at the summit of honor, that his humility sends forth its brightest rays. It was for the humble priest the access to court and rank. It brought homage from the ambitious. It was a certain controlling power over the affairs and the wealth of the Church of France. Judge of his grief at his appointment and of the efforts he made to rid himself of such an honor! He wrote immediately to Rome: "I never more deserved compassion than now, nor had more need of prayers than at present in my new office I hope it will not be for long. Pray to God for me."

This hope sustained him for more than a year. "I pray to God every day" he said to one of his priests, "that I may be considered the simpleton that I am, so that I may not be employed in that kind of commission and may have more opportunity of doing penance for my sins." In truth, he prayed to both God and man. From the day of his appointment he never said Mass without asking the grace to be restored to his former condition. He continually importuned the Queen, the cardinal and all others from whom he could expect this novel kind of protection. Towards the end of 1644, it seemed as if his prayers were heard; on the occasion of a journey he was obliged to make the rumor run that he was in disgrace. An ecclesiastic, informed of the falsehood of the report, came to compliment him. "Oh, my God, would it were true!" he exclaimed, raising his eyes to Heaven and striking his breast, " but so miserable a creature as I am does not deserve such a favor." On the fourth of January, 1645, in similiar strains to Mr. Codving, his superior in Rome: " God be praised for what you say! It is true there was an appearance that I would be no longer tolerated in that office; but my sins have effected otherwise and have caused God not to accept the sacrifices I have offered Him for His purpose. In the name of the Lord I place my trust and I will not be confounded."

He went to court in the same equipage that brought him to his missions in the country and wearing the cassock which may be still seen, a cassock of coarse stuff, threadbare, and patched. He never would change it, not even when he went to the Louvre. If a new one were put in his room he took the old one, and when he could not find that, he looked out for one like it on the back of some one of his priests who was nearly his size and, under one pretext or another privately effected a change. His dress, though poor, was neat and clean. His answer to compliment or banter on the subject was: "Stainless and without rent." He thus replied to Mazarin who, one day, taking hold of his poor cincture showed it to the Queen, saying: "See, Madame, how Mr. Vincent comes dressed to court, and look at his beautiful cincture." This cleanliness he believed conciliated his obligation to propriety with his habit of poverty and simplicity. The brilliancy of the Louvre did not dazzle him and when the mirrors reflected back his image, he cried out: "Oh, the big booby!"—contrasting in his mind, no doubt, the splendor of the royal apartments with the poverty of the cottage of his childhood; then raising his thoughts higher he said to himself: "Oh my God, if by means of this mirror, which is the product of earth, we can see whatever passes in the room, what do not the blessed in Heaven see in that magnificent mirror of Thy Divinity that embraces all and in which are contained all things."

But it was not only in the secrecy of his interior that he delighted to humble himself in expiation for an involuntary grandeur; he, moreover, abased himself in the presence of all in atonement for distinctions that were to him a martyrdom. The Minister of State, Le Pelletier, deposed in the process of his canonization: "I was yet young when I first saw the servant of God at the Louvre, and I saw him there many a time after. His modesty and prudence were full of dignity. Courtiers, prelates, ecclesiastics and others rendered him, out of pure esteem, great honor; he received it all with great humility. On leaving the council, where he had decided upon what was greatest in the kingdom, he was as kind and as easy of access as he was when among the slaves of Tunis, or on the bench of the galleys. A virtuous bishop who had not seen him since his entrance to court, and having found him equally humble and affable, and equally disposed to do a favor as before, could not refrain from saying to him: "Mr. Vincent is always Mr. Vincent."

In the beginning, when first summoned to court, the Prince of Conde desired him, one day, to take a seat beside him. "What! my Lord," answered the humble priest, drawing back, "it is already too much honor that your highness suffers me in your presence. But make me sit beside you! Are you, then, unaware that I am but the son of a poor villager?" This was his defence, his watchword, against all attacks on his humility. "Manners and life ennoble a man," answered the prince. "Moreover, Mr. Vincent, it is not to-day that we learn your merit." And, the better to judge, he brought about the conversation to some point of controversy. Vincent handled it with so much precision and clearness that the prince cried out: "Ah, Mr. Vincent, Mr. Vincent, what do you say, you preach everywhere that you are ignorant, and look, you have resolved, in two words, one of the greatest difficulties proposed by the sects." Then the Prince went into some question of Canon Law, and, more and more charmed with the answers of the *scholar of the fourth form*, he rose from his seat without a word, and, hastening to the Queen, congratulated her on her choice of a man so well versed in what pertained to ecclesiastical matters.

More than once he was the butt for bitter jests and the blackest of calumnies. Persons endeavored to ruin him with the Queen, with the Minister of State and with people of merit. To him all this was a happiness and a recompense for zeal. A young noble, whom Vincent, doubtless, had frustrated in his culpable hopes, said to him once: "You are an old fool." "You are right, my son," answered the holy man, at the same time falling on his knees, "and I ask pardon for whatever may have given you cause to speak so." "Are you aware, Mr. Vincent, of what is said of you," the Queen laughingly said to him one day. "Madam, I am a great sinner." "But you should justify yourself." "Far worse things have been said of our Lord, and He never justified Himself."

He never justified himself. An unworthy ecclesiastic whom Vincent had debarred from a benefice, attempted revenge in spreading dishonorable reports about him. "If Mr. Vincent," he represented among people of quality, "did not favor me, it was simply because I was unwilling to purchase. But that man, so hostile to simony in others, is quite reconciled to it in himself; and I know one to whom he gave a benefice for a library and a good round sum of money." This time the saint was moved, and in the first moment of excitement he seized the pen to write a letter of justification. But he had barely traced the first words when he exclaimed: "Oh wretch! of what are you thinking? What! you want to justify yourself! And the news has but just come that a Christian, in Tunis, falsely accused suffered tortures for three days, and, finally, though innocent of the accusation, died without a word of complaint! And you, you wish to excuse yourself! No, indeed; it will not be so." And he tore the letter which he had already begun. Some days after, the calumniator died miserably, and all saw in it the vengeance of Heaven.

Once, noticing that a certain lord, who had previously been his friend, no longer manifested for him anything but aversion he went to him, and said with a serene countenance: "Sir, I am so wretched as to have given you displeasure without in the least intending it, and, not knowing in what way, I come to humbly beg you to tell me, that I may repair my fault." In the presence of such candor and humility the nobleman could not dare to complain, and friendship was re-established. In like manner did he act in regard to a religious who retained ill-feeling towards him. He was vesting, at the college *Bons Enfants*, and ready to say mass, when the words of the Gospel came to his mind: "*If thou offerest thy gift at the altar and there shalt remember that thy brother hath anything against thee; leave then thy gift before the altar and first go to be reconciled to thy brother.*" (Mat. v., 23.) Suddenly he lays aside the vestments, betakes himself to the religious, is profuse in excuses and protestations of esteem for him, and his order, and then returns to the altar to offer up the sacrifice of reconciliation and of love.

If he did not succeed the first time, his inventive charity invariably finished in discovering some means for disarming ill-will. Having cast himself at the feet of a superior of a religious community, to ask pardon for some imaginary offence, he found himself spurned with scorn and contempt, and he withdrew elated with joy in having been ill-treated for justice' sake. Some days after, some ornaments being wanting at St. Lazarus, he sent to borrow from this self same superior just as if he had been his best friend. The superior, confounded and touched by such a request, cried out: "This is, indeed, the mark whereby I recognize the man of God." The ornaments were sent, he follows, and soon he and the holy priest are at the feet and in the arms of one another.

He sometimes disconcerted those who insulted him and put them to flight by an unexpected act of humility. Publicly abused, one day, at the very gate of St. Lazarus by a noble whose son he had refused to recommend, he threw himself at his feet and said: "You are right, sir, I am but a wretch and a sinner." The noble immediately escaped into his carriage. But he could not so easily evade the humble priest; Vincent immediately arose, ran after him, and did not leave before making a profound reverence.

We see that his humility did not manifest itself merely in vain words that often signify nothing, but that it produced acts of the most profound humiliation. How often did he not fall on his knees before his priests to publicly avow what he termed the crimes of his past life! How often, again, did he not accuse himself of some supposed dereliction of duty and even of secret movements which he had so effectually curbed that nothing appeared exteriorly! How often, finally, did he take upon himself all the blame for the faults committed in the congregation, always believing himself to be their first cause, and looked upon the death of his missionaries and all loss of goods suffered by the institution as a punishment for his sins! Every year, on the anniversary of his baptism, he knelt before his community and asked pardon of God, and of men, for all the sins he had committed and for all the scandals he had given during the many years that Divine Goodness had suffered him upon the earth, and he recommended himself to the prayers of all to obtain his conversion and mercy from God.

He abased himself in this manner before the least of his brothers. When he thought he had offended any one of them he sought him everywhere, in the garden, in the kitchen and even in the cellar, threw himself at his feet, kissed them, and asked pardon. In 1649, being taken sick at Richelieu, they sent to him from Paris the infirmarian of St. Lazarus, who, better than any other, knew his constitution, and how he should be treated. Vincent, without doubt, received him with his usual kindness; yet he thought proper to say to him in a sad tone of voice: "My old carcass was not worth so long a journey." Instantly fearing lest the brother infirmarian saw in this only a reproach and not a protestation of humility, he cast himself at his feet and asked his pardon. But this was not enough for this man of insatiable humility, trembling before the shadow of wounded charity. On his return to St. Lazarus, he seized, or brought about an opportunity to make more ample and honorable amends; and, one day, the brother infirmarian and his assistant being together in his room, he said to the latter: "Would you believe, sir, that when this good man went to Richelieu for my sake, I did not give him my heart as I was accustomed? And for this, in your presence, I very humbly ask his pardon, and I beg you to pray to God for me that I may not again fall into a like fault."

All superiority and all distinction should necessarily wound a humility so profound. Hence, as we see in his *Life*, the efforts he made in 1642 to lay aside the office of superior. Forced to retain it, he, at least, refused all its advantages and honors. He complained of the marks of honor with which respect for his virtue inspired his children; and when they objected to him that such was the custom in all communities, he answered: "I know that very well, and we must respect their reasons for so doing; but I have still greater reason for not suffering it in my regard — I, who ought not to be compared to the most unworthy of men, since I am worse than all others."

He would not allow the place which he occupied in the church to be covered with a mat, much less would he allow the chair to be elevated. "That is," he said, "the privilege of bishops and not of a miserable priest as I am."

Under the influence of the same spirit of humility he always selected for himself the poorest vestments for mass. In 1638, on the birth of the king, Ann of Austria sent to St. Lazarus a magnificent vestment of silver cloth. It was near the feast of Christmas, and all were glad to think that Vincent, who was to officiate on that solemnity, would be the first to wear it. But ornaments so rich frightened him and it was absolutely necessary to bring him others more common.

Whilst he delighted in abasing himself in performing the most humble service for others, even washing the dishes, and cleaning the shoes of an ordinand, he refused for himself all that his position, his age and his infirmities demanded. He dressed his ulcerated limbs himself, and the carriage of which he was obliged to make use he called his ignominy.

His love for humility in himself he extended to his congregation, always terming it little, the very little, and the sorry congregation. He wished it to be considered as the least of all, as holding, in every instance, the last rank among the clergy, whether regular or secular. He limited its ministry to the poor country people. Once, in a letter to St. Jane Frances Chantal, something that might redound to the honor of his congregation slipped from his pen. He felt remorse and wrote to her: "I have told you many things to the advantage of this little congregation. Truly, my dear mother, that makes me fear. Hence, I beg you, lessen a great deal what I have said, and mention it to no one. Alas! my worthy mother, did you but know our ignorance and the little virtue we possess you would greatly pity us. . . . . With tears in my eyes I say this, feeling but too well the truth of what I say, and the abominations of my poor soul. I beseech you, then, my dear mother, to offer to God my shame and the confession I make of it to you in the presence of the Divine Majesty." And this is why, too, when any one asked admission into his congregation, he said: "What! sir, you wish to be a missionary? And how came you to cast your eyes on our little congregation? For we are only poor people." One of the greatest astonishments of his life was when the Abbe of Tournus, Louis de Rochechourt de Chandenier, wished to clothe himself with the name and the rags of the poor mission in presenting himself before God. And when, in his presence, any one persisted in praising his congregation, he would say: "It is your kindness towards us that induces you to think in that way; but it is, nevertheless, true that all other communities are holy, whilst we are miserable, and worse than miserable." Also, when he learned that the labors of the congregation were ignored, or calumniated, he rejoiced and refused all defence. He said: "I will never justify myself, save by my works. Moreover, it is a blessing to be treated as our Lord was."

It is useless to add, when speaking of St. Vicent de Paul, that his humility in no way impaired his constancy or generosity. St. Thomas has well said that humility, far from destroying greatness of soul, on the contrary, strengthens it, by giving it a solid foundation in God, whilst, at the same time, it regulates and orders it in preventing it from losing itself amid the violence of vanity and human activity. When there was question of sustaining the interests of God or of the Church, no one was more active and firm than Vincent. He showed, from the example of St. Louis, at once so humble and so magnanimous, how easily humility accords with generosity and true greatness of soul. He proved it by his own example. None made himself so little, none did greater things.

II.

It was of humility, his favorite virtue, that the Saint spoke lovingly and grandly. And hence, we find in no spiritual writer anything comparable to his conferences on humility. To show its excellence and necessity, he first, according to his constant custom, brought forward the lessons and example of our Lord: "If I called upon any of you to speak, no matter whom, he could advance a number of authorities, and reasons touching on this subject; but to honor the words and sentiments of our Lord we will only say that He Himself recommended it to us: '*Learn of Me because I am humble of heart.*' (Mat. xi., 29.) If it were an apostle, if it were St. Peter or St. Paul who gave us that lesson, if it were the prophets or some saint, we might say they were, like ourselves, only disciples. If it were philosophers, alas! they know not this virtue! And Aristotle himself, he who has spoken so nobly of all the other moral virtues, does not even mention humility.

"Therefore, only Jesus Christ could say: 'Learn of Me.' Oh, what words! Learn of me, and not of another, not of a man, but of a God! Learn of Me! What, then, Oh Lord, is this thing so dear in Thy eyes? 'Because I am humble.' Oh, my Savior, what a word! *I am humble.* 'Yes I am so, not simply externally, or from ostentation, or through vanity, but humble of heart; not with a slight and passing humility, but with a heart truly humbled in the presence of My Eternal Father, with a heart always humbled before men and for men, sinners, loving lowly and abject things and embracing them always with joy and love. *Learn of Me.*' This is so contrary to the spirit and maxims of the world, so removed from the inclinations of men, and from the heart of each one, that did not a God say it and exemplify it in His own person, none would be willing to listen to it; for all so love what is in them and what they produce externally that there is not one who, naturally, does not wish to be in good repute, and who does not make every effort to obtain esteem and praise.

"And yet, all love humility above all other virtues, at least in theory, and this is a fruit of the grace of baptism and of the spirit of our Lord. All love it and none possess it, for we have an astonishing bent for pride. Oh, my Savior! how differently do Thy actions teach! What is the life of this Divine Savior, if not a continual humiliation, both active and passive? He so loved it that He did not leave it for an instant while on earth; and even after his death, He has wished that His Church would represent to us His Divine person in the figure of the crucifix, that He might appear to us in a state of ignominy, as having suffered for us the death of a criminal, and a death the most shameful and most infamous that could be imagined. And why this? Because he knew the excellence of humiliation and the malice of the opposite sin, which not only aggravates other sins, but even vitiates works that, of themselves, are not evil, and which may taint and corrupt those that are good, yes, even the most holy. Because He knew the height, the depth, the length and the breadth of humility, and saw the relations it bears to the perfections of God, His father, in dealing with sinful man.

"All His life, then, was but a continued series of humiliations. That wonderful body, formed by the Holy Ghost, to remain for so long enclosed in the womb of a Virgin! To wish to have it said that he was refused a lodging and that, thus, He was reduced to take shelter in a stable! Having received the homages of Heaven and of earth to immediately thereafter fall into contempt, being obliged as an infant, to miserably fly into Egypt! What do I say? As an infant! Ah, as an impotent and feeble God! His life was one continual affection for contempt. His soul was so filled with it that had any one dissected His heart he would have found engraved on that adorable heart, humility, above every other virtue.

"Humility, therefore, is the virtue of Jesus Christ; it is the virtue of His Blessed Mother; the virtue of the greatest saints; it is the virtue of missionaries. But what do I say? I mistake, I would that we possessed it, and when I said that it was the virtue of missionaries, I meant that it is the virtue of which they have the greatest need, and which they should most ardently desire. For, this sorry little congregation, which is the least of all, should have no other foundation than humility, which should be its own peculiar virtue; otherwise, we will never do anything effective, either within or without; and without humility we can never expect either progress in ourselves or profit for our neighbor. Oh, my Savior, give us, then, this holy virtue which is so suited to us, which Thou hast made known to the world, and which Thou hast cherished with so much affection! And you, gentlemen, know that he, who wishes to be a true missionary, should labor without ceasing to acquire this virtue and become perfect in it, and should especially guard against all thoughts of pride, of ambition and vanity as against the greatest enemies he can have; as soon as they appear he should attack and exterminate them, being most vigilant to give them no entrance. Yes, I say it anew, if we be true missionaries, each one of us, in his own particular case, will be glad to be considered as of poor and mean intellect, as a person of no virtue, will be content to be treated as ignorant, to be insulted and contemned, to have his defects cast in his face, and to be proclaimed as insupportable by reason of his wretchedness and imperfection. I go further and affirm that we should rejoice when it is said that our congregation, in general, is useless in the Church, is composed of poor, simple persons, that it succeeds but poorly in all that it undertakes, that its labors in the country bear no fruit, that the missionaries are devoid of the grace of God and that the ordinations are conducted without order. Yes, if we possess the spirit of Jesus Christ we should be satisfied to be reputed such as I have mentioned. 'But, sir,' some one will object, 'what do you say? *This word is hard.*' It is true, I acknowledge, that that is hard to nature and that it is very difficult to persuade nature that it has done badly and still harder for it to suffer that such be believed and made a reproach. But also it is very easily understood by a soul that is truly humble and knows itself as it really is; and so far is it from being saddened, that, on the contrary, it rejoices and it is well content that God be exalted and glorified by its humiliation and its insignificance. I know very well that our Lord has given to many in the congregation the grace to hasten on in the practice of this virtue, has given them the grace to animate their actions with the desire of their own abasement, and a love to be unknown and despised. But we must ask God to grant the same grace to all the others, so that our only ambition will be to abase ourselves, to annihilate ourselves for the love and glory of God and that the special, distinctive virtue of the Mission be humility. That you may the more cherish it, take note of what I am about to say, namely, that if you ever heard any strangers relate any good done by the Congregation, you will find that they do so because they discovered in it some little image of humility, and because they witnessed it practice lowly and humble actions, such as instructing the simple peasants and serving the poor. So, too, when you see the ordinands come out of the retreat edified with the house, you will recognize, should you examine, that it is because they noticed a simple and humble manner of acting which for them is a novelty, and for every one a charm and a pleasure."

It was, then, not simply individual humility that Vincent recommended; it was, moreover, and with reason, humility as a body. He said: "Our Lord was humble not only in Himself, but He was also humble in His little congregation. He formed it out of a few poor rustics without knowledge or manners, who even did not agree among themselves, who, in a word, all abandoned Him, and who, after His death, were treated as Himself, hunted, despised, condemned, and put to death. Is it not a strange thing to see how readily it is understood that Peter, James and John, particular members of a congregation, should fly honor, and love contempt, whilst at the same time the congregation, they maintain, the community must acquire and preserve esteem and honor in the world? For I ask you, how is it possible that Peter, James and John can truly love and seek after contempt, and yet that the congregation composed only of Peter, James and John, and other particular members, should love and strive after honor? It must certainly be admitted and acknowledged that these two things are incompatible. And hence it is that all the missionaries should be content not only when they find themselves in their own persons, contemned and humbled, but also when they see their congregation despised, for that will be a sign that they are truly humble. The Apostles agreed upon a symbol whereby they might know each other, and by which they might distinguish who were Christians; so that when they were asked: 'Who are you?' 'I believe in God, I believe in Jesus Christ!' was their answer. So with us, let humility be the distinctive mark of the congregation, and let it be known by that virtue rather than by its name, so that, should we be asked what is our state, we may say: 'Humility,' if we be summoned with: 'Who goes there,' let humility be our watch-word."

Influenced by these sentiments he ordained that the missionaries, when assisting at any public exercise at the universities or in colleges, should take the lowest, as their proper place, and be very careful to make no show of learning. One of the most distinguished of his first missionaries, James de La Fosse, failed in this order, one day, and thereby drew upon himself compliment upon compliment. But there was one who had no idea of felicitating him; it was Vincent, who soon heard of this incident: "Knowing, sir," he said to him, "that a truly humble man and a poor missionary never seeks either the first places in assemblies, or to have himself spoken of, I require you, therefore, to go and ask pardon of those whom you have disedified."

In what does humility consist? First, in the contempt of one's self. "In truth, if each one of us would study to know himself he would find that it is very just and very reasonable to despise himself. For, if we, on the one hand, seriously consider the corruption of our nature, the levity of our mind, the darkness of our understanding, the disorder of our will and the impurity of our affections; and if, on the other, we weigh well in the scales of the sanctuary our works and our productions we will find all worthy only of contempt. 'But what!' you may say to me, 'do you include the sermons we preach, the confessions we hear, the care and trouble we take with our neighbor for the glory of God? Yes, gentlemen, if our best actions be reviewed, it will be discovered that in most of them we have failed in the manner of doing them, and often, in the end proposed, and that in whatever way we look at them, we will find as much of evil as of good. For, tell me, I pray you, what can be expected from the weakness of man? Who is it that produces nothingness and who is it that produces sin? And what else have we within us but nothingness and sin? Let us, then, look upon it as certain, that, in all things and everywhere, we deserve to be rejected, and are very despicable by reason of the opposition we have in ourselves, to the sanctity and other perfections of God, to the life of Jesus Christ and to the operations of His grace. If, then, we study to know ourselves thoroughly, we will find in all we think, in all we say, in all we do, regarding either the substance or the circumstances, that we are fully and completely surrounded with cause for shame and confusion; and if we be unwilling to flatter ourselves, we will perceive that we are not only worse than other men, but even, in a certain fashion, more wicked than the demons in hell. For, if these unfortunate spirits had had, at their disposition, the graces and means that have been given us to become better they would have made a thousand times better use of them.

"And more; we ought to be pleased when others know our faults and despise us. We ought to receive with satisfaction the contempt that our state of life, our person, our manner of acting or our mode of speech may bring upon us. Our Lord could have avoided the insults, the jeers, and the reproaches he received from the Jews, and yet He did not. Let us beget within us an affection for humiliation, and thus God will give us humility, He will preserve it in us, and He will increase it by the acts He will inspire in us to perform; for one act of virtue well done disposes for another, and the first degree of humility is the stepping stone to the second, the second to the third, and so of the others. Remember, gentlemen and my brothers, that Jesus Christ, speaking of the publican who humbled himself, said that his prayer was heard. If, then, He rendered this testimony to a man, who, all his life, had been wicked, for what should we not hope provided we be truly humble? But, on the countrary, what happened to the Pharisee? He was a man separated from the rest of the people by his state of life, which, among the Jews, seems to have been a kind of religious order, in which he prayed, fasted and did many other good works, and yet, notwithstanding, he is rejected by God; and why? Because he regarded his good works with complacency, and took pride in them just as if he had performed them by his own virtue. See, then, a just man and a sinner before the throne of God. And because the just is without humility, he is rejected, and with all his good works condemned, and that which, in him, appeared virtuous was really vice; on the other hand, see the sinner who, recognizing his wickedness and touched with a true sentiment of humility, remains at the door of the temple, strikes his breast and dares not raise his eyes to heaven; and by this humble disposition of his heart, although he was guilty of many sins going to the temple, yet he left it justified, and one single humiliation was the means of his salvation. From this we may perceive that humility, when true and real, introduces all the other virtues into the soul, and that by sincerely and profoundly humbling ourselves, from sinners, that we were, we become just. Yes, were we even the most wicked, did we but have recourse to humility it would make us just; on the contrary, were we like unto angels and did we excel in the greatest virtues, yet, were we devoid of humility, these virtues, having no foundation, could not subsist, and they, being thus destroyed from want of humility, we become like the damned who have no virtue. Understand well, then, this truth, gentlemen, and let each one engrave it on his heart, and say within himself: 'Though I had all virtue, if yet, I have not humility I only deceive myself, and, thinking myself virtuous, I am but a proud Pharisee, and an abominable missionary.' Oh, my Savior, Jesus Christ, shed upon our minds those lights that filled Thy holy soul and made Thee prefer contumely to praise! Inflame our hearts with those holy affections that burned and consumed Thine, and which caused Thee in Thy own confusion to seek the glory of Thy heavenly Father. Grant, by Thy grace, that we begin from the present moment to reject all that does not tend to Thy glory and our shame, all that savors of vanity, of ostentation and self esteem! Grant that we renounce, once for all, the applause of men, who are deceived and, in their turn are deceivers, and all vain imaginations of the good success of our works! In a word, Oh, my Savior, by Thy grace and Thy example, grant that we may learn to be truly humble of heart."

Such is an abridgement of the great conference of the 18th of April, 1659. But he continually returns to this dear humility. One morning, during a repetition of prayer, one of the community having humbled himself for his poor thoughts, the Saint said: "It is a good practice to enter into details in humiliating things when prudence allows them to be publicly declared, on account of the profit we derive from overcoming ourselves in the repugnance we feel in disclosing and making known what we would keep secret. St. Augustine published the secret sins of his youth, composing a book on them, that thus the entire earth might learn the extravagance of his errors and the excess of his licentiousness. And that vessel of election, St. Paul, that great apostle who was ravished to the third heaven, has he not avowed that he persecuted the Church? He has even left it in writing, so that it may be known to the consummation of ages that he was a persecutor. Indeed, if we be not watchful over ourselves and do not do some violence to ourselves in declaring our misery and our failings, we will soon confine ourselves to what may occasion esteem, and we will conceal what will give confusion. We inherit this from our first father, Adam, who, after having offended God, went and hid himself.

"I have made different visits to some houses of religious women and have often asked of them what virtue they esteemed and loved the most; I asked it even of those who, I knew, had the greatest repugnance for humiliation. Yet out of twenty I found scarcely one who did not tell me it was humility, so true is it that every body finds this virtue beautiful and amiable. Whence is it, then, that so few embrace it and that still fewer possess it? It is because they content themselves with admiring it and take no pains to acquire it. In theory it is charming, but in practice its visage is disagreeable to nature; its acts offend, because it would have us always select the lowest place, put ourselves beneath others and even beneath the least, would have us bear with calumny, seek contempt, and love abasement, for all which things we naturally have an aversion. Hence it is necessary to overcome this repugnance and to make some effort to actually exercise ourselves in this virtue, for, otherwise, we will never acquire it. I know well that, through the mercy of God, there are those who practice this divine virtue, and who, not only have no good opinion of themselves nor of their talents, nor of their learning, nor of their virtue, but even, regard themselves as very miserable and wish to be considered as such, and esteem themselves beneath all creatures. And I must confess, I never behold these persons but they cause confusion in my soul, for they secretly upbraid the pride that is within me, wretched as I am. But they themselves are always content, and their joy is reflected in their countenance, for the Holy Ghost, who resides in them, so fills them with peace that nothing has the power to disturb them. When contradicted, they humbly acquiesce, when calumniated they bear with it, when forgotten they think it but just, when overburdened with occupation they willingly do their best, and how difficult soever the thing commanded be, they devote themselves to it with a good heart trusting in the power of holy obedience. The temptations that assail them only serve to strengthen them the more in humility, and to make them have recourse to God; and thus they easily obtain the victory over the evil one. And so the only enemy they have to combat is pride which, never in this life, declares a truce, but attacks even the greatest saints on earth, some in one way and some in another. Some it surprises with vain complacency in the good they have done, whilst it inflates others with the knowledge they have acquired. The latter are tempted to consider themselves the most learned, the former to believe themselves the most virtuous and most constant. Hence, we have great need to pray to God that He may be pleased to secure and preserve us from this pernicious vice which is all the more to be feared since we have for it a natural leaning. We should, moreover, be vigilant over ourselves and do just the contrary of what corrupt nature wishes. If it desire to elevate us we must abase ourselves; if it excite esteem for ourselves let us think of our weakness; if it make us desirous of appearing, we must hide all that may attract notice and must prefer humble and lowly actions to those that are important and honorable. In fine, we must frequently recur to the love of our own abjection, an assured refuge against all like agitations which this unfortunate tendency to pride constantly excites within us. Let us pray our Lord, by the merits of the adorable humiliations of His life and death, to be pleased to draw us after Him. Let us, each one for himself, and mutually for each other, offer to Him all the humiliations we may suffer, and let our practice of humility be solely for the honor of God and for our own confusion."

Another day, in speaking of a conference at St. Lazarus, he said again: "These gentlemen, the ecclesiastics who meet here, took for the subject of their conference, Tuesday last, what virtues each had remarked in the late Mr. Olier who had been a member of their association. Among other things that were said the most important was that this great servant of God aimed, ordinarily, to belittle himself in his words, and that, among all virtues, he particularly endeavored to practice humility. As they were speaking, I regarded those holy persons' portraits that are hung up in the hall, and said to myself: 'Oh, Lord, my God, if we could penetrate the Christian truths as those persons have done, and conform our lives to this knowledge. Oh! how differently we would act.' For example, having rested my eye on the portrait of the blessed bishop of Geneva, I thought that were we to look upon the things of this world in the same light that he regarded them, were we to speak of them as he did, and were our ears, like his, open only to eternal truths, we would be careful not to allow vanity to occupy our minds or our hearts.

"But above all, gentlemen, if we attentively consider this beautiful portrait which we have before our eyes, this admirable original of humility, our Lord Jesus Christ, can it be possible that we will give to our minds admittance of any good opinions of ourselves, seeing how far we are from His marvellous self abasement? Seeing Him reputed as a murderer, will we be so rash as to prefer ourselves to others? Will we have any fear of being esteemed miserable when we see the innocent treated as a malefactor, and dying between two thieves, as the most guilty? Let us pray God, gentlemen, to preserve us from this blindness, let us ask the grace of always tending to lowliness, let us confess in His presence, and before men, that of ourselves we are but sin, but ignorance and malice; let us wish that it be so believed, that others say such of us and on that account despise us; in fine, let us lose no opportunity of subduing ourselves by the practice of this virtue. But it is not enough to have an affection for it, and to resolve to practice, as so many do; we must do violence to ourselves and actually come to the exercise of its acts, and of these there never can be too many."

Following the counsel of the apostle he insisted *in season and out of season* on the humility proper to his congregation: "God has not sent us to assume honorable charges and employments, nor to act and speak with pomp and authority; but He sent us to evangelize and serve the poor and to perform the other functions of our institute in an humble, sweet, and familar manner. Hence, we may apply to ourselves what St. John Chrysostom said in one of his homilies, that as long as we remain sheep out of a veritable and sincere humility, we not only will not be devoured by the wolves but will even change the wolves into sheep; whereas, the instant we depart from this humility and simplicity, the spirit of our institution, we will lose the grace which is attached to it, and we will find none other in the most brilliant actions. And, indeed, is it not just that a missionary, who has made himself worthy, in his little profession, of the blessing of Heaven and the approbation of men, should lose both one and the other when he applies himself to works which, by the renown that is sought in them, savor of the spirit of the world, and are opposed to the spirit of his state? Is there not reason to fear that he will vanish in open day and fall into disorder, as is said of the servant, who, becoming master, became, at the same time, haughty and insufferable? The late Cardinal Berulle, that great servant of God, was accustomed to say that it was good to keep one's self lowly, that the more humble conditions in life were the safer, and that there was a certain indefinable danger in high and elevated positions, that that was the reason the saints have always tried to fly dignities, and that our Lord, to convince us by His example as well as by His word, had said, in speaking of Himself, that He was come into the world to minister and not to be ministered unto."

The humble founder would not suffer strangers, much less members of the congregation, to sound its praises. A person lately admitted and still ignorant of the spirit and usages of the community having called it the holy congregation, Vincent abruptly said: "Sir, when we speak of the congregation we should never make use of this term or of any other term equivalent or elevating, but we should employ the following: the poor congregation, the little congregation, and such like. In this we will imitate the Son of God, Who called the congregation of His apostles and disciples, little flock, little congregation.

Oh! how I wish that God would be pleased to give the poor little congregation the grace to establish itself strongly in humility, to make this virtue the foundation whereon it may build, and that it may remain fixed in it as in a frame. Gentlemen, we must not deceive ourselves; if we have not humility we have nothing. I speak not merely of exterior humility. I speak principally of that of the heart, and of that humility that makes us really believe there is not a single person on the earth more pitiable than you and I: that the Congregation of the Mission is the meanest of all congregations, and the poorest, both in number and quality of subjects: and a humility that gives us pleasure to know that the world so thinks of us. 'Alas! what is it to wish to be esteemed unless to wish to be treated otherwise than was the Son of God? It is an insupportable pride. When the Son of God was on the earth what did they say of Him? And for what was He pleased to pass in the minds of the people? For a fool, for a seditious person, as stupid, as a sinner, though he was none of these; He even wished to be passed over and to have a Barabbas preferred — a brigand, a murderer, a wicked person! Oh, my Savior, my Savior! how Thy holy humility will, on the Day of Judgment, confound all sinners, such as I, miserable. Let us be vigilant in regard to this; and you, who go on missions, you, who speak in public, take care. Sometimes, and often enough, the people are touched with what has been said to them, they are seen to weep; and even there are some among them who, in their excitement, cry out: 'Blessed is the womb that bore thee and the paps that gave thee suck!' We have, sometimes, heard similar exclamations. Nature hearing this is satisfied, vanity is engendered and nourished, unless these vain complacencies be suppressed, and unless we seek purely the glory of God, for which alone we should labor. Yes, we should labor solely for the glory of God and the salvation of souls. To do otherwise would be to preach ourself and not Jesus Christ. And he, who preaches for applause, for praise, for esteem, to have his name on everybody's tongue, what does he do, what does such a preacher do? What is it that he does? He commits a sacrilege; yes, a sacrilege! What! make the word of God and divine things the means to acquire reputation! Yes, it is a sacrilege! Oh, my God, my God, give this poor little congregation the grace that no one of its members fall into this misfortune! Believe me, gentlemen, until we have a profound humility and an entire contempt for ourselves we will never be fit to do the work of God. No, if the Congregation of the Mission be not humble, and if it be not pursuaded that it can do nothing good, that it is more suited to spoil everything than to succeed in any good work, it never will do much; but when it will possess and live in the spirit I have mentioned, then, gentlemen, it will be ready for the designs of God because such are the subjects God makes use of to effect great and lasting things.

"Some theologians, explaining the Gospel of the day, in which mention is made of the five wise virgins, and of the five foolish ones, think that this parable should be interpreted of persons in community who have retired from the world. If, then, it be true that the half of these virgins, of these persons are lost, ah! what should we not fear? And what should not I, first of all, dread? But now, gentlemen, let us take courage and not lose heart, let us give ourselves properly to God, let us renounce ourselves and our satisfactions, our ease and our vanity; let us look upon ourselves as our greatest enemies; let us do all the good we can and let us do it with all the requisite perfection. It is not enough to assist our neighbor, to fast, to meditate, to labor on the missions. All this is good in its way, but it is not enough; we must, moreover, do all this well, namely, in the spirit of our Lord, after the manner of our Lord, humbly and with an upright intention, that the name of His Father be glorified and His will accomplished.

"The fruit that plants bear is not of a nature more excellent than that of the stalk. We are the stalks of those who will come after us, who, very likely will not carry their works to a higher degree of excellency than we do ours. If we have done well, the example will go from one to another. Those who remain teach those who follow the manner the first practiced virtue, and these, in their turn, teach others who come after; and this results from the grace of God which the first merited. How is it that we see in the world certain families who, for generations, live so well in the fear of God? I have just now in my mind one, among others, of which I knew the grandfather and the father, who both were very good men, and I know to-day the children, who are likewise good. Whence does this come? It is because their parents, by their good and holy lives, have merited this grace from God. For God, according to His promise will bless such families even to the thousandth generation. But again we see husbands and wives who are good and live virtuously, and yet everything melts away and goes to ruin in their hands, nothing succeeds with them. And whence comes this? It is because the punishment of God, which their parents merited by their grievous faults, passes to their descendants, according to what is written, that God will chastise the sinful father in his children to the fourth generation. Although this is understood principally in regard to temporal goods, yet we may, in some manner, take it in relation to spiritual things. Consequently, if we faithfully observe our rules, if we practice well all the virtues proper for a true missionary, we will merit, in some sort, the same grace from God for our children, that is, for those that will come after us, who, likewise, will do well. If we do badly, it is to be feared that they will do the same, and even worse, for nature always carries us along with itself and ever tends to disorder. We can consider ourselves as the fathers of those who will come after us. The Congregation is still in its cradle, it has just been born, it is only a few years since it began to exist, and is not this to be in the cradle? Those, who, two or three hundred years from now come after us, will look upon us as their fathers and even those who have only just now come, will be considered as among the first, for all those of the first hundred years will be regarded as the first fathers. When you wish to give more weight to a passage that is found in some one of the fathers of the first ages, you say: 'This passage is taken from such a father, who lived in the first or second century.' In the same way it will be said: 'In the time of the first priests of the Congregation of the Mission such was done, they lived in such a manner, such and such virtues flourished among them.' This being so, gentlemen, what example should we not leave to our successors, since the good they will do depends, in some manner, on that which we perform? Some of the fathers of the

Church maintain that God shows damned parents the evil their children do on earth in order to augment their torments; and that the more these children multiply their sins so much the more do the parents, who are the cause by the evil example they left them, suffer the vengeance of Heaven. On the other hand, St. Augustin says that God makes known to the fathers and to the mothers who are in heaven the good that their children do on earth, that their joy may be increased. Then, gentlemen, what consolation and what joy will we not receive when God will deign to show us that the Congregation is doing well, abounding in good works, observing faithfully the order of time and employments left it, living in the practice of the virtues and good examples which we will have willed to it! Oh, wretched man that I am, who says and does not! Pray to God for me, gentlemen; pray to God for me, my brothers, that He may convert me! But now, let us all give ourselves to God, but in earnest, let us labor, let us assist and aid the poor country people who are awaiting us."

One of his priests, who was stationed in Artois, having published, without previously obtaining permission, a short notice of the Congregation, its progress and its works, sent a a copy to Vincent thinking that he would, in return, receive some mark of gratitude.

The humble founder, on the 7th of February, 1657, wrote to him: "The pain this has occasioned me is so sensible that I am unab'e to express it. To publish what we are, and what we do is very much opposed to humility . . . . If there be any good in us or in our method of life, it is from God, whose also it is to manifest it, should He judge it expedient. But for us who are poor, ignorant and sinful men, we ought to hide ourselves as being unfit for any good and unworthy the consideration of any one. Hence it is that, thus far, God has given me the grace, to refuse to allow to be printed anything that could make the Congregation known and honored, though I have been warmly urged, particularly in regard to correspondence from Madagascar, from Barbary and the Hebrides. Still less would I have permitted the publication of what relates to the essence and spirit, the birth and growth, the functions and the end of our Institute. And would to God, sir, it were yet to be done! But since there is no longer a remedy, I will say no more. Only, I beg you, do nothing that concerns the Congregation before informing me."

When it was impossible to conceal from himself and others the virtue and the success of the Congregation, he wished, at least, to protect humility and even that it should receive its share of the profit, and would say: "We ought never turn or fix our eyes on what is good in us, but rather strive to know what is bad and defective; this a great means to preserve humility. we ought not to dwell on the gift of converting souls nor on whatever other exterior talents we may have, for they are not ours, we are only the bearers of them, and even with those gifts we can lose our souls. For this reason no one should flatter himself, nor take any complacency in himself, nor conceive any self-esteem because God works grand things by his instrumentality; he should rather humble himself and acknowledge that he is but a wretched instrument which God deigns to make use of just as He did of the rod of Moses, which, though working wonders, was none the less a piece of fragile wood.

"I pray you to adopt these sentiments and to seek in your labors nothing but humiliation and ignominy, and, if it please God, death at the end. Ought not a priest, who aims to acquire a reputation in the service of God, die of shame? Ought he not to be overwhelmed with confusion in dying in his bed, he who has seen Jesus Christ receive opprobrium and a gibbet as the recompense of His labor? Recall to mind that we live in Jesus Christ to die the death of Jesus Christ, and that we ought to die in Jesus Christ to live the life of Jesus Christ; that our life should be hidden in Jesus and full of Jesus, and that, to die as Jesus died, we must live as Jesus lived. Now, these principles established, let us devote ourselves to obloquy and ignominy; let us disapprove of the honors rendered us, of the good name and applause given us, and let us do nothing to acquire them. . . . Humble yourselves profoundly in the thought that Judas received greater graces than you, that these graces produced more effect than yours, and, notwithstanding, he is lost. And what will it profit the greatest preacher in the world, and one endowed with most excellent talents, to have the praise of his sermons sounded throughout an entire province or even to have converted thousands of souls, and lose his own?"

With St. Vincent, humility was the source whence flowed all other virtues, especially charity. "During the sixty-seven years that God has suffered me to be on earth, I have thought and thought again on the means the most proper to acquire and preserve union and charity with God and our neighbor; but I have found none better or more effectual than holy humility, than the abasing of ourselves beneath all, judging evil of none and looking upon ourselves as the least and as the worst of all. For it is self-love and pride that blind us and induce us to maintain our ideas against those of our neighbor. Consequently, the more a person is humble, the more charitable will he be. Charity is the paradise of communities. But charity is the soul of virtues, and it is humility that attracts and guards them. As with valleys that receive the mountain rains so with communities that are humble. Once we are void of ourselves, God will fill us with Himself, for He cannot bear a vacuum. Let us, then, humble ourselves, my brethren, seeing that God has cast His eyes on this little congregation, to render it of service to His Church, if, however, we can call a congregation a hand-full of men poor in birth, in learning, and in virtue, the dregs, the sweepings and the refuse of the world. I pray God, two or three times every day, that He may destroy us if we prove unserviceable for His glory. What! gentlemen, would we desire to remain in the world without pleasing God and procuring His glory?"

CHAPTER XIII.

OBEDIENCE

I

Vincent's obedience was profound, entire, and admirably ordered. First of all he kept himself in a constant and absolute dependence on God, and sought to do His adorable will in everything. Hence, hardly arrived in Paris, he places himself under the direction of Berulle and obeys him as he would God Himself, assuming, on a word from him, either pastoral duty, or service in the house of Gondi

He saw God in all spiritual and temporal powers, and submitted to them alike in sorrow as in joy, in humiliation as in honor.

In his judgments, in his affections and in his undertakings, he obeyed the Pope, as Vicar of Jesus Christ and Sovereign Pastor of the Church, he obeyed the bishops, as the successors of the apostles, never performing or permitting any functions of his institute without their consent. If a bishop refused the service of his missionaries, he immediately withdrew them, and simply wrote: "We are entirely unworthy to serve God under so great a prelate as you are; when I seek for the reasons Providence has had to cause us to be considered so, I find none other but my sins." (To the Bishop of Perigneux, April 1st, 1657.) It was in obedience to a bishop, St. Francis de Sales, that he accepted and continued for so long, notwithstanding the press of duties, his infirmities and his age, the direction of the Nuns of the Visitation; in obedience to the Archbishop of Paris, he reassumed the burden after having laid it aside, and continued to carry it until his death. "I am the child of obedience," he wrote one day, "it seems to me that should the bishop command me to go to the extremity of his diocese, there to remain all my life, I would do it just as if our Lord had commanded me, and that that retirement, or the employment he would give me would be a foretaste of Paradise, because I would in this be accomplishing the good pleasure of God."

He still obeyed the parish priests even after he had received the mission and full power from the bishop, and would never undertake anything in their parishes save with their consent and according to their pleasure.

He obeyed the King in the smallest, as well as in the greatest things, and sometimes in the most *naive* manner. A brother found some partridge eggs within the enclosure of St. Lazarus. He took them and put them under a hen. As soon as they were hatched he put them in a cage and brought them to Vincent. The latter, at first, seemed to make no acknowledgement, but presently he said to the brother: "Come, let us take a walk in the enclosure." As soon as they reached the field he told him to open the cage and let the birds loose. "My brother," he then said, "you knew well that the king forbade the taking of partridges whence you found these eggs. I beg of you, do so no more."

One day, a noble said to the Queen: "There are few persons, like Mr. Vincent, attached to the service of the King and state with such a sincere, constant, and disinterested fidelity." "You are right," answered Ann of Austria, "Mr. Vincent is a true servant of God and of his Prince.'" It was, in a special manner, in obedience to the Queen that he undertook the missions of St. Germain and Fontainbleau; and when in this last royal residence his priests had met with certain obstacles, he would not withdraw them without the permission of the Queen.

He obeyed his inferiors, and even all classes of persons. In obedience to the Reverend Doctor Duval he entered St. Lazarus; through obedience to the former prior he made the acquisition of that farm of Orsigny that brought a distressing and ruinous lawsuit. In general he condescended to listen to the advice and wishes of others, even those of a weak mind, when the object was indifferent, and when neither truth nor charity was interested. In such cases, for the sake of obedience and humility, he sacrificed to them his superior intelligence and experience. He never either contradicted or contended; he, himself, when contradicted, invariably, after having adduced his reasons, maintained an humble silence. But when the service or glory of God was the subject, then he showed himself firm and unshaken in his opinions and resolutions: " I will condescend as much as you wish," he would say, "provided God be not offended." And still, even in such instances, he refused with such grace, such gentleness and humility that his resistance was more acceptable than the deference of others.

II

Such was the obedience that he preached to his confreres, and counselled every one. He wrote in his constitutions: "We will obey exactly all our superiors, and each one of them, considering them in our Lord, and our Lord in them; and first of all our holy father, the Pope, to whom we will sincerely and faithfully render reverence and obedience."

He taught obedience to the Pope, especially in regard to foreign missions. He wrote: "The power of sending to the nations residing in no one on earth, save in the person of His Holiness, he, consequently, has the power of sending ecclesiastics throughout the entire earth for the glory of God and the salvation of souls, and ecclesiastics are, in this, obliged to obey. In accordance with this principle I have offered the little Congregation to God to go whithersoever His holiness may ordain. We ought to be, in regard to the Pope, as were the servants in the Gospel, in regard to their Master, so that when He tells us: 'Go there,' we will be obliged to go; 'Come here,' we will come; 'Do this,' it will be our duty to do it. This little Congregation ought to live in the disposition to obey, even to the neglect of all else; it should be so disposed that were the Pope to send its members, from the superior down to the last brother, to the extremities of the earth, they would willingly go."

Whilst reserving for himself and his successors the internal government of the Congregation, he asked the Holy See to make it subject to the bishops in all those functions that pertained to the assistance of the neighbor, such as missions, conferences, retreats, and seminaries, so that in these nothing might be done but with their permission and consent.

He also recommended his priests to do nothing in parishes, not even, he said, to remove a single straw, without the consent of the pastors. And he wrote: "We hold it as a maxim, to labor in the service of the public according to the good pleasure and under the direction of the pastors, and never to go against their sentiments; and at the opening and at the close of each mission we ask their blessing in a spirit of dependence."

He preached obedience to kings, and confirmed it by the example of the first Christians: "We should, after their example," he said, "always render to kings a faithful and simple obedience, without ever complaining of them, or murmuring against them under any pretext. And even when there is question of loss of property, or of life, let us yield them from a spirit of obedience rather than gainsay their wills, provided the will of God does not oppose, for kings represent in our regard the sovereign power of God on earth."

And carrying his doctrine of obedience further, he said again: "We should not confine our obedience simply to those who have the right to command us, but we ought to extend it still further; for if, as St. Peter recommends, we submit to every living creature for the love of God, we will be far from the danger of failing in what is of obligation. Let us, then, try to do so, and let us regard all others as our superiors, and, for this purpose, let us esteem ourselves below them and even inferior to the least, showing them deference, condescension and kindness. Oh, what a happy thing it would be were God to firmly establish us in this practice!"

He counselled, particularly, this condescension among children of the same religious family: "In a community," he said, "all those who compose it and are members should exercise condescension towards each other; and in this spirit the learned ought to descend to the weakness of the ignorant in all that is not sin or error; the wise and prudent ought to condescend to the humble and simple: '*Not high-minded, but condescending to the humble.*' (Rom. xii., 16). In this same spirit of condescension we should not only approve of the sentiments of others in things good or indifferent, but we ought even prefer them to our own, believing that others possess more light and have better natural or supernatural qualities than we. But in things that are bad we must be on our guard against any condescension, for, in such a case, it is no longer a virtue but a serious fault and one that can only come from a licentious mind, or from cowardice and pusillanimity."

So obedient himself, and so penetrated with the necessity of obedience he could not suffer the least infraction of this virtue. Lambert Aux-Conteaux was his assistant, that is to say, he was after Vincent, the first in the Congregation. The Saint, one night, kept him up very late working, and, when he was leaving the room, told him to take a rest in the morning. The next morning Lambert was the first at prayer. Vincent perceived him, and, in the presence of the entire community, brothers and young seminarists included, he ordered him to kneel down, and then said: "Sir, obedience is better than sacrifice. A fault less serious than yours nearly cost Jonathan his life and created disorder in the army of the children of Israel."

Finally, obedience to rules and to superiors. He said to the Sisters of Charity: "You have, doubtless, heard tell of what sailors do when they are on the open sea, and, sometimes, more than five hundred leagues from land. Well, they have perfect confidence as long as the laws of navigation are observed; but when these are neglected and the sails become unmanageable then they run great chance of being lost. It is the same in every community. A community is a little vessel that floats in an open sea, but a sea extremely perilous, and where dangers are multiplied. Your fidelity to your vocation, your good behavior and constant observance of your rules, give all assurance of safety. Do not fear, then; your are in the very vessel God inspired you to sail in; there is need of a good pilot who will watch while you sleep.

"And who, do you think, are those pilots so necessary to

guide your ship? Your superiors, whose duty it is to direct you in what you have to do to arrive happily at port. This happiness will be yours, provided you obey them punctually and be faithful in the practice of your rules."

The obedience he taught his own community, he preached to all others of which he had charge. Among all the virtues—the religious of the first house of the Visitation in Paris have testified—he frequently recommended to us the virtue of obedience and exactitude to regularity, even in the slightest points of the rule. He took a special delight in forming our community well in these virtues of obedience and exactitude, and said to us: "These two virtues, when practiced perseveringly, constitute the religious state. To incite ourselves to their practice it is good to talk of them familiarly when together, and entertain ourselves with the idea of their excellence and beauty. We should have an affection for them on account of the pleasure God takes in the religious who are faithful in them, and because He, Who is their Divine Spouse, so loves these virtues that the least delay in obedience is disagreeable to Him. A truly religious soul, having vowed obedience in the presence of the entire Church, ought carefully accomplish what she has promised. If we give way in little things we will soon give way in something greater. All the creature's good consists in doing the will of God. But this will is found particularly in the faithful practice of obedience, and in the exact observance of the rules of the institute. We cannot render a more agreeable homage to God than by practicing obedience, whereby He accomplishes His designs in our regard. In it is found His pure glory, together with the destruction of self-love and all other interests, and this is what we should have mainly in view. The practice of obedience gives the soul the true and perfect liberty of the children of God."

He strongly recommended us to renounce our own judgment, and to mortify it by submitting it to that of our superiors, and he said to us again: "Obedience consists not only in doing immediately what is ordered, but it also requires that we keep ourselves entirely disposed to do all that may be commanded on any occasion. We must look upon our superiors as holding in our regard the place of Jesus Christ, and in view of that, we should render them a very great respect. To murmur against them is a certain interior apostasy. For, as exterior apostasy consists in quitting the habit of religion, and separating from the community, so interior apostasy exists when we separate from superiors, contradicting them in our own minds and adhering to our own particular views which are contrary to theirs; this is the greatest of all evils that can happen in communities. That religious avoids this evil who remains in a holy indifference and allows herself to be guided by her superiors."

He said to us still further on the subject of obedience: "As the basis for the true submission that ought to exist in a community the following should be well weighed:

"First: The position of superiors who hold in our regard the place of Jesus Christ on earth.

"Second: The trouble they take and the solicitude they have for our perfection; sometimes passing the entire night in unrest, and often deeply troubled in heart, whilst inferiors enjoy, at their ease, the peace and tranquility procured for them by the care and toil of the superiors, whose anxiety is all the greater because they have reason to dread the account that they will have to render to God.

"Third: The recompense, even in this life, promised souls truly obedient; for, besides the graces this virtue merits, God delights in doing the will of those who, from love for Him, submit their will to their superiors.

"Fourth: The punishment that those, who are unwilling to obey should apprehend, a terrible example of which God gives us in the chastisement His justice inflicted upon Core, Dathan and Abiron for having contemned Moses, their superior, and for having, by this contempt, grievously offended God, who has said, speaking of the superiors whom His Providence has established in the Church: 'He, who hears you, hears Me, and he, who despises you, despises Me.'

"Fifth: The example of obedience Jesus Christ came to give man, having preferred death to disobedience. And surely it would be a great hardness of heart to see a God obeying even unto death for our salvation, and we, poor, miserable creatures, refusing to subject ourselves for love of Him."

But all this doctrine is found more amply and more eloquently developed in the conferences of the Saint whether to the Sisters of Charity or to the missionaries. Following his ordinary method he first adduced the motives of obedience, and first the example of the Son of God: "There certainly must be something very great and divine in this virtue since our Savior so loved it from the first moment of His birth to the time of His death, since all the actions of His life were done through obedience. He obeyed God, the Father, in becoming man; He obeyed His mother, and St. Joseph, His foster father: 'And He was subject to them.' He obeyed all those who were in dignity, whether good or bad; so that His entire life was but one continued act of obedience. He began His life, and finished it through obedience. He made Himself obedient unto death, even unto the death of the cross, and *wherefore* it is His Father exalted Him.

"Oh, my Savior, what then is this virtue of obedience? How excellent must it be since you have found it worthy of a God! Oh, the beautiful example of obedience our Lord has left us! What need of other motives after that? If there be anything more it is what our Lord has said: 'He who does not renounce himself is not worthy of me, nor worthy to be my disciple.' We cannot, indeed, go out of ourselves nor leave our soul or our body. To renounce one's self then is to renounce one's judgment and one's will, and this is obedience.

"Second: In disobeying, we sin more or less grievously according to the gravity of the disobedience, and particularly, according to what is commanded by the rules, since these are all taken either from the scriptures, or from the commandments of God; and when the disobedience is in important matters it gives scandal; and particularly, when it is through contempt, we may sin mortally."

He then asked himself in what this virtue consisted, and answered: "In a disposition to do what those, to whom we are subject, wish. God is the God of virtue. But virtue has its principle and its root in the interior, for, as what appears man is not man himself, so what seems obedience is not always the virtue of obedience which consists in a constant disposition to obey, to renounce one's own judgment. With such a disposition we go direct to God. A superior, who ordains a certain thing, can, indeed, fail in ordaining. Alas! he is not infallible nor impeccable—but he, who obeys, provided the thing be not evidently sinful, is sure of doing the will of God, for God cannot deceive. How could our Lord exact obedience from the Scribes and Pharisees, from the priests of the ancient law who, for the most part were filled with vice, and with which he frequently reproached them. And yet He told the people: 'Obey them, do as they tell you, but do not imitate their works.' And how could He have obeyed them Himself, were He thus doing wrong, or did not know how to practice great acts of virtue? Because they were in authority and dignity; they, therefore, should be obeyed according to the rule: *He who hears you hears me* . . . . Theirs it was to guide souls.

"Let us then follow the beautiful example that our Lord has given us: '*For I do always the things that please Him.*' (John viii, 29). Yes, *I do always;* and this obedience which He rendered endured not only whilst he was on earth, but continues even to-day when He is glorious in heaven. He is obedient to the priests, even those who are wicked, allowing them, in the Holy Eucharist, to elevate or lower Him as they please. Oh, what an obedience that endures even after death! Oh, my Lord, Thou hast, from all eternity, taken the resolution to obey! Grant us the grace to enter into Thy sentiments, the grace to obey our rules, to obey the order of our superiors, their will expressed by word or sign, and even their intention."

In the third place how are we to obey? The answer to this question is read particularly in a conference to the Sisters of Charity, given on the 25th of June, 1642: "We must obey promptly, cheerfully, with submission of judgment, and with the intent of pleasing God. Obedience should be prompt; for sluggishness and delay in obeying greatly diminish the merit, disedify our neighbor, sadden superiors, who, in such case, would far prefer to do the thing themselves, than command it. We should obey willingly and not through force and constraint, fearing to displease and then be reprimanded We should obey with submission of judgment, doing what is commanded and in the manner it is commanded, and considering it to be for the best, notwithstanding any contrary ideas we may have; and all the more so as our judgment is blind and the knowledge of what is best is often hidden from us by the preoccupations of our passions, as clouds hide the rays of the sun. Finally, we should obey in order to please God, enlivening our obedience with thoughts like these; 'In obeying I render myself acceptable to God, it is the same as if I said I do a pleasure to God.' Oh! what a happiness for a poor and wretched creature to have the power to do a thing that pleases God! This is doing His holy will, this is doing what the angels do. On the other hand, whatever we do of our own choice, let the thing be ever so excellent, we always incur the danger of doing the will of the devil, who transforms himself into an angel of light, and desires to deceive us by the appearance of some little good."

In the conferences of April 7th, 1650, and May 23d, 1655, he returns to the subject and recompense of obedience: "There is a double merit in an action performed through obedience: there is the merit of the work, when it is good, in itself, and, moreover, there is the merit of obedience by which the action is done. We may compare actions done through obedience with a painting from the hand of some great master, as, for instance, Michael Angelo. The painting is in itself worth, say, no more than ten crowns, but being the work of a great artist its value is greatly enhanced and may be sold for twenty or thirty crowns. Or again, we compare them to ornaments destined for the service of the altar. You will see fine linen, very white, nicely folded, and of sweet odor, that is highly esteemed in itself, but is prized far more since it is to be used for the service at mass. Thus, a good action which we perform has its own merit, but obedience gives it an additional merit, and, moreover, renders meritorious the most indifferent actions, and even those that of themselves have no value.

"It is just as if we united precious stones with other precious stones. Imagine a dress made of beautiful silk. The silk alone makes the dress beautiful, but it is still more stiking if gold lace be added. Thus it is with good actions performed out of obedience; and for each such action we receive two rewards. Even the indifferent actions are more agreeable to God than good works without obedience. This virtue is a sort of philosopher's stone, and all it touches becomes gold."

It is readily understood that, in his correspondence, the Saint placed this same doctrine within the reach of each of those under his charge according to the state or dispositions in which they were. He wrote to Mademoiselle Le Gras who, through obedience, had renounced one of her pious undertakings: "Our Lord will, perhaps, draw greater glory from your submission than from all the good you could have done. A beautiful diamond is of more value than a mountain of stones, and one act of the virtue of acquiescence and submission is worth more than a number of good works performed in behalf of others." (1631).

He wrote to one of his clerics (May 28th. 1655): "Your letter has informed me of your trouble. I fully believe that God makes you feel the unhappy results of a change sought by your own will, for it is His custom to make those, who have undertaken to serve Him, know that their repose is in obedience, and never in the accomplishment of their own will. And, remember, you will never find calmness of mind in following our Lord, unless you renounce yourself, because He Himself has said that, in order to follow Him, this renunciation must be made, and the cross carried every day. You have heard this a hundred times and yet you do not apply the lesson; at least you have manifested the contrary by the frequent requests you have made to be changed, and notwithstanding that you were begged to have patience where you were, you still had your objections and difficulties, and I told you that you would have them everywhere. It was necessary to content you, but the contentment did not last long: you tell me so yourself. Our Lord calls obedience to His maxims a yoke to show us that it is a state of submission, and a hard one for those who wish to withdraw from it, but sweet and easy for those who love it and are enamored of it. My dear brother, do you wish to find peace of heart and thousands of blessings from God? Listen no more either to your judgment or your will. You have already sacrificed them to God; be careful not to resume them. Let yourself be guided, and rest assured that it will be God who will conduct you, and He will lead you to the liberty of His children, to an abundance of consolation, to great progress in virtue and to your eternal happiness. I say all this to you

because you propose still another change; otherwise I would have imitated the kindness of God who never reproaches us with faults once pardoned. I would have thought of yours no longer, had I not seen you in the danger of committing the like again; this is why I represent to you the trouble and anxiety that will come upon you if the experience of what you have already suffered do not make you more submissive. Consider it as certain that, if you are changed because you demand it, you will no sooner arrive at your destination than you can say, as you now say where you, at present, are. that you are there by your own choice rather than by the will of God, having obliged your superiors to send you against their better judgment, and this thought will constantly disquiet you. And now, to take away this sting of conscience in regard to the place you are in at present, remain there because holy obedience ordains it, and no longer look upon your being there as by your own will, but by that of God. Ask His pardon for the past and think no more of it. Resolve to give ear no more to your own spirit, if you do not wish to be led astray, for it is of such a nature that it will trouble you wherever you go, unless you believe me. I pray our Lord to animate you with His spirit, our Lord who was so submissive that He compared Himself to a beast of burden, which is so indifferent that one can do with it as he wishes, no matter when or where. Were we in such a disposition God would soon lead us to perfection.'

Everything furnished him a subject and an occasion to preach obedience: "A captain told me, a few days ago, that, were he to perceive that his general gave a wrong command and that he would lose his life in obeying it, though he could, with one word, have the order changed, yet he would lose his honor were he to say that word, and he would prefer to die than utter it. See, gentlemen, how great our confusion will be before Heaven in witnessing such perfection of obedience in war, and our own so imperfect in comparison."

And suddenly, reflecting on his position as Superior and on the obligation he had just imposed on his children of obeying himself, he cried out in his humility: "Oh, wretch that I am! To obey one who disobeys God! Who disobeys our holy Mother the Church! One who was disobedient to his father and mother from his infancy! for almost all my life has been but disobedience. Alas! gentlemen, to whom do you render obedience? To one, who, like the Scribes and Pharisees, is full of vice and sin. But this will give your obedience all the greater merit. I was reflecting a little while ago on my disobedience and I remembered that, when a small boy, my father brought me to the city and I was ashamed of him because he was badly dressed, and limped a little. Oh, miserable wretch that I am! How disobedient have I been! I ask God's pardon for it and for all the scandals I have given you. I will also ask pardon of the entire congregation, and I conjure you to pray to God for me that He may pardon me these faults, and give me also a sincere regret for them."

GETHSEMANI ABBEY,
GETHSEMANI, P. O. KY.

CHAPTER XIV.

SIMPLICITY.

I

Simplicity shone in Vincent in all its modest brightness. It gained all those with whom he came in contact; it contributed, in a great measure, to the success of his immense undertakings, because, besides the blessing of God, it won for him the confidence and affection of men. With humility and charity it, of all his virtues, is the one that struck his contemporaries the most, and they all unite in rendering it a most touching and unanimous eulogy. It was simplicity, the character of the great in all things, the common character of true virtue as well as of real genius, that, in St. Vincent de Paul, especially charmed Bossuet. Hence, it is to this simplicity, to this *admirable simplicity* of the holy old man that, with manifest feeling, he rendered testimony all his life, and to which, grown old himself, he pays a last tribute in his letter to Clement XI. A simplicity all the more wonderful, since it maintained itself, and thrived in dealing with the world, amid the hypocrisy of a Court, in the windings of business, that is to say, in the midst of dissimulation, deceit and duplicity, which naturally should have withered and destroyed it. His simplicity was the ornament of his discourses, the secret of his direction, the charm of his person, as also the counselor of his humility in avowals of forgetfulness or fault.

II

Hence, he preached it with love, and indignantly stigmatized the contrary vice. He said: "To appear good externally, and to be far otherwise internally, is to do as the hypocritical Pharisees, it is to imitate the demon who transforms himself into an angel of light. And since prudence of the flesh and hypocrisy especially reign in this corrupt age, to the great prejudice of the spirit of Christianity, we cannot better combat and overcome them than by a veritable and sincere simplicity." "God is simple," he said again, "or rather He is simplicity itself; and wherever you discover simplicity, there, too, you find God. And, as the Wise Man says, he, who walks in simplicity, walks in confidence, while, on the contrary, those, who make use of craft and simplicity, are in constant dread lest their cunning be detected, and lest others, having found out their dissimulation, place no further confidence in them."

But let us hear him in a special conference on this subject, given March 14th, 1659: "Our Savior, in sending the apostles to preach His Gospel throughout the world, recommended to them particularly this virtue of simplicity as one of the most important and most necessary to draw down upon them the grace of Heaven, and to dispose the hearts of those upon earth to hear and believe them. Now, it was not only to His apostles that he spoke, but also, in general, to all those Whom His Providence predestined to the work of preaching the Gospel, of instructing and converting souls. Consequently, it is to us Jesus Christ spoke and recommended this virtue of simplicity so agreeable to God. '*And His communication is with the simple.*' (Prov. iii., 32.) Imagine, my brothers, what a consolation, and what a happiness for those, who are of the number of the truly simple, to be assured by the very word of God that His delight is to dwell and entertain Himself with them.

In these words, which He addressed to God, His Father: "*I give thanks to Thee, Oh Father, Lord of Heaven and earth, because Thou hast hid these things from the wise and prudent, and hast revealed them to little ones,*" (Mat. xi., 25). Our Lord shows us how agreeable to Him is simplicity. I acknowledge, Oh, my Father, and I thank Thee for it, that the doctrine, which I have learned of Thee, and which I diffuse among men, is known only to the little and simple, and that Thou permittest not the wise and the prudent of the world to understand it, the sense and spirit of this Divine doctrine being hidden from them. Certainly, these words, if we reflect on them, ought to alarm us who run after knowledge as if all our happiness depended upon it. Not but that a priest and a missionary should have learning, yet it should be such as is required to satisfy the duties of his ministry and not to content his ambition and his curiosity. He should study and acquire knowledge, but soberly, as the Apostle says. There are others who plume themselves on their understanding everything, and who wish to pass for persons accomplished, clever, and capable in all things. These, too, as well as all the learned and wise in the knowledge of the world, are of the number of those from whom God takes away the understanding of the truths and virtues of Christianity. To whom, then, does He give the understanding of His truths and His doctrine? To the simple, to the artless, and more frequently, even to the poor people, as is verified by the difference remarked in the faith of the poor people in the country and that of persons in high life. For my part, I can say a long experience has proved to me that a lively and practical faith, and a true spirit of religion are more ordinarily found among the poor and among the simple. God takes a pleasure in enriching them with a fervent faith; they believe and relish the words of eternal life which Jesus Christ left us in His Gospel; we see them, generally, bear patiently their sicknesses, their privations and their other afflictions without murmuring and even without complaining, save little and rarely. How comes this? It is because God is pleased to infuse into them, in abundance, the gift of faith and all other graces, whilst He refuses them to the rich and wise of the world.

"Add to this that all love simple and candid persons, who use neither cunning nor deceit, who act ingeniously and speak sincerely, and whose lips, thus, are ever in accord with their hearts. They are everywhere esteemed and loved, even at Court when met with; and in all well regulated communities every one bears them affection and places confidence in them. And what is very remarkable, even those, who do not possess either candor or simplicity in their speech or their thought, love it in others. Let us strive, then, my brethren, to become pleasing in the sight of God by the practice of this virtue, and imitate those in the little congregation, who, by the grace of God, give us in this so bright an example.

"But, to understand and appreciate the excellence of this virtue, we must know that it brings us to God, and, by producing conformity, renders us like to Him, He being but simple spirit, and His essence admitting no composition. Hence, what God is by essence we ought to be by means of this virtue in as far as our weakness and misery will permit. We must have a heart simple, a mind simple, a simple intention and simple action; we should speak simply, act straightforwardly, without dissimulation or guile, looking only to God, whom alone we ought to desire to please.

"Simplicity, then, comprehends not only truth and purity of intention, but it possesses, moreover, a certain property of removing us from all deceit, cunning and duplicity. And, as it is principally in the use of words that this virtue manifests itself, it obliges us to declare with the tongue just as it is in the heart, speaking and uttering what we have to say, simply, and with the pure intention of pleasing God. Yet simplicity, notwithstanding all this, does not oblige us to disclose all our thoughts; for this virtue is discreet, and it is never in opposition to prudence, which discerns what is good to say from what is improper, and knows when to observe silence and when to speak. If, for instance, I advance a proposition, good in its substance and good in all its circumstances, I ought to express it simply as it is; but if, among the things I have to say, some improper or useless circumstance is met with, it must be omitted; and, in general, those things should not be said which are known to be against God or our neighbor, or which tend to our own praise, or aim at some carnal or temporal gratification, for otherwise we would sin, at one and the same time, against many other virtues.

"In regard to simplicity in action, it is of such a nature that it acts openly, straightforwardly, and keeps God always in view, whether in business transactions, or daily avocations, or ordinary exercises of piety, rejecting all hypocrisy, all artifice, and all vain pretence. For instance, a person makes another a present, pretending it is through affection, and yet he gives the present solely in expectation of receiving something of more va'u? from the other. Though, according to the spirit of the world, that seems to be permitted, it is nevertheless opposed to the virtue of simplicity, which cannot suffer a pretending of one thing whilst meaning another. For, as this virtue induces us to speak according to our interior convictions, so, too, does it cause us to act with candor and Christian rectitude, and do all for God, Who is the sole end it has in view; whence we must infer that this virtue does not reside in those who, through human respect, desire to appear other than they are, nor in those who do good externally that they may be esteemed virtuous, who keep a number of superfluous books that they may be regarded as learned, who study to preach well in order to obtain applause and praise; nor, final'y, in those who have other than the proper motives in their exercises and practices of piety. Now, I ask you, my Brethren, is not this virtue of simplicity beautiful and desirable, and is it not just and reasonable to guard against all dissimulation and artifice in word and action? But, to acquire it, we must practice it; and we can become truly simple only by frequent acts of simplicity, aided, certainly, by the grace of God, which we should frequently ask."

The particular and written instructions of the Saint in regard to this virtue were absolutely the same as his public or spoken teachings. On one occasion, when sending a missionary to a province where the people were noted for their shrewdness, he gave him this advice: "You go into a country where, they say, the people are for the most part clever and cunning. Now, if such be the case, the best way to be of use to them will be to act with them in the greatest simplicity. For the maxims of the Gospel are totally contrary to the spirit of the world. Hence, as you go there in the service of Our Lord, you ought to act according to His spirit—a spirit of rectitude and simplicity." To another of his priests who regulated his friendly relations with externs in the interest of the Congregation, and wished to have published what he wrote of certain persons, he answered: "Alas, sir, with what are you amusing yourself? Where is that simplicity of the missionary which aims directly at God? If you do not recognize any good in these persons, do not say you do; but if you see good, speak of it in order to honor God in them, for from Him proceeds all good. Our Lord reproved a man who had called Him good because his intention was not pure. How much more reason will He have to reprove you when you praise sinful men through complaisance, to gain their favor, or through some other temporal and imperfect end, though there be other motives which may be good! For I am convinced that you do not seek to gain the affection of any sa e as a means to promote the glory of God. But remember, God does not like duplicity, and that to be truly simple we must consider only Him "

But it was in preaching, especially, that he insisted on simplicity, wishing all to absolutely discard all hankering after esteem and praise. He said : " We desire to shine and have ourselves spoken of; we love to be praised, and to hear people say we succeed well and are doing wonders ; behold the monster, the infernal serpent, that conceals itself under fine pretexts and empoisons, with its deadly venom, the hearts of those who listen to it! O, accursed Pride! What good dost thou corrupt and destroy! Of what evil art thou the cause! Thou makest the preacher preach himself, and not Jesus Christ, and thus, instead of edifying, he destroys and ruins. I was present to-day at the instruction that a prelate gave the ordinands ; after which, going to his room, I said to him : 'My lord, you have to-day converted me.' He answered: 'How is that?' 'Because,' I rejoined. 'you have spoken, in what you said, so plainly and so simply, that it seemed to me very touching, and I could not refrain from thanking God.' 'Ah, sir!' he replied, 'I must confess to you with equal candor that I might easily have said something more polished and more elevated ; but had I done so, I would have offended God.' See, gentlemen, the sentiments of the prelate, sentiments which all those, who truly seek God, and desire to procure the salvation of souls, should possess, and then, I can assure you, God will not fail to bless what you say, and give force and power to your words. Yes, God will be with you, and will operate in you, for He delights in the company of the simple. He assists them and He blesses their labor and enterprises. On the contrary, it would be an impiety to think that God would wish to favor or aid a person who seeks the glory men give and who nourishes himself on vanity, as do those who preach themselves, and who, in their sermons, speak neither with simplicity nor with humility. For, how can it be said that God would desire to assist a person in destroying himself? Such a thought cannot enter the mind of a Christian Oh, if you knew how great an evil it is to intrude oneself into the office of preacher for the purpose of preaching otherwise than Jesus Christ has preached, otherwise than have preached the Apostles and many great Saints and servants of God, and still do preach, you would be horror-stricken! God knows, that three times, during three consecutive days, I knelt before a priest, who then was, but now is not, of the Congregation, to beg of him, with all the earnestness I possibly could, to preach and speak with simplicity, and to follow the directions that were given him, but I never could induce him to consent. He gave the instructions of the Ordination but produced no fruit; and all that beautiful collection of thought and selected periods went off in smoke, for, in truth, it is not the pomp of words that profits souls, but simplicity and humility, which draw down and instil into the hearts of men the grace of Jesus Christ. And if we will recognize and confess the truth, what is there in us to attract all these gentlemen, the ordinands, the theologians, the bachelors and licentiates of Sorbonne and Navarre, who come here? It is not the learning nor the doctrine which we offer them, for they have more than we. No; but it is the humility and simplicity in which, by the grace of God, we act towards them. They come here only to learn virtue; when once they see its light grow dim in us they will withdraw. Hence, we ought to desire and pray to God that He may be pleased to grant the grace to all the Congregation, and to each one of us in particular, to act simply and plainly, and to preach the truths of the Gospel in the way Our Lord has taught them, that thus, all may understand them, and each one profit by what we say."

He said to those who preferred a more elevated and ornate style to simplicity and familiarity: "Why all this vain display! Does any one desire to show himself an elegant rhetorician? a learned theologian? Strange! he, surely, takes the wrong way. Perchance, he may be esteemed by a certain class of persons who hardly understand anything about it; but to acquire the esteem of the wise, and to win the reputation of being an eloquent speaker, he must know how to persuade his auditory to embrace what he desires, and to dissuade it from what he wishes it to void. But that does not consist in a dainty choice of words and rounded periods, in an unusual manner of expressing the subtlety of his conceptions, and in delivering his discourse in an elevated and dramatic tone of voice, which overshoots the mark. Do such preachers attain their end? Do they strongly persuade the love of piety? Are the people touched, and is the confessional crowded? And yet such is the supposed aim of these great preachers! But here is their real object: to acquire a name, to have it said: Truly, that man declaims well; he is eloquent; he has beautiful thoughts and he expresses them agreeably. Behold to what the fruit of their sermons amounts! You then ascend the pulpit not to preach God, but yourselves, and, —oh, what a crime! you make use of a thing so holy as the word of God to nourish and cherish your vanity! Oh, my Divine Savior!"

He then went on to answer the objections: "We will forfeit all honor and esteem by this too simple and too trivial a method." And he answered: "You will thereby lose your honor! Oh! in preaching as Jesus Christ has preached, you will lose your honor! What! to speak of God as the Son of God has spoken of Him is to lose one's honor! Oh! Jesus Christ, the word of the Father had, then, no honor! To deliver sermons with simplicity, in familiar language as our Lord has done, is to have no honor! To do otherwise is to be a man of honor! To weigh down the word of God with affectation and to cloak it with a mask is to have honor! Oh, my Divine Savior! Oh, gentlemen! To say that we lose our honor in preaching the Gospel as Jesus Christ has preached it! I would just as soon say that Jesus Christ, He, Who is eternal wisdom, did not know exactly how to manage His speech, that He did not very well understand himself! Oh, what a blasphemy!"

In this connection, he said again: "As things of natural beauty possess far more attraction than those that are painted and artificial, so, simple and familiar discourse is better received and finds a more favorable acceptance with minds than those that are affected and labored."

He exercised his children in this simple style of preaching and practiced it himself even in his old age. Each one, in his turn, had to speak before him. In the evening he gave an account of the sermon, and had it analyzed publicly by the chief members of the community. When any showed great research and studious care he took pleasure in pointing out the vanity displayed therein and then he concluded in his ordinary charity: "Believe me, sir; try to preach as Jesus Christ has done. This Divine Savior could, had he so desired, have said marvellous things concerning our most sublime mysteries, and with conceptions and terms corresponding, being, as He was, the Word and the Wisdom of His Eternal Father. And, yet, we know in what manner he preached, simply and humbly, in order to accommodate Himself to the people, and to give us a model and a method how to treat His holy word."

When he was sending the ecclesiastics of his conference on a mission in the Faubourg St. Germain, these latter took the liberty to represent to him that there was a great difference between a mission given in a city, and a city like Paris, and missions in the country. With different enemies, different arms, they said to him; and this simple and familiar language which succeeds with the country people, would, here, excite only laughter and ridicule. "What is that I just heard, gentlemen?" interrupted Vincent. "behold words inspired by human prudence, and, perhaps, by self-love. You, then, wish to destroy the power of the cross by relying on means purely natural Believe me, the method which God has blessed in your mission to the country people is the only one He will bless in the mission you wish to undertake. You go to combat the spirit of the world, which is a spirit of pride, and you will overcome it only by attacking it in the spirit of Jesus Christ, which is a spirit of simplicity and humility. Like this Divine Savior, seek not your own glory, but the glory of His father; after His example, be ready to suffer contempt, and, if need be, contradiction and persecution. In speaking the language which the Son of God has spoken, it will not be you who speak but Jesus Christ through you. Thus, you will merit to become the instruments of that mercy which alone touches hearts the most obdurate and converts souls the most rebellious."

Let us terminate this chapter with the admirable letter the Saint wrote to Mr. Martin, Superior in Turin, who was anxious to inaugurate, with some grand mission, his ministry in Piedmont. "Oh, no, my dear sir." Vincent immediately wrote to him, "you must, on the contrary, begin by some little mission that will have no great show. To commence so meanly will seem to you unfortunate; for, to acquire esteem we ought, it seems, come out a little by a complete and splendid mission which will, at once, display all the fruits of the spirit of the congregation. May God preserve me from the thought of such a desire! What conforms to our poverty and to the spirit of Christianity is to fly all ostentation, and love retirement, is to seek contempt and humiliation as Jesus Christ has done; and when we have this resemblance to Him He will labor for us. The late Bishop of Geneva understood this well. The first time that he preached in Paris, on the occasion of the last visit he made. the people flocked to hear him, from all quarters of the city; the Court was present, and all, who could render an audience worthy so celebrated a preacher, were present. Every one expected a discourse befitting the power of that genius by which he was accustomed to rivet the attention of all. But what did this great man of God do? He simply recited the life of St. Martin. and he did this on purpose to abase himself before so many illustrious personages, whose presence alone would have aroused the enthusiasm of any other preacher. He was the first to profit from his sermon by reason of this heroic act of humility. He related this, shortly after the occurrence, to Madam de Chantal and myself. He said to us: 'Oh, how I have mortified our sisters. They were sure that I would be wondrously eloquent before such good company.' During the sermon a girl said: 'Just look at the mountaineer, how poorly he speaks! It was well worth his while to come so far to say what he says, and weary the patience of so many!' This is how the saint repressed nature which loves distinction and renown; it is thus we should do, preferring the common and lowly to great and important occupations. preferring abjection to honor. I hope, indeed, that you and those of your house will build upon this holy practice as a foundation, so that your edifice may be established upon the rock, and not upon moving sand."

CHAPTER XV.

PRUDENCE.

I

Vincent did not, any more than the Gospel does, separate simplicity from prudence: two virtues equally necessary to each other, and which he practiced in the same degree of perfection. His prudence and his wisdom obtained for him universal confidence. During his entire life, St. Lazarus was known as the house of the *Seer*, and people came to consult him on all affairs pertaining either to Church or State, to the public in general or to private individuals. During half a century there was nothing of importance done in France, whether in the political, or religious order, without his participation or his counsel. In the height of the civil troubles he was equally esteemed and consulted by both parties, by the Court, and by the Princes, by the adherents of Mazarin and by the Frondists. In the troubles of Jansenism he again it was to whom they addressed themselves, and to his prudent intervention is principally due the triumph of truth, the preservation of faithful communities, and the return to the faith of a number of the seceders. The nuncios, Bagni and Piccolomini, were accustomed to seek his advice in relation to important questions concerning the Church of France, and even the Universal Church. Bishops, abbots, directors of souls, submitted to him their most serious and most delicate affairs. Heads of religious orders, superiors of communities sought his concurrence for the reformation of their orders and of their houses; or again, an individual religious, a simple novice would consult him on his vocation, or his change of state. Numbers of pastors, of priests, proposed to him the difficulties of their ministry, or of their conscience. Great lords and noble ladies left to him the decisions of their projects for the glory of God, the solace of their neighbor, or their own sanctification. There was not a generous soul, not a family, not a community in which his prudent action was unfelt; not a reunion for a good object of which he was not the inspiration and the guide.

Whence came this universal recourse to him? No doubt, from his reputation for sanctity; from the confidence placed in the grace attached by God to his intervention; but also from the knowledge of his natural and acquired prudence. For he was a wise man by excellence, a man, possessing in an eminent degree that good sense which Bossuet terms the master of human life; and consequently, he was a man always keeping himself in that middle where the true and the good have fixed their throne, preserving himself with equal care from both extremes which end in error and ill success. Even the pretext of good could not deceive his prudence. From necessity he had originated the adage: "The better is the enemy of the good," for that was among his maxims. He said again: "The human mind is active and restless. The most enlightened are not always the best, if they be not as well the most circumspect. We walk safely when we do not depart from the path trodden by the majority of the wise."

He founded his prudence on God, whose will he was careful to consult in everything; on Jesus Christ, whose lessons and examples he studied, in order to conform his counsel and his conduct to the virtue of a holy analogy, ever asking himself: "What would Our Lord have said, or done in like circumstances, or in such a difficulty?"

"There is a time to speak and a time to keep silence" the Divine Wisdom has said. Vincent had learned it and practiced it. None knew better how to maintain silence, when speech would either violate a secret, wound charity, compromise an affair, or when it was simply useless. He knew how to listen, a virtue rare, though necessary, without ever interrupting. Interrupted himself, he instantly ceased speaking; but, as nothing could bend his inflexible wisdom, the interruption once ended he resumed the thread of his discourse and went straight to his point. His speech was slow from habit of reflection. His reasonings were pure, clear, and convincing, expressed in terms plain and precise, animated with a gentle warmth, and carried persuasion to the heart while convincing the mind. If he spoke the first, he unraveled and explained the question with such order and precision, such depth and reach, that each one, even the most clever, said to himself, "That is it,"—an homage to his infallible good sense. Moreover, good sense taught him to adapt himself to all styles and all language, according to the minds he dealt with, so that the man of moderate parts believed himself his equal, whilst the highest genius did not find him his inferior.

And this was because he had the power of discernment in men as well as in doctrine and affairs. He immediately perceived the ability of each one, and adjusted his language and conduct in accordance. He divined the strong and the weak, the good and the bad qualities of all, and he knew how to regulate thereupon their position and their occupation. In everything he distinguished the true from the false, the good from the bad, the better from the less good, under appearances the most deceptive, or the most clearly hypocritical.

This is what made his direction so sure, his decision so infallible, his action, when once he had formed his mind, so firm and so resolute. When consulted, he sometimes was slow to answer, for he, himself, required to previously consult God and the wise; but the answer which he finally gave was stamped with the mark of wisdom and experience.

He was, likewise, slow to resolve and undertake, always in virtue of that good sense which felt the need of previously penetrating and combining the nature, the means, and the end in all things. His children, particularly the younger, used to complain to him of it, and he ordinarily answered as he did on the 7th of December, 1641, in the following letter, addressed to Mr. Codoing, Superior of the Mission at Annecy: "You will object that I am too slow, that you have to wait sometimes six months for an answer that might be given within a month, and that, meanwhile, the occasions pass, all remains stationary. To which, sir, I answer that it is true: I am too long a time in answering, and in doing things; but, notwithstanding, I have never yet seen any affair spoiled by my delay; on the contrary, everything has been done in its good time, and with the necessary foresight and precaution. Still, I purpose, for the future, to answer your letters as soon as possible after their receipt, and after having considered the thing before God, who is greatly honored by the time we take to weigh maturely what concerns His service. You will, then, in your turn correct yourself, if you please, of your promptness in resolution and action, and I will labor to correct my negligence. . . . . Will I dare tell you, sir, without blushing? . . . There is no remedy; I must. It is thus, that, reviewing all the principal things that have been done in this congregation, it seems to me, and it is easily demonstrated, that had they been done before they were, they would not have been so well done. I say this of all, without a single exception. And this is why I have a special devotion to following, step by step, the adorable Providence of God, and the sole consolation I have is, that it seems to me it is our Lord alone Who has done, and constantly does, all in this little Congregation."

He was then the friend of slowness, or rather, the enemy of precipitation. This was an effect of his prudence. This slowness had, moreover, as a cause, his fear of going in opposition to God, the desire of being assured of His concurrence, and the need he felt of never laying the foundation of a work without the certainty, or, at least, the probable hope, of being able to carry it to completion. From this arise the wise combination, the continuance and permanence of all his works.

But, once assured of the Divine Will and of the resources of His Providence, nothing had the power to stay him. He was dismayed neither at the number nor the difficulties of the undertakings. He followed them with a force of mind and an intrepidity of courage that no obstacles could weaken, whether they came from persons or things, from the combination of the elements or of human passions. He applied himself with a sagacity full of order and light; he sustained the burden, the trouble, the delays, with a calm that came from a holy security, with a perseverance which he derived from his religious certainty of success.

His was a soul truly superior in its admirable prudence, whose passions did not, as with most men, arise to disarrange his calculations; whose virtue, on the contrary, inspired, directed, and brought to a successful termination all his projects.

Such he has shown himself in the establishment and guidance of the Congregations of the Missionaries and the Daughters of Charity, to which he gave rules only after twenty-five and even thirty-three years, wishing thereby to imitate Our Lord, Who began to do before He taught, and also, to avoid the inconveniences of premature Constitutions. Hence there was nothing unforeseen, nothing provisional, and consequently, nothing to be reformed in these rules; nothing that did not have existence in fact before being formulated in words, nothing which weakness or cowardice can tax as impracticable or even difficult.

Such, too, he showed himself in the Council of Conscience, where, with an admirable wisdom, he veered amid so many intrigues and ambitions, where he knew how to reform so many abuses, where he succeeded in conciliating things often the most incompatible, namely, the interests of the Court and of individuals with the superior interests of the Church.

Such, in fine, he showed himself when obliged to admonish, to reprehend, or to correct. His prudence knew how to suit itself to character and circumstance, so as not to dishearten pusillanimity or to push pride to revolt, so as not to wound either the dignity of the person or the charity due to secret faults. Mr. Soure, pastor of St. John en Greve, exiled to Compiegne, wrote to him on the 17th of August, 1659, to obtain information concerning a priest who formerly belonged to the Mission, and to whom he wished to confide for a time the care of his parish. "Sir," Vincent answered him, "I do not sufficiently know the ecclesiastic whom you mention to give any recommendation, though he did enter and leave our Congregation twice." Messrs. Portail, d'Horgni and Almeras, who were present when he dictated this letter, observed to him that this pastor would have reason to be surprised if he wrote that he did not know well enough a priest who had been twice under him. "I see that very clearly," replied Vincent, "but Our Lord, though He had a perfect knowledge of all classes of persons, has, nevertheless, said to some, 'I know you not;' and he will say the same on the Day of Judgment because he does not know with approving knowledge." What is most to be admired here, his charity or his prudence?

Vincent sometimes employed no less prudent address than persevering zeal in his efforts with ecclesiastics who were sus pected in matters of faith. One, learned, a great preacher, of aristocratic family, often came to see him. "Sir," the Saint one day said to him, "as you are learned and eloquent I want to ask an advice. In our missions in the country it happens that we find persons who do not believe the truths of our holy religion, and we do not know how to go about convincing them, what must we do in such circumstances?" "Why do you ask me that," replied the abbe with feeling. "Because, sir, the poor apply to the rich in their necessities, and, as we are but poor, ignorant persons, we have recourse to you who are rich in knowledge." Flattered and reassured, the abbe enumerated the proofs of religion—Scriptures, the fathers, reasoning, the common consent of peoples and of ages, the testimony of the martyrs, miracles, etc. "Very good, sir," returned Vincent. "Reduce all that to writing, I beseech you, simply and without study, and send it to me." Two or three days after the abbe himself brought the writing. "Thank you, sir," said Vincent. "It is a singular pleasure for me to see you with such good sentiments, and to learn the fact from yourself. For, besides the profit I will derive from this paper myself, it will serve me for your justification. You will, with difficulty, believe it, but it is, nevertheless, true, that certain parties are persuaded, and say you have not proper ideas in regard to things of faith. Complete, then, sir, what you have so well begun, and, after having so worthily defended the faith in your writing, profess it by an edifying life. You are all the more obliged as you are a man of rank; for it is with virtue joined to birth as with a precious stone. When the stone is enchased in gold it is incomparably more dazzling than when set in lead." This manner of action and these words had their effect, and Vincent had the consolation of seeing the abbe enter into himself and persevere in his holy resolutions.

To prudence he joined respect, ingenuity, and, at times, courtesy when he had a wise advice to give to bishops. A bishop, one of his friends had several times protested to him that he would never abandon his spouse, meaning his church, for any other no matter how beautiful or how rich; and in pledge of his fidelity he showed him his pastoral ring, saying: *If I forget thee, let my right hand be forgotten.*" (Ps. cxxxvi-5.) Some time after the tempting offer of a rich and grand archbishopric was made, and the bishop felt inclined to yield to the seduction. Vincent met him by chance: "My Lord," he said to him after the compliments of the day were passed, and with his eyes fixed on the bishop's hand, "I pray you remember your ring." "Ah! Mr. Vincent," answered the bishop, "you catch me there."

We must not forget to mention with what a happy union of prudence and humility he extricated himself, on his journey to Mans in 1649, from the embarrassment he was occasioned by the presence in the city of the Bishop, Lavardin de Beaumanoir, — the very one about whose consecration, for an unthinking word, so many ridiculous fables were invented after his death. Far from being of service to him in the council, Vincent had opposed his promotion to the episcopacy. Lavardin knew it, had frequently complained of it, and even bitterly. Judge, then, the surprise, and the delicate position of the servant of God when he learned that this prelate, who had not yet received the bulls, was already at Mans! How was he to act towards the bishop? It was unbecoming to leave without seeing him, dangerous to see him without previously preparing him, impolite to ask him if he would receive a visit. "If I go to salute him," said the Saint, "very likely he will be surprised, and, perhaps, touched and moved; if I send to inquire whether he would be pleased with a visit I do not know how he will receive the compliment; if I neither go nor send, this good lord will have reason to be still more incensed against me, and this must be avoided. What, then, is to be done?"

The humility of the Saint came to his rescue. The very next morning he sent two of his priests, the superior of the seminary and another priest, to inform the bishop, that, having arrived in his diocese the previous evening, he did not dare to make any delay without his permission, and he very humbly besought him to be pleased that he remain seven or eight days in the house of the seminary.

This compliment on the part of a man whose rectitude and sincerity Lavardin, notwithstanding his resentment, knew better than any other, completely disarmed him: "Say to Mr. Vincent," he answered the messengers, "that he is free to remain in Mans as long as he thinks fit, and that had he no house in my episcopal city I would take a pleasure in offering him mine."

So courteous an answer required a return of thanks. Vincent was preparing to go to the bishop's palace when he was apprised of the abrupt departure of Lavardin.

II

And now we will listen to the Saint speaking to us on prudence, in his conference of the 14th of March, 1659: "It is the duty of this virtue," he said, "to regulate and guide our words and actions. It makes us speak wisely and in proper season, directing us in our conversations in selecting, with circumspection and judgment, those subjects that are good in their nature and in their circumstances, suppressing and retaining in silence those that are against God, or that injure our neighbor, or that tend to self-praise or any other unworthy object. This virtue, again, causes us to act with discretion, and only after mature deliberation, and with pure motives in everything we do, not only in regard to the substance of the action but also its circumstances; so that the prudent man acts as he should, when he should, and for the purpose he should. On the contrary, the imprudent man adopts neither the proper manner, nor time, nor motive, and this is wherein his fault lies, whereas the prudent man, acting with discretion, does all things in weight, number and measure.

"Prudence and simplicity tend to the same end which is to speak well and to do well, and all with a view to God; and, as the one cannot exist without the other, our Lord has recommended both together. I am aware that, by a distinction of reason, a difference may be found between these two virtues; but they have, in reality, a very close connection both in their substance and in their object. The prudence of the flesh and the world, since it has for its object the quest of honors of pleasures, and of riches, is diametrically opposed to Christian simplicity and prudence which alienate us from these deceptive goods and impel us to embrace the solid and enduring. They are as two good sisters who are inseparable, and are so necessary for our spiritual advancement that he, who has learned to make proper use of them, will certainly amass great treasures of grace and merit. Our Lord, on several occasions, practiced both in an excellent degree, and particularly when that poor woman, caught in adultery, was brought to Him to be condemned; for, not desiring to take the place of judge at that time, and wishing to deliver her from her enemies, He said to the Jews: '*Let him who is without sin, among you, cast the first stone at her.*' (John viii, 7). Herein he practiced in an eminent degree these two virtues: simplicity, in the merciful design He had of saving this poor creature, and thus doing the will of His Father, and prudence, in the manner He adopted to effect His purpose. And so, again, when the Pharisees came, tempting Him, asking if it were lawful to give tribute to Cæsar; for, on the one hand, he wished to maintain the honor of His Father, and do nothing to the prejudice of His people, and on the other, He did not want to put Himself on record as being in opposition to the rights of Cæsar, nor to give His enemies an opportunity to publish Him as in favor of exactions and monopolies. What, then, does He answer them so as not to say anything out of place, and to avoid all surprise? He requests them to show Him the money of the tribute, and, learning from the lips of the very ones who show it, that it is the image of Cæsar that is engraved upon it, He says to them: '*Render, therefore, to Cæsar the things that are Cæsar's and unto God the things that are God's.*' (Mark. xii, 17). Simplicity appears in this answer in its relation with the intention Jesus Christ had in His heart of teaching that the honor due should be given to the king of Heaven and the king of earth respectively; and prudence also appears, since by this answer He wisely avoids the snare these wicked men set to surprise Him."

"It is, then, the nature of prudence to regulate words and actions; but it has, moreover, another duty, and this is the choice of the proper means to attain the end proposed, and this end being none other than God it takes the paths the most direct and most certain, that lead to Him. We do not here speak of political and worldly prudence which, aiming at only temporal and sometimes unjust success, makes use, likewise, of but human, and, therefore, very doubtful and uncertain means. But we speak of that holy prudence, recommended to us by our Lord in the Gospel, which induces us to select the proper means to arrive at the end He proposes to us, and, this end being entirely divine, it is necessary that these means bear with it a relation and a proportion. Now we can choose the means adapted to the end we propose in two ways; either by our reason alone, which is often weak enough; or, guided by the maxims of faith that Jesus Christ has taught us, which are always infallible, and which we can follow without any fear of being deceived. Hence it is that true prudence subjects our reason to these maxims, and proposes to us, as an inviolable rule, to always judge of all things as our Lord has judged; so that when occasions present themselves, we ask ourselves: 'How has our Lord judged of such and such a thing? How did He act in such and in such circumstances? What has He said and what has He done in such and such cases?' And then we conform our conduct to His maxims and to His examples. Let us, then, gentlemen, take the resolution to act in this wise, and walk with assurance in the royal path wherein Jesus Christ will be our guide and conductor, and remember what He has said, that Heaven and earth will pass away but His words and His truths never. Let us bless our Lord, my brothers, and let us endeavor to think and judge as He, and do all He has recommended either by word or by example. Let us put on His spirit in order to co-operate with Him in His works; for, to do good is not all, we must, moreover, do it well, in imitation of our Lord, of whom it is said: '*He did all things well.*' (Mark. vii, 37). No, it is not enough to fast, to observe our rules, to perform the functions of the mission; we must, further, do these things in the spirit of Jesus Christ, that is to say, with perfection, for the ends and objects He Himself has instituted. Christian prudence consists, then, in judging, in speaking, and in acting as the eternal Wisdom of God, clothed in our weak flesh, has judged, spoken, and acted."

The Saint again said: "Where human prudence fails and sees nothing, there the light of Divine wisdom begins to dawn."

Finally, he made his prudent slowness the rule for others: "The works of God are done little by little; they begin and they progress. When God wished to save Noah with his entire family from the deluge, He commanded him to construct an ark that could have been completed in a short time; and yet, that he might do it little by little, He orders him to consume a hundred years in building it. God, similarly, wishing to conduct and introduce the children of Israel into the Promised Land could have had them make the journey in a few days, yet more than forty years went by before He granted them the grace to enter it. Again, having the design to send His Son into the world to atone for the sin of the first man, as that sin infected all other men, why did he delay more than three or four thousand years? Because He does not hurry in His works, and He does all things in their proper time. And, too, our Lord, coming upon the earth to work our redemption, could have come in perfect age without consuming thirty years in retirement, which might seem superfluous. Nevertheless, He has willed to be born a little child and to increase and grow in age, just as other men, in order to approach, little by little, the consummation of His purpose. Did He not sometimes say, speaking of what He had to do, that His hour had not yet come? And this to teach us not to advance too much in things that depend more on God than upon us, He could, even in His own time, have established His Church throughout the entire earth; yet He contented Himself with laying the foundations, leaving the rest to be done by His Apostles and their successors. Accordingly it is not expedient to wish to do everything at once and immediately, nor to think all is lost because everyone does not manifest an eagerness to co-operate with us in the little good will we have. What then must we do? Go on sweetly and calmly, pray to God a good deal; and act in concert."

CHAPTER XVI.

JUSTICE AND GRATITUDE.

I.

Vincent regulated and ordered his justice in accordance with the words of Our Savior: "Render, therefore, to God the things that are God's, and to Cæsar the things that are Cæsar's."

To God, above all, he, as a man, as a Christian, as a priest, faithfully rendered all the duties of religion. To men likewise, according to their rank and their relations with him, he paid every debt of justice. "Tribute to whom tribute; custom to whom custom; fear to whom fear; honor to whom honor; owing no man anything save charity, which he so tenderly exercised towards all that thus he might accomplish the entire law." He said to his community: "Gentlemen, let us care for the interests of others as well as for our own; let us be upright in our dealings, act loyally and equitably." With himself, justice went before everything else. He wrote one day: "Remember particularly to pray to God for me. Yesterday I found myself obliged to select between two duties, one to fulfill a promise I made, the other to do an act of charity to one who can do us a great deal of good, or a great deal of harm, and unable to satisfy both. I left the act of charity to fulfill my promise, and the person to whom I refer is very much displeased. But I am not so much concerned about that as to having yielded too much to my inclination, as, it seems to me, I did in doing the act of justice."

He scrupulously paid the debts of his community without waiting to be asked: and often he had the amount sent to the house of the creditor. "It is not just," he used to say, "to give them the trouble to come to demand what is legitimately due them."

He largely indemnified those who had to suffer from any accident on his part, no matter how involuntarily. One day his coachman having upset in the mud some loaves that were in front of a baker's shop, he immediately paid for them and ordered them sent to St. Lazarus.

The same coachman, another time, having broken a rotten bar that served to close a carriage entrance, he made him replace it with a new one worth four times as much.

He never received recompense for his good offices; never especially would he cast a favor in the way of equity to arrest its course. In a certain large city the missionaries were threatened in the possession of their establishment by some powerful persons, who had summoned them before the law. The governor offered to protect them on consideration that Vincent would befriend him at Court. "If it be in my power to serve you," the Saint wrote to him, "I will do so; but, I beseech you, leave the affair of the priests of the Mission in the hands of God and of justice to decide; for I do not desire to be in any place either by the favor or authority of men."

Though enjoying seignorial rights he was the enemy of discord and litigation. Yet he dispensed justice gratuitously and recommended that kindness and mildness should be exercised in his courts. He, himself, intervened whenever, for example, he learned there was danger of dissension between any two families of his domain, and his charity rarely failed to conciliate both interests and hearts. He dissuaded all those who counselled him from trying the law. "A lawsuit," he said, "is a morsel hard of digestion, and the very best is not worth the poorest accommodation." He said again: "A mutual agreement in actions at law is so acceptable to God, that He says to each one, '*Seek after peace and pursue it.*'(Ps. xxxiii.15.) He does not merely say we should accept this divine peace when offered us, but that we should seek it and run after it.

Much less would he patronize the law either for himself or for his houses. He wrote to one of his priests who had tried the law and had been defeated: "We have reason to go to law as little as possible; and when forced to do so, it is only after having taken counsel both within and without. We prefer to relinquish what we have than to disedify our neighbor."

His conduct in suits he could not avoid was full of charity. If on these occasions he approached the judges or had them visited, it was less for the purpose of recommending to them his own cause than to pray them to consider only justice. Plaintiff and defendant at the same time, he alleged without omission all that was in favor of his adversary as well as what availed himself. One would have said that he was an impartial councilor whose interest in the case had not been secured; or rather, he was partial only towards his opponent, whose points he brought out in far stronger light than his own. Besides, he went to see the magistrates as little as possible. All solicitation appeared to him as a violence done to justice. "A judge who fears God," he would say, "should pay no attention to any such. I, myself, when in the Council of the Queen, counted all representation as nothing, contenting myself to examine if the requests were just or not."

He spared the purse of the party opposed to him more than his own. Some of his priests, having an affair with certain tenants who were intractable and of bad faith, begged him to procure for them a *committimus,* in order to intimidate those men so addicted to chicanery. "Help yourself as best you can," Vincent answered. "I would be very sorry, for my part, to see these poor people forced to come so far to defend themselves."

The inhabitants of the valley of Puiseaux wished to levy a tax on the little farm of Fresneville, which belonged to the Congregation, and, in spite of his friendly efforts to the contrary, they invoked the law. They, therefore, came to Paris. The Saint received them as people associated with his own cause. He lodged them at St. Lazarus, had them placed by his side in the refectory, and defrayed the expenses of their return home. When the suit was on the point of being decided, he sent them notice that they might adduce in time their last arguments. In effect, they returned to Paris and betook themselves straightway to him as to the patron of their cause. He, himself, brought them to the attorney, where he aided them to establish their pretended rights. Much against his will, as it were, they were defeated; but he bore all the expenses of the proceedings, gave them their supper, once more lodged them for the night, and only allowed them to depart when he had put into the hands of each twenty sous for his journey home.

When he, himself, lost a case he submitted to the decrees of justice as to a judgment of God. No murmur, no complaint against either Providence or men; and he required his priests to imitate him in this. "Long live justice," he wrote on the 24th of October, 1659, to one of his missionaries in Genoa, "long live justice. You must believe that it is found in the loss of your cause. The same God Who gave you the good has taken it away; blessed be His holy name! Good becomes evil when it is not where God wishes it to be. The more we resemble our Lord naked on the cross the more will we partake of His spirit. The more we seek, as He did, the kingdom of God, His Father, in order to establish it within ourselves and in others, the more will those things that are necessary for life be given us. Live in this confidence and do not anticipate those years of sterility of which you speak. Should they come and you lack either the means of subsistence, or occupation, or both together, well, *in the name of the Lord*, let them come. It will not be through your fault but by the order of Providence whose conduct is always adorable. Let us, then, leave to our Father in Heaven the duty of guiding us, and let us, whilst on earth, strive to will as He wills and reject what He rejects."

Gratitude is a part of justice, for it is justice to be rendered to benefactors. Vincent, who was so just, could not therefore, be but grateful both to God, the source of all good, and to men who, for us, are the channels of His mercies. Every morning he returned thanks to God for His glory, for the glory He gave His Son, for that which He gave the Blessed Virgin, the holy angels, the apostles and all the saints. He, again, thanked Him for the graces conferred upon the Church, on all religious orders, and particularly for those conferred upon his own congregation. Finally, he thanked Him for the assistance given the poor, for the happy success accorded the arms of the king, for the victories won by Christian princes over infidelity, misery, or schism; in a word, for all events advantageous to Church or State. And as he believed himself unable to testify to God a complete acknowledgement, he invited his children, devout persons, and religious communities, to unite with him in this pious duty and would say: "*Praise the Lord with me!* Nothing gains the heart of God sooner than gratitude. We ought to employ as much time in thanking God for His benefits as we occupied in asking them." And then he would lament over the ingratitude of men; he would repeat the complaint of our Lord in reference to the nine lepers who did not return to thank Him. He strongly urged the flight from a vice which, he said, makes us unworthy to receive any favor either from God or men.

He tenderly thanked God for all the gifts conferred upon himself; and every year on the anniversary of his baptism, he requested the aid of the homage and prayers of his community so that his thankfulness might not fall short of the favors he had received from the Divine Bounty.

Grateful towards God, he was, likewise, thankful towards all who had rendered any service either to himself or to his community. Always believing that none owed himself anything he regarded all honor, all kindness done him as a favor, and he poured forth his thanks with a touching humility and an effusion of heart. "How good of you," he would say, "not to despise my old age! to support a poor miserable sinner! to listen to me so patiently and to suffer me in your presence! May God bless you! And thus he acted towards the least of his brothers. One of them having procured some holy water for him and kneeling for his blessing, he said: "Yes, my brother, may God bless and reward you." That was his customary formula. "In my inability," he always said or wrote, "to suitably thank you, I pray God to be Himself my thanks and your reward."

He acted in the same manner towards strangers, and even towards little children, thanking them for the slightest service, such as having helped him to mount his horse, and he would blame his companion for too much coldness in his thanks.

Still more, he considered, in example of our Lord, as done

to himself what was done to the least of those belonging to him, and was equally grateful.

He was even grateful towards those who rendered no direct service to either himself or his children; for instance, towards the poor country farmers, who, by their labors furnished the clergy with the means to live solely for the sanctification of the people. After having, one day, pictured a vivid representation of their sufferings in the public calamities, he said: "Alas! my brethren, while they slave themselves thus to nourish us we seek the shade and take our rest. Even in the missions where we labor the churches shelter us from the inclemency of the weather; we are not exposed to the wind, or rain, or to the rigors of the seasons. Surely, living thus by the sweat of these poor people, and on the patrimony of Jesus Christ, we should always reflect, in going to the refectory, whether we have actually deserved the food we are going to take. For my part, that thought often enters my mind and gives me great confusion. I say to myself: 'Wretch! have you earned the bread you go to eat? the bread you receive from the labor of the poor? At least, my brethren, if we do not gain it as they do, let us pray to God for them, and not allow a day to pass that we will not offer them to our Lord that He may be pleased to give them the grace to make a good use of their sufferings. We said, some few days ago, that God looks to the priests, particularly, to arrest the course of his indignation; He expects that they will do, as Aaron did, and station themselves with censers in their hands between Him and these poor people; or else, like Moses, they will make themselves intercessors to obtain a cessation of the evils they suffer for their ignorance and their sins, evils they, perhaps, would not have had to undergo had they received the necessary instruction and had care been taken of their religious welfare. To these poor, then, we should render these offices of charity as much to satisfy the duty of our condition as to manifest gratitude for the benefits we receive from their labors. Whilst they struggle against want and all the misfortunes that encompass them we must, like Moses, constantly raise our hands to Heaven for them; and if they suffer for their sins and ignorance, we ought to be their intercessors with the Divine Mercy, for charity obliges us to give them a helping hand to withdraw them from their misfortunes; and, moreover, if we do not occupy ourselves, even were it to cost us our lives, in instructing them and assisting them in their perfect conversion to God, we become, in some manner, the cause of all the evils they commit."

Much more did he manifest a lively gratitude towards his personal benefactors and those of his congregation.

His voyage from Maine to Anjou, in 1649, was signalized by two remarkable instances of gratitude. The young missionary, who accompanied him and had rescued him from a very great danger whilst crossing a river that was much swollen, little by little grew tepid, and less and less observant of rule, and his superiors soon found him indocile. Finally, tired of the yoke, he wished to cast it off entirely, and, notwithstanding all the ordinary efforts of Vincent to retain him in his vocation, he left.

At the end of a year he repented, and like the prodigal son he cried out: "I will rise and go to my father." He thereupon wrote to Vincent letter after letter, asking pardon and beseeching him to receive him among the number of his most humble servants, if not of his children.

Both to try him, and from repugnance to receive anew those who once had left, Vincent, for long, failed to answer. The missionary multiplied his letters and redoubled his importunity: "I am forever lost, my father, unless you reach me out a helping hand." At this, Vincent responded, not, however, to grant him his request, but to lay before his eyes the fault he had committed, and the impossibility of again receiving him.

Repulsed in all his assaults and exhausted in methods of attack he tried a final effort against the side the most accessible, and the most vulnerable of the heart of Vincent: "Sir," he wrote him, "I once saved the life of your body, save now that of my soul!" This opened the breach. "Come, sir" was he immediately answered, "come and you will be welcomed with open arms." It was not, however, into the Congregation of the Mission on earth, according to Vincent's beautiful expression, but into that of Heaven, that he was to enter. On the point of setting out, he fell sick and died, full of the hope he found in repentance and in the generous pardon so graciously accorded him.

The second instance is no less touching. On getting out of the water St. Vincent entered the farm house of the Goualeric to dry his clothes. Always at home among the poor, he entered into conversation with the farmer and learned that he was afflicted with rupture which caused him cruel torments. The holy priest, whom God had cured of a like evil, promised him, as soon as he returned to Paris, to send him a certain bandage that would give him instant relief. After having paid his host of the moment most liberally, and thanked him for the hospitality of his cottage with more earnestness than he would a noblemen for the hospitality of his castle he resumed his journey. His travelling was prolonged far beyond his calculations or desires. Nevertheless, he has scarcely set foot in Paris when he recalls his host and his promise. He sends the bandage and adds a letter wherein he reiterates all his thanks. And, as there was no sure way of reaching the poor peasant, he addresses all to the lady of the Marshall of Schomberg, of whose lands the Goualeric formed a portion, with the request to co-operate in the good work and recommend the peasant to the good will of her people.

Loving, esteeming those belonging to him more than himself he could not entertain less grateful feelings for the benefactors of his houses.

He provided for the support and settled for the rent of a poor woman for twenty-five, or thirty years, because she had nursed one or two of the plague-stricken of St. Lazarus.

The Jesuit Fathers of Bar had received into their house a missionary of Lorraine. He died with them and was buried in their church. Touched with this hospitality accorded to his child whilst living and when dead, the saint gave his community, for subject of conference, the necessity of gratitude. "I feel two things within me," he said, "gratitude and inability to refrain from praising the good."

Even those, to whose generosity obligations were attached, did not find him wanting in gratefulness. "We must not on that account," he said, "fail to show ourselves very thankful and pray to God for them as for our benefactors. We see that the Church, even, has had such a feeling of gratitude for her benefactors as to relax her discipline in their favor, granting to lay persons the right of patronage, such as we see existing in many places, though this right belongs to the Church alone. Why has she done this if it be not to prove her gratitude for those who have benefited her?"

A doctor of the Sorbonne, named Louis Calon, had given a considerable sum to the Congregation, and finished by founding a house of the Mission at Aumale, the place of his birth. Exhausted by labor, penance and mortification, more than from old age, he retired to Vernon, to the children of St. Francis, who received him as an apostle and as an emulator of their poverty. About a year before his death, Aug. 28th, 1646, Vincent de Paul, who learned of his destitution and the desire he had of going to St. Lazarus, wrote to him: "I thank God for the hope you give us of soon seeing you here, where you may take your rest after your great labors. Oh, sir, how welcome you will be, and with what joy I will embrace you! Come, then, and, I beg of you, do not delay. And I can assure you, we will take a very special care of your health, and you will be the master of all in the house, saying and doing just as you desire, but particularly will you have all power over me, who ever loved you with greater tenderness than I did my own father. If you need the four thousand francs with which you endowed the religious of St. Bernard, but which are appropriated to the Mission, we will with pleasure return them to you; it being but just, it seems to me, that a founder who is in want should receive assistance out of the revenue of the foundation he made. We will do more, for if you have need of the principal to maintain yourself in your old age, we will restore it to you, as we did to the pastor of Vernon. He gave us a revenue of six hundred francs, and afterwards, believing himself in want, requested its return, and we gave up both the income and the fund. But if you do not desire the principal, still, sir, enjoy the rent as you have done up to the present and we will continue the Missions which you have commenced and maintained with such blessings." But the children of St. Francis did not wish Mr. Calon to have recourse to the disinterestedness of the holy priest; they retained him with pleasure, and closed his eyes in death.

Vincent always acted in this manner towards the founders of his establishments and the benefactors of his Congregation. In September, 1654, he wrote to one of his priests: "We can never be sufficiently thankful, nor grateful enough to those who have founded our establishments. God has lately given us the grace to offer to a founder of one of our houses the money that he donated, because I believed him in want; and it seems to me I would have been greatly consoled had he accepted. And I believe that, in that case, the Divine Goodness itself would have been our founder and would not have permitted us to want. But even, were that not to happen, what a joy, my dear sir, would it not be to impoverish ourselves to relieve him who had wished to benefit us? God has already given us the grace to do this once, having actually restored to a benefactor (the pastor of Vernon) what he conferred upon us; and every time I revert to it I feel an unspeakable joy and consolation." And, the year following he wrote to a benefactor whom he imagined to be in straightened circumstances: "I beg you to use the property of the Congregation as your own. We are ready to sell all we have, even our chalices, to assist you. In this we would only do what the holy canons ordain, namely, to return to our benefactor in his need what he gave us in his abundance. I say this, sir, not for form's sake, but in the presence of God and as I feel it in the bottom of my heart."

In 1654, the Cardinal de Retz succeeded in escaping from his prison in Nantes, and fled to Rome. Son of the General of the Galleys, pupil of Vincent de Paul, Retz, even amid his intrigues, his political escapades, and gallantries, always showed himself the protector of St. Lazarus, and St. Lazarus, grateful as its founder, was inclined to sustain Retz in his disgrace. Vincent de Paul, without money, owing to the condition of the Congregation at that time and of France, borrowed three thousand francs to send the Cardinal. Retz, knowing the straightened circumstances of St. Lazarus, refused. He then was offered at least personal service. The Missionaries of Rome, therefore, received the proscribed Cardinal; but on whose order, and under what circumstances, and at what cost, the following letter, written to Ozenne, in Genoa, the 12th of March, 1655, will show: "Our house in Rome is in distress, as you may have learned by the Gazette of that Court. And the reason is because, by order of the Pope, they received the Cardinal de Retz, before they were aware of the King's prohibition to have any intercourse with him. The King, displeased at this act of obedience to the Pope and of gratitude to our archbishop, has had orders sent to Mr. Berthe and the other French priests to leave Rome and return to France. They have done so, and Mr. Berthe is now in France, or on the point of arriving, and through pure obedience. The affair may turn out as God pleases; but it is better to forfeit all than lose the virtue of gratitude."

We have elsewhere recounted what the affectionate gratitude of Vincent did for Adrian le Bon, the former prior of St. Lazarus. A part of this gratitude was exercised towards the old religious of St. Lazarus. Vincent desired that they be granted as much as conscience would permit, and made participants in the good works of the Congregation. "All our little merits," he said, "come from their gifts." He himself gave the example, and on every occasion showed them both in word and deed a singular deference. The sub-prior having been prostrated by a contagious disease, then prevalent at St Lazarus, he went to see him, consoled him, offered him his services, served him in reality, remaining with him and inhaling his infectious breath, and would have stayed with him night and day had he not been forced away.

The gratitude of Vincent towards the prior descended even to his servant. This man, after fifteen or sixteen years of service, left his master in spite of all the efforts and the liberal offers of our Saint to retain him. Having returned to his own province, he there almost entirely lost his mind. Without subsistence, without relatives, he fell into misery, wandering at hazard, and gaining his mouthful in any and every way, without knowing distinctly whither his steps led him. But Providence, which was conducting him, guided him one day to Paris, and his intelligence, awakened by the sight of so many objects that recalled ancient memories, discovered the way to St. Lazarus. He asked to speak with Vincent who, occupied at the time, sent him to dinner, promising to see him afterwards at leisure. At the first interview, and almost from the first words, the holy priest saw the sad state of the poor man. "It is the domestic of our benefactor," he said to himself, "and we must have pity on him and consider him as one of the family." And, in fact, he gave him a room at St. Lazarus and provided for all his wants till death.

The virtue of gratitude accompanied Vincent even into the arms of death, for two days before his end he profited of his little remaining force to pay a last tribute of gratitude to his two most illustrious benefactors, the Cardinal de Retz and the reverend Father de Gondi, the venerable General of the Galleys.

CHAPTER XVII.

DETACHMENT FROM EARTHLY GOODS, AND LOVE OF POVERTY.

I

The entire life of Vincent de Paul, considered either as a Christian, or as a founder and superior of a religious community, was one act of continual detachment. Having overcome the desire—legitimate, for that matter—of obtaining a benefice, having renounced one of the best parishes in the diocese of Acqs because he did not wish to acquire possession on the strength of the law's introduction, he no longer obeyed but the secret impulse that led him to possess nothing of his own. He lived poor among the poor at Clichy and Chatillon, poor again in the house of Gondi; after that he consecrated himself by poverty to the service of the poor.

Poverty inaugurated all his works. He accepted the foundation of Mister and Madame de Gondi only on the refusal of several communities; he refused, for long, the priory of St. Lazarus, and took possession of it only through obedience. And in that rich house, possessed of seignorial rights, superior of two congregations, in favor with the rich and the great, he was captivated anew with love for poverty, and he embraced it with a greater passion than does the miser riches.

He was poor in his room, a room more than modest, small and bare. Its walls were whitewashed, the floor devoid of carpet; for furniture, a deal table with a cover; two straw chairs; for a bed, a hard straw tick without a mattrass, and during the last years of his life without even linen; for all ornament a wooden crucifix and some paper pictures which a brother had, at different times, placed upon the walls, and which the Saint, retaining but a single one, had had removed as being contrary to poverty. There was neither fire nor fire-place, and that up to the age of eighty, when his children forced him to take another room because he had need of a little fire in order to dress his ulcerated limbs. But how he humbled himself for it! How he accused his sins as being the cause of subjecting him to such a misery which he called scandalous! With what parsimony he used the wood which, as everything else, he claimed to be the property of the poor! So, too, when in condescension to the entreaties of his children, he finally consented to permit a curtain on his bed, with what reproaches did he overwhelm himself for this *luxury*, which resembled the coarse serge that is seen on the beds of the poorest peasants in the country! And still he feared that his room was too luxuriously fitted up. Hence, when they made the visit to the rooms he required them also to visit his, in order to remove whatever might be superfluous. He said one day: "There are two coverlets in my room which I use in perspiring; let them be removed." The same bareness was visible in the lower room where he received persons of the highest rank. A brother had once placed a piece of old carpet before the door to keep out a cold wind that blew through; he had it taken away the very same day. The poverty of the clothes he wore at Court has been noticed; at home they were still poorer. If he were told that his collar was worn, or that his hat was too old, he would answer with gentle pleasantry: "Oh, my brother, the King can have no more than a collar that is not torn and a hat that is not worn." Equally poor were all the objects destined for his use: his umbrella, for instance, is still preserved, and is made out of a coarse stuff dipped in wax, not unlike the rude canvass the poor women, who sell their wares on the street, use as a protection against the weather.

Poor in his costume, he was not less so in his food; and yet, every day when seating himself before his poor pittance, he exclaimed: "Ah, wretch, you have not labored for the food you eat." When he found himself in the country without money he was delighted because he could then go to the house of some poor peasant and ask a piece of black bread for the love of God.

His poverty included even the ornaments and vestments used in the church of St. Lazarus; he would have them plain and cheap, save on grand solemnities. He was liberal only in what concerned the glory of God, and the spiritual and corporal benefit of the poor; then he became prodigal, and scattered money as so much dust, and was never troubled with fear in contracting even large debts.

His detachment embraced his Congregation as well as himself. "This tongue that now speaks to you," he one day said to his community, "has never, through the mercy of God, asked for anything of all that the Congregation now possesses; and were it necessary only to take a single step, or to pronounce one solitary word to have the Congregation established in the provinces and in the large cities, to have it multiplied and called to important duties, I would not wish to pronounce that word, and I trust Our Lord would give me the grace not to utter it. This is the disposition of my heart, which is to let the Providence of God do everything."

His action in regard to the Daughters of Charity was similar. He never made any effort to maintain them in places he had sent them, against the wishes of those who had called for them, and on the slightest intimation of their pleasure he withdrew them. The administration of the hospital of Nantes having manifested a desire to substitute for the Daughters of Charity the Hospitaller nuns, he, ever disinterested, immediately wrote to the gentlemen that he knew a great deal of good concerning these nuns, and that if they wished to dismiss the Daughters of Mademoiselle Le Gras, he very humbly begged them to do it without ceremony. At the same time he wrote to Mademoiselle Le Gras, who then was at Nantes: "This is what our Lord would do were He still living on earth. The spirit of Christianity wishes that we should enter into the sentiments of others, and God will, if we place no obstacle, turn this change to His greater glory."

Not only was it his maxim, and his practice to solicit nothing, not even a place to dwell in, after the example of our Lord "who never had a house and did not wish to have any," but, during the public misfortunes, he even refused the rich donations that were offered him, protesting that the poor had greater need than he. He once refused as much as eight hundred thousand francs which were offered him to build a church, because he believed he could not accept them without doing an injury to the poor of Jesus Christ.

His disinterestedness shone particularly in the Council of Conscience. Admirable disinterestedness, of which, according to the testimony of the minister of state, Le Pelletier, the secretary, Le Tellier, said: "In quality of secretary of state I was in position to have a great deal of intercourse with Mr. Vincent. He has accomplished more good works in France for religion and the Church than any one I ever knew; but I have particularly remarked that in the Council of Conscience where he was the principal actor, there was never question either of his own interests, or of those of his congregation, or of the ecclesiastical houses he had established." A disinterestedness all the more praiseworthy, as his houses, nearly all poor, were moreover burdened by the gratuitous nature of their chief functions. The acquisition of a few benefices would have placed them in ease. He never thought of it. And if sometimes benefices were attached to his seminaries this occurred only at the earnest entreaties of the possessors, or of the legitimate collators. And even then it was difficult to obtain his consent, the only share he ever had in securing them. And, moreover, he imposed the law that revenues should be devoted, not to the services of the houses, nor to the advantage of his members, but to the education of young ecclesiastics. If he learned that the Queen was about to confer some favor on him, he immediately had it given to another. What was his dismay when the rumor got abroad that she intended to demand for him the Cardinal's hat! He would have listened to his death sentence more willingly than he did to the compliments some that of his friends addressed to him on that occasion. The Roman purple would, truly, have been for his humility the purple of martyrdom.

Is it necessary to add that this disinterestedness was proof against all corruption! One of his most intimate friends came to him, one day, to offer him, in the name of certain parties, one hundred thousand francs to obtain his influence in the Council in favor of certain projects that contained nothing burdensome in regard to the people, but which could hurt the interests of the clergy. Vincent might have said as did St. Peter to Simon: "*May thy money perish with thee . . . . for thy heart is not right in the sight of God*," (Acts. viii, 20). He contented himself in saying with more gentleness: "God preserve me from it! I would rather die than say a word on the subject."

Disinterested in acquiring, he was indifferent in preserving what he already possessed, having no attachment to anything here below. Troubled in his title to St. Lazarus by the priests of St. Victor, he preferred to abandon all rather than maintain his right in law, and came to the determination of defending his title only out of deference to wise counsels.

He was the same in regard to all his houses, whether intrigue or armed force disputed his possession. After the battle of the Faubourg St. Antoine, when his house was in danger of being pillaged by both armies, he ordered the entire community to repair to the church, and there, prostrate in the presence of the God of the poor, to offer Him all its possessions, and, in case of ejection, thank Him very humbly for having despoiled them.

But his detachment won its triumph in the proceedings relative to the Orsigny farm. He had acquired this farm on very onerous conditions, and had quite considerable expense in improving it. He was on the point of enjoying the results when an unjust sentence deprived him of all.

Brother Du Courneau, his secretary, brought the news of the decision. "God be blessed," he exclaimed, and he repeated this cry of loving resignation five or six times with increasing fervor. From his room he repaired to the Church and remained a long time in adoration and prayer; in coming out he again repeated: "God be blessed, only one thing causes me sore trouble and it is to have, by my sins, caused such a loss to the congregation."

Again in his room, he immediately wrote to a friend. "Sir, good friends impart to one another the good and the evil that befall them, and, since you are one of the best we possess in the world, I must inform you of our loss of the suit and of the Orsigny farm, not, however, as an evil but as a grace that God has bestowed upon us, and I beg you to aid us in returning thanks. I term graces from God the afflictions He sends us, especially when they are well received. But His Infinite Goodness, having prepared us for this loss before the judgment was rendered, has also given us the grace to submit to it with resignation, and, I presume to say, with as much joy as if the decision were favorable. This would seem a paradox to one not blessed, like you, sir, in the things of Heaven and who would not know that conformity, in adversity, to the good pleasure of God is greater good than all temporal gain. I humbly beg you to permit me thus to pour into your heart the sentiment of my own."

As the case was lost by the dissent of only three or four judges out of twenty two, Vincent was advised to renew the proceedings and take up an appeal: "No," he wrote, "we would be accused of too much attachment to wealth, a charge already made against ecclesiastics, and we might, in causing ourselves to be accused in court, do a wrong to other communities and scandalize our friends. Besides, I have extreme difficulty in going against the counsel of our Lord, Who wishes that those, who have undertaken to follow Him, would not entangle themselves in the law. That we have already done so was because I could not, in conscience, abandon a property so legitimately acquired, a property, moreover, belonging to the community, and of which I had only the administration, without doing all in my power to preserve it. But now, since God has discharged me of His obligation by a sovereign decree that has rendered my further care unnecessary, I think we ought to do no more. And all the more so, as, should we fail a second time, it would be a sort of dishonor which might prejudice the duty and the edification we owe the public. . . . Moreover, as one of our practices in missions is to settle all disputes and difficulties among the people, it is to be feared that, were the congregation to become obstinate and renew the suit by an appeal to a higher court — the last resource of all chicanery — God would deprive it of the grace to further effect reconciliations.

Vincent, therefore, renounced a new prosecution of his rights. He gave up the farm of Orsigny, but not the obligations he had contracted in accepting it, and he continued the prayers and other spiritual obligations of the donation.

II

It remained to inspire the members of his community with his own detachment and induce them to acquiesce in this unjust judgment as if it were the sentence of Heaven. He gave them a spiritual conference on the subject, wherein, having related the advice given him to have recourse, for his protection, to a higher court, he cried out: "Oh, my God, we will take care not to do so! Thou Thyself O, Lord, hast pronounced this decree; it will be, if pleasing to Thee, irrevocable. And, not to delay the execution, we now make a sacrifice of this property to Thy Supreme Majesty. And you, gentlemen and my brothers, I pray you to add a sacrifice of praise; let us bless the Sovereign Judge of the living and the dead for having visited us in our day of tribulation; let us return Him infinite thanks, not only for having withdrawn our affections from the goods of this earth, but also for having in reality stripped us of what we had, and let us beg of Him the grace to love this deprivation. I love to believe that we are all joyful in this temporal loss; for since our Lord says in the Apocalypse: '*Those whom I love I chastise,*' (Apol. iii., 19,) must we not love chastisements as we would the tokens of His love? But it is not enough to love them; we must rejoice in them. Oh, my God, who will give us this grace! Thou art the source of all joy, and outside of Thee there is no true joy! It is of Thee, then, we demand it. Yes, gentlemen, let us rejoice since it seems that God has found us worthy to suffer. But how rejoice in sufferings, since they naturally displease, and we try to avoid them? In the same manner as we do, when sick, in remedies. We know that medicines are bitter and that the very sweetest of them create an involuntary shudder. And yet we swallow them gladly; and why? Because we love our health which we hope to preserve, or recover by means of the medicines. These afflictions, which of themselves are disagreeable, contribute, nevertheless, to the good condition of a soul or of a congregation; by them God purifies it as gold is purified by fire. Our Lord in the Garden of Olives felt only agony, and on the cross only sorrow which was so excessive that it seemed, deprived as He was of all human succor, as if He were abandoned also by His Father. Yet, in these terrors of death and these excesses of His passion, He rejoices in doing the will of His Father, and, rigorous though it be, He prefers it to all the joys of the world; it is His meat, His delight. My brethren, such should be our gladness when we see His good pleasure accomplished in us by means of the humiliations, losses, and troubles, that may come upon us: '*Looking*,' as St. Paul says, '*on Jesus, the author and finisher of faith, Who, having joy proposed to Him, underwent the cross, despising the shame.*' (Heb. xii., 2.) The first Christians were imbued with these sentiments, according to the testimony of the same Apostle. '*And received with joy the plundering of your goods.*' (Heb. x., 34.) Why will we not, with them, rejoice, to-day, in the loss of our property? Oh, my brethren, how great a pleasure it is to God to see us assembled for that purpose, to behold us entertaining ourselves with it and to see us exciting this joy within us. We are become, on the one hand, a spectacle to the world by the disgrace and the shame arising from this sentence which publishes us, it seems, as unjust detainers of another's good. '*We are made a spectacle to the world and to angels and to men.*' (I Cor. iv., 9.) '*By reproaches and tribulations made a spectacle.*' (Heb. x., 23.) But, on the other hand: '*My brethren, count it all joy when you shall fall into divers temptations.*' (James i., 2.) Let us look upon our loss as a great gain; for God has, with this farm, deprived us of the satisfaction we felt in possessing it and of the pleasure we took in sometimes going to see it; and this recreation, being agreeable to the senses, would have been like a slow poison that kills, as a knife that cuts, like a fire that burns and destroys. But now, through the mercy of God, we are delivered from this danger; and the Divine Goodness wishes to inspire us, now that we are exposed to want in temporal things, with more confidence in His Providence, and to oblige us to abandon ourselves to it entirely for all the necessities of this life, as well as for the graces of salvation. Oh, were it pleasing to God that this temporal loss were recompensed with an augmentation of confidence in His Providence, with greater abandonment to its direction, with a greater detachment from earthly goods and renunciation of ourselves, oh, my God, my brethren, how happy we would be! I will hope in His paternal bounty, which does all for the best, that this grace be accorded us.

"What, then, are the fruits we ought to gather from all this? The first is to offer to God all that remains of our goods and consolations, as well temporal as spiritual. To offer ourselves to Him in general and in particular, but in the proper spirit, that He may absolutely dispose, according to His good pleasure, of our persons and of all that we have. To offer ourselves in such a manner that we will always be prepared to leave everything and accept any inconvenience, ignominy, or affliction that may come upon us, that thus we may imitate Jesus Christ in His poverty, His humility, and His patience.

"The second is never to have recourse to law, no matter what our right may be, or, should we see ourselves obliged to call in its aid, to do so, provided our title be entirely clear and evident, only after having essayed every imaginable means of settlement; for he who trusts in the judgment of men will often find himself deceived. We will put in practice the counsel of our Lord, who says: '*If anyone will take away thy coat let him have thy cloak also.*' (Matt. v. 40). May God grant the Congregation this disposition! We must hope that, should it prove faithful in this practice and steadfast in never departing from it, His Divine Goodness will bless it, and if with one hand He takes away He will give with the other."

Whether the family of Vincent was dispossessed of any piece of property, or its services no longer required in any locality, he always preached the same detachment. On these occasions he wrote to those whom he was obliged to recall: "After having rendered your account to the Grand Vicars, and received a receipt for what you have, as according to inventory, you will deliver all into their hands and gracefully take leave of them, without a single word of complaint, or any expression of content to leave the place, and you will pray that God may bless the city and the diocese. I would especially beg of you not to say anything in the pulpit, or elsewhere, that could show the slightest discontent. You will ask the blessing of these gentlemen, and have all your little family do the same, and, at the same time, ask it for me who desires to prostrate myself at their feet in spirit with you."

He taught them, when in the greatest distress, to be reassured in regard to the future, and to place all their trust in Providence. One of his priests representing to him, one day, the poverty of his house, he asked him: "What do you do when necessaries fail the community? Do you have recourse to God." "Yes, sometimes," answered the priest—"Well," he replied, "that is the effect of poverty; it makes us think of God and elevate our hearts to Him, whereas, were we in comfortable circumstances we might, perhaps, forget Him. For this reason I am rejoiced that poverty, both voluntary and real, is practised in all our houses. There is a hidden grace in poverty that we do not know." "But," rejoined the priest, "you procure for others what they need, and you neglect your own." "I hope God will forgive you these words," returned Vincent, "I see you said them simply without meaning anything; but know that we will never be rich until we become like to Jesus Christ."

His priests, having as yet no fixed abode in Rome, he wrote to them: "Can we be better off, or more agreeable to God, than when we are just as God wants us to be, provided, indeed, we will acquiesce in submission to His holy guidance, acknowledging that we are unworthy a more convenient abode, that the one we have is far better than our deserts, and more suited to the designs that God has on us? For, if we are not destined to remain, we have no need of a fixed habitation, nor, if we wish to follow our Lord who had none, should we have a house of our own? If we do not love humiliation when God gives us the occasion to practise it, will we seek it when in more honorable circumstances? Let us remain humble and be content in poverty, because, then, people seeing our mean condition will despise us. Then we will begin to be true disciples of our Lord. '*Blessed are ye poor: for yours is the kingdom of God.*' (Luke vi, 20). It is, then, in Heaven they will be lodged. Is it not a beautiful place for us? Oh, my God, give us the grace to prefer the means that conduct thither to the pretentions and conveniences of earth."

Such was the spirit of the Mission from the very beginning. The Saint said one day: "The Congregation, still in its infancy, being composed of only three or four, went to Mount Martyr (with the exception of the miserable man now speaking, he being indisposed) and recommended itself to God through the intercession of the holy martyrs, that it might enter into the practice of poverty, then and since so well observed by a great portion of the community."

To maintain this spirit of poverty among them, the Saint often gave it as the subject of their conferences: "You should know, gentlemen," he said, "that this virtue of poverty is the very foundation of this Congregation of the Mission. Alas! what would become of this Congregation should attachment to the goods of the world creep in? What would become of it did it give entrance to the desire of riches which, the Apostle says, is the root of all evil? Some great saints have said that poverty is the bond of religious orders. We are not, in truth, religious, it having been found inexpedient to have us such, and, moreover, we are not worthy to be, though we do live in common. Still it is, nevertheless, true, and we can say it also, that poverty is the bond of communities, and particularly of ours; it is the bond which, releasing us from all earthy things, unites us perfectly to God. Oh, my Savior! Give us this virtue which binds us inseparably to Thy service, so that, henceforth, we may desire and seek only Thee and Thy glory."

He then indicated more clearly and more completely its necessity and its excellence. "Our Lord," he said, "being the sovereign master of all riches, having created them all, and, therefore, being their legitimate possessor, witnessing the great disorder the desire and possession of these riches occasioned on the earth, wished to remedy it by practising poverty. And for this purpose, He became so poor that He had not whereon to lay His head. He desired, too, that the Apostles and Disciples whom He admitted to His company, should practise the same poverty, as also the first Christians, who, as we read, possessed nothing in proper but had all things in common. Our Lord, then, seeing the great ruin the evil spirit caused in the world by the possession of riches, which were for a great many a source of destruction, has wished to repair the evil by a contrary remedy, namely, by the practice of poverty.

"'Blessed are the poor in spirit: for theirs is the kingdom of Heaven,' (Matt. v. 3.) This is the first lesson of Our Lord. What first escapes the lips is that which most fills the heart. But the first words of Our Lord are these: 'Blessed are the poor'— a mark of his great love and esteem for poverty. More, still, in what does the good pleasure of God consist? In this, that He desires that those, who love Him, love without reserve. Now, those who have made a vow of poverty have severed all ties and retain affection for nothing. They are, then, forced, as it were, to direct their affections and their love towards God; for life is impossible without love. But, since, by the vow of poverty we have no longer affection or love for earthly and created things, we must have both for the Uncreated Good, and for things of Heaven. Having, therefore, made this vow of poverty we are no longer attached to anything; neither to honors, nor to riches, nor to pleasures. And then, will our heart be devoid of love? It must, therefore, direct its love to God. Consequently, the vow of poverty is but a sovereign and perfect means of properly loving God. Let us well understand this truth, that we abandon the riches of earth to possess those of Heaven. I desire to make profession of it; and, in withdrawing my love from false gods, to love and enjoy the only true God, I reject trifles, and corruptible and perishable riches that I may possess those that are eternal and enduring. Oh, my Saviour, what a happiness!"

Another day he compared the soul, not free from all attachment, to a man firmly bound, hand and foot, to a tree, that can neither liberate himself, nor go and seek necessary sustenance. He will, consequently, die of hunger or be devoured by wild beasts. Image of a soul fastened with the love of the goods and conveniences of this world! It thinks of them, night and day, and the thought will not away; it seeks none who may deliver it and give it life; it is, then, in great danger of being devoured. Oh, my Saviour, is it possible that we will not endeavor to cast off such bonds? What! a little bird, ensnared in a trap, struggles night and day to regain its freedom, and we, when entangled in an evil attachment, will take no pains to free ourselves! The example of that little bird will condemn us before the tribunal of God."

And, arming his charity with invective and anathema, he added one day: "Woe, woe, gentlemen and my brothers, yes, woe to the missionary who shall allow himself to be attracted by the perishable goods of this life! For he shall be ensnared; these thorns will remain imbedded in him and these ties continue to fret him. And should this misfortune happen the Congregation, what, then, will be said? And what sort of life will be led in it? Individuals will say: 'We have so many thousand francs income, we ought to take our ease. Why go teach in the villages? Why labor so much? Let the poor people of the country alone; their parish priests, if such be their good pleasure, will tend to them for us; we can live quietly without giving ourselves all that trouble.' See how idleness will follow in the train of avarice; the only thought will be how to preserve and augment temporal goods, to gratify self. And then may be said farewell to all the exercises of the Mission, and to the Mission itself, for it will no longer exist. You need but consult history to find an infinity of examples of how riches and abundance of temporal possessions have brought about the ruin, not only of many ecclesiastical personages, but also of entire orders and communities, because they had lost the spirit of their first poverty."

And, falling back on himself, in one of his ordinary returns of humility, he exclaimed: "Oh, my Savior, how can I, who am so miserable, speak of this! I who have had formerly a horse, a carriage, and who, now, have a fire in my room, a curtain on my bed, and a brother to wait on me; I, of whom such care is taken that I want for nothing! Oh, what a scandal I give the Congregation by my abuse of the vow of poverty in all these and other like things! I ask pardon of God and of the Congregation, and I beg it to bear with me in my old age. I have difficulty in bearing with myself, and it seems to me I have deserved to be hung at Montfaucon. May God grant me the grace to correct myself, though too old, and to retrench as much as I can in all these things."

CHAPTER XVIII.

MORTIFICATION.

I

Detachment from things of earth and love of poverty include mortification. But we must study more directly in our Saint the special virtue designated by this name.

So faithful a disciple of the Savior, Vincent could not fail to bear in his body and in his entire being, according to the counsel of the apostle, the mortification of Jesus Christ. Therefore, like the Savior's life, His was but a continual sacrifice. And this sacrifice was all the more meritorious and agreeable to God as it was the more humble and the more secret. For, founder and head of a congregation destined to serve as a model both to clergy and people, and therefore obliged to show externally only those virtues which true Christians and good ecclesiastics might emulate, he confined himself entirely to a life well regulated, equally removed from culpable weakness and from a rigor too severe and forbidding. But the cross of Jesus Christ did not lose any of its claims; he paid to it, interiorly and in secret, the tribute of homage and imitation which, in public, he seemed to refuse.

He sacrificed to it all the love of man: the love of honor and self-esteem, unveiling before the eyes of all, as we have seen, his lowly birth and his pretended weaknesses whether in the order of nature, or of grace; the love of reputation, and of gratitude on the part of others, the desire of friendship which he always forced to yield to duty, fearing neither contempt, nor hatred, nor vengeance; the love of parents and of country, constantly calling to mind that, priest according to the order of

Melchisedech, he should forget all genealogy; that, priest of Jesus Christ, he should know neither mother, nor brother; that, apostle of the Gospel, he should prophesy everywhere save in his native land. Having become priest, and, in particular, when once intrusted with the portfolio of benefices, he made it a law to ask nothing either temporal or spiritual for himself, or for his family. In vain did the priests of the locality, and even some of his missionaries represent to him the straightened circumstances of his relations and the severe labor to which they were condemned, and urged him to do something for them: "What," he asked, "are they poorer than before, and can their arms no longer suffice to procure a living for them suitable to their condition in life?" And reassured on these two points, he added: "They are, then, indeed happy, for they execute the divine sentence which has condemned man to gain his bread in the sweat of his brow."

The only share which the family of Vincent ever had in the immense charities that passed through his hands was the sum of a thousand francs, and then it owed it to extraordinary misfortunes. This sum had been given the holy priest for his relations by his friend, Du Fresne. Vincent accepted it; but he said to Du Fresne: "My family can live as it has up to the present, and this increase of wealth will not render it more meritorious. Besides, it alone would profit by it. Do you not believe a good mission given to all the parish would be of more value before God and men?" Du Fresne could not deny this, and the money was laid aside for that purpose. But occasion failing to present itself, the civil wars intervened and desolated the provinces, especially Guienne. None suffered more than Vincent's relations; they lost their little all, and some even their lives. This was about the year 1656. Vincent received the most distressing information concerning his family. His friend, the canon of St. Martin, the Lord of Pouy, wrote to him that they were reduced to beggary; the Bishop of Acqs, who visited Paris that year, told him: "Your poor relatives are badly off, if you do not take pity on them they must experience great difficulty in procuring the necessaries of life. Some of them died during the war, and there are others who are living on alms." "See in what state my poor relations are," added

Vincent in relating this to his priests, "they are reduced to beggary! to beggary! And I, myself, had not God given me the grace to be a priest, and to be here, would be as they are. But what is to be done? The property of the community does not belong to me, and it would be giving a bad example to dispose of it." It was then that he remembered the money handed him by Du Fresne. "Blessed be the Divine Providence," he cried out, "that did not permit me to send missionaries to Pouy! It evidently reserved this alms for my poor family. And, full of joy in being able, this time, to reconcile his disinterestedness with his tenderness for his family, he hastened to place the thousand francs at the disposition of the canon St. Martin whom he begged to distribute it.

This soul, so loving, could not exclude from its universal charity those whom time and the order of God had inscribed on it even before the poor themselves. And, consequently, was he obliged to make use of the most cruel efforts of virtue to suppress and extinguish in it the explosions of a love that ever tended to manifest itself in benefits, and no mortification cost him more. "Do you imagine," he said one day when pressed to assist them, "do you imagine I have no love for my relations? I have for them all the feelings of tenderness and affection that anyone can have for his family, and this natural love impels me sufficiently to aid them. But I must act according to the movements of grace and not of those of nature, and I must think of the poor the most abandoned, without stopping at ties of friendship or relationship."

There came a day when the Saint had especial need to call to his aid his principles of mortification in order to struggle against his love for his relatives. In 1623, after a mission at Bordeaux, finding himself at the very door of his family, he determined, by the advice of his friends, to pay them a visit. He had for a long time resisted this advice, objecting the example of many good ecclesiastics who had at first done great good away from their native place, but, having revisited their home, were, on their return, entirely changed, had become useless to the public, and were as much immersed in the affairs of their family, as before they were devoted to the works of their holy ministry.

He obeyed, however. In doing so, he yielded less to the needs of his heart, charmed nevertheless to revisit his own, than to the design of strengthening them in virtue, of teaching them to love and prize their lowly condition, and of declaring to them, once for all, that in the future, as in the past, they should count for their livelihood on the labor of their hands alone. He wished to reawaken the reminiscences of his humble childhood, of his infant piety, and to consecrate his priesthood and his mature years to the God of his childhood. On the morning after his arrival, he renewed, in the parish church, the promises of his baptism, and offered himself anew to the Lord on the very spot where he received, with the seal of a Christian, the breathings of the apostolic spirit. During his stay at Pouy, he greatly edified his relatives and all the honest villagers by his piety, his prudence, his temperance and his mortification. These good people remarked especially,—let us not draw back in presence of these simple details — that he drowned his wine in water, and that at night he removed the soft bed they had prepared for him, and lay down on the hard straw. On the day of his departure he went barefooted on a pilgrimage from the Church of Pouy to the Chapel of Our Lady of Bugloose. It was the same path that he, as herdsboy, often took with his beasts; to day, he, a priest, is escorted by his brothers and sisters, by his poor relatives, and by almost all the villagers justly proud of their compatriot. Vincent celebrated solemn mass in the chapel. After the ceremony he gathered all his relatives around a modest board; then he rose to take his leave of them. All fell on their knees to ask his blessing. "Yes, I bless you," he exclaimed with emotion, "but I bless you poor and humble, and I ask for you from our Lord the grace of a holy poverty. Never leave the condition in which He has been pleased to have you born. This is my most earnest recommendation and which I beg you to transmit as an heirloom to your descendants. Farewell, forever."

But Vincent had scarcely set out before he felt his heart breaking, and tears streamed from his eyes. He had just been the witness and the guest of the poverty of nearly all his people, and he left them so, when he had but to open his hand, to say a word, to bestow upon them wealth. There then arose within him between, the law he had imposed upon himself and his fraternal tenderness, a struggle the issue of which was long uncertain. "Wretch!" he cried out in this cruel agony, "this is the punishment of your disobedience to the spirit of detachment and abnegation so frequently recommended in the Scriptures to the ministers of the Gospel. Before this journey you thought only of the service of God, of works far removed from flesh and blood, and now all your thoughts turn on your people." But we must listen to him, fully relating this contest between nature and grace, in a conference he gave on mortification on the 2d of May, 1659. He said: "Having spent some eight or ten days with my relations in order to instruct them in the way of salvation and to remove from them all desire of riches, even telling them that they must expect nothing from me, that had I chests of gold and silver, I would give them nothing, because an ecclesiastic who possesses anything owes it all to God and the poor. The day I departed I was so overcome with grief in leaving my poor relations that I did nothing but weep the entire way, and weep almost without ceasing. To these tears succeeded the desire to assist and better them; to give such a one this, such a one that; thus, my heart softened by pity portioned out what I did have and what I did not have. I say this to my shame, and I say it because God, perhaps, permitted that, in order to make me the better understand the importance of the evangelical counsel of which we are speaking. This importunate passion to advance the well being of my brothers and sisters lasted for three months; it was a constant weight upon my poor mind. During it, whenever I experienced a little freedom, I prayed to God that He would be pleased to deliver me from this temptation, and I prayed so earnestly that, finally, He had pity on me. He took away from me all this immoderate tenderness for flesh and blood; and, though they have since then been reduced to live on alms, and are so even to-day, He has has given me the grace to commit them to the care of His Providence and to consider them happier than were they in abundance.

"I say this to the community because there is something grand in this practice so much recommended in the Gospel, excluding, as it does, from among the disciples of Jesus Christ all those who do not hate father and mother, brother and sister, and because our rule, following that counsel, exhorts us to renounce all immoderate affections for those belonging to us. Let us pray God for them; and if we can assist them in charity, let us do so; but be firm against nature, which always tending in that direction, will, if it can, turn us away from the school of Jesus Christ. Let us be firm."

From the time of this journey up to the day of his death, Vincent never again saw but a single member of his family, the nephew whose story we have related in the chapter on Humility, and whom he dismissed as he came, on foot, and with only ten crowns for his long way. And, moreover, he received this modest sum from the Marchioness of Maignelay— the only alms he ever solicited for his family. Later, he had a scruple for having even kept his nephew a few days, and he asked pardon on his knees for having given him to eat of what belonged to the poor.

Notwithstanding the ill-success of that journey some years after one of his brothers, the father, possibly, of this young man, had the thought of trying his chance. He had just lost a ruinous lawsuit and wished to reestablish his affairs. But in a letter of the 29th of August, 1635, written to a Mr. de Fontenay, Vincent, after having thanked him for what he had done for his brother during the trial, eagerly added: "In relation to his intention, as I have been informed, of coming to Paris to see me, I beseech you, sir, to dissuade him from the idea, as well on account of his age, as from the fact that when here I could not relieve him, since I have not the disposal of a single thing that I could give him."

He extended this mortification in matters of family to his native place. Once, when he had the idea of establishing there some of the priests of his Congregation, fearing this thought to be inspired by a natural feeling rather than by a movement of grace, he immediately said to himself: "Oh, wretch! of what are you thinking? Should not all places and countries be indifferent to you, and have not all souls equally cost the Son of God? Why then incline to succor some in preference to others?" And he abandoned his project.

The soul disclosing itself especially in speech, the interior mortification of Vincent manifested itself in the absolute empire he held over his tongue. A useless word never escaped him; still less a word of detraction, of boasting, of vanity, of ridicule or of impatience that could betray in him a vicious or undisciplined temper. He never spoke of himself save from a motive of charity; and when he sometimes did, it was without any feeling of self-love and simply to maintain the conversation, and he soon ceased, warned by the interest of his hearers, struck his breast and exclaimed: "I am a wretch, full of vanity and pride, who do nothing but speak of myself." He then asked pardon on his knees for the scandal he thought he had given.

But he gave willing ear to others relating what he already knew, both to mortify self-love which always delights to appear knowing, and not to deprive the speaker of his pleasure in narrating. He listened, particularly, without interruption or reply when reproaches and insults were addressed him that he might imitate the Savior in His passion; and like the Savior again, he prayed with gratefulness from the bottom of his heart, for those who outraged him.

In the perplexities of affairs, in losses, in misfortunes, never a complaint, never a murmur escaped him; only a loving acquiescence in the Divine Will, expressed ordinarily in these words: "God be praised! God be blessed! We must submit to His good pleasure and accept all that He will please to send us."

His exterior mortification was not less. Up to extreme old age he sought out all occasions wherein he could suffer. It was one of his maxims that mortification could be practised at every moment either in maintaining a painful, though modest, position, or in depriving the senses of the sight of agreeable objects, or in willingly suffering the inclemency of the weather and of the seasons. And he constantly reduced this maxim to practice. In 1649, in a journey he undertook for the purpose of visiting the houses of his Congregation, he condemned himself to the most rigorous penance and the most excessive privations. It was winter, and a very severe winter, which alone ought to have been sufficient and more than.

sufficient to satisfy the desire of suffering in an old man of seventy-three wandering from farm to farm, badly housed, and poorly clad. To the rigor of the season, he would add a still more rigorous abstinence. Rye bread, or bread made of beans was almost his only food, for all else that was placed before him he distributed to the peasants whom he invited to eat with him; and of this he partook so sparingly that he had time to read for the others during the greater part of the dinner hour.

He did not look on beautiful landscapes, nor at magnificent buildings. He never plucked a flower. To their perfume he preferred the fetid odor of hospitals, or of the sick room. Notwithstanding his sensibility to extreme temperatures he never took any precaution against cold or heat; he never wore gloves in winter, and his hands, like his limbs, were swollen and chapped.

He closed his ear to harmony of sound and to agreeable discourse in order to mortify the hearing as he did the sight. As to taste, he seemed to resemble the holy precursor, who neither ate nor drank. He would permit no distinction between himself and his brethren in the quality of his food, not even in the infirmities of old age. Coming in very late in the afternoon from his charitable expeditions, he directed his steps to the refectory only after he had long partaken of his spiritual food at the foot of the altar, the only nourishment for which he exhibited any eagerness. If the common repast was over, his mortification was overjoyed, for then he would have only what remained, and the more meagre and less appetizing it was, the more delicious and savory it appeared to him. For that matter, he seemed to have taste for nothing, still less did he have any preference. He was served with raw eggs by mistake; he ate them without a word, and it was known only the next day through the cook. If everything had already been served and nothing was left, he contented himself with a little bread. Were his wine removed he never asked for it, he drank the water. And yet this, so sober a repast, was his first, and often his only, meal in the day, for he entered very late, and, according to his habit, had taken nothing in the morning. When very old he was urged to take some broth before going out. "You tempt me, sir," he said to the priest who presented it to him. "Is it not the evil one that induces you to persuade me to thus nourish this miserable body, this vile carcass? Is this right? May God forgive you." Still, in his last days, he consented to take a drink in the morning, but by way of medicine; for it was a broth without meat, made of wild chicory and pearl barley, with no seasoning either of lard, butter, or oil.

And yet he had a strong appetite. One day, pointing to a loaf of bread weighing two or three pounds, he said: "If I yielded to my appetite, I could eat all that." But poor nourishment, and little of it, was not sufficient for his mortification; he held in reserve bitter powders which he sprinkled over what he ate to render it more disagreeable to the taste. Nature sometimes gave way, and at night they were obliged to bring him, when overcome by weakness, a morsel of dry bread, the only refreshment he would accept.

Such was the repast destined to repair the strength lost in a long day of work, and even for this, we have seen, he reproached himself, believing he had not merited it.

It was a constant fast with him. Nevertheless, he fasted more regularly twice every week and on all days ordained by the Church. When more than eighty years of age, he contented himself with the salt fish served to the community. When he came in after the others had finished they sometimes tried to deceive him, and served him fresh fish, but he asked what had been given to the others, and if he were not served the same he would not touch anything. In the evening a little bread, an apple, and water colored with wine formed his collation. He abstained from even this when he came a little late from the city; then, without taking any nourishment, he would retire to his room, or repair to the church to preside at a spiritual conference. He was so severe with himself that it was necessary to request the interference of the highest authorities to induce him to moderate his austerity, and at the prayer of his children, the Cardinal de Rochfoucault commanded him to take more care of a health that was precious to the Church.

After meals, his brethren had an hour for recreation; he never took any. Finally, all retired to rest, and soon St. Lazarus was buried in sleep; he alone watched. His nights were almost as laborious as his days. On entering in the evening he found a number of letters awaiting him; it was at night he answered them.

Most frequently, midnight struck and he was still at work. He, finally, thought of taking some rest. But not before taking a severe discipline as a chastisement for the many good works of the day, in which he discerned nothing but imperfections and sin; in the morning he had prepared himself for the work of the day by a like penance. A brother, whose room was adjoining, affirmed that that had continued for twelve years. It was for more than that; this practice went as far back as Chatillon, at least, where his hosts had often heard him go through this rough gymnastic, and where they found under his pillow, after his departure, a forgotten instrument of penance. From that time he never omitted it, not even when traveling, or whilst sick. But all this was only his ordinary and daily practice of mortification. He imposed upon himself extraordinary penances during the public calamities, in the general and particular needs of his Congregation, and particularly when he learned of some fault committed in any of his houses. Then, he began by giving himself the discipline twice every night for a week, to expiate the faults of others, which he always imputed to himself. "My sins," he said, "are the cause of all the evils that happen; is it not just that I should do penance for them?" After that, he sought a remedy for the evil and applied it. At all times he joined to the discipline the wearing of bracelets and pointed wire cinctures, which he sometimes replaced by a hair shirt, still preserved, the sight alone of which is enough to make one shudder.

At last he fell on his knees to say his final prayers, and make his daily preparation for death. He turned down his bed. What kind of bed this was, we have seen. For forty years, at least, it was the same; for, at the time of his journey from Macon, in 1617, the Oratorians, with whom he had stopped, entering his room early in the morning, noticed that he had removed the mattrass from his bed. If, as we have seen, he consented towards the end, to have a curtain hung around it, he still continued to sleep upon the straw. Very often on this wretched pallet he found neither rest nor sleep. Fever consumed him, his sores tortured him, he was bathed in sweat: no matter, at four o'clock in the morning, he was the first to rise; and, notwithstanding the swelling in his aged limbs, which he had to bandage after rising, he was in the church before the youngest, and the most healthy to commence anew the same round of labors and mortifications.

II

This habitual mortification was also with Vincent de Paul an habitual subject of discourse: "Be firm," he said continually, "be firm against nature: for if we once give it an inch it will take an ell. Let us be convinced that our advancement in spiritual life will be measured by the progress we make in this virtue of mortification, a virtue particularly necessary for those who are to labor for the salvation of souls. It is vain to preach penance to others if we ourselves do not practise it and if it do not manifest itself in our actions and in our conduct."

He redoubled his exhortations during the public evils; and to give effect to his words, he sometimes retrenched a dish at table, and, at others, ordered the substitution of black for white bread. He would say: "God afflicts His people. Ought not we, priests, be at the foot of the altar bewailing our sins? This is our duty. And, further, should we not forbid ourselves something in our ordinary nourishment in order to relieve them, to suffer with them, and share in the general misfortune?"

He said again, in a more general way: "Our Lord has so loved affliction and suffering that He wished to lead a life of sorrow; He became man that he might have the means of suffering. All the saints have embraced the same state, and those, to whom our Lord did not send severe sickness, sought out, themselves, opportunities to afflict and chastise their bodies. Witness St. Paul, who said, speaking of himself: '*But I chastise my body and bring it into subjection.*' (1 Cor. ix., 27.) This is what we, too, should do, we, who are in perfect health: we should punish and mortify ourselves to atone for the sins we have committed and for the daily sins of the world against the Divine Majesty. But alas! man is so wretched and miserable that not only does he not punish himself, but even often suffers with impatience the sickness and afflictions it pleases God to send, though they be for his good."

Mutual forbearance was one of the crosses and mortifications he especially recommended to his missionaries and Daughters of Charity.

He wrote to the missionaries, on the 13th of August, 1650: "It is with difficulty we succeed in loving the evil that comes to us from others. We are more susceptible of grief than of pleasure; the sting of the rose remains longer than its scent. The means to equalize this disparity is to embrace, with as much willingness, whatever may mortify nature as what may deprive it of pleasure, to incline our heart to suffering by the advantage it brings, and to be prepared to receive it, so that, when it does come, we may neither be surprised nor saddened.

"The Spiritual Combat counsels to represent to oneself all the untoward accidents that can arise, to struggle against them, and exercise oneself in the combat until one feels himself the victor, that is, resolved to suffer all willingly should they, in reality, come. However, we should not imagine extreme evils of which the bare thought affrights, such as certain tortures of martyrs, but rather picture ourselves in contempt, calumniated, down with a fever and the like."

He wrote to the Daughters of Charity, on the 8th of March, 1648: "I pray you, bear with one another. You go in company to eternity, and you are all spouses of Jesus Christ, our Savior; be united, then, more and more. Let no one take it to heart if another contradicts her, or if others speak and murmur against her. There is not a person in the world who has not something to endure from his neighbor. Even our Lord, Himself, among His disciples did not escape. We must pass by this way, or else live in a desert, separated from all. But woe to him who is alone! Let us, then, go together cheerfully and sweetly. We belong to God and are obliged to accept what He ordains and what He permits. We are repulsed, our actions are criticised, we are treated worse than servants; again, we are informed on, superiors listen to what is said to our disadvantage, the very worst is done against us.

Oh, Lord, my God, what beautiful opportunities to acquire humility, to exercise sweetness and patience, to make ourselves agreeable in the eyes of God, to become beloved of the glorious Virgin Mary, and all the heavenly court, and finally, to gain the hearts of those who made us suffer, for, sooner or later, they will recognize their fault, if we only do our little duty, and this we should do diligently and carefully. Let us, then, do it in the presence of God, with calmness of mind, with sweetness and condescension towards everyone; in this way, our actions will become golden and our recompense will be very great. But what must we do to make proper use of the contradictions and vexations which God sends us? We must love them. And the means to love that which is disagreeable? First, we must reflect that such was the constant practice of our Lord, while on earth, and, generally, such was the practice of all the saints; secondly, none go to Heaven save by way of tribulation and penance; thirdly, to suffer in this world is a necessity whether we will or not and only those, who love to suffer, do not, suffer; fourthly, if the Sisters of Charity, those whom our Lord has chosen among thousands to elevate to his love, do not wish to honor His passion in anything, who, then, will do so? You are Daughters of Charity: mortification is also a daughter of charity and ought, therefore, be your sister. Caress her, then, visit her often in prayer, and be mindful of her on occasion."

With the intention of mortifying an excessive tenderness for parents, he rarely gave permission to visit them. "I cannot advise you," he would write, " to go visit your parents, because our Lord has left us an entirely different counsel, not wishing one of his disciples to go home to bury his dead father, nor another to return and sell what he had to distribute it to the poor. And yet these were motives very holy and urgent. To this counsel He added His example. He returned to His own country but once, and then his countrymen endeavored to precipitate Him from the summit of a mountain. He permitted this, I think, to represent to us the spiritual dangers we incur by similar visits. Hence, you will perform an action very agreeable to God by mortifying nature in refusing it the journey. At the hour of death you will experience an indescribable consolation for having remained steadfast at your post, when flesh and blood united to divert you from it. I assure you, the advice I give you is what I would follow myself. We ought to have a very great difficulty in leaving the works of God for temporal affairs, and still more when it is only for a passing gratification, such as revisiting our home and to be seen by our family. For, when the time of separation comes, there is nothing but grief and tears; and, what is worse, these often remain afterwards subjects of distraction to servants of God, and, having received impressions and ideas but little conformed to their state of life, they sometimes lose the affection they had for their exercises."

The Saint has left us two conferences on this subject of mortification, the one of the 6th of January, 1657, to the Daughters of Charity, the other of the 2d of May, 1659, to the missionaries. In the conference to the Daughters of Charity he identifies mortification with Christian perfection: "Rivers," he said, "have their currents, and the boats that follow the stream constantly move, even without labor, because the river carries them on. But, if you wish the boat to go against the current you must employ horses, or oars, and if the oar be not constantly in the hand, the boat recedes in the direction whence it came. Now, it is the same with those who wish to serve God. If they desire to approach Him and advance in His good graces, they must labor, without ceasing, to make new progress in virtue; otherwise, they will discover that, instead of nearing Him, the distance insensibly increases, themselves falling back and drifting away. For, the practice of virtue is not according to nature. Nature inclines to the possession of beautiful objects, to the enjoyment of sensual pleasures and the craving after esteem and praise. This is our bent, and we follow it without difficulty, because it is as a current that sweeps us along. The sentiments of grace are totally opposed to those of nature. Grace leads towards things of Heaven and to the practice of virtue; it wills that the appetite be mortified, and satisfactions renounced. Nature tends towards things of earth, wills that we follow our passions, that we enjoy our pleasures, and drain their cup to the last drop. It is, therefore, certain, that if we do not continually labor to mortify ourselves and resist our passions, they will obtain the upperhand, and we will follow the propensities of corrupt nature. During life we must not cease laboring to mortify ourselves; and, even though we had already one foot in Paradise, we should not relax in our efforts to place the other there also, lest the foot outside succeed in withdrawing the one within, and thus ruin all."

The Saint then explained the practice of mortification, both interior and exterior, almost as we see in the following conference given on the 2d of May, 1659.

On that day he took as a text these words of Our Savior: "*If any man will come after Me, let him deny himself, and take up his cross.*" (Matt. xvi. 24. Luke ix. 23.) And he commented thus: "Our Lord says to us, you wish to come after me? Very well. You wish to conform your life to mine? Very good, again. But do you know that you must begin by renouncing yourself, and continue by carrying your cross? And this is not given to all; very few receive this grace. Hence it is that the many thousands, who followed to hear, abandoned Him and withdrew, not being found worthy to be His disciples because they did not possess the necessary dispositions to overcome themselves, to deny themselves, and to carry their cross.

"What is meant by denying oneself? It is the renouncing of our judgment, our will, our senses, and of our relations. What a life! To renounce one's entire self for the love of God, to conform one's judgment to that of another, to submit one's will, through virtue, to whom we should, and submit to the judgment of God in all things! It is thus that our Savior did. By judgment we understand knowledge, intelligence, and understanding. The Son of God was pleased to have it known that He had no judgment of His own, that His judgment was that of His Father, as He gave us to understand by these words: '*My doctrine is not Mine, but of Him that sent Me.*' (John vii. 16.) I attend to the judgment He passes on things and I judge the same.—How profitable it is for a Christian to submit his lights and reason for the love of God! Who denies himself better than he who surrenders his judgment? A question is proposed and each gives his opinion. Now, to renounce oneself in such a case it is not required to refuse to say what we think; we ought to present our reasons; but he, whose judgment is submissive, prefers to follow that of another rather than his own. Let us, then, as did Our Savior, accord our judgment with that of God, which is known to us by the sacred Scriptures, and let us use it only when our rules and our superiors are silent. In that case, *in the name of the Lord*, we can form our reasoning according to the sense most conformed to the spirit of the Gospel.

"Our Lord has equally renounced His will: '*For I always do the things that please Him.*' (John viii, 29). If we do the same we will be worthy to belong to His school. But, as long as we enjoy our own will, we cannot be in a proper disposition to follow Thee, O my Savior; we will obtain no merit in bearing with our trials, nor have any part with Thee.

"We should mortify our interior and exterior senses, watch continually over them and take especial care to subject them to God. Curiosity of the eyes is frequent and dangerous. And curiosity in hearing, oh! what a power it has to run away with our minds! Curiosity was the ruin of our first father, and he would have been totally lost had he not found the path of penance. Curiosity of touch may also have unfortunate results. We must, then, have a guard over ourselves that we give no rein to our passions, nor satisfy our senses.

"There is another thing which seems hard; still we must bow the head and yield. The Son of God has said in precise terms that, to renounce ourselves, we must hate our parents. But this is understood when they wish to hinder us from going to Him; for when they themselves conduct us to Him, or leave us free, He does not require of us this hatred. Again, it is not, properly speaking, to hate them, but to behave as if we did, I mean we must abandon them, and disobey them when they interpose to prevent us from obeying God and following Jesus Christ.

"¶Let us then renounce our parents, our country, . . ." Then the Saint cited himself as an example to prove what danger there is in too great a tenderness for family, and recalled that voyage of 1623, which we have already recited; he then proceeded: "Let us renounce the recollections of our past lives. Otherwise, we will turn with a lingering pleasure to our youthful follies, we will dwell on the affections we had, and on the vexations and sorrows we experienced. Now, nothing so much inflames the appetite for forbidden things as the recollection of their false joys.

"Let us renounce the devil and his pomps. 'But, sir,' you will say to me, 'we are poor priests who have already done so; we have but plain clothing, poor furniture and nothing that savors of pomp!' Oh, gentlemen and my brothers, let us not be deceived in this! Though we have poor raiment and mean rooms, can we not have a pompous spirit? Alas! yes. To aim to preach fine sermons, to be spoken of, to publish the good we do, to grow proud, this is to have the spirit of pomp. And, to combat this vice, it is preferable to do a thing less well than to take complacency in having done it well. We must renounce vanity and human applause; we must give ourselves to God, my brethren, so that we may separate ourselves from self-esteem and from the praise of the world, in which the pomp of spirit consists. It were better to be bound hand and foot, and cast into a burning fire, than to do or say anything to please men. In this connection, a celebrated preacher said to me, some days ago: 'Sir, when once a minister of the Gospel seeks after the honor and applause of men, he delivers himself up to the tyranny of the public, and, thinking to make himself important by his beautiful discourses, he becomes the slave of a vain and frivolous reputation.' To this we may add that he, who utters forth rich thoughts in a pompous style, is opposed to the spirit of Our Lord, who said: '*Blessed are the poor in spirit.*' (Matt. iii. 5.) Herein the eternal Wisdom shows how carefully evangelical laborers should avoid grandeur in action and word, and adopt a simple, humble, and common manner of speech and conduct, whereof He Himself has been pleased to give us the example. It is the evil spirit that delivers us to this tyranny of desiring to gain applause, and who, perceiving us disposed to go simply about performing our duty, whispers to us: 'That is, indeed, mean; it is too trivial, and very unworthy the grandeur and majesty of Christian truth!' Beware of such suggestions, my brethren; reject these vanities, I pray you by the bowels of the mercy of Our Lord, renounce this worldly and diabolic ostentation. Keep constantly before your eyes the simple and humble manner of Our Lord, of Him Who could have given renown to His works and sovereign efficacy to His word, and yet did not wish to do so; but, going still further, the more to confound our pride by His admirable humiliations, He has willed that His disciples should do greater things than He Himself. *You will do,* He says to them, *what I do, and you will do still more.* But, O Lord, why dost Thou wish that, doing what Thou hast done, they do still more? It is, gentlemen, because Our Lord permits Himself to be outdone in public actions in order to excel in those that are humble and secret; He desires the fruits of the Gospel, and not the noise of the world, and hence He has done more through His servants than by Himself. He has wished that St. Peter should convert, at one time, three thousand, and at another, five thousand persons, and that the entire earth should be enlightened by His Apostles, whilst He, Himself, though the Light of the World, preached only in Jerusalem and its neighborhood; He preached there, knowing that He would succeed less than elsewhere; yes, He addressed Himself to the Jews as the people most likely and capable of contemning and contradicting Him. He, then, has done but little, and His disciples, ignorant and uncouth, animated with His spirit, have done more than He. Why this? To give us an example of perfect humility. Oh, gentlemen, why not follow the example of such a Divine Master? Why not always yield to others the advantage, and choose for ourselves the worst and most humiliating works? For, assuredly, this is the most agreeable and the most honorable to Our Lord, and He ought to be our only aim and object. Let us, then, adopt His example. Here is a public action I perform; I can, in doing it, attract great attention; I will not do so, I will omit such and such which might give it some brilliancy, and draw on myself some praise. Two thoughts come to my mind: I will give expression to the less fine for humility's sake, and retain the more beautiful to sacrifice it to God in the secret of my heart.

"There is still another certain passion that is dominant in

many, and which we must carefully renounce: it is this immoderate desire of health and of being well, and this excessive care for its possession that urge us to do both the possible and the impossible for the well-being of our body. For this undue solicitude and this fear of suffering any inconvenience, which we perceive in certain persons, who apply their whole mind and entire attention to the care of their poor little life, are great impediments in the service of God, for they take away the liberty to follow Jesus Christ. Oh, gentlemen and my brothers, we are the disciples of this Divine Savior, and yet He finds us enchained slaves! And bound to what? To a little health, to an imaginary remedy, to an infirmary where all our desires will be attended to, to a house wherein we will be satisfied, to a walk we take to recreate ourselves, to a repose that savors of laziness. 'But,' some one will object, 'the doctor counselled me not to apply myself so much, to take the air, he advised a change in the climate.' Oh, misery and weakness! Do the great in the world leave their ordinary abode because they sometimes are indisposed? Does a bishop leave his diocese? A governor, his province? The citizen, his city? The merchant, his house? Do kings, themselves, do this? Rarely; and when they are taken sick, they remain where they happen to be. The late king fell sick at St. Germain-en-Laye, and, without having himself removed elsewhere, he continued there four or five months, in fact up to the time of his death, which was truly Christian, and worthy of a king most Christian. Attachment to life does not lack for pretext. I will be told: 'It is a participation of the Deity, and therefore must be preserved.' Yes, but it is self-love that seeks to conserve it. This is why our Lord has said: '*For whosoever shall save his life shall lose it*,' (Matt. xvi, 25). And elsewhere He adds that there can be no greater proof of love than to give one's life for his friend. But is not God our friend? And our neighbor, is He not also our friend? Would we not be unworthy to enjoy the existence He has given us, did we refuse to employ it for objects so noble?

"Another way to renounce ourselves is to put off the old man and clothe ourselves with the new, and this we do when we endeavor to free ourselves from our passions and imperfections. In this way he who was in the filth of sin becomes purified. I was addicted to pride. I delivered myself by making acts of humility. Whilst engaged in remedying my past negligence and combating my present cowardice, what do I? I purge myself of the old leaven that corrupts the entire mass, and I infuse life into all my actions by my vigilance and attention. Consequently, to labor thus a whole life-time, not only in correcting the vile and evil inclinations, but also in elevating our habits and our occupations to the level of the new man, Our Lord Jesus Christ, is to put away incessantly the old Adam and to clothe ourselves with the new.

"May it please God to give us the grace to become like to a good vine-dresser, who has his pruning knife always about him that he may cut away whatever he meets hurtful to the vines. And if they sprout more than he desires, and continually shoot out useless wood, he has his knife always ready, and often he holds it in his hand to lop off, as soon as he perceives it, whatever may be superfluous, that the sap may mount to the branches which are to bear fruit. It is thus we ought to cut away the unwholesome productions of depraved nature that never wearies in putting forth the shoots of its corruption; and then, they will not prevent Jesus Christ, Who is compared to the vine and Who compares us to the branches, from rendering us abundantly fruitful in the practice of holy virtues.

"Courage, then, let us work at mortification. Let no day pass without our making three or four acts of it, and thus we will become true disciples of Jesus Christ."

CHAPTER XIX.

CHASTITY.

I.

Chastity is the daughter of mortification. By mortification, in truth, the flesh is so reduced that the body seems no longer to exist, and, on the ruins of the sense, purity, like a heavenly flower, springs up. It is the life of angels under a material envelope. Such was the modesty of Vincent de Paul, and it was reflected from his heart on his countenance, and passed into his every word and his entire conduct. Whether he spoke or wrote, his words were always charitable; but never, when addressing a female, whether secular or religious, did he use a word too soft or too tender. He even refrained from the use of any expression which, though proper and becoming, might yet inspire the slightest evil thought. The word chastity was too expressive for his sensitiveness, because it suggested the thought of the contrary vice, and he preferred the more comprehensive term of purity. If he had occasion to speak of any fallen creature he designated her crime only by the vague expressions of weakness and misfortune, in order to remove all impure imagination, and herself he never termed other than fallen creature.

Pure as an angel, and so confirmed in grace that he no longer felt the sting of the flesh, he, nevertheless, made use of all the precautions of a man still subject to the assault of corrupt nature. We have told of his mortification. Who will describe his subjugation of the senses, particularly of his eyes, which he never fixed on any woman? With none did he confer alone, in private, but always before witnesses, and with the door of the apartment open. Be the condition of the person, who wished to speak with him, what it might, he never went, save accompanied by a brother who had a standing order to keep him in sight. One day, the lady of the Marshall of Schomberg came to the parlor of St. Lazarus, and the brother, out of respect and consideration, withdrew, drawing the door after him. Vincent immediately called out to him: "What are you doing, my brother? You know your duty is to keep the door open and your eyes on me."

He acted in the same manner with his ladies and even with his Daughters of Charity; he never, without necessity, visited either. "I must soon go to La Chapelle," he one day wrote to Mademoiselle Le Gras, "if there be any need of my going to your house you will please send me word. I am well pleased not to go otherwise, according to the decision we agreed on from the very beginning."

And, at another time: "If you desire I should have the benefit of seeing you in your sickness, acquaint me. I have made it a law never to visit you unless called for some necessary or very useful purpose."

When obliged to confer with Mademoiselle Le Gras or with her Daughters, he observed the same rules of prudence as with persons of the world.

The purity of Vincent, as are all Christian virtues, was expansive and conquering. One of his devotions was to withdraw women and young girls from the perils to which he knew them to be exposed. Thus, he brought from Lorraine to Paris a number of young girls whose virtue was, at the same time, a prey to the temptation of hunger, always an evil counselor, and the brutality of an undisciplined soldiery. He placed them with Madmoiselle le Gras, who, with the assistance of the Ladies of Charity, succeeded in obtaining for them situations, in the best families in Paris, some as maids in waiting, others as house servants, each according to her qualifications

He was no less devoted in snatching from vice those who had already fallen. He favored and encouraged all the institutions for penance that existed in his time, and more particularly the Magdalene, where he sent the Daughters of the Visitation, whose sweetness and charity seemed the virtues most proper to win over the poor penitents.* He, himself, toward the close of his life, formed the project of building a vast hospital for young girls and abandoned females, and especially those who make an infamous traffic of their honor. He held on the subject numerous and long consultations with persons of piety; and, notwithstanding the difficulties of such an enterprise, he would, doubtless, had not death intervened, have carried it into successful execution. Others inherited his idea and realized it under different forms.

II

Having such a love of purity, what must he not have done to infuse and foster it in his children? "It is not enough for Missionaries," he said, "to excel in this virtue; they are obliged moreover to do their utmost so to comport themselves that none can have the slightest cause to entertain, in their regard, the faintest suspicion of the contrary vice, because, this suspicion, though totally false, would tarnish their reputation and prove more prejudicial to their holy occupations than all the other crimes that could be falsely imputed to them. Hence, we must not rest satisfied in using all ordinary means to guard against this evil, but we must, moreover, if necessary, employ extraordinary precautions, such as omitting, at times, to perform certain actions, though otherwise lawful, and even good and holy, as visiting the sick poor, when, in the judgment of superiors, such actions might furnish occasion to these suspicions."

And for this reason he answered those who asked if they should take with them a companion when visiting the sick: "O, my Jesus! Sir, you must be vigilant not to fail therein. When the Son of God ordained that His disciples should go two and two together, He saw, no doubt, the great danger that would result in sending them alone. Now, who would be rash enough to derogate from a usage which He introduced among

---

* That was before the Sisters of the Visitation were cloistered. In the beginning of their institute their duties were similar to those of the Sisters of Charity.—TRANSLATOR.

His disciples, and which the Congregation has always followed? Experience has taught a number of communities of religious women that it is necessary, on account of the abuses that have arisen at such times and places, to leave the door of the infirmary open, and have the curtains of the bed drawn back, while the confessor administers the sacraments, and remains by the sick sister."

He wrote to another: "I have recommended to the Daughters of Charity never to permit men to enter their rooms, either lay persons or ecclesiastics, and no more those of the Congregation than others; and I have begged them to close the door even on myself, should I wish to enter. I except, of course, cases of sickness; for, in case of necessity, the sister infirmarian can conduct the priest, or a brother may accompany him, but never otherwise."

One of his priests having, one day, asked him in simplicity, if it were expedient to feel the pulse of the sick so as to be able to judge of the necessity of administering the last succors of religion, he replied: "That practice must be carefully avoided, for the evil spirit might easily make use of it to tempt the living and even the dying. The devil, in this last passage, forges arrows of all woods wherewith to strike the soul. The strength of the passions may remain though the body be emaciated. You should call to mind the example of that Saint, who, having separated from his wife with her consent, would not, while sick, allow her to touch him, crying out with what voice he had that there was still fire under the ashes. Besides, if you wish to know the symptoms of approaching dissolution, ask some attendant or some other person present to do you that favor, there being less danger for him; or else inform yourself of what the doctor says. But, on no account, run the risk of touching either girl or woman under any pretense whatever."

In the same sense, he wrote one day to one of his brothers to abstain from all intercourse, though his motives and intention were pure, with a person of the other sex: "Because," he said, "in such particular conversations, if there be no evil, there is always the occasion of thinking evil; and, moreover, the means to preserve purity is to shun the occasions that may sully it."

However, the Saint would not have the temptations against this virtue alarm them, still less be the occasion of their abandoning their vocation. He wrote to a brother, thus tempted, who desired to become a hermit: "On the one hand, I have been consoled by your letter, in seeing the candor with which you disclose what passes within you; but, on the other, it has given me a pain similar to that St. Bernard formerly received from one of his monks, who, under pretext of greater regularity, desired to leave his vocation and enter another order, though the holy abbott assured him it was a temptation, and told him that the evil one desired nothing better than this change, knowing well that, could he force him to abandon his first state, it would be an easy matter to withdraw him from the second, and then precipitate him into a disorderly state of life, as it actually happened. What I can say to you, my dear brother, is that, if you be not continent in the Congregation of the Mission, you will not in any condition in the world, and of this I assure you. Be careful lest there be levity in your desire for change; if not, then, after prayer, which is always necessary in all needs, the remedy will be to reflect that there is no state in life in which there are no dryness and weariness, and, at times, longings for change. After this consideration, think that, God having called you to the congregation in which you are, He, very likely, has attached to it the grace of your salvation, which, not having called you, He will refuse you elsewhere. The second remedy against temptations of the flesh is to fly all communication with and the sight of those persons who give rise to them, and, moreover, to reveal them immediately to your director, who will give you other remedies. I would, besides, advise you to have a great confidence in Our Lord, and in the assistance of the immaculate Virgin, His mother, to whom I will frequently recommend you."

Treating, one day, of this subject of chastity, after his usual fashion, that is, in its motives, its nature, its means, he adduced as the principal motive the great aversion of Our Lord for whatever seemed contrary to this virtue: "So much," said he, "that, intending to become man, He did not wish it to be in the ordinary manner, but by the operation of the Holy Ghost, in a way entirely supernatural, so that He, being true man, as other men, His Mother remained always chaste and a Virgin. Oh, my Lord! there must be something grand in this virtue, since the Holy of Holies has for its sake willed to abrogate in His conception and His birth the laws of nature.

"Our Lord has been pleased to permit Himself to be calumniated, to be called a seducer, a drinker, one possessed by the devil, and so on; but He never allowed even His greatest enemies to reproach Him with the least thing against chastity.

"Oh, my Savior! to Thee we address ourselves to obtain this so rare a virtue. Nature has not the power to grant it; on the contrary, it excites within us thousands upon thousands of impure temptations.

"Our Lord goes farther, and says: 'He who does not leave his wife is not worthy of Me.' Hence, the Apostles and the Disciples, who were married, separated from their wives to follow Him, and so did the wives from their husbands. Many of the first Christians followed this example, and had no further matrimonial intercourse. But the demon, the enemy of this virtue, soon succeeded in breaking down in men this beautiful resolution. Worldly intercourse and the immense weakness of nature induced some to return to a life less pure. This is the reason why a great number, fearing they did not possess strength sufficient to live in a state of chastity in the world, fled into the deserts of Lybia and Egypt, there to lead the life of angels. Since that time, monasteries have been established where those who, tearing themselves away from sin and the pleasures of the flesh, and wishing to live a chaste life, are received.

"There are two kinds of chastity. The first is a virtue; which, in general, moderates the desires of carnal pleasures. It concerns married persons and is termed conjugal chastity. But there is another chastity which consists in extirpating from the heart all impure affections. A virtue rare, and one which the demon does his utmost to snatch from the most holy souls especially. The most holy things serve him as means to tempt us with impurity. Oh, Lord, what is to be done in these terrible moments? Fly to God, take refuge in the wounds of our Lord Jesus Christ. Help us then, O, my God, to pluck from our hearts these accursed affections, to erase from our memories all these wicked remembrances!

"There are, also, two kinds of purity, purity of the body and purity of the heart. He who possesses purity of the body has not, therefore, chastity. He must add purity of the heart, which is the form and essence of this virtue. Chastity, in truth, drives away all evil thoughts from the imagination, from the memory and from the mind. We should, then, direct all our efforts against our heart in order to become masters, and root out all that can give rise to any image contrary to this sublime virtue.

"The means to preserve chastity are, first, vigilance over the senses, and particularly over sight and hearing. A guard over the eyes: O, sight how dangerous thou art! O how evil it is to allow the eyes to wander here and there and rest on all kinds of objects! David, that holy man, by this became an adulterer and a homicide. A guard over the hearing: very many would never have known what impurity was had they not seen and heard those comedians and buffoons, who represent unbecoming actions and rehearse evil discourse. Oh, what danger there is in listening to such things! We must, then, employ the greatest vigilance over our senses; over the sight, the sight, I say, yes, the sight; over the hearing, and so of all the other external senses, the touch, too, and as far as possible make ourselves masters. Secondly, to fly all private conversation with persons of the other sex. Thirdly, to practise sobriety, especially in the use of wine. Fourthly, to shun idleness; when the devil finds a person idle, he does everything to make him succumb. Oh, what a fine opportunity he has to tempt and torment him by impure representations! Fifthly, to avoid all tender relations and expressions both in conversations and in letters."

CHAPTER XX.

COMPOSURE OF SPIRIT.

I

With a mortification both interior and exterior, such as we have seen, with so absolute a submission to the Divine Will, Vincent could not but possess his soul, and maintain over himself an empire that retained all his faculties in perfect equality. And he did maintain this equality in all things and at all times.

He was composed in his manner of life, always humble and inclined to piety and charity from infancy to old age.

He was composed in his holy undertakings; he sustained and prosecuted them to their termination amid contradiction of every description and trials of every quality.

He was composed in the inequalities of occupations and affairs, in humiliations and honors, in the slave-pen of Tunis and at the Court of Anne of Austria, which forced a bishop to exclaim, as has been mentioned: "Mr. Vincent is always Mr. Vincent."

He was composed in losses of property and in those of law, during disorder and wars, which could wring from him only this cry: "God be praised;" or this humble and submissive plaint: "We will be obliged to go act as curates in the village if God do not have pity on us."

He was composed in misfortunes at sea which deprived his children of their all, save life, but which could not turn him from the maintenance of the foreign missions.

He was composed in the losses, still more sensible, of his

He has finished as he lived, in the good use of suffering, in the practice of all virtues and in the desire to consume himself, like our Lord, in the accomplishment of the will of God. He was one of the first two who labored in the Missions, and he always contributed to the other functions of the Congregation, to which he has rendered very great service in every way, and in losing him it would have lost greatly, did not God dispose all things for the best and cause us to find our profit, where we imagine only injury. There is reason to hope that this, His servant, will be of more benefit to us in Heaven than he could have been on earth. I pray you to render him the customary suffrages."

He wrote, in the same spirit, a month after, on the occasion of the loss of Mademoiselle Le Gras; and generally, in every instance, on the death of his best and dearest subjects. A last quotation: "You have not, then, heard of the losses we have undergone? Oh, Sir, but they are great, not only in the number of men whom God has taken from us, but also in the quality of persons, all being priests, and of the best workers in the Congregation. And so, too, they proved themselves, meeting death whilst serving their neighbor, and a death most holy and extraordinary. Six of them, without counting a brother, died of the pestilence, in Geneva, whilst assisting the plague-stricken, and the others have given their temporal life to procure that of eternity for the islanders of Madagascar and the Hebrides. They are so many missionaries in Heaven. There can be no doubt of it, since they have consumed themselves for the sake of charity, and since there can be no greater charity than to give one's life for his neighbor, as Jesus Christ Himself has said and done. May God, then, Sir, be glorified with the glory He has bestowed upon our confreres, as we have reason to believe, and may His good pleasure ever be our peace and the calm of our afflicted hearts! I do not tell you what was our grief on receiving such news coming almost all at the same time; it would be imperishable to express it. You, loving the Congregation so tenderly, will be able to judge, by the pain you will experience, whether we could receive a greater stroke without being crushed."

CHAPTER XXI.

FORTITUDE AND PATIENCE.

I

The man so meek, so humble, so gentle, was for all that, whenever the interests of truth and justice required, as strong and invincible as a wall of brass or a column of iron.

It is, again, in the Council of Conscience, on that more public theatre, where his fortitude distinguished itself, as did his equanimity, his humility, as did all his virtues. Without a doubt, his natural kindness led him, when he could in conscience do so, to oblige every one from the humblest plebeian to the highest lord or peer; but did any ask what was against his rules, then he opposed an insurmountable refusal. In vain did intrigue, cupidity, and ambition assail his virtue; without taking counsel of either hope or fear, he, as far as in him lay, repulsed them from the sanctuary without mercy. For long, he struggled even against Mazarin himself, becoming more and more powerful, who, forgetting his ecclesiastical character and obeying only the calculations of his personal ambition, or what he termed a reason of state, wished to make friends, not with the Mammon of iniquity, as the Gospel has it, but with the sacred goods of the Church. In his letter to Clement XI., Fenelon wrote: "An incredible discernment of spirits and a singular firmness were conspicuous in this man of God. Having regard neither for the favor nor the hatred of the great, he consulted only the interest of the church, when, in the Council of Conscience, by order of the Queen, Anne of Austria, mother of the King, he gave his advice in relation to the choice of bishops. Had the other councilors adhered more constantly to this man,

who seemed to read the future, certain men, who afterwards created great trouble, would have been far removed from the episcopal charge." Such, too, was the sentiment of Victor de Meliand, Bishop of Alet, who speaks in similar terms of the invincible firmness and fortitude of soul with which the man of God neither permitting himself to be moved by entreaties nor alarmed by threats. refused his vote, in the promotion to prelacies and benefices, to those, whose unworthiness was known to him, no matter what their rank, their condition, or their dignity. The laity rendered to Vincent, on this point, the same testimony as the clergy. "It was the public esteem in which he was held," the president of the parliament, de Lamoignon, has deposed, "that induced the Queen to call him to the Council of Conscience; but this honor did not change his mode of life. In difficult circumstances he spoke with a firmness worthy the apostles; no human consideration could persuade him to dissemble the truth in the smallest degree, and he never made any other use of the confidence reposed in him by the great, than to inspire them with the sentiments they should have."

The instances of this constancy are innumerable. A lady of high rank, having besought him to obtain from the King a benefice for one of her children, he answered: "Pardon me, madam, I can have nothing to do in the matter." Astonished at first in being less favorably received by a poor priest than she would have been by the greatest lords, then carried away by pride and passion, she said: "Indeed, sir, your assistance is unnecessary, I know of other ways to obtain my request. I have done you too much honor to address you, and it is readily seen that you do not, as yet, understand how to behave towards ladies of my rank.' Vincent's further answer was silence over which even insults had no power. In similar circumstances, if he did answer anything it was simply: "Madam, our rules and my conscience do not give me the liberty of obeying you in this; therefore, I beg you, hold me excused." Or, again, it was a personal argument he opposed to the solicitor, as he did to a judge of a superior court who, meeting him on the street, thought to gain him to his interest. To pretended friendship and to anger, to flattery and to insult, the Saint contented himself with answering: "Sir, you endeavor, as I wish to believe, to acquit yourself worthily of your duty, and I ought to do the same in mine."

He needed still greater fortitude when they came to him on the part of the Queen. A young man of family had asked of the Queen an abbey. He obtained his request on condition that Vincent would not object. He, then, accompanied by his tutor, went to St. Lazarus. They opened with the ordinary compliments of politeness, then expressed the anticipated thanks of the entire family and recounted a long list of present and future qualities of the claimant; all which proved more the desire to obtain the benefice than the presence of the required merit. To this picture, Vincent, previously informed, meekly opposed another of contrary hues, and concluded with a refusal which he couched in his accustomed phrase: "I, therefore, beg you, sir, not to take it ill if I refuse my consent to a thing of which God will demand of me an account." At these words the tutor rose and advanced towards the Saint with clenched fists, pouring out at the same time a torrent of abuse; then, seeing that he could not even disturb his tranquility he departed, but Vincent accompanied him, and, with more than ordinary politeness, reconducted master and pupil as far as their carriage.

But what was to be done when Mazarin, now all powerful, with his policy for his only counselor, alone named to the ecclesiastical benefices, and no longer proposed but the ratification of an accomplished fact? Even then fortitude did not abandon Vincent. He strove to enlighten the religion of the Queen, and obtained from her the choice, at least, of worthy bishops.

This is how he merited the following testimony from Clement XI., in his bull of canonization: "When the nobles recommended to him their sons and solicited him by prayers or threats, he disdained their offers as he trampled under foot their menaces. Never did this soul, strong and robust, wish to make powerful friends to the detriment of the inheritance of Christ and at the expense of the cross, or compromise, through fear, the evils wherewith his enemies threatened him."

He showed himself strong, again, in the direction of the communities confided to his care, and notably of those of the

Visitation. He courageously closed them to all that could introduce either the spirit of the world or the errors then prevailing. With a holy and disinterested firmness he refused admission to ladies of the highest rank, to princesses, even, who sought his consent to be received as boarders, some to gratify their curiosity, others to satisfy a mistaken devotion. The lady benefactors were the only exception and he had an exact list of their names. And generosity alone could not acquire with him the title of benefactress; a pure faith and solid virtue were moreover necessary. For example: the monastery of St. Antoine street could hope for great advantages from a lady, who had already, during the two years she was with the nuns, donated a sum of fifty thousand livres, and who had given to another monastery, less scrupulous, the sum of three hundred thousand. But she desired to be guided by the advice of the new sectaries, and wished to introduce into the convent her Jansenist director. Vincent had the fifty thousand francs returned, and then dismissed her. To all temporal advantages he preferred the spiritual good of communities. He often reaped only hatred and persecution. Thus a high born dame, to whom he had closed the door of the house at St. Denis, would not permit him to give a mission on her lands; but that did not influence him, he remained inflexible. In 1658, a messenger came to inform him that Madam Payen, mother-in-law of Mister Lionne, was at the gate of the monastery of St. Antoine street, and demanded admission to see a little daughter of the minister, who was dangerously ill and could not be removed. He answered: "I am Madam Payen's most humble servant, and desire greatly to serve her. But my rule is to grant admission to none. I have refused Madam de Nemours, Madam de Longueville, and the Princess de Carignan, who will never forgive me. What would these ladies say were they to learn of the exception? Besides it would be against my conscience. And the sight of Madam Payen will not recall the child to life."

He was firm even against gratitude. Never did he manifest such fortitude as on one occasion when he was obliged to resist the entreaties of Adrien Le Bon, former prior of St. Lazarus, to whom he had vowed so much respect and gratitude. Through

Vincent's advice, and by order of the queen, an abbess of high family, but who had given her scandals a renown equal to that of her high birth, was imprisoned. The prior, who was under great obligations to the abbess, was charged by her with obtaining her freedom. He accepted, and all the more willingly, as, in this case like in others, he believed he had but to say a word to Vincent to attain his purpose. What, then, were his surprise, and astonishment, when he saw that not only his first request, but all his continued persistence, fell before the steady refusal of the holy man! Tranquil and respectful, but resolute, Vincent simply answered: "I cannot betray my conscience; I beg you to excuse me." "What, sir," cried the prior wounded, "is this the treatment I receive at your hands after having given you my house? Is this the return for all the benefits I have rendered you and your Congregation!" "It is true," replied Vincent deeply grieved, "it is true you have laden us with goods and honors, and our obligations to you are those of children to their father; but be pleased, sir, to take it all back, if we merit it only at the sacrifice of God and our conscience."

Finally, the entire life of Vincent de Paul, so many persistent efforts against error and evil, so many religious and charitable institutions established and maintained in spite of a thousand difficulties that would deter and dishearten the most generous, abundantly testify to his heroic fortitude and constancy.

In some of the incidents above related we have seen his patience in company with his fortitude, for he ever found means to practise several virtues at the same time.

His patience was remarkable under the abuse and evil treatment his courageous resistance to ambition and cupidity brought down on his devoted head. As, for example, on that day when, having obtained from the queen the retraction of the promise of a bishopric made to a dutchess, and being commissioned by her to notify the lady of this decision, he was received with an outburst of rage. The dutchess, not feeling herself sufficiently revenged by the torrent of abuse she had lavished on him, seized a foot-stool and threw it at his head.

making a gash from which the blood flowed freely. Vincent, unmoved whilst the storm raged, was almost felled by this stroke. He withdrew without a word, covering his face, all blood, with his handkerchief. From the noise he had heard and at the sight of Vincent, the brother, who had accompanied him and whom he had left in the ante-chamber, divined all.

Fired with indignation, he cried out that his father, a priest, and a minister of the king, should not be thus treated with impunity, and he rushed towards the apartment. Vincent threw himself before him: "You have no business there, my brother; this is the way. Come, let us go." And he led him with him. "Is it not," he added on leaving, "a wonderful thing to see how far the tenderness of a mother for her son can go?" This was all his vengeance. Witness, again, that other day when, publicly maltreated at the very gate of St. Lazarus by a lord whose son he had refused to recommend: "You are right, sir," he said to him throwing himself at his feet, "I am a wretch and a sinner."

Again, all those numerous instances of evil treatment and abuse at the hands of the poor, who laid at his door the public distress, or complained to have not received enough, to which he quietly returned only these words: "Go, and pray to God." And, finally, witness his behavior towards his adversary in the Orsigny farm lawsuit. The latter was prodigal in his slanderous abuse of Vincent and his Congregation. Vincent could have exacted reparation of honor. He would not permit his lawyer to reply. "Our Lord has suffered far more," was his only answer to those who urged him to defend himself; and, as in the passion of the Savior, this patience and silence excited the admiration of the court and of his opponent himself.

He was patient in the importunities, the urgent solicitations, the inconsiderate requests, and the offensive answers to which he was every day subject, and which, instead of drawing from him a bitter or a sharp word, or any sign of impatience, served, on the contrary, to induce him to act and speak, if possible, with more calmness and more meekness.

He was patient in the losses, oftentimes not inconsiderable, of the Congregation when they brought him into contempt.

His patience, in such cases, was not only resigned, but joyous, for he saw an opportunity of practising humility, poverty and all other virtues.

His patience was heroic in the loss of subjects as well as of property, and of subjects the most dear and most necessary. He then wrote: "Through the mercy of God, my soul is in peace, because this loss happens by the good pleasure of God. It is true, I sometimes fear, that my sins are the cause; but, recognizing, even in this, the good pleasure of God, I accept all with a good heart."

The good pleasure, the will of God was, in effect, the first foundation of his patience. He said with the prophet: *"Shall here be evil in the city which the Lord hath not done?"* (Amos iii. 6.) Another motive for his patience he found in these words of St. Paul: *"And God is faithful, who will not suffer you to be tempted above that which you are able; but will make also with temptation issue, that you may be able to bear it."* (1. Cor., x–13.)

II

"Afflictions," he taught, "are not an evil. God sends them to us to exercise our patience and to teach us to have pity for others; He Himself having been pleased to endure them in order that we might have a pontiff, who knew how to compassionate with our miseries, and encourage us, by his example, in the practice of this virtue. One of the most certain marks that God has great designs on a person is when He sends desolation on desolation, and sorrow upon sorrow. The true time to discover the spiritual progress of a soul is the time of temptation and tribulation, because such as a person is in these trials, such, ordinarily, will he be afterwards. In a single day of temptations we can acquire more merit than in many days of peace." And he illustrated this doctrine by pointed comparisons. "A captain," he said in one of his conferences of the year 1645, "first payed twenty francs a piece for his soldiers, and then he supplied them with army bread; but after that he placed them in the ranks where they had to undergo great fatigue, instead of nourishing them delicately and making cowards of them, and thus rendering them useless. Thus God gives sweetness in the beginning, but afterwards He sends the fatigues and torments of temptations and trials. When on sea the traveller remarks the dolphins follow each other in regular order and divert themselves in the water, and notices the flocks of little birds clinging to the masts, he is delighted and amused, but when the water, the bread and provisions give out, then there is only anxiety and terror. The water in a pond being always at rest becomes stagnant, muddy, and offensive; on the contrary, rivers and springs, which flow with rapidity among stones and rocks, have beautiful and sweet waters. Now, who would not prefer to be a river at this price than a stagnant pool?"

He wrote (March 9th, 1657): "The difficulties you experience in your management are not proof that it is not good. On the contrary, our Lord wishes to show that it is, since He puts it to the test. It is not surprising that a good vessel is safe in calm weather, since even a bad one could not then sink; but its quality is determined when it, exposed, weathers the tempest. You would be very happy had you nothing to suffer in your position; but you will be still more so, if, for the love of Our Lord, you remain firm in the midst of the agitations which He sends. I have before counseled patience, and I again renew the recommendation.'

He said to the Daughters of Charity in a still more vivid manner: "See the sculptor who wishes to carve a beautiful figure out of a rough and ugly looking stone He takes his hammer and gives such heavy strokes that, looking at him, one would imagine that he was going to break it into pieces. Then, when he has cut away the roughest part, he uses a smaller hammer, and after that he begins with the chisel to fashion the figure in its different parts. When it is rough formed he takes more delicate tools to bring it to that state of perfection which he intends. This is how God does. See the poor Daughter of Charity and the poor Missionary: when God withdraws them from the corrupted mass of the world they are still carnal and unpolished; they are unwrought stones. God, however, wishes to make of them beautiful images, and for this purpose He goes to work and applies heavy strokes of the hammer. And how does He do it? In making them suffer, now heat, again cold, and then the hardships of visiting the sick in the country, where, in winter time, the wind is biting sharp, and where they should go in bad as well as in fine weather. Well, these are the heavy strokes of the hammer that God gives a poor Daughter of Charity; and whoever would consider merely the surface would say that that Daughter is to be pitied. But if we cast our eyes on the designs of God we will see that all these blows are only for the purpose of fashioning that beautiful soul. And when, after having sent great afflictions as well of body as of mind, He perceives that what was the most coarse has been removed from the soul by the patience which it has practised, oh, then He takes up the chisel to perfect it. He commences to delineate the features; He adorns and embellishes it; He takes a delight in enriching it with His graces, and He does not rest until He has rendered it perfectly acceptable."

In twenty different letters he returns to this subject, especially in regard to temptations; for example, in the following letter addressed, in 1624, to a missionary in Rome: "Such is the conduct of God in regard to those whom He destines for something great, or for something special in His service, that He, previously, exercises them in troublesome dislikes and repugnances and movements of inconstancy. At times, His object is to try them, again it is to let them feel their own weakness, at other times to detach them more from created objects, and occasionally to dissipate the vapors of self-complacency, and ever and always His object is to render them more agreeable in His eyes. Do not doubt, provided you resist, that the temptations you suffer will contribute to your advancement. There is not a man, be he ever so perfect or so steadfast in his vocation, that is not subject, at times, to like temptations. The enemy was even so rash as to attempt to induce the Son of God to adore him, a temptation the most horrible his malice could have invented. Was there any among the Apostles, or among the saints, who had no need to do violence to Himself in order to resist the attacks of the flesh and the world? Courage, then; be firm! Can it be possible that a little repugnance will cause us to abandon all? God forbid, since the Apostle says that it is impossible for those, who were once enlightened and have become unworthy of the light, to return to the state whence they fell.

For, though their intentions be good and their resolutions strong, still when it comes to the execution of these resolves, when the question is to overcome the difficulties grace fails them because they have failed grace. Their scruples wear and harass them, and the desire of calm and rest forces them to form their conscience which will easily accommodate itself to sensuality, and nature assumes the mastery."

He wrote similarly to a young novice Sister, June 25th., 1658: "I am not astonished at the repugnance you feel in your exercises of religion; on the contrary, I would be, did you not experience any. Sooner or later, God always tries the souls He calls to His service by similar pains, and it is preferable to undergo them in the beginning than later, or towards the end. Because thereby you early learn to know and humble yourself, to distrust yourself and to place all confidence in God; in a word, you lay in a fund of patience, of fortitude and of mortification, virtues of which you will have great need all your life.

"I have no doubt you would be glad to remain free as you are, but this content would come from nature, and would not last. We cannot serve two masters. If you wish to enjoy the liberty of the children of God you must follow Jesus Christ in the narrow path of subjection which conducts to salvation. For so great is human inconstancy, notwithstanding the dispositions you may have to do right in going by the broad way of liberty, you may mistake, as ordinarily they do, who are attached to God only by silken cords.

"Consider, for a moment, I pray you, the Son of God, Who came into the world not only to save us through His death, but also in order to submit to every will of His Father and to draw us to Him by the example of His life. He was still in the womb of His Mother when He was obliged to obey an edict of an emperor; He was born out of His own country, in a tempestuous season of the year, and in extreme poverty. Shortly after His birth, see how Herod persecutes Him, and how He has to fly, how in His exile He suffers not only His own discomforts, but also, through compassion, those of the Blessed Virgin and St. Joseph, who endure a great deal on His account. Having returned to Nazareth and grown up, He submits to His parents, and to the rules of a hidden life in order to serve as a model to religious souls who, having embraced the like, ought to obey their superiors and the observances of their state. And without doubt, He had you in view then, in the eternal design He had of saving you by means of the absolute retreat you have begun. If you, in your turn, will look at this Divine Savior you will see how He suffers without ceasing, how He prays, how He labors, and how He obeys. '*If you live according to the flesh,*' St. Paul says, '*you shall die.*' (Rom. viii., 13.) But to live according to the spirit that vivifies, you must live as our Lord has lived, you must renounce self, must do rather the will of another than your own, make good use of contradictions, and esteem suffering preferable to self-satisfaction. He, speaking of His passion, asks of His disciples: '*Ought not Christ to have suffered these things?*' (Luke xxiv., 26.) This is to give us to understand that as He entered into glory only through afflictions, we should not pretend to enter without suffering. There are different kinds of suffering. The Apostles and the first Christians suffered the persecution of tyrants and endured every species of hardship, and it is said that all those, who wish to follow Jesus Christ, will suffer temptation. If you revert to your past life you will find that you have not been exempt, and in whatever condition you may be, even were you married, and advantageously, you would still find crosses and troubles. There are few persons in the world that do not complain of their state, even though it seems happy. Truly, the best is that wherein we become like our Lord, tempted, praying, working and suffering, and this is the path by which He leads those souls whom He wishes to raise to a high degree of perfection. You must not, then, be disheartened if you find no attraction for the practice of virtue. Virtue is not virtue, save in as much as we do violence to ourselves to practise it. The life of man, according to Job, is a combat. We, then, must combat if we do not wish to be vanquished. And, as the devil is a roaring lion going about seeking to devour us, he will not fail to attack you in order to weaken you in your determination of being all to God, to discourage you in its prosecution and to completely dishearten you if possible, foreseeing that should you persevere he will be confounded. It is, therefore, necessary to resist him resolutely by prayer and by exactitude in the practices of the community, and, especially, by a filial and entirely singular confidence in God. His grace will not fail you; on the contrary, it will abound in you in proportion to your trials, and to your resolution, with its help, to overcome them. God never permits us to be tempted above our strength.

"For all these reasons, it seems to me, you will do well to be resolute in your difficulties. The more you give our Lord, the greater graces will you receive. His yoke is sweet to those who willingly embrace it, and your burden will be light if you compare it with that of Jesus Christ, Who has so suffered for you, or if you consider the consolation and recompense He promises those who serve Him constantly, without regret, in the place and in the manner He desires, as I trust you will do."

Speaking in a more general manner he said: "The wisdom of God has so well ordered everything that night succeeds day; sadness, joy; and contradiction, applause; and this He has done that our minds would rest only in Him, Who alone is above all change. We must all, without exception, be prepared to suffer in one way or another; otherwise, we will not be disciples of the Divine Master, Who has wished to be persecuted. Regard it as a blessing to be treated as He was, and endeavor to follow His example in the virtues He practised when maltreated."

Or again: "Your pains, which are various and of long continuance affect me sensibly. They are a cross with outstretched arms, embracing both body and soul; but also a cross that elevates you above earth, and this gives me consolation. You ought to be consoled in seeing yourself treated as our Lord was, and honored by the same marks whereby He proved His love for us. His sufferings were both interior and exterior, and the interior were, beyond comparison, far greater than the others. But why, think you, does He try you in this manner? For the same object He had in wishing Himself to suffer, namely, to purify you of your sins and to clothe you with His virtue, in order that the name of His Father be sanctified in you. Remain in peace, then, and have perfect confidence in His goodness. Give no heed to any contrary feelings; be shy of your own sen-

timents, and believe rather what I say and the knowledge I
have of you, than all that you yourself may think or feel. You
have every motive to rejoice in God and to hope for everything
from Him through our Lord, Who dwells in you; and after the
recommendation He has given you to renounce yourself, I do
not see anything that could give you cause for apprehension,
not even sin, which is the only evil we should fear; because in
the state of religion, which you have embraced, you do penance
for the past, and in regard to the future your great horror for
whatever may displease God is your safeguard."

To one of his missionaries, who had suffered for justice sake,
he wrote: "Is not your heart greatly comforted in seeing that
you have been found worthy before God to suffer in His service?
Certainly, you owe Him special thanks and are bound to ask of
Him the grace to make good use of your trial."

To an abbess, who complained of the contradictions she met
with in endeavoring to reform her abbey, he said: "The sufferings undergone in the establishment of a good work draw
down the graces necessary to succeed."

To missionaries prevented in the work of their mission by
some popular outbreak against them: "Blessed be God for
the difficulties He is pleased to have you encounter! You must,
on this occasion, honor the contradictions the Son of God experienced when on earth. Oh, how much greater they were,
since through aversion for Him and His doctrine they forbade
Him entrance to certain places and, at last, deprived Him of
life! It was for occasions just like these that He prepared His
disciples when He told them they would be ridiculed, affronted
and maltreated, that fathers would take sides against their
children and children would persecute their fathers. Let us
derive our profit from them, and bear with patience, as did the
holy Apostles, the contradictions we may meet with in the service
of God. Or rather, when we experience them, let us rejoice as in
a great good, and let us begin with the present occasion to
make that use of them which the Apostles, after the example of
their Head, made of theirs. If we conduct ourselves in this
manner, you may rest assured that the very means by which
the devil wished to thwart you will turn to his own discomfiture;

that you will give joy to Heaven and to all good souls who may witness or may hear of your action; that, in fine, even those, who now oppose, will at last bless you and recognize you as co-operators in their salvation. But what! '*This kind of demon is not cast out but by prayer and patience.*' The holy modesty and interior recollection which are practised in the congregation will also be of service to you; and, again, it will be well to inform yourself of the causes that led to the aversion which this people exhibits towards the missionaries in order to avoid whatever may have given any occasion, and even, if judged expedient, to do the contrary."

Writing to one who complained of one of his confreres, he said: "You must not look upon his action as coming from himself, but rather as a trial wherein God wished to test your patience; and this virtue will be all the more real virtue in you as you are more alive to resentment, and as you have given less cause for the injury you received. Prove, then, that you are a true child of Jesus Christ and that it is not in vain you have so often meditated on His sufferings; but that you have learned to overcome yourself by bearing patiently the things that wound your heart the more."

"In a word, sir," he said to another by way of conclusion, "we must go to God *through infamy and good name;* and His Divine Goodness shows us a mercy when He is pleased to permit us to fall into reproach and public contempt. I have no doubt you have received in patience the confusion arising from what has happened. If the glory of the world be but smoke, the contrary is indeed solid when received in the proper spirit; and I hope you will derive great profit from this humiliation. May God grant it, and may He deign to send us many more of them that thereby we may merit to become all the more agreeable to Him."

The advantage, the happiness of suffering was one of His favorite doctrines. "Ah! sir," he wrote to one of his priests in trouble, "would you desire to be without suffering? Would it not be preferable to have a devil in the body than to be without a cross? Yes, for in that case the devil could not hurt the soul; but having nothing to suffer, neither soul nor body would be conformed to Jesus suffering; and yet this conformity is the mark of our predestination. Therefore, be not astonished at your pains. since the Son of God has chosen suffering for our salvation."

Under this admirable conviction, he, at times, complained as have done so many saints, that God did not try his congregation by afflictions. "I have," he said one day, "for some time back, and indeed very often, dwelt on the thought that the congregation does not suffer anything, that everything smiles on it in success, and that it is in a certain prosperity; let us say rather that God blesses it in every way without its experiencing either obstacle or annoyance. I commenced to have a doubt of that inactive tranquility, knowing that God proves those who serve Him and chastises those whom He loves. '*Whom God loveth He chastiseth*' (Heb. xii–6.) I recalled to mind what is related of St. Ambrose, how, when once traveling he came to a house where the master, he learned, did not know what sorrow was. And thereupon, enlightened from above, he judged that a house so gently dealt with was near its destruction, and said: "Come let us leave this place, for the wrath of God is about to fall on this house." And, in reality, he had no sooner departed than the lightning of heaven struck it and enveloped in ruin all who were within. Again, I saw many orders troubled from time to time, and particularly one of the greatest, and most holy in the church, which is, at times, in consternation, and is even now undergoing a terrible persecution; and I said to myself: 'See how God acts towards the saints and how He would treat us were we strong in virtue.' But, knowing our feebleness, He nurses us and feeds us on milk just like little children, and gives us success almost without our lifting a finger in co-operation. I had, therefore, reason from these considerations, reason to fear, that we were not acceptable to God, nor worthy to suffer anything for His love since He turns aside from us all afflictions and all those tests which prove His servants. True, we have met with some disasters at sea in our embarkation for Madagascar, but here again God has come to our relief; and in the year 1649 the soldiers occasioned us a loss of altogether forty-two thousand francs: but we alone did not suffer; every one felt the effects of the public troubles; the evil was common, and we were not treated otherwise than others.

But, blessed be God, my brethren, because now it has pleased His Adorable Providence to deprive us of the piece of property just taken from us! The loss is considerable for the community; yes, very considerable. Let us enter into the sentiments of Job when he said: '*The Lord gave these goods, and the Lord hath taken them away: blessed be the name of the Lord!*' (Job 1-21.) Do not consider this deprivation as coming from a human judgment; but let us say it is God Who has judged us, and let us humble ourselves under the hand that strikes, as David who has said: "*I was dumb, and I opened not my mouth, because thou hast done it.*" (Ps. xxxviii-10.) Let us adore His justice, and regard it as a mercy that He treats us in this manner. He does it all for our good. *He did all things well*, St. Mark relates."

He taught, moreover, (June, 1659) how to make a good use of calumnies, persecutions and other trials: "They are never wanting," he said, "to those who are faithful to God. They are graces that God lavishes on those who serve Him with fidelity. Without a doubt, He is not the author of them, He only permits them; but, in as much as they are tests and exercises for our patience and meekness, they are His work. He wishes thereby to wean His servants from all that might impede their going to Him. Therefore, whenever it pleases His Divine Goodness to send us these opportunities for suffering, let us elevate our hearts to Heaven, let us adore and praise His holy and ever adorable conduct; let us receive them with joy, as favors shown us, and say in the fullness of our hearts: Welcome, dear persecutions! Welcome, dear calumnies, dear crosses sent from Heaven! I propose to profit by this visit you make me on the part of God! Poor nature will suffer, it will grumble. No matter, we must suffer, and suffer with joy what God wishes us to suffer. Oh! had we but a lively faith, did we look upon these things with a Christian eye, did we regard them not as oppositions coming from men but as graces on the part of God, and did it but please His goodness to disperse from our minds the clouds of the maxims of the world, which hinder faith from penetrating to the depths of our hearts with those of the Gospel, we would, indeed, have far different views and other ideas; and when question of suffering injury and persecution arose, we would esteem and look upon them a**i** a great blessing and a happy condition. Yes, to be calumniated and persecuted is, indeed, a happy state.

"What! to be maligned and suffer persecution a happy state? Yes, for it is Jesus Christ Who has said: '*Blessed are they who suffer persecution for justice' sake.*' (Matt. v. 10.) Remark the words: '*For justice' sake.*' For, when we give cause to speak and act against us, we must humble ourselves under the avenging hand of God, Who leaves nothing go unpunished, and Who, sooner or later, chastises the transgressors of His law. In this case the contradictions we suffer at the hands of men come from God irritated against us; they are the effects of His justice, and men are but the ministers. But, when calumny falls on those who serve God faithfully, it is a great happiness, since it is a means to sanctify them more and more.

"When a physician prescribes a remedy in order to drive away the unhealthy humors of the body, we call it a purgation; and when the gardener lops off the useless branches of a fruit tree it is also called a pruning; but with this difference: the doctor purges to take away the evil or its cause, while the gardener prunes the tree and cuts away live branches that it may bear more fruit and less wood. So with us; if God sends us persecutions when our behavior is not such as it ought to be, then the persecution is a purgation. But if we suffer from men without having given them reason, then it is the gardener who lops off the quick branches in order to have the tree bear more fruit than leaves. Such a person has attained to two degrees of virtue; God wishes to advance him to four; he has reached four and the Lord wishes him to have six; for this purpose He employs the rod of calumny and persecution. It is, then, a very happy state; it is one of the evangelical beatitudes; it is a Christian beatitude, a happiness begun here below and completed in Heaven: '*Blessed . . . for theirs is the Kingdom of Heaven!*'

"Wretches, indeed, on the contrary, are those who do not suffer persecution! Let us, then, await with firmness the occasions for suffering that it shall please God to send us, and endure them in the spirit of Jesus Christ.

"The means to derive profit from affliction are: First, to prepare ourselves for them by a faithful use of the little daily occasions that arise, and make them serve us in our apprenticeship. For, if we behave cowardly in such trifling annoyances, how can we expect to patiently endure great sufferings? If we cannot endure a rough word, a cross look, how can we receive unmoved, much less with joy, calumnies, affronts, and humiliations? Second, on the very instant to close our lips, so that no word of ill-will, of irritation against those who calumniate and persecute may escape. *'I was dumb, and I did not open my mouth."* Is it not just that we maintain silence, since it is God Who speaks to us and sends us these visitations? Is it not reasonable that we accept this cross with submission since such is His good pleasure? Ought we not even thank and praise Him for persecutions, seeing that He permits them for our sanctification? Third, we are to defend ourselves neither by speech nor by writing. We should not fear to lose the esteem of the world. True esteem is but the gleam from a good life; its source, its foundation, is virtue, which can be taken from us neither by slander nor by persecution, provided we make a good use of them and remain faithful to God. Calumny can, indeed, eclipse the lustre of our virtue for a time; but virtue remains all the same, and will recover its brilliancy when it shall please God to dissipate the clouds that conceal it from the eyes of men."

CHAPTER XXII.

PATIENCE IN SICKNESS.

I

Patience in sickness! Another exercise of almost the entire length of the long life of our Saint, but particularly of the last fifteen years. Already, in 1645, his life was hanging by a thread. Old diseases, and ever new afflictions, the weight of labors that had neither rest nor respite, the martyrdom of the Council of Conscience, all these exhausted nature, which was soon reduced to extremity. But faith and charity retained all their vigor. To keep these alive, he daily received his God, and, even in delirium, he still found their accents and their ardor. He was found in this condition, one day, by Father St. Jure, who, like so many worthy people, had, on the news of his sickness, hastened to visit him. To the question which the father asked him, of the thoughts that flitted through his ravings, the aged man, without however recognizing him, seemed to answer: "*In a contrite and humble heart, let us be accepted, O Lord!*" (Dan. iii. 39.)—the cry of humility, the echo of his entire life, rather than an answer to a question he likely had not heard.

Snatched from death on this occasion by the devotedness of one of his children, he, however, retained a painful weakness. Henceforth, his infirmities, which in reality began at the time of his residence in the house of Gondi, or, rather, at the time of his captivity in Tunis, were continual. He had ever been very sensitive to the weather, and subject to a light fever, which sometimes continued for three or four days, and, at other times, even fifteen or more. During these attacks he would do nothing for relief, nor would he interrupt either his labors or his exercises.

"It is nothing," he would say; "it is only my little fever." The only remedy he had recourse to, and a remedy far more painful than the evil itself, consisted in forced sweats, lasting for successive days, particularly in summer, which made his short nights a kind of martyrdom. During the greatest heats, when even the linen of the bed is a burden, he would cover himself with three blankets and place at his sides two large vessels of boiling water. He thus passed the night with neither rest nor sleep, and in a suffocating heat. In the morning, always at the stroke of four, he arose from his bed as from a bath. Bed and bedding, all was steeped and steaming. He dried himself alone, never accepting the assistance of anyone, and went to prayer.

What could days succeeding such nights be? Enervation and drowsiness overcame him amid his occupations and visits. Instead of yielding to sleep, he arose from his chair and remained standing, or assumed some painful position; and when sleep did conquer, he begged pardon for what he termed his misery, instead of alleging in excuse sickness and the necessity of nature.

To his habitual *little fever* was added a quartan fever that seized him once or twice every year. He treated it no better than the other, and it was precisely during this time that he rendered the greatest services to God and the poor.

He was already an octogenarian when the evil became greater than his courage. He had long suffered from erysipelas, and this was followed by a continuous fever for some days, which terminated in a severe inflammation of one of his legs. Then, notwithstanding his will, he was forced to keep his bed for some time, and his room for two months. For the first time they succeeded in inducing him to take a room where there was fire. He could no longer resist, for his weakness was such that he had to be carried from the bed to the fire, and back again, just as a child.

The Lent of the following year, 1657, was marked by an universal loathing which prevented him from taking scarcely any nourishment. In 1658, he suffered from his eyes and for a long time did not wish to apply any remedy. The physician had prescribed an application of the warm blood of a pigeon; but when the brother brought the pigeon and was about to kill it, St. Vincent cried out: "No, no, I will never consent! That innocent bird represents to me my Savior, and God will readily find another means of curing me."

Besides, indifferent to life and death, to health and sickness, he was the same in regard to remedies. When a medicine was prescribed and he suspected it to be unpleasant, he took it and seemed content with the evil effect as if it had been an entire success.

Towards the end of the same year, as he was returning from the city in company with one of his priests, the braces of the carriage breaking, he was thrown out and his head dashed against the pavement. He received a severe wound and a renewal of his fever, and there was increasing danger of his death.

All these ills, borne with fortitude so sweet and so quiet, are as nothing in comparison with what he had to endure, especially from 1657, on account of the swelling and ulceration of his legs. It was forty-five years before, as we already know, that is during his captivity in Tunis, that he experienced the first symptoms. In this long space of time he had moments of such painful weakness and such agony from this inflammation that he could neither walk nor support himself, and was obliged to remain abed. This is the reason that, from 1632, the year of his taking possession of St. Lazarus, so removed from the centre of Paris and from business, he was necessitated to travel on horseback to the different scenes of his charity, and, in 1649, after his long journey into Brittany and Poitou, he was forced to abandon the horse for the famous carriage which he called his ignominy.

After this the evil made alarming progress. In 1656 it reached both knees. The Saint could no longer bend them but with extreme difficulty, nor rise up again without terrible pain, nor walk save with the aid of a crutch. Finally, the swelling broke in his right leg near the ankle; two years after, the humors collected there anew and the pain in the knees continually increasing. It was impossible for him, from the beginning of 1659, to leave the house. He, nevertheless, contrived for some time to descend to the church for prayer and mass, and to the conference hall, to preside at the meetings of his community, or of the Tuesday conferences, or of the Ladies of Charity, who preferred to go to that extremity of Paris than miss the happiness of seeing and hearing him.

Soon, unable longer to either ascend or descend the steps of the sacristy, he was obliged, in order to celebrate holy mass, to vest and unvest at the altar. "See how I am become a great lord," he would say smiling, alluding to the privilege, belonging to bishops alone, of vesting at the altar.

Towards the close of 1659, he was deprived of the consolation of celebrating mass in the presence of the people, and he could say mass only in the chapel of the infirmary; some months after, his limbs no longer bearing him, he saw himself reduced to the necessity of simply hearing it, which he did every day up to his death, but at the price of what sufferings! To go from his room to the chapel he had to drag himself along on crutches, and this movement reopened his wounds and aggravated all his pain. Nothing could be read on a countenance always serene; but the sight alone of his painful tottering walk carried the counter-stroke of his suffering to the hearts of all.

Moreover, they feared a fall at any instant, which, in his condition, might prove fatal. They, however, conjured him, in the middle of July, 1660, to consent to have the room adjoining his fitted up as a chapel so that he might be able to hear mass without leaving his own. "No, no," he said, "domestic chapels should not be allowed except in case of great necessity, and I do not think that mine is such a case." "Consent, at least," they said to him, "to have a chair to carry you from your room to the chapel of the infirmary; a thing that will cost but little, is contrary to no rule, and will preserve you from all danger and will spare your children extreme anxiety." This proposition, too, failed in the presence of his humility and his love for suffering. Finally, on the day of the Assumption of the Blessed Virgin Mary, six weeks only before his death, unable even to drag himself on his crutches, he permitted two of the brothers to carry him; but it was to his great confusion, and only to the chapel, about thirty or forty steps from his room.

What a martyrdom! And to all this supervened a disorder of the kidneys, an infirmity no less painful to him, than inconvenient and humiliating. Not wishing to accept any aid, he would grasp a cord pendent from the ceiling of his room, and in the most frightful pains he was heard to utter this cry only: "Ah, my Savior! My good Savior!" At the same time he would cast his eyes on a small wooden crucifix, still preserved among his relics, which he had placed before him, to inspire himself by this sight with fortitude and consolation.

His nights were even more cruel than his days. Even then, he would have no other couch than the hard straw whereon he passed five or six hours less in rest than in new torments. During the day his sores flowed in such abundance that the floor was stained, yet this was in itself some relief; but, at night, the humors and serosities, hardened by the heat of the bed, coagulated in the joints of the knees and occasioned terrible torture. He himself acknowledged it, first in a letter, and afterwards to one of his priests. "I have concealed my condition from you as much I could," he wrote to a person in his intimate confidence, "for I did not wish you to know of my illness, lest it might sadden you. But, O my God! how long will we be so tender that we dare not tell of our happiness in being visited by Thee? May it please Our Lord to make us stronger and cause us to find our happiness in His good pleasure!" And one of his missionaries having said to him: "It seems to me that your pains increase from day to day," he replied: "It is true, that I feel them augment from the sole of the foot to the top of the head. But, alas! what an account I will have to give at the tribunal of God, before which I have very soon to appear, if I do not make good use of them!"

But he did not wish to be pitied, more particularly if the expression of pity seemed a murmur against Providence. The missionary above mentioned having entered his room one day as they were dressing his sores, and perceiving that he was suffering very much, said: "Oh, sir, how grievous are your pains!"—"What!" interrupted the holy old man, "do you call grievous the work of God, and what He ordains in inflicting suffering on a miserable sinner like me? God forgive you, sir.

for what you have just said, for the language of Jesus Christ does not admit of such speech! Is it not just that the guilty suffer, and do we not belong more to God than to ourselves?"

Meanwhile, he grew weaker and wasted away day after day, yet continuing the same vigorous treatment with himself and ingeniously turning aside in his greatest distress all the solace and comfort they wished to procure him. Madam d'Aiguillon and other Ladies of Charity, horrified at his changed appearance and his ever-increasing weakness, and informed of the objection he made to the strengthening meats offered him, came to an understanding with the physician to draw up a daily regimen in which were included broth and fowl; then they presented this plan of diet to him for his signature in order to oblige him to follow it in every point. He signed it through a motive of charity, and resolved to keep his word. But, after the first or second day, his stomach, unused for so long a time to such delicate nutriment, could not bear it, and he begged, in pity, the Ladies and his brethren to permit him to live after his own fashion. They were obliged to allow him to return to the community fare.

His mind, always free and clear, his soul, ever strong and active in a wasted body, continued to direct his Congregation and its works. In his arm chair where pain tied him down, he was present and presided over all. There, he received visits of every description from within and without, and was ever smiling, always calm, ever meek and affable in tone of voice, in words and manner. If asked concerning his sickness, he would answer: "It is nothing" or "What is it all in comparison with the sufferings of Our Lord, or with the pains of hell which I have merited," and then he would adroitly change the subject and from his own troubles which he desired forgotten, would turn to those of his visitors to compassionate with them and offer consolation. And, notwithstanding his difficulties in speaking, he would protract the conversation and continue to talk for more than half an hour with as much grace, vigor, and unction as in his better days.

It is unnecessary to add that, amid these occupations so burdensome for a dying old man, his exercises of piety followed in their usual course. He even multiplied them in his last days as a more immediate preparation for death. And yet many a long year before he had begun to prepare himself for his final passage, not only by his wonderful labors, but also by special acts. Every day after mass he recited the prayers of the dying; and at night he placed himself in condition to answer, that very night itself, were it necessary, the call of God.

All these practices were known only by chance, or rather through a special permission of Providence. A little before the death of Vincent one of his priests wrote to a confrere concerning his bad state and the fears of the congregation, and without thinking, went according to the usage to hand Vincent the letter to read. The venerated superior did read it. At the words in the letter: "Mr. Vincent is wasting visibly, there is every appearance that we will soon lose him," he became agitated and ceased reading. Far from manifesting displeasure at the imprudence of the missionary, he said to himself: "It is a salutary counsel this good priest has wished to give me and a warning to hold myself in readiness." A moment after, he, in his humility, troubled, asked: "May I not have had the misfortune of giving this priest some cause of pain and scandal?" He immediately sent for him. "Sir," he said to him, "I very humbly thank you for the good advice you have given me. I assure you, you have done me a kindness; and I beg you to complete your charity by informing me of any other faults you may have noticed in me." "Oh, sir," answered the poor missionary, disconcerted and confused, "I assure you, in my turn, that I have not thought of either directly or indirectly giving you a lesson, and I have failed only through inadvertence." "Do not annoy yourself, and let your mind be at rest," replied the Saint, "I would only have loved and honored you the more. And in regard to the admonition I thought you wished to give, I will tell you in all simplicity that God has given me the grace to avoid its necessity; I tell you this, in order that you may not be scandalized in seeing me make no extraordinary preparations. For eighteen years I have never gone to bed without having previously disposed myself to die that very night."

It was for a still longer time even that the Saint lived in

this thought and in this practice, for the following little note, written with his own hand, twenty-five years before, was found: "I was taken dangerously ill two or three days ago, and that made me think seriously of death. Through the mercy of God I adore His Will. I acquiesce in it with all my heart; and examining myself on what could give me any regret, I have discovered nothing unless it be that we have not as yet finished our rules."

This faithful servant had, then, for long, as he of the Gospel his loins girt and his lamp lighted ready to go meet His master and open for Him, as soon as He knocked at the door. This supreme moment was constantly before his eyes, and he ever recalled it to the minds of his children. "One of these days," he repeated to them, "the miserable body of this old sinner will be placed in the earth. It will crumble to dust and you will trample it under foot." And when he was asked his age, he would answer: "For many years I have been abusing the grace of God. '*Woe is me that my sojourning is prolonged!*' (Ps cxxix., 5). Alas! O Lord, I have lived too long, because there is no improvement in my life, and because my sins multiply with my years." Whenever he announced the death of a missionary, he added: "Thou neglectest me, O my God, and ca'lest to Thyself Thy servants. I am the tare that spoils the good grain which Thou gatherest, and see, I always uselessly occupy the earth. '*Why do I take up the earth?*' (Luke xiii., 7) But yet, my God, let Thy Will be done and not mine."

Meanwhile habitual and increasing weakness, and sleepless nights brought on a heaviness against which he could no longer struggle. He saw in it the image and precursor of approaching death. "It is the brother," he smilingly said, "that comes to await his sister." A few days after, the sister, Death, did come in effect, and the holy old man received her with the same gentleness and the same patience that he had received all the sickness she had sent in advance of herself.

He took occasion from his own condition to lead others to the thought of death, a thought most salutary, provided it be animated with confidence in the goodness of God. He wrote to a person who had a too vivid and exclusive apprehension of death: "The thought of death is good, and Our Lord has counselled and recommended it; but it ought to be moderated. It is not expedient for you to have it constantly present to your mind. It suffices if you reflect on it two or three times a day, without, however, delaying very long; and, even should you find yourself disturbed, not to delay on it at all, but gently put it aside."

II

The example of his own ills served him as a means to encourage the sick, especially if they were young. "Do not fear, my brother," he would say, "I had the same disease when young, and I recovered; I have had asthma, and now I have it no more; I have had rupture, and God cured me; I had neuralgia in the head, and it has disappeared; I had oppressions of the chest and weakness of the stomach, and all I have outlived Have patience for a time; there is every reason to hope that your sickness will pass away and that God still wishes to make use of you. Let Him act, and do you peacefully and tranquilly resign yourself."

He also spoke of his own maladies in letters and in conferences, in order to exhort his disciples to patience in their illness. "It is true," he wrote, "that sickness, more clearly than health, shows us better what we are, and that, in suffering, impatience and melancholy attack the most resolute. But as they only hurt the weakest, you have derived rather an advantage than an injury from them, because Our Lord has strengthened you in the practice of abandoning yourself to His good pleasure. This strength appears in the resolution you have taken to combat them with courage. And I trust it will appear still more in the victories you will gain by enduring your pains henceforth for the glory of God, not only with patience, but also with joy and gladness."

He said to his community: "We must admit that the state of sickness is a troublesome state, and one almost insupportable to nature; and yet it is one of the most powerful means that God employs to bring us back to our duty, to remove us from sin, and to shower down upon us His gifts and graces. O, my

Savior! Thou Who hast suffered so much and Who hast died to redeem us, and to show us how greatly affliction may glorify God and promote our own sanctification, do Thou grant us, if it please Thee, to know the immense good and the great treasure that are hidden in sickness! It is, gentlemen, by it that our souls are purified, and it proves a most efficacious means to acquire the virtue we do not possess. There is no more suitable condition for the practice of all virtues. In sickness faith is wonderfully exercised, hope acquires new lustre; resignation, love of God, and all virtues find abundant opportunities for manifesting themselves. It is there we learn what is in us, we know what we are; it is the gauge wherewith to sound and know unerringly the virtue of each, whether he has much or little, or none at all. You can never see what the man is better than whilst he is in sickness. That is the surest test whereby to recognize the most virtuous, or those who are less so. And this proves how important it is that we thoroughly know how to properly conduct ourselves in sickness. Oh, if we knew how to act like a certain servant of God, who of his sick bed made a throne of merit and grace! He surrounded himself with the mysteries of our holy religion; to the canopy of his bed he attached an image of the most Holy Trinity; at the head he placed one of the Incarnation; on one side, the Circumcision; on another, the blessed Sacrament; at the foot, the Crucifixion, so that no matter how he turned, to the right or to the left, or in what direction he cast his eyes, whether above or below, he always found himself environed by these divine mysteries, and, as it were, encompassed by and full of the presence of God. Oh, what a beautiful thought, gentlemen, what a beautiful thought! How happy we would be were God to give us a like grace! We ought to praise God because through His mercy and grace we have in the Congregation sick and infirm persons who manifest in their indispositions and their sickness, as on a stage, patience and all other virtues in their brightest lustre. We will thank God for having given us such members. I have often said, and I can not refrain from repeating, that we ought to consider those who are sick as a blessing to the Congregation.

"Let us regard ill health and afflictions as coming from God. Death, life, health, disease, all come by the order of His Providence; and be the manner what it may, it is always for the benefit and salvation of man.

"Yet, there are those who, very frequently, bear their sufferings with impatience. This is a serious fault. Others permit themselves to be mastered by the desire for change of place; they wish to go here, to go there, to this house, to that province, to their own country, under pretext that the climate there is better. And what does this indicate? It shows that they are men attached to themselves, childish spirits, persons who wish to suffer nothing, just as if bodily ailments were evils that must be avoided. To fly the condition wherein it has pleased God to place us is to fly our own happiness. Yes, suffering is a state of happiness, and it sanctifies the soul.

"I have seen a man, named Brother Anthony, who knew neither how to read nor write. We have his portrait in our hall. He possessed the spirit of God in abundance. He called every one his brother, or, if a female, sister; and when he spoke to the queen he called even her his sister. Every one wished to see him. He was asked one day: 'What do you do when sickness comes upon you? How do you act when sick?' 'I receive them,' he said, 'as trials sent by God. For example, when a fever comes I say to it: ah, now, my sister malady, or my sister fever, you come on the part of God, be, therefore, welcome; then I suffer God to do His will in me.' Behold, gentlemen and my brothers, how he acted. It is thus the servants of Jesus Christ, those lovers of the cross, are accustomed to do. But they do not neglect to employ the remedies prescribed for their relief and for the cure of each disease, and in this, too, they honor God Who has created the plants; and given them healing properties. But to have such tenderness for oneself, to be so exceedingly delicate in our least indisposition, O, my Savior! this is what we must reject; yes, we must renounce this tenderness in regard to ourselves."

And coming back, as usual, to himself, he cried out in finishing: "Oh, wretch that I am! What a poor use I have made of the sickness and the little inconveniences it has pleased God to send me! Of how many acts of impatience have I not been guilty! Oh, miserable that I am, what scandal have I not given those who have seen me behave in that manner! Help me, my brethren, to ask forgiveness of God for the past, and grace to make a better use, in the future, of whatever His Divine Majesty will please to send me in my great age, and during the little time that remains to me of life."

CHAPTER XXIII.

METHOD OF DIRECTION.

I.

If we study St. Vincent de Paul in his conduct in general, we will see united as in one single picture all those virtues we have successively admired. Moreover, it will afford the opportunity of gathering together certain teachings of the Saint that could not be classified under any of the preceding titles.

The sole end of his conduct was the greater glory of God and the accomplishment of His will on earth as in Heaven; the way followed to attain this was He Who defined Himself as the Way, the Truth and the Life, Our Lord Jesus Christ, taken as light in His doctrine and as guide in His examples.

Like Jesus Christ, Vincent began by sanctifying himself; then his own sanctification he made the instrument of the sanctification of others.

From this may be learned the basis of his conduct, a conduct that was always humble, ever doubtful of the most vivid personal lights, seeking always to be directed by the light of God, and even according to the counsels of men.

His was a conduct attentive and vigilant, arranging all, watching over all, and foreseeing all. And at the same time this conduct was prudent and circumspect in word and in deed, especially in the direction of others; never absolutely determining anything, but proposing simply thoughts and submitting them in some manner to the judgment of those who sought his counsel; never inspired by that spirit of sufficiency and presumption which decides without hesitation: "This is true, this is the right way," but adopting in preference these more humble phrases: "This is my advice, this is what seems to me conformable to the order of God;"—except, however, where a maxim of the Gospel answered directly the question proposed, for there can be no hesitancy possible in the presence of a Divine oracle.

His conduct was slow and willingly dilitory, save when necessity absolutely required an immediate answer or action; and even then, he still took time to quickly consult God, or seek for something analagous in the lessons or examples of Jesus Christ.

Having need of a counsel at Tunis, Vincent cast his eyes on Martin Husson, a lawyer who practised before the superior court of Paris, who then, was living in retirement in Montmirail. He wrote to him, but, with his usual prudence and reserve, confined himself in his letter to a simple enumeration of the reasons for and against, without adding a word that could influence his will. Much perplexed, Husson came to Paris, and left the decision in the hands of the holy priest. Vincent directed him to consult some wise and prudent persons, but Husson assured him he awaited his word as the expression of the will of God. Forced into his last intrenchments, Vincent had recourse to prayer, and on Easter Sunday, in the year of 1653, he said to Husson: "I have offered to our Lord, in the mass, your anxieties, your lamentations and your tears; and after the consecration I cast myself at His feet begging Him to enlighten me. Having done that, I considered attentively what, at the hour of my death, I would have wished to have counseled you to do. It seems to me, then, that if I were summoned at this very instant I would be consoled in the thought of having told you to go to Tunis, on account of the good you can do there, and I would, on the contrary, extremely regret to have persuaded you not to go. This is my inmost thought. You may, however, go, or not go as you choose." "God wishes it," exclaimed Husson moved by such disinterestedness, "and I go." Vincent immediately procured his credentials from the king. A few weeks afterwards, Husson departed for Tunis.

We see from this example that the Saint did not like himself to designate the subject to be sent to foreign missions. He ordinarily waited until a person had manifested, and had repeatedly shown a decided vocation for that sort of apostolate. He acted in this way notably in regard to Madagascar.

His conduct was strong and firm in the maintenance of exactitude and regularity, and at the same time full of suavity and gentleness, in imitation of the conduct of God Himself, Who, says the Wise Man: *'reacheth from end to end mightily, and endureth all things sweetly'* (Wisdom, viii–1). This conduct was consequently tempered with kind consideration, with humble excuses in refusals to intemperate demands; by entreaty, or kindness of expression in commands; and, on this very account, more effective and more obeyed than the most imperious authority.

It was not only in regard to foreign missions, but also in relation to any difficult employment that Vincent previously desired to know the dispositions of his subjects: "I write you," he said to one of his priests, "to know the state of your health, and with what God will inspire you in relation to the proposition I am about to make you. We are called to N., to take charge of an establishment, and, having determined to send four or five missionaries, we have thought of you as their guide. Hence sir, it only remains that you raise your heart to God to listen to what He will say to you on this subject, and I beg you to send me immediate information of the disposition of your body as well as of your soul in regard to this holy enterprise, and pray Our Lord to grant us the grace to ever and in all places correspond with His holy will."

He sometimes adopted a charming gaiety "Are you the man," he, one day, said to a priest, "to undertake a long voyage for the service of God?" "I am ready," rejoined the other. "But it is out of the kingdom." "That's no difference." "But you must cross the sea." "To go by sea or land is all the same to me." "But, indeed,", added the saint, smiling, "the place is twelve hundred quarter leagues distant!" "Were it two thousand I am willing to go." "Depart then, sir; you are wanted in Rome."

Finally, his conduct was edifying and exemplary, always in imitation of Our Lord, Who commenced to do before He taught.

Hence the admirable care of the venerable old man to attend **exactly** all the exercises of the community, especially those the most painful for him, such as the morning meditation, and that after a cruel sleeplessness, when harassed with perplexities and with business, when sick and whilst undergoing treatment for the recovery of his health.

Let us now consider this conduct applied to the spiritual as well as temporal interests of his communities. We will dwell awhile here on fraternal correction, which was one of his triumphs. He possessed the authority of example, which guarded him from the severe retort, "Physician heal thyself;" the patience that defers the bitter remedy and employs it only in the last extremity: the charity that applies it in a manner proper to heal the wound instead of irritating it or inflicting a fresh one; the humility which, by accusing itself the first, commences by drinking the cup of shame and leaves to others but a few drops; the prudence, which measures the strokes in accordance with character, so as neither to discourage weakness, nor drive proud ardor to revolt; the meekness that sweetens correction, deceives and lulls nature to sleep; and with all this, the firmness that does not hesitate to put the axe to the root of the evil when the cure is at no other price. All these virtues conspired to give an incomparable charm to his manner of correction. Ordinarily, he delayed his reprehension, until nature had become calm both in himself and in others. He reflected on it before God and, like a skillful physician, he studied both the moral temperament of the sick and the medicinal property of the remedy, in order to render the correction effective; and, when he saw a refractory subject, he made his meditation, for even three days in succession, on how he should act.

The moment arrived, he approached his object by a profession of esteem for him whom he wished to reprehend. At one time he would praise the qualities of the person, at another, find, at first, an excuse in the first movement of nature and of passion. Then, he would accuse himself, always taking upon himself the greatest share of the fault. "Oh," he would say, "how you and I both need to labor to acquire humility, to exercise ourselves in the practice of patience, to bear with others as we wish they would support us, to accustom ourselves to exactitude, and to regularity." Sometimes he took the role of the accused before acting the judge. Once having remarked a young seminarist carrying to the church a strange book, he called him aside and said: "Have you not remarked something in me that has scandalized you?" Receiving an answer in the negative, he continued, "Well, my dear brother, would you like me to tell you something that I have observed in you?' And he sweetly informed him, adding: "May God bless you, my brother."

When the individual was conciliated by all these humble and charitable precautions, when he was in a disposition to recognize, with the Wise Man, that the wounds of a friend are preferable to the deceptive caresses of an enemy, he went straight to the fault, and with firmness pointed out all the circumstances of time, of place, and of person; he rendered palpable its gravity and its consequences in regard to God, to the good of the neighbor, to the future of the congregation or of a special work. He, then, would not hesitate to add with severity: "If you say you have not remarked these defects in yourself it is a sign you have but little humility, for had you as much as Jesus Christ requires of the Priest of the Mission, you would believe yourself the most imperfect of all and would readily acknowledge yourself guilty of all these things, and would attribute to some secret blindness the fact of your not perceiving what others see, all the more so as you have already been admonished of them. And, in speaking of admonition, I have also been informed that you can scarcely bear to be reprehended. If that be the case, O sir, how your state is to be feared, and how far removed you are from the saints, who loved to humble themselves before all and rejoiced in having their slightest faults pointed out. It is, indeed, a poor imitation of the Saint of Saints, Jesus Christ, Who has permitted Himself to be reproached publicly with evil that He did not do, and yet uttered not a word to avoid the resulting shame. Let us learn of Him, sir, to be meek and humble of heart. These are virtues which you and I should demand of Him without ceasing, and to which we should give special attention in order that we may not be carried away by the opposite passions which, with one hand, throw down the spiritual edifice that the other builds. May it please this same Lord to enlighten us with the light of His Holy Spirit so that we may see the darkness of our own, and submit it to those whom He has appointed to conduct us, and may we be animated with His infinite meekness which, inspiring our words and actions, will render us agreeable and useful to our neighbors."

The correction finished, he reanimated fallen courage, renewed his protestations of esteem and affection, and as a final sedative, added words like the following: "I experience the most intense pain in saying the least thing to wound you. In the name of God, bear with me;" or again. "I am unable, no, I cannot express the sorrow I feel in grieving you. I beg you to believe that were it not for the importance of the thing I would a thousand times have preferred to bear all than to give you the slightest pain." Such tenderness was irresistible. Self love died almost without feeling its wound; and this is what gave rise to the saying: "Mr. Vincent is like the grand Turk, because he strangles self-love with a silken cord."

Notwithstanding his absolute detachment from things of earth the Saint took the greatest care to preserve and manage with economy the temporalities of his congregation. As man, he knew that all are condemned to eat their bread in the sweat of their brow; as Christian, he knew that Providence, even in its designs the most generous, desires to be seconded by us; as head of a family and general of a spiritual army, that it belongs to fathers to provide for their children and to captains to furnish arms and rations to their soldiers.

Therefore, he first sought to turn to best account the little property that the congregation possessed. Not content with appointing intelligent procurators, he reserved to himself the general superintendence and the chief administration, permitting nothing to be done without his advice, designating in advance, often, every day, the specific duty of each, and requiring an account. When he learned that his orders had been anticipated, exceeded, or violated, he deposed the unfaithful agent, even were he a particular superior; for he said: "If every one were to do as he thinks fit the dependence established by God would be destroyed and there would no longer be but change and disorder in the houses."

He appointed brothers to superintend the cultivation of the farms of the congregation; and they had under them husbandmen and shepherds. He himself entered into the most minute details in regard to the crops and flocks, the kitchen garden and orchard, and as formerly Charlemagne did, he even attended to the accounts of the barn-yard of St. Lazarus.

He was thrifty in the use of these revenues, augmented by such skillful management, by procuring his stores at the times and places the most favorable, recommending to allow nothing to go to waste, to use the most rigorous economy, and, in bad years and during public disorders, even to retrench in the ordinary expenditures. Charity alone knew no calculations; therein, though ever acting prudently, he displayed a holy prodigality. But, for himself and his priests, in his houses, in clothing and at table, he confined himself to the strictly necessary and shunned every superfluity. This was why he was such an enemy to change, which necessitated costly journeys, when these changes had no other reason than the pretended unwholesomeness of the climate, the difficulty of the occupation, or the incompatibility of disposition.

II

For him, too, time was a rich capital of which he was severely economical. That he might consecrate it entirely to his pious undertakings, he never gave a moment to idleness. Moreover, he augmented it by adding the two hours' recreation he permitted his community, but which he himself refused, and each night by two or three more hours taken from his sleep. He never paid a visit save through a necessity of business, gratitude or charity. In the discharge, even, of his duties, in charitable reunions, notwithstanding all his condescension, he avoided useless words and digressions and always led the others back to the question by this ordinary word: "Come, let us to the subject; we must try to finish." This is how, according to the remark of Mademoiselle de Lamoignon, he alone had done more good works than any twenty other saints.

Vincent, we have said, required in all those who wished to unite themselves to him first a real vocation, and then perseverence in that vocation. On this two-fold subject he said, one day, to the Daughters of Charity (22nd of September, 1647): "A vocation is a call from God for the purpose of doing something. God says: 'I wish this soul to sanctify itself in serving Me in such an occupation.' Though His Divine Goodness often calls us by means that are unknown to us, yet He most frequently employs the strong desire, which He gives us, to be received into such a state, and the perseverance we manifest in our request. After this, we must no longer doubt that our vocation comes from God; for when you allow yourselves to entertain the doubt, it is, ordinarily, because you find difficulty in the practice of poverty, of humility, and of obedience which the demon endeavors to make appear to you impossible. But God is immovable in His judgments, and the salvation of souls is not of such little consequence to Him that He does not take all the necessary care to place them in the way the most sure and most easy for them to secure it. But we must not leave that way, for should a person who is on a long journey turn aside and leave the high-road he runs the risk of meeting only by-ways that will lengthen the distance. A man, with his orchard planted with good fruit-bearing trees, would incur the risk of not only gathering no fruit, but also of killing the trees, were he to change them constantly and yearly transplant them. Judas, having been called to the apostleship and having had a participation in the graces of God, imagined he was not right when he was, and thought to better himself elsewhere. You know his history and how he was lost. Let us, then, remain where God has called us. Have you ever heard of a soldier who, without an order, left the post assigned him by his captain? When a soldier is on duty, whether it rains or blows, whether it hails or freezes, even when cannon balls are falling on every side, he is not permitted to retire. He must remain even at the risk of death; and, should he prove so cowardly as to abandon his post, he is put to death without mercy, he is taken out and shot; and why? Because he did not remain where his captain placed him. It is the same with the soul. Faithless to its vocation it no longer knows any rest. Far better for it would it have been, had it never begun, for then, at least, it would not have to answer for so many graces received and abused. On the contrary, the soul that perseveres drives the demons back into hell when it resists their temptations. And it, at the same time, gives great joy to God; for He is looking on, and takes a singular pleasure in witnessing its perseverance in what it has undertaken for His love, notwithstanding all the combats of flesh and blood, and all the wiles of the evil spirit.

"A good means to preserve us is to take resolutions, and to write them down for future use whenever the occasion presents itself. Afterwards, to re-read them and say to yourself: 'Was it not God who inspired me with that thought? Was it not a good motive that influenced me to take that resolution?'—For we must expect temptations.

"There are two classes of persons, however, who are never troubled with them: those who never resist, and those who find the things of God so sweet and so agreeable that they never experience any repugnance. Hence, instead of being astonished if sometimes we see ourselves tried, let us employ the means proper for resistance, and, above all, let us ask the grace rather to die a thousand times, were it necessary, than consent to temptations against our vocation."

He desired a still more serious vocation for the priesthood. On the 5th of March, 1659, he wrote to a lawyer in Laval: "It is a misfortune for those who enter the priesthood by the window of their own choice, and not by the door of a legitimate vocation. Yet the number of the former is very great; because they regard the ecclesiastical state as an easy manner of life, in which they seek their comfort rather than labor; and hence have arisen the fearful ravages we see in the Church. For, to the priests are attributed the ignorance, the sins, and the heresies that lay it waste. This it was that forced St. John Chrysostom to declare that few priests would be saved; and why? Because God does not give the graces necessary to fulfill the obligations of this sacred state but to those whom His goodness has called, and It never calls any in whom it does not perceive the proper qualifications, or on whom it does not intend to bestow them. As for all others, God allows them to advance, and permits them, in punishmen for their temerity, to do more evil than good, and finally to destroy themselves. The call, then, to this holy profession must come from God, and this we see in the case of Our Lord Himself Who, being eternal priest, yet did not presume to exercise its duties until the Eternal Father had declared: '*This is my well beloved Son, hear Him*' (Luke ix-35). This example, together with the knowledge I have of the disorders occasioned by priests, who have not lived up to the holiness of their character, induces me to caution those who seek my advice in regard to receiving orders, against engaging themselves unless they have a true vocation from God, a pure intention of honoring Our Lord by the imitation of His virtues, and other marks showing that His Divine Goodness calls them; and this feeling is so strong within me that, were I not a priest, I never would become one. This is what I frequently say to such aspirants, and I have repeated it over a hundred times in preaching to the country people."

To confirm his own children in their vocation he said: "See the design of God in your regard in causing you to be born precisely at the time of the institution of the Congregation. You are the first called. If a king selected certain soldiers to lead in the assault, would not this honor be a motive powerful enough to make them face death rather than give way?" And then, addressing the brothers, he added: "You, too, as well as the priests, lead a life conformed to that of Our Lord: You imitate Him in His hidden life, during which he was engaged in corporal labor, working in a carpenter shop and performing household duties just like a domestic. Thus you imitate His life of thirty years, whilst the priests, in their functions, imitate only that of three and a half years; you honor the dependent life of Our Lord and the priests His priesthood. Moreover, by reason of the union that exists between the members of the same body, an effect of which is that what one does the others are considered as doing, it is certain that you labor in the confessional with the confessors, that with the preacher you preach, and that you evangelize the poor with the priests who evangelize them." (29 Oct. 1638.)

He concluded in a general way: "Let us continue our

voyage to Heaven in the ship in which God has placed us. The grace of perseverance is the most important of all ; it crowns all others, and the death that finds us with arms in our hands is the most glorious and most desirable. Naturally, we desire to die at home, in the arms of those we love and surrounded by our relations and friends; but all do not yield to such tenderness; it is only those souls that are over-delicate. Our Lord wished to terminate His life as He lived : His life having been severe and painful, His death was hard and cruel, without any human consolation. This is why many have desired to die alone, abandoned by men, trusting to have God only to aid them."

What sorrow and fear seized him when he learned that certain of his subjects had the thought of abandoning their vocation! He wrote, July 18th, 1659 : "May God grant them the grace to open their eyes, to see the danger to which they expose themselves in thus following the inclination of rebellious nature, which never accords with the spirit of Jesus Christ. Oh, how difficult, says the Scripture, for those who have fallen after having been enlightened to rise again! Indeed, they have every reason to fear that they will miserably wander if they leave the path in which God has placed them. For, how will they fulfill their duties in the world, where there are so many snares and obstacles, if they do not perform them in the state in which they are, and in which they are assisted by so much grace from God, and have so many spiritual and temporal helps, all which will be wanting to them outside their vocation? Yet we must not be surprised to see persons thus waver and turn back. The like are met with in the most holy communities, and God permits it to show men the weakness of man, to give the most determined and resolute a subject for fear, to try the good, and to give both an occasion for the practice of many virtues. Let them, at present, conceive a regret for past faults, let them purpose amendment, humble themselves, and become submissive and repair the bad example they have given; do you take special pains to assist them."

We have seen in another chapter the charitable efforts the Saint made to retain them ; but we must cite again that letter, so admirable for its longanimity : "It would be but justice to the Congregation to cut off the diseased members. This is true, and prudence demands it. But, to give an opportunity for the practice of all virtues, we now exercise patience, forbearance, and charity, even without the hope of their improvement. We try, as remedies for the evil, different applications of meekness, of menaces, of prayer and admonition, and all with the hope of no other good than that which it may please God to work by Himself. Our Lord did not drive away St. Peter for having denied Him more than once, nor even Judas, though he was to die in his sin. Therefore, I judge His divine bounty is much pleased to see us extend the kindness of the Congregation to those who are froward, that thus we may satisfy justice and omit nothing that can gain them to God." (July 15th, 1650, to Almeras, Rome.)

When any had left he consoled himself with the following consideration: "After Mr. —— had left, I commenced, in my sorrow, to say my Office. But it pleased God to console me by the understanding He gave me of what He had done in having the trumpets sounded in the armies of Israel before battle, and having it proclaimed that those who were afraid, or had married, or had planted a vineyard, or built a house that year should retire, considering that such classes of persons would be of more injury than benefit in battle. And then it struck me what great evil some of those who had left, having become dispirited in their vocation by the example of a single one, who loved the things of the world, could have occasioned in the Congregation had they remained in it all their life-time. In this way God was pleased to comfort me very much. Perhaps, He took into account the fact that I was for a full half-hour on my knees before one of the parties, trying to change his mind, and was unsuccessful.

"*In the name of the Lord!* We must remember how many followed Our Lord and how few persevered with Him. I say we should remember this, in order that we may honor His feelings on these occasions." (Aug. 26th, 1642, Annecy.)

Under the influence of such considerations, he did not wait until the subject left of his own accord, but took, himself the initiative either by refusing to receive those whom he foresaw would not persevere, or by dismissing the incorrigible. He wrote: "Where is the community that does not refuse applicants who do not possess the requisite qualifications, or that does not send away those who do not behave well? I was, some time ago, in the company of a great prelate, one who thoroughly understands what communities are. Some one was speaking of a certain community, and was praising it because it never sent away any it had once received. Thereupon the prelate expressed astonishment, and said, 'O, poor community! Thou scarcely tendest to thy perfection, since every description of subjects is suited to thee.' Every tree that is planted does not take root, nor does every grain sowed come up. The Kingdom of God is compared to a net cast into the sea that takes both good and bad fish, and the fisherman retains the good, and casts the bad back again into the sea. The Son of God did not receive into His company all those who presented themselves. He did not enforce His authority to retain those who wished to withdraw; but He offered those who remained their choice in saying to them: '*Will you, also, go away?*' (John vi. 68.) If he did not dismiss Judas, it was because Judas was to be the principal instrument in His passion.

"I say all this in order that you may impress it upon those who think differently, and on those who are disposed to enter the Congregation, as well as on their parents. The Son of God informed His apostles of the dangers they would incur, and I think the missionaries would do well to act in the same way to honor the simplicity and candor of our Lord in this as in all other things. Yes, but many will be scandalized by this manner of acting, and will not enter the Congregation. I answer: First, it will be a scandal taken, if what is in vigor in all well regulated communities in the church of God can be called scandal; second, if it be our Lord Who calls them the fear of being sent away will not deter them from coming; and if it be not He, we ought to be well pleased that they do not enter the Congregation, for it ought to desire only those whom God sends, because all others will never be of any advantage." (Aug. 28. 1656).

He wrote in a still more decided tone in relation to the dismissal of dangerous subjects: "Our seminary is being filled up; I think our Lord grants us this as a reward for the fidelity of the Congregation in purifying itself of refractory members. One of our priests here told me that six of the best could not do as much good as one who was beyond correction could do evil . . . . We must purge the Congregation. Ten of the right sort are worth a hundred, and a hundred, that are not called, or who do not correspond with the designs of God, are not worth ten. (25th of December, 1642) . . . . . . Purify, yes, let us purify the Congregation of those who are profane and of those who are not agreeable to God and He will increase and bless it. God, having wished to put to death three thousand men because they had adored the golden calf, answered Moses, who wished by his prayers to stay His hand: '*Let me alone that my wrath may be kindled against them, and I will make of thee a great nation.*' (Exodus xxxii., 10). According to this, then, to diminish in a community the number of those who offend God is to augment it both in virtue and number. for well-regulated and virtuous communities attract subjects. Yes, but those sent away will write and otherwise incense the public against the Congregation! They will occasion no more harm than God will permit them to do; and the injury they may do us will turn to our benefit. And, moreover, would we not be unworthy to serve God in the state in which we are, if, to hinder a person from doing us an evil, we were willing to suffer him to vitiate the service and glory of God among us? Remember that the decay of most of the communities comes from the cowardice of superiors who are too weak to hold a strong hand and who neglect to dismiss the froward and those who are unwilling to be corrected." (20th of March, 1643, Rome).

To forestall the sad necessity of such extreme measures, we have said that the Saint watched most sedulously over the training of those whom he admitted to the internal seminary. He did not neglect to animate and sustain all by his living and powerful word: "Whoever desires to live in community," he said, "should resolve to live as a pilgrim on earth; he should be satisfied to become foolish for Christ's sake; should make up his mind to change his manners and habits, to mortify his passions, to seek God solely, to subject himself, as if the least, to every one; he should fully persuade himself that he came to serve and not to be served, to suffer and labor, and not to live in delight and idleness. He should know that one is tried as gold in the furnace, that perseverance is only at the price of humbling himself for God's sake, and he should be convinced that in doing thus he will obtain true content in this world and eternal life in the next."

Everything furnished him with an occasion to instill into their minds the most heroic dispositions. When he learned that a missionary had been maltreated in a foreign country, he recounted the affair, and added: "May God grant that all, who seek admission into the Congregation, may come with the thought of martyrdom, and with the desire to suffer death and to consecrate themselves wholly to the service of God, either in foreign countries or in the their own or where else soever it will please God to make use of the little Congregation! Yes, with the thought of martyrdom! Oh, how we should often ask this grace from our Lord! Ah! gentlemen and my brothers, is there anything more reasonable than that we should be consumed for Him Who has so generously given His life for us? If our Lord has so loved us as to die for us, why will we not have a like affection for Him and prove it when occasion offers? We see so many popes, who, one after the other, were martyred Is it not strange to see merchants traverse seas and incur an infinity of dangers, all for a little more gain? Last Sunday I was speaking with one, who told me that a proposition to go to the Indies was made him, and that he had resolved to go. I asked if there were no danger: he told me that there was very great danger; that though it was true such a merchant whom he knew had returned, yet such another had not. I then reflected: if this person, for the purpose of seeking some precious stone or for the sake of gain, is thus willing to expose himself to so many dangers, how much more should not we brave in order to carry the precious gem of the Gospel, and gain souls to Jesus Christ!"

He wanted studies to be prosecuted with moderation and humility. He wrote, on the 18th of July, 1659: "The desire to learn is good, provided it be moderated. . . Remember the advice of St. Paul, who recommended us to use sobriety in learning. Mediocrity suffices, and whatever is aimed at beyond this is rather to be feared than desired for the laborers of the gospel, because it is dangerous, it puffs up, it leads them to show off, to become self-conceited, and finally to shirk the humble, simple and ordinary duties, which, nevertheless, are the most useful. Hence, our Lord selected disciples who were capable of doing but the humblest things. If we labor for the salvation of souls in the spirit of our Lord, He will give us the lights and the graces necessary to succeed. If you desire to know only Jesus Christ crucified, if you wish to live only His life, doubt not that He Himself will be your science and your guide." He said again in a conference: "The learned, and, at the same time, humble, are the treasure of the Mission, as good and pious doctors are the honor of the Church."

He dreaded the transition from the purely spiritual exercises of the seminary to the distractions of studies, and he multiplied his instructions in order that the students might not diminish in fervor according as they advanced in knowledge. He said: "Glass, when taken from the furnace and placed in the cold, is in danger of breaking; so a young man, who passes from a place of recollection, vigilance and prayer, to the tumult of a class-room runs the risk of becoming disturbed in his practices of piety. Strive, then, to maintain your first fervor and prevent nature from assuming the upperhand. Incite your will in proportion as your understanding is enlightened with new knowledge, and make use of your study as a means to elevate yourselves to God. Let the light of the mind become a fire in the heart. Be firmly convinced that the science most useful for our neighbor is that which has its foundation in piety. Fly curiosity, that pest of a spiritual life, which has introduced so many evils into the world. Fly the inordinate desire of knowing, which dries up devotion and closes the soul to the lights of Heaven. I have remarked that common and ignorant persons ordinarily make their prayer better than men of learning. God delights in communicating Himself to the simple, because they are more humble than the learned, who are always so full of themselves. Would that you all had the learning of St. Thomas, but on condition that you also had the humility of the holy doctor! Pride ruins the wise, as it ruined the angels, and knowledge without humility has ever been baneful to the Church. Love, then, humility and do not become conceited. The most insignificant demon in hell knows more than the most subtle philosopher, or the most profound theologian on earth. God does not need the learned to do His work; He rejects them, on the contrary, when they are proud, prefers the simple, and even women, as He did in the last century for the reformation of a very celebrated order in the Church. In conclusion, employ your youth in fitting yourselves for the service of your neighbor. Do not lose your time, for the work is urgent, and infinitely exceeds the number of workmen. The people in the country are being lost for want of instruction, and the greatest portion of the earth is still buried in the darkness of infidelity. Study, therefore, labor to acquire knowledge, but without losing humility."

Whilst he condemned a vain curiosity he cautioned the community against sensuality. "Wo," he said, "to him, who seeks his own satisfaction! Wo to him, who flies the cross! For he will find others so heavy that they will overwhelm him. He, who makes light of exterior mortifications under pretext that the interior are much more important, sufficiently shows that he is mortified neither interiorly nor exteriorly."

He said, at another time: "I have remarked in the most of those, who suffer shipwreck in their vocation, a remissness in two things: the first is rising in the morning in which they are not exact; and the second is effeminacy in regard to the hair, letting it grow too long, and insensibly allowing themselves to become attached to other like vanities."

We see what importance the saint attached to rising, and morning meditation. Here is a long letter he wrote, on this subject, on January 15th, 1650, to the superiors of his houses:

"You know that everything in this world is subject to some change, that man himself is never in the same condition, and that God often permits abuses to creep into the most holy communities. This has happened in some of our houses, as we have lately become aware by the visits that have been made to them, without, however, knowing at first the cause. To discover it required patience and study on our part. At last, God has shown us that the liberty on the part of some to repose longer than the rules allow has produced the evil results; all the more so as they, not being in prayer with the others, deprive themselves of the advantages that exist in making it in common, and they frequently make none at all or very little in private. Hence it is that such persons, being less vigilant over themselves, become languid in their actions, and the community becomes irregular in its practices.

"To remedy this disorder the cause must be removed; and for this purpose, exactitude in rising must be recommended, and firmness in maintaining it shown; so that, little by little, each house may come to change its appearance, exhibiting more devotion to rule, and individual members, in their own particular, may become more solicitous for their spiritual advancement. This has furnished us with the occasion to take for the subject of our first conference, this new year, the first action of the day, in order to strengthen ourselves all the more in the resolution of invariably rising at four o'clock. The felicitous results of fidelity in this, and the inconveniences arising from the contrary having suggested to us the motives, I have considered it my duty to communicate them to you, I have added the objections and answers that may be advanced in relation to this matter, and the means that may be made use of, in order that you may acquaint your community and thus strengthen it in this practice, or, if it be not already existing, introduce it that thus it may participate in the same happiness.

"The first advantage, resulting from promptitude in rising as soon as the signal is heard, is that we fulfill our rule, and consequently do the will of God. Second, the obedience shown at that hour, being so much the more pleasing to God as it is the more prompt, draws down likewise His blessing on the other actions of the day, as appears from the example of Samuel, whose alacrity in rising three times in one night was praised by Heaven and earth and merited great favors from God. Third, the first of good works is the most honorable. But, all honor being due God, it is only reasonable to give Him our first good action. If we refuse, we give the devil the first share, and prefer him to God. Hence, this lion lies in wait around our bed in the morning ready to receive this action, and thus be able to boast that if he cannot obtain anything else from us during the day, he has had, at least, the very first action. Fourth, in accustoming ourselves to the hour, we contract the habit. In a short time we become quick to respond to the signal, the habit even serves as an alarm where there is none, and we experience no difficulty in promptly leaving our beds. Whereas, on the contrary, nature is encouraged by the indulgence we allow it: having reposed one morning, it demands like gratification the next, and will continue to demand it until all hope be absolutely taken away. Fifth, if Our Lord left Paradise and became so poor here on earth as not to have whereon to lay His head, how much more ought not we leave a bed, and go to Him? Sixth, well regulated sleep is beneficial to both body and mind, but he who sleeps much becomes effeminate. Moreover, temptations arise during that time. Seventh, if the life of man is too short to worthily serve God and repair the evil use he has made of his nights it certainly is a deplorable thing to wish to still shorten the little time left for that object. A merchant rises early that he may become wealthy; his moments are precious; thieves do as much, and lay in wait the entire night to surprise the passers-by; will we be less diligent in good than they in evil? Worldlings make morning calls, and are careful to be present at the levee of the great. My God! what a shame, if laziness will cause us to lose the hour assigned for converse with the Lord of Lords, our Support and our All! Eighth, when we assist at prayer and at *repetitions* we share in the blessings of Our Lord, Who then abundantly communicates Himself, being Himself present, as He assures us, in the midst of those assembled in His name. The morning, being the most tranquil portion of the entire day, is the most proper time for prayer. Hence, the ancient hermits and the saints, after the example of David, always devoted the morning to prayer and meditation. The Israelites were obliged to rise early in the morning to gather the manna; and we, who are without grace and without virtue, why should not we do in like manner to acquire both? God does not bestow His favors equally at all times. And, indeed, since He has granted us the grace to all rise at the same time, we see among us here greater punctuality, more recollection and modesty, and this inspires the hope that, as long as this beautiful order will endure, virtue will make constant progress, and each will become more confirmed in his vocation. Indolence and negligence have induced many to leave us, because they could not love a life wherein they were not able to satisfy themselves as they would like. How is it possible to willingly go to prayers if we rise with reluctance? To meditate properly when we are only half in the church, or are there simply for the sake of appearance? On the contrary, those, who love to rise, ordinarily persevere, rarely become remiss, but rather make happy progress. The grace of vocation is attached to prayer, and the grace of prayer to that of rising. If, then, we be faithful in this first action, if we all meet together before Our Lord and present ourselves to Him, as did the first Christians, He, in turn, will give Himself to us, He will enlighten us with His light, and will Himself operate in us and by us the good we are called to do in His Church; in a word, He will grant us the grace to attain to that degree of perfection which He desires of us, that we may one day fully possess Him during an eternity of ages. See, sir, of what importance it is that the community rise exactly at four o'clock, since prayer derives all its value from this first action and since all our other actions possess only what prayer gives. He, who said that he judged from the manner of his prayer how all the other actions of his day would be, well knew this.

"But, in as much as the delicacy of some will not surrender without a struggle, for it has a pretext, I foresee that it will tell me the rule of rising ought not to equally oblige persons of feeble constitution and those who are more robust, and that the former require longer sleep than the latter. To this I oppose both the opinion of physicians, who maintain that seven hours' sleep suffices for such persons, and the example of all the orders in the Church. All limit themselves to seven hours and there is not one that takes more. Some have not even that much, and the greater number have it broken, for they rise once or twice to go to choir. And what condemns our cowardice is that the Daughters of St. Mary—I except those who are in the infirmary—though weak and tenderly educated, have not a greater privilege. But, do they not at times rest longer than usual? No; I have never heard so.

"Another will ask: 'Sir, must a person rise when he feels indisposed? I have had a severe head-ache, a tooth-ache, a fever, that prevented me from closing an eye almost the entire night long.' Yes, my dear friend, you must rise, unless you be in the infirmary or have permission to remain longer in bed. For, if seven hours of rest have not relieved you, neither will one or two taken of your own accord cure you. Moreover, though in effect your pain might be alleviated, it is expedient that you give glory to God in union with the others by rising, and then you can represent your indisposition to the superior: otherwise we will always have to begin, because frequently many feel some inconvenience, and more may imagine sickness in order to indulge nature. All this would give rise to constant disorder. If a person has not slept one night, nature will know how to supply for it the next.

"But, sir, do you likewise mean that those who arrive, after a journey, be also deprived of the extra rest?"

"Yes, the morning rest. Should the superior judge that the fatigue is such as to require more than seven hours' sleep he will have them retire earlier than the others." "But should they arrive very late and very much exhausted?" "In such a case there will be no harm to allow them to repose in the morning, for here necessity answers for rule."

"What! rise every morning at four o'clock! And the custom is to take a repose once a week, or at least once every fifteen days in order to recruit ourselves a little! That is very hard, and liable to render us sick." "Such is the language of self-love, and here is my answer: both our rule and our custom require that we all rise at the same hour. If laxness has crept in, it is only recently, and it is confined to a few houses, and has been occasioned by the abuse of individuals and the toleration of superiors; for, in other houses, the practice of rising has always been faithfully observed. Hence, they have ever been in benediction. To suppose that any will become sick because no intermission in this exactitude is permitted is simply an imagination; experience proves the contrary. Ever since all began to rise regularly at the appointed time we have here none sick who were not so before, and we have none elsewhere. And we know, and the doctors declare, that too much sleep is injurious to those of phlegmatic constitution and those whose humors are vitiated.

"Finally, if it be objected that there may be some necessity preventing a person from retiring to rest at nine, or even at ten o'clock, and that then it is but reasonable he should take in the morning what he lost at night, I answer that we must, as far as possible, avoid whatever may prevent us from going to rest at the appointed hour; and if this cannot be done, it is so seldom that the loss of one or two hours' sleep is slight in comparison to the scandal that is given by remaining in bed whilst the others are at prayer.

"Have I not done wrong, sir, in dwelling so long on the importance and utility of rising, since, perhaps, your community is one of the most fervent and most regular in the entire Congregation? If it be so, my purpose is no longer to persuade any anything else than gratitude for the faithfulness God gives. But if it have fallen into the abuse we are combating, I am right, it seems to me, in inviting it to correct itself, and in praying you, as I do, to see that it does. Now, here are briefly the means to be employed by you and your community.

"Those for the community are: First, it should convince itself that exactitude in rising is one of the most important practices in the Congregation; for, as is the beginning, such will be the remainder of the day. Second, to offer itself to God at night before retiring, and ask of Him the strength to overcome itself in the morning without delay, and for this purpose to invoke the assistance of the Blessed Virgin by the recital of a Hail Mary, kneeling, and recommend itself to its angel guardian. Many have found this means of very great advantage. Third, each one should represent to himself that the sound of the bell is the voice of God, and as soon as he hears it he should rise immediately, and, making the sign of the cross, prostrate himself, kiss the floor, and adore God in unison with the rest of the community; and when he fails in this he should impose a penance on himself. There are those who give themselves the discipline for as long a time as they lost in disputing with the pillow. Finally, the last means for each individual is never to swerve from this exactitude; for the more we give way the more difficult it becomes.

"The general means which are dependent on your care, and that of the officers for the house, are: First, that a person be appointed who will go from room to room, give a light when necessary, and say in a loud voice, *Benedicamus Domino*, and repeat it until he receives an answer; that, after, another go the round of the rooms, and even a second time, where the community is large. Those designated for these purpose should be exact in their duty.

"Second, that those who make the visit be strict, and under no pretext whatever allow any, not in the infirmary, except in case of necessity, to rest later than four o'clock. This exactitude in rising has been found so beautiful and so beneficial, that the conclusion has been arrived at that those who are unfaithful ought not be intrusted with any offices in the congregation, because their example would soon produce laxness in this point, and they could with ill grace take for themselves what they would be obliged to refuse the others. May it please God to forgive us our past failings and grant us the grace to correct them, that we may become as those faithful servants whom the Master, when He comes, will find watching! '*Amen, I say to you,*' says Our Lord, '*He will make them sit to meat, and, passing, will minister to them; and if He shall come in the second watch, or if He shall come in the third watch, and find them so, blessed are these servants. Verily, I say unto you He will set them over all He possesseth.*'" (Luke, xii. 37.)

The Saint again recommended uniformity in sentiment, in will, and in action. "We will be on our guard," he said, "against elevating ourselves above others, or aiming to surpass them, for this destroys affection, introduces envy, and engenders aversion. If, heretofore, we have striven to excel, in the name of God, let it happen no more. If I find myself capable of great depth in penetration, or great elevation in my discourse, I will confine myself, externally, to one-half; should I find myself able to perform any action exceedingly well, or display more than ordinary learning or erudition—ah, away with all that! Our Lord has not acted after that fashion. He, all powerful as He was, accommodated himself to the understanding of the weak. Should two thoughts present themselves to me, the one beautiful and ingenious, the other common and less striking, I will adopt the latter and reject the former. Let us adjust ourselves to mediocrity. Let the learned appear so with moderation, and let the strong, who labor, labor humbly. For all that is said and all that is done in regard to the poor people, in an elevated spirit, is vain and useless; it all passess above their heads, the wind sweeps it over the housetops. What do these preachers, who exhibit new, curious, and strange wares in grave and lugubrious tones of voice? What do they do? They stir the feelings of nature a little, but they neither give life to the dead, nor shed the light of the Gospel on the people living in the darkness of ignorance. Let us aim to give our exhortations with the least show of learning possible, and with less of eloquence, in order to conform ourselves to others who preach but who have less learning and less talent. . . . Every one can approach mediocrity, but to sublimity only few can attain. He who has a superior mind can descend to a certain degree to which he who has less talent can ascend. This will banish far from us envy, rivalry, and detraction, and will produce union and uniformity among ourselves, and in our actions.

"Let us form ourselves in this spirit if we desire to have within us the image of the Blessed Trinity, if we wish to have a holy relation with the Father, the Son, and Holy Ghost. In what do the unity and conformity in God consist if not in the equality and distinction between the three persons? And what constitutes their love, if not their resemblance? And, asks the holy bishop of Geneva, were there no love among them what amiability would they possess? Uniformity, then, exists in the Holy Trinity: what the Father wishes that the Son desires; what the Holy Ghost does, the Father and Son both do. They act alike. Their power is one and the same. They have but one operation. Such is the origin of perfection, and our model. Let us render ourselves uniform, and then we will be many, and yet as one, we will possess a holy unity in plurality. Let us examine in what we differ, one from the other, that we may strive to resemble and make ourselves equal, each to each; for likeness and equality engender love, and love tends to unity." (May 13th, 1659.)

To induce his subjects to mutually aid each other in the observance of the rules, to establish among them a certain solidarity in fidelity, so as afterwards not to be obliged to employ harsh measures against transgressors, Vincent enjoined them, whether in private or in public, to admonish each other.

On the advantages of admonitions, he said: "Had we a stain on our face and none told us of it, would we not take it ill, and would we not feel thankful to the person that would draw our attention to it and thus spare us the mortification of the laughter of those who, but for the kindness of that person, would see us in that condition? Also, we are blinded in what concerns ourselves, and often we do not know our own faults. Hence, have we not reason to complain of those who are charged with our direction, when, knowing our faults, they do not mention them to us, judging that we are unable or are not sufficiently mortified to bear an admonition? Where is the person, who, considering on one side the advantage of being admonished, and on the other the disadvantage of being deprived of that charity, will not say: 'Oh, I wish to be admonished, and it is the greatest favor that can be done me! What! All know my faults and I alone remain in ignorance!' Of course, you must not be astonished to feel a repugnance to be admonished, for there are few who are not moved when their faults are mentioned, because nature, loving itself so well, cannot but be pained thereby. But it must be habituated to it, and we must punish ourselves when we perceive we have fallen into any fault and have not well received the admonition. . . . Oh! one of the keys to a spiritual life is to consent to receive admonitions, to accept them properly, and to believe that were we known as we really are, many other faults could be pointed out. For, if we look closely at ourselves we will perceive that there is not one on earth more wicked than we are. And since we neglect to do so on account of the ugliness we might perceive, the admonitions disclose what self-love conceals, and if we take them in good part, we will, little by little, attain to great perfection. Were we sick, would we not be pleased to have our father informed, to have the physician notified and minutely instructed concerning the nature of our disease, and to have it made known to the entire house? And why, if not to receive comfort and relief? But sin renders our souls ill with a mortal sickness; why, then, not be glad that information of our condition be given our superiors, who are our spiritual physicians, and who can apply the proper remedies?" (March 15th, 1648, to the Daughters of Charity.)

And he added: "But," some one will say, "such a one informed that I committed such a fault, and yet it is not so; or he added something not in accordance with the truth." I answer: the thing is true or not; if true we have no reason to be put out because we are admonished; we should, on the contrary, humble and correct ourselves. If it be not true, well, we have an opportunity presented by Divine Providence to uffer, and to practise an act of heroic virtue. If the fault be somewhat exaggerated, or a circumstance be added we should also suffer it patiently. Tell me, my brethren, how did the Son of God, who was innocence itself, suffer the false accusations lodged against Him? You yourselves know, and I have no need to tell you. And why, then, will we be so wretched and mean spirited as not to be willing to receive the advices given us? It is true that we are not always masters of ourselves and cannot hinder the first movements of nature. When certain persons are admonished you see them change color. What is that but a first movement of nature, a movement which is not culpable and of which, though one were a St. Paul, he cannot always be master? But if the mind, regaining itself, does not repress it, ah, then, there is sin. Herein we perceive the distinction between the animal and the rational parts of man. Ah, me! how miserable I am! I have great cause to humble myself before God, and all the more so as there is not a sin committed in the house of which I am not culpable. Even this very day I permitted myself some little complacency. It is self-love that prevents us from properly receiving admonitions. Destroy self-will, says St. Bernard, and hell shall be no more. Let us earnestly give ourselves to God that we may properly receive the advices that may be addressed to us." (June 9th., 1656.)

The Saint wished that even superiors be admonished. One of these having complained to him of one of his subordinates, he answered: "It is a little exercise Our Lord sends you to form you in the proper manner of conducting those under you. This will give you a glimpse of the greatness of Our Lord's kindness in bearing with, when He was on earth, His apostles and disciples, and will give you an idea of what He had to suffer from both good and bad. It will, also, prove to you that superiority has its thorns like all other conditions, and that superiors who are anxious to do their duty, both in word and by example, have much to suffer, not only from the froward but even from the very best of their subjects. Hence, let us give ourselves to God to serve Him in this state without any hope of satisfaction from men. Our Lord will give us abundance, provided we labor properly to become more exact in the observance of our rules, and to acquire the virtues fitting true missionaries, especially those of humility and mortification. It seems to me, you would do well, sir, to tell this good priest, on the occasion of his communication, or at some other suitable opportunity, that you beg him to inform you of your failings; for in your position it cannot be but that you commit many faults, not only in your capacity of superior, but also in that of missionary, and as a Christian. You would also do well to declare from time to time to your community that not only you consent to be admonished by the member of your house designated for that charity; but, moreover, that you would be pained were he to neglect it, or did he fail to write to the superior general according to the practice established in all well regulated orders. You will, moreover, assure them that you will not read the letters they write me nor those I write them. Oh, sir, how great is human misery and what patience superiors need! I close in recommending myself to your prayers, and I beseech you to offer them to God that He may pardon me the incomparable faults I every day commit in my position—a position of which I am, of all men, the most unworthy, worse than Judas in regard to our Lord."

We see that the humble Saint was far from wishing to make himself an exception in this. Hence, he said one day: "I affirm that those, who notice faults that tend to irregularity and the ruin of the Congregation, and do not inform, are guilty of that ruin and disorder. I, therefore, should be content to be admonished myself; and if I did not correct myself of any scandalous failing which could bring disorder and destruction on the Congregation, or again, if I taught or maintained anything contrary to the doctrine of the Church, the Congregation, in assembly, should depose me and then send me away."

The following is the manner of giving admonition. Ought they be public? Yes, in three cases: "First, when the evil is so inveterate in the guilty person that a private admonition is judged useless. For this reason our Lord did not reprimand Judas save in the presence of the other apostles, and then, even, in obscure terms. On the contrary, He upbraided St Peter who wished to dissuade Him from His passion, and called him Satan, knowing well that thereby he would be benefited; second, when the persons whom we wish to advise, are good but weak and unable to bear correction, no matter how gently given: a general recommendation suffices to correct them; third, when there is danger that others will, unless the fault be noticed, fall into the like. Beyond these, I think the admonition should be given in private.

"In regard to faults committed against the person of the superior the inferior should be admonished, but, in doing so, attention should be paid to two or three things. First, the admonition should never be immediate unless in necessity; second, it should be gentle and suitable; third, it should be more by manner of reasoning, representing the inconveniences that result from the fault, and the superior, in reprimanding should make it plain to the inferior that the correction is given not through injured feeling or because he himself is concerned, but simply for the subject's own good and that of the Community." (13th of Aug. 1650).

Vincent said further: "The first reprimand should be given in great gentleness and kindness, and at a time well selected; the second with somewhat more severity and gravity, and yet with meekness, making use of entreaty and charitable remonstrance; and, finally, the third time, with zeal and firmness, declaring to the culprit what will have to be done as a final resort. On every occasion we must avoid reprehending through antipathy, through self interest, or from a spirit of vengeance; otherwise, we fail in truth when we say we admonish in a spirit of humility and charity." (29th of Oct. 1638).

Naturally, to impress such direction on his congregation it was to the superiors of particular houses charged with the application of its principles that he addressed his most frequent and most precise instructions.

He first spoke of positions and offices in general, and dwelt on the heavy responsibility they imposed, in order to remove from imprudent ambition the desire of assuming so great a burden: "I do not know how I shall speak to you on this subject, because it concerns myself." Here the Saint made a pause and humbled himself before God. "Nevertheless, I will lay before you my little thought. Although our Lord was the natural Master of all creatures, He yet made Himself the last of all, the opprobrium, and the outcast of men, taking in all places, and always, the lowest rank. You, perhaps, believe that a man is very humble and has lowered himself very much when he has taken the last place? What! a man humble himself in taking the place of Our Savior? Yes, my brethren, the place of Our Lord is the last. He who desires to command cannot possess the spirit of Our Lord. This divine Savior did not come into the world to be ministered unto, but to minister to others; and He has wonderfully practised this not only during the time He spent with His parents and those whom He served in order to gain His livelihood, but, even as several of the fathers have taught, whilst the Apostles dwelt with Him, serving them with His own hands, washing their feet and making them rest after their fatigue. In fine, he reprehended His Apostles when they disputed among themselves as to who should be the first, saying to them: '*And whosoever will be the first among you shall be the last and the servant of all.*'

(Mark, x. 44.) It is the accursed spirit of pride within them that urges men to aim to be in high position and have the direction of others. I know of no other way of expressing this deplorable condition than by stating that these persons have the evil one in themselves. For the devil is the father of the pride with which they are possessed. Oh, how dangerous is position, even when not ambitioned! How difficult to maintain virtue therein unless by laboring constantly to annihilate oneself before God, and to mortify oneself in all things! For the care and the troubles of business distract and divert the mind from the love of God and from union with Him in prayer and recollection. To-day I said to a superior, who told me of some persons whom he destined for positions: 'Alas! You send them to their destruction.' But, what! It is a necessary evil. I heard one of the most holy men I knew (the Cardinal de Berrulle) say, and I have experienced the same myself, that the state of authority is so malignant that it leaves, by itself and of its nature, a base and detestable stain, which infects the soul and all man's faculties, so that, when not in office, he has all the difficulty in the world to submit his judgment, and obey. His arms, his gestures, his carriage, and his looks, always retain something savoring of sufficiency, unless, a thing very rare, he be a man thoroughly consumed in God.

"And then, what should cause one to tremble is the strict account God demands of those who have charge of others, even were it a brother they had for a companion in their office. Oh, poor me! What will I answer to God for myself, especially since my time has been so long? But yet, may God pardon me, if it be pleasing to Him. Yes, an account must be given of words, of actions, of postures that may have scandalized inferiors, and of the faults they will have committed through our weakness and our negligence. In this connection it is related of Cardinal Bellarmin, that, whilst he was archbishop of Capua, he was informed of the dangerous illness of a bishop of his province. He went to see the sick prelate, and finding him in great peace and tranquility of mind, was surprised, and feared some fatal illusion. He resolved to undeceive him, and, therefore, said to him: 'Whence is it, my lord, that you are in such great peace, and a peace so unknown to persons of our position in like circumstances? Have you carefully reflected? Have you maturely weighed the words of the Apostle: *Reprove, entreat, rebuke, with all patience and doctrine?* Is it really possible that you do not find yourself guilty in this so important a point? If you do not, disabuse yourself, for undoubtedly there is illusion on your part.' This touched the bishop, who, melting into tears, excited himself to contrition, or, rather. became so perturbed that the archbishop was obliged to return and restore his peace of mind. O my God! Who will not tremble at the awful moment of death, particularly if he has sought after office? I asked a bishop recently if he did not feel the weight of his charge. 'Alas, sir,' he answered, 'the burden has not waited until now to make itself felt, for, three weeks after my consecration, I experienced so bitter a remorse that I would willingly have wished to have had the power of beginning anew.' Such is, sooner or later, the state of those who have thrust themselves into dignity. What, then, shall we do to totally banish from the Congregation this detestable and diabolical spirit of ambitioning authority?

"First. If any one among us feel this accursed appetite for office and superiority, he ought to have constant recourse to the hair cloth, the discipline, and to mortification until God will have shown him mercy. He should go before the Blessed Sacrament and lament before God: 'Ah, my God, what have I done? In very truth I am filled with sin, but, my God, why dost Thou permit me to stray so far from Thee by so deplorable and diabolical a spirit? My God, forgive me!' Second. We should return thanks to God for the grace he has given us of not allowing this spirit of authority and superiority to take possession of those who are in charge. On the contrary, all the superiors of this little Congregation write me pressingly to release them; and whenever I accede to their request they again write with such professions of joy and gratitude that it is impossible to suppose any lack of sincerity. Oh, my brethren, what blessings the Congregation will receive as long as God will please to continue in it this spirit, which is the spirit of humility, the spirit of Our Lord. We must thank God for it, and I pray our brothers to do so in their communions and the priests in their masses; it would even be well to celebrate mass for that purpose. Third. When obedience, at a suitable time, calls us to an office, we should submit. This is what the bishop of Geneva ordained: 'Whenever a sister,' he says, 'shall be elected to any office, though she consider herself unworthy, let her submit and receive the blessing, and let her place her trust in God for the grace necessary to acquit herself properly of her duties. For, when God calls us to any employment, He either sees the necessary disposition in us, or He is determined to confer it."

" Our Saint said again: " Those who are in charge groan under the weight, because they feel that they are feeble, and they believe themselves incapable of conducting others. If any presume the contrary he would be a source of affliction to his inferiors, for he would lack humility and the other graces necessary to give consolation and good example to them. The gifts of God are manifold and He bestows them as He thinks proper. Such a person is learned, but unsuited to govern, and such another makes progress in sanctity, but is not the one to guide others. Therefore, it belongs to His Divine Providence to summon us to the employment for which He has given us a fitness and not for us to insinuate ourselves into them." (May 5th. 1658.)

On those who were legitimately appointed to office, he afterwards lavished instructions. He first recommended them to share their responsibility with others by taking counsel. He wrote: "Very far from it being wrong to take advice, it is, on the contrary, expedient and even necessary to do so when the subject in question is important, or when we cannot ourselves come to any determination. In regard to temporal affairs, the counsel of some good lawyer or other intelligent person outside should be sought; and in what concerns the interior of the house we should confer with the proper officers, and also with others of the community whenever it seems proper. And when this is done with all the necessary precautions, the authority of God, which resides in superiors, suffers no detriment, but, on the contrary, the good order which results makes it more loved and respected. I pray you to act in this manner, and remember that, in regard to changes, or extraordinary matters, you are first to propose them to the superior general."

He wrote to another: " Live cordially and simply with your confreres, so that any one, seeing you all together, may not perceive who is the superior. Do not take any decision in affairs of little moment even, without their advice, especially the advice of your assistant. For my part I call mine together whenever any difficulty as to how I should act arises, whether in spiritual and ecclesiastical matters, or in temporal things; and in regard to the latter, I also consult those who have charge. I even seek advice from the brothers in whatever relates to their department, on account of their knowledge of those things, blesses the decision taken in concert."

Having taken counsel, and having formed a decision, he would have them go directly and perseveringly to its execution. "When once we have recommended anything to God, and have taken counsel, we ought to adhere steadfastly to what has been decided, and reject as a temptation whatever may arise against it, being confident that God will not be displeased nor reprehend us. For we can say in legitimate excuse: 'O, Lord, I have recommended the affair to Thee, and I have taken counsel; I could do no more to discover Thy will!' The example of Pope Clement VIII. is a good case in point. An affair of grave importance, concerning an entire kingdom, was submitted to him. Several couriers were dispatched to him and an entire year passed without his wishing to come to any decision, notwithstanding all their representations. He, meanwhile, recommended the affair to God, conferred with those in whom he had the greatest confidence, and whom he regarded as the most capable and enlightened, and, finally, after several consultations, he came to a conclusion favorable to the Church. And yet, after this, he had a dream wherein it seemed to him, our Lord appeared with a severe countenance reproaching him for what he had done and threatening to punish him. On awakening, being greatly distressed by such a vision, he communicated it to Cardinal Tolet, who, having considered the matter in the presence of God, told the Pope not to be at all annoyed, that it was but an illusion of the devil, and that he had no cause for fear, since he had recommended the affair to God and had taken counsel, which was all that he could do. This good Pope, accepting the Cardinal's advice, experienced no further misgivings on the subject."

He recommended firmness particularly in maintaining the rule: "Those who are in office must be firm in seeing that the rule be observed, and must use great caution so as to not give occasion for a falling off in this respect, through want of resolution and exactitude. Among all things that can occasion, in communities, a decline in their first discipline, I have seen nothing more dangerous than their government by weak and easy superiors or other officers who desire to please their inferiors and gain their affection. As disasters in war are usually attributed to the general of the army, so the faults committed in a community ordinarily arise from the negligence of the superior, and, on the contrary, the good state of the members depends upon the wise direction of their head. I have seen one of the most regular communities in the Church fall away in less than four years, through the negligence and supineness of a superior. If, then, all the good of a community depends on the superiors, we ought, certainly, pray fervently to God for them, intrusted as they are with the guidance, and obliged to render an account of all under their direction."

On the superior depends not only the good conduct of his confreres, but also, in seminaries, the proper education of young ecclesiastics : "Train them, sir," he wrote to a superior, "in the true spirit of their calling, which consists especially in an interior life and in the practice of prayer and virtue. For it is not sufficient to teach them chant, ceremonies, and a little moral theology; the principal thing is to form them to solid piety and devotion. But for this, sir, we ought ourselves, the first, possess these, for it would be almost useless to give them instructions without the example. We ought to be reservoirs always full, so that the water may flow without exhausting the supply. We should, ourselves, be imbued with the spirit with which we desire them to be animated, as no one can give, what he does not possess. Let us, then, earnestly beg it of our Lord and give ourselves to Him that we may endeavor to conform our direction and our actions to His. Then your seminary will diffuse a sweet odor both within and without the diocese, that will increase its numbers and draw down the blessings of

Heaven. But, were you to act the master towards those under your charge, or were you to neglect or disedify them, it would, on the contrary, prove a serious obstacle to such a good. This will result if we seek too great an elegance in manners, too great a nicety in dress, too much delicacy at table, if we aim at consideration and honor, if we seek to recreate ourselves, to spare ourselves in labor, and hold too much converse with externs. We must be firm, but not austere, in our government, and should avoid childish meekness which serves no purpose. We will learn from our Lord how our rules should ever be accompanied with humility and affability in order to win over all hearts and offend none."

To superiors again it belongs to insure the success of the missions: "My great hope is that, with the grace of God, you will contribute very much to the salvation of these people, and that your example will serve to enkindle in your confreres an affection for this good work, which will induce them to devote themselves to it in the places, at the times, and after the manner prescribed by you, who, like another Moses, will consult God and receive from Him the law which you will transmit to those whom you lead. Remember that the government of this holy patriarch was gentle, patient, forbearing, humble and charitable; and that in the conduct of our Lord, these virtues appeared in their perfection in order that we might conform thereto."

Consequently it was the superior's duty to regulate the conduct of his subjects both on the journey thither, and during the labors of the mission: "You will have charge, sir, of the direction of those who accompany you, and I pray our Lord to inspire you with His spirit and His manner of directing. Undertake, then, this holy work in His spirit; honor the prudence, the foresight, the meekness, and the exactitude of our Lord. You will do a great deal if you have the rule observed as it should be, because fidelity in it will draw down the blessing of Heaven on all the rest. Begin, then, with exactitude in the hours of rising and retiring to rest, in prayer, the Divine Office, and the other exercises. Oh, sir, how rich a treasure is the habit acquired in these, and what inconvenience the contrary occasions! Why, then, will you not take the pains to acquit yourself of these duties for God's sake when you see people in the world, for the most part, so faithfully observe the order they have established for themselves in their affairs? We rarely see judges fail in rising, in going to court, and returning at their usual hours, or tradesmen, in the hour for opening and closing their shops. We, ecclesiastics, who are so given over to our own ease, are the only persons who follow the movement of our inclination."

If the Saint imposed on superiors so heavy a burden he likewise aided them to bear it, by his encouragements, and by the consolations he lavished on them when in difficulties: "I compassionate with you in your trials," he would write on these occasions, "you ought not to be astonished at difficulties, still less become disheartened, for they are met with everywhere. Two men living together are enough to try each other's patience; and even were you entirely alone you would prove a burden to yourself, and would have in yourself abundant to bear with, so true is it that our wretched lives are full of crosses; I thank God for the good use to which you turn yours as I am persuaded you do. I have perceived too much wisdom and meekness in your character to think they will fail you in these untoward circumstances. If you do not satisfy every one, you should not therefore allow yourself to be annoyed: for our Lord, Himself, did not please all. How many have there been who have criticised His words and actions, and how many will still be found to do the same?

On another occasion, he wrote: "I well know there is suffering in the office you fill, and I pray our Lord to strengthen you in your difficulties. These are the occasions wherein we acquire virtue, and when there is no trouble there is but little merit. Would it were pleasing to God to give us a great indifference for all offices. Oh! then, what an assurance we would have of doing His holy will, which ought to be our only aim, and what peace and content would be ours." (Dec. 8, 1649.)

He loved to see superiors humble and diffident of themselves, and when so, he hoped everything from their labors: "I have remarked the humble idea you have of yourself. This is very necessary for those who govern. But you know this diffidence in your own strength, ought to be the foundation of the confidence you should place in God. For, without this confidence we often discover that we are far worse than we thought, and with it we find we can do a great deal, or rather God himself does what He requires of us. Do not, therefore, fix your attention on what you are, without, at the same time, regarding our Lord near you and within you, ready to give you a helping hand as soon as you turn to him for assistance, and then you will see that all will prosper. Do not doubt but that, having placed you in position, He will give you the graces necessary to fill it properly, if you, for His love, undertake it with courage. (Dec. 19, 1646.)

He comforted them especially, when they suffered from the conduct of their subjects, and recommended a charitable forbearance. "You should bear with your confrere. If he had not these faults he would have others; and had you nothing to suffer from him or from others, your charity would have very little exercise and your direction not sufficient resemblance to that of our Lord. He was pleased to have rude disciples and subjects who had many defects, so that he would have the opportunity of manifesting towards them meekness, humility, and patience, and thus, by His example, show us how those should act who have charge of others. Let this Divine Model be your rule, and he will teach you at the same time how to bear with your brethren, and how to help them to correct their fault. Evil must not be tolerated, but the remedy must be gently applied."

And again: "The virtue of such and such a one is a reproach to the others; but this is because these have less regularity, less punctuality and solicitude for their own advancement and that of their brethren. Yes, their zeal and their exactitude are eyesores to those who have neither, because the courage and strength of the former condemn the cowardice of the latter. I acknowledge that virtue has two vicious attendants, defect and excess; but, in comparison with defect, excess is praiseworthy and should be encouraged. Job complained to God of the rigor of His chastisement, his friends, who had been witnesses of his righteousness, considered that his lamentations were unbecoming a just man. It seemed to them they were excessive, and they, consequently, reprehended him. But God became incensed against them, and, to appease Him the Saint was obliged to offer sacrifice for them. His virtue was so pleasing to God, that he had a right to say what he did say, and yet these friends blamed him. And why? Because they were as persons who, with eyes bleared and sore, cannot gaze upon the rays of the sun without being dazzled. In like manner, those, who cannot attain to the virtue of these two good missionaries, imagine there is excess, when before God there is not. They find fault with their conduct, because they have not the courage to imitate them. May God give us all the grace to consider as good everything which is not evidently evil." (July 18th, 1659.)

Impressed with such ideas how he must b'ame those who did not exercise meekness and patience! A superior having written to him that he would prefer to rule animals than men, the Saint answered: "What you write will bear explanation. Yes, your words are true in regard to superiors, who desire that everything bend beneath them, that nothing resist them, that everything succeed according to their inclination, that they be obeyed without reply or delay, and, so to say, that all adore them; but they are not true in regard to those who love contradiction and contempt, who look upon themselves as the servants of all, and who strive, in their government, to imitate our Lord, Him who bore with rudeness, rivalry, want of faith and the like from the members of His company, and who declared that He came to serve and not to be served. I know, sir, that, thanks to God, this same Lord has given you the grace to act with humility, and patience, and that you have made use of this language only the better to express the difficulties you encounter, and the more to persuade me to relieve you. We will try, however, to send some one in your place."

He, sometimes, released superiors, but more frequently he answered their request : "So far from the reasons you allege for your discharge from superiority inducing us to seek another that, on the contrary, they confirm us in the determination of giving it to you altogether. The knowledge of your defects and your incapacity should serve to humble you as it does, but it should not discourage you in the work Our Lord wishes you to perform. He possesses enough virtue and ability both for you and for Himself. Let Him guide, and rest assured that whilst you remain in the humble sentiments in which you are at present, and place a special confidence in Him, His direction will sanctify yours. I trust in His goodness and in the holy use you will make of His grace." (April 10th, 1648.).

He answered another: "In regard to your request I pray you not to think of it, but rather hope that, under the ashes of that humility, which inclines you to submission to another, is hidden the spirit of our Lord, who Himself will direct your rule, will be your force in your weakness, your science in your doubts, and your virtue in your difficulties. On your part, sir, give yourself to Him that you may be a burden to none, that you may act towards each one with meekness and respect, and, that your language may be always entreating and amiable, never severe and imperious. For there is nothing so capable of wining hearts as this amiable and suave manner of action, and, consequently, none so proper to attain your object which should be to have God served and souls sanctified."

He did not neglect to recommend in temporal things the economy, modesty and mortification he himself so well practised. In times of scarcity and want, he said: "We must lament over the distress of the poor, and weep with those who weep, else we are not disciples of Jesus Christ. But what else should we do? The inhabitants of a beleaguered city examine from time to time what provisions still remain. How much grain have we, they ask? So much. How many mouths are we? So many. And thereupon they regulate the quantity of bread each is to receive, and say: "With two pounds of bread a day we can continue for so long. And when they perceive the siege is to last longer, and that the provisions diminish, they limit themselves to one pound, to ten ounces, to six, to four, in order to hold out the longer and prevent capitulation through hunger. And how do they manage at sea when it happens that the ship is tossed and driven by the winds, and remains a long time from port? They count the biscuit and measure the fresh water and if there be not enough, with the usual allowance, to last till they arrive in port, they give less; and the more they are delayed the more they diminish each person's share. Now, if governors of cities and captains of ships act in this wise, and if wisdom even requires they should use these precautions, lest they might perish, why will not we do similarly? Do you think that the people in cities do not retrench something in their ordinary expenses, and that the very wealthiest establishments, seeing that the vintage is over, do not economise in their wine, in the fear that next year they might not be able to procure a supply? Yesterday, some persons of quality from the city were here and they told me that most of the houses would entirely cut off the servants' wine. They will tell them: 'Provide for yourselves; the wine in the house is only for the master.' All this, my brethren, has made us think of what we should do, and, yesterday, I assembled the ancient priests of the house to hear their advice. We, finally, came to the conclusion to reduce, for this year, the community's allowance of wine at each repast to one gallon. This will pain some who think they have more need of a little more wine; but, as they are accustomed to submit to the orders of Providence, and overcome their appetites, they will turn this privation to their own profit as they do all other causes of mortifications. There will, perhaps, be others who will complain because they are attached to their own gratification; carnal spirits, sensual and inclined to their own pleasure, unwilling to deny themselves the least satisfaction and who murmur against everything that is not in accordance with their taste. Oh, my Savior, protect us from this spirit of sensuality?

He answered a superior who wished to build, under pretext of the good he could effect in a more commodious dwelling: "You speak of commencing to build. Oh, my Jesus! My dear sir, you must not think of it. It is a great mercy of God that the congregation has even so good a house whilst waiting till it please His Divine Goodness to send us aid. As regards the inconveniences you adduce I must say that since we cannot prevent them, we will not be the cause of them. And, moreover, all this seems to me to bear some resemblance to the conduct of God in regard to His people. He permitted great disorder for many ages, and the loss of an infinity of souls that He might establish an order all divine, and save all by the advent, the life, the passion and the death of His Son whom He sent when He saw His people, prepared by so many warnings, so many prophecies, and so many ardent aspirations, disposed to receive

Him. If this be a false view, I withdraw; and if you offer a better I will adopt it with pleasure."

Economical of his own time the Saint preached the grand law of labor. He first gave the motives: "First, God has given an express command to man to gain his bread by the sweat of his brow; that is to say, by a labor so painful that the perspiration will flow from his face. This command is general and there is none who may claim exemption. God has not simply said: 'Thou shalt make use of the industry of thy mind to obtain thy livelihood,' but 'Thou shalt labor with thy hands, with thy arms, and with thy entire body, and with such an energy and in such fatigue that the sweat will fall in drops from off thy brow. Second, it is said in Holy Writ that the just man liveth by the labor of his hands; the Holy Ghost giving us to understand thereby that the greatest obligation of man, after that which he owes to God, is to labor to gain his livelihood. He likewise intimates that, in reward for the hardships thus borne, he will bless him, and none will see him reduced to necessity and become a burthen to any; but that he will always have sufficient to support himself and maintain his family; everything will prosper with him, for God will second his efforts and labor with him. The unjust, on the contrary, not working, is frequently a burthen to others, because he is forced to beg his bread, or else is in the occasion of taking what belongs to others. Third, God Himself constantly works; He has never ceased and never will cease to labor. He is active within Himself from all eternity: the Eternal Father engenders from all eternity His only Son: from the Father and the Son, mutually loving each other, the Holy Ghost from all eternity proceeds, through whom are conferred upon us all celestial gifts: God does not cease to labor in time and outside Himself in the production and conservation of this grand universe. The heavens are ever in movement, the stars constantly exert their influence, the earth continually produces, the seasons are all regulated; but all this beautiful order which we see in nature would instantly return to its original nothingness were God to remove His hand; more, God labors with each individual creature. He works with the artisan in his shop, with the woman in her household duties, with the bee and the ant in their gatherings, and He does not rest a moment from labor. But for whom does He work? For man; yes, for man alone, in order to procure him the means of preserving his life and to provide for all his wants. This being the case, it is quite reasonable that we, His creatures, should labor, and labor until the perspiration pours, according to the command He has imposed upon us. Fourth, Our Lord during His mortal life was always at work. Up to the age of thirty He worked at the carpenter's trade in the shop of St. Joseph, thus living by the labor of His hands, and in one of the most humble and painful occupations in the world. And we, pitiable and miserable creatures, will we want to pass our time in laziness? What did not Jesus Christ do from the age of thirty up to the moment of His death! He was always occupied; He was frequently in the holy temple instructing the people; He went about preaching from village to village and gave Himself no rest. His poverty was such that He did not have even a stone for His pillow; He ordinarily lived on the alms given Him by Magdalene and other pious women who followed Him to hear His sermons; He sometimes went to eat with those who invited Him; but He was engaged night and day and at all hours in doing some good work. At one time He went to such a place when He knew there was a soul to gain, again He visited a sick person to give first, corporal, and then, spiritual health. Thus we should do. The apostle St. Paul, notwithstanding his numerous occupations, lived by the labor of his hands, taking the time for this work either from the day or night, in order thus to be a burden to none, as he himself informs us in one of his letters. And yet, he was not a man of the common people; he was by birth of good condition, and eminent in virtue and in science; but he held the poverty of Jesus Christ in such high esteem that he scrupled to eat a mouthful of bread without having labored for it; and when, by reason of his great duties, he could not work during the day, he took the time from his rest at night. In the beginning of the primitive church everybody worked. The monks, after having assisted at the divine office, made mats and baskets out of rushes, as a means to procure themselves the necessaries of life. In the time of St. Bernard this custom was still in vigor, and the religious lived very holily; but, since it has been abolished, there has been a great falling away in the discipline of the regular orders. For, idleness is the mother of vice; yes, it is the nurse.

"But in what disposition should we labor? First, we should have the intention of pleasing God, for He delights to see us occupied in good things, and for a good purpose. Second, to honor the painful labors of Jesus Christ, Who, during His mortal life, did not spare Himself, but engaged in the greatest labors. Third, for the service of our neighbor, who is so dear to Our Lord that He regards as done to Himself whatever we do for the relief of His poor members." (To Daughters of Charity, Nov. 1649.)

In the following advices given to a newly appointed superior we find, admirably abridged, both the Saint's own method of government and that which he prescribed for others.

"Oh, my dear sir, what and how great, think you, is this office of governing souls to which God has called you? What profession, imagine you, is that of the Priests of the Mission, who are obliged to manage and guide minds whose movements God alone knows? *The art of arts, the government of souls!* This was the employment of the Son of God while on earth; for this He descended from Heaven, was born of a virgin, gave every moment of his life, and finally suffered a most ignominious death. You, consequently, should conceive a very great esteem for what you are about to undertake.

"But what are the means to properly fulfill the duties of this office? To lead souls to God! To oppose the torrent of the vices of a people, or the faults of a seminary! To inspire sentiments of Christian or ecclesiastical virtue in those whom God will confide to your care, to contribute to their salvation or their perfection! Certainly, sir, in this there is nothing human; here is not the work of man, it is the work of God. *A great work.* It is the continuation of the work of Jesus Christ, and, consequently, human industry, can do nothing here but ruin all, unless God interferes. No, my dear sir, neither philosophy nor theology, nor eloquence operates in souls. Jesus Christ must unite with us, or we with Him; we must work in Him and He in us; we must speak as He spoke and in His spirit, just as He Himself was in the Father, and preached the doctrine which the

Father had taught Him. This is the language of Sacred Scripture.

"You must then, sir, divest yourself of yourself, and clothe yourself with Jesus Christ. You will easily understand how ordinary causes produce effects of like nature; for instance, a sheep begets a sheep, and man begets man. So, too, if he who guides others, who forms them, who speaks to them, is animated only with a human spirit, those, who will behold him, who will listen to him, who will aim to imitate him, will become all human. He will infuse into them, no matter what he says or what he does, only the shadow, and not the substance of virtue; he will communicate to them the spirit with which he himself is animated, just as we see masters impress their maxims and their manner of action on the minds of their disciples.

"On the contrary, if a superior be all in God, if he be thoroughly imbued with the maxims of our Lord, his every word will be efficacious, there will go out from him a virtue that will edify, and all his actions will prove so many salutary instructions which will influence all those who may become cognizant of them.

"But to attain to this, sir, our Lord, Himself, must imprint on you His mark and His character. For, as the grafted wildstock bears fruit according to the nature of the graft, so we, miserable creatures, who are but flesh, hay, and stubble, do what our Lord has done on earth, when once he imprints on us His character; He gives us, so to speak, the sap of His spirit and of His grace, and unites us to Himself as the branch of the vine is united to the vine. I mean that we do divine actions, and, like St. Paul, who was full of His spirit, we beget children for our Lord.

"A very important thing, and one to which you must devote yourself with care, is to have frequent communication with God in prayer. This is the reservoir wherein you will find the instructions necessary for you in the duties of the position you are about to assume. When doubt arises, have recourse to God, and say to Him: 'Oh, my Lord, Thou Who art the Father of light, teach me what I must do in this circumstance.

"I advise this not only in regard to difficulties that will occasion you trouble but also that you may learn directly from God what you will have to teach, in imitation of Moses who announced to the people of Israel only what God had inspired him : '*Thus saith the Lord.*'

"And again, you should have recourse to God in prayer to preserve your soul in His fear and in His love; for, alas, sir, I am bound to tell you, and you ought to know, a person is often lost whilst contributing to the salvation of others. Such a one does very well in private, but, occupied outside, he forgets himself. Saul was found worthy of the kingly dignity, because he led a good life in the house of his father; and yet, after having been raised to the throne, he miserably fell away from the grace of God. St. Paul chastised his body, lest, after having preached to others and having shown them the way of salvation, he himself should become a reprobate.

"But, to avoid falling into the misfortune of Saul and Judas, we must unite ourselves inseparably to our Lord, and, raising our minds and hearts, often say: 'O, my Lord, do not permit that in saving others I should become miserably lost myself; be Thou Thyself my pastor, and do not deny me the graces which Thou hast bestowed on others by my agency and through the functions of my ministry.'

"You should again have recourse to prayer to demand of our Lord the graces necessary for those under your charge. Be firmly persuaded that by this means you will reap more fruit than by any other. Jesus Christ, Who should be your example in all your actions, was not content with preaching, with laboring, with fasting, with shedding His blood, or even with dying; to all that, moreover, He united prayer. He had no need for Himself; it was therefore for us that He prayed so often, and to teach us to do the same as well in our own needs, as for the necessities of those of whom, with Him, we ought to be the saviors.

"Another thing which I recommend to you is the humility of our Lord. Often say: 'O, my God, what have I done to merit such an employment? Where are the works that correspond to the burden placed upon my shoulders? Ah, my God, I will spoil all if Thou, Thyself, dost not direct all my words and all my works.' Let us always look at all that is human and imperfect in us and we will find only too much reason to humble ourselves not only before God, but before men, and in the presence of our inferiors.

"Above all, do not give way to the desire of appearing the superior or master. I am not of the opinion of a person who said to me, some days ago, that to govern well and to maintain authority, one should show that he was superior. Oh, my God! Our Lord Jesus Christ has not thus spoken; He has taught us the entire contrary both by word and example, declaring to us Himself that He had not come to be ministered unto, but to minister, and that he, who would be master, must become the servant of all.

"Be inspired with this holy maxim, and act towards all with whom you will dwell *as one of themselves*; tell them, first of all, that you have not come to be their master, but rather to be their servants. Do this both within and without, and you will experience its good effects.

"Still more, we ought always refer to God the good that is done through our instrumentality, and, on the contrary, attribute to ourselves all the evil that happens in the community. Yes, bear in mind that all the disorders arise principally from the superior, who, by his negligence or his bad example, introduces irregularity, as the members of the body languish when the head is unsound.

"Humility should also induce you to shun all complacency, which easily insinuates itself, especially in occupations that attract attention. Oh, sir, how dangerous to all good works is the poison of vain complacency! It is a bane that corrupts the most holy actions and that soon superinduces a forgetfulness of God. In the name of God, beware of this defect; I know of none more dangerous to progress in spiritual life, and to perfection.

"For this purpose give yourself to God that you may speak in the humble spirit of Jesus Christ, avowing that your doctrine is neither yours nor of you, but of the Gospel; imitate, especially, the simplicity of language and comparison which our Lord employs in the Holy Scriptures when speaking to the people.

Ah! what marvellous things He could have taught the people! What secrets He, Who was the Eternal Wisdom of the Father, could have told of the Divinity and its admirable perfections! And yet, you see how intelligibly He speaks, how He makes use of familiar comparisons, of a husbandman, of a vinedresser, of a field, of a vineyard, and of a grain of mustard seed. Thus you must speak, if you desire to be understood by the people when you announce to them the word of God.

"Another thing to which you must give special attention is dependence on the conduct of the Son of God. I wish to say that when you are called upon to act, you should make this reflection: 'Is this conformable to the maxims of the Son of God?' If you find it to be, say: 'Very well, let us act.' If the contrary, say: 'I will not touch it.'

"Again, when there will be question of doing some good work, say to the Son of God: 'O Lord, wert Thou in my place how wouldst Thou act in this case? How wouldst Thou instruct this people? How console this person, sick both in body and in mind?'

"This dependence should also include a great deference to those who represent Our Lord and who hold the place of superiors in your regard. Believe me, their experience, being derived from their position, has taught them a great many things relative to their manner of conduct. I say this to induce you neither to do anything of importance, nor undertake anything extraordinary without acquainting us. If the thing be so urgent that you have not the time to await our decision, address yourself to the nearest superior, and ask him: "Sir, what would you do in such circumstances?" We know from experience that God has blessed those who have thus acted, and, on the contrary, those who have done otherwise have embarked in affairs that have not only placed themselves in difficulty but also have embarrassed us.

"I pray you also to banish the wish of distinguishing yourself in your government. I desire that you affect nothing singular, but that you always follow *the royal road*, that grand route, in order to walk surely and without blame. I mean by this that you conform in all things to the rules and pious customs of the

Congregation. Introduce nothing new, but follow the instructions that have been drawn up for the use of those who are charged with the government of the houses in the Congregation, and abridge nothing of what is practised in it.

"Be not only faithful yourself in the rules, but also be exact in having them observed, for if you fail in this all will go wrong. And, as you will hold the place of Our Lord, so must you, in imitation of Him, be a light that both lightens and warms. 'Jesus Christ,' says St. Paul (Heb. 1--iii) 'is the splendor of His Father' and St. John says that He is 'The light which enlighteneth every man that cometh into the world.'" (John 1--ix)

"We see that superior causes influence inferior. For example: The angels that belong to a superior hierarchy enlighten, illumine, and perfect the intelligence of an inferior hierarchy. So too, should the superior, the pastor, or director, purify, illumine, and unite to God the souls whom He commits to them.

"And, as the heavens diffuse their beneficent influence on the earth, so must those who are above others infuse into them the chief spirit that is to animate them. To do this you will require to be replete with grace, with light, and with good works; just as we see the sun, of its plenitude, communicate to the other luminaries their brightness.

"Finally you must be like salt: *You are the salt of the earth,* preventing corruption among the flock of which you are the pastor."

At this point of the conference a brother, who had something to say about some temporal concerns, entered. The brother, having left, Vincent took occasion to add the following remarks: "You see, sir, how from the things of God, of which we were just now speaking, I must turn my attention to temporal matters. From" this you should understand that not only is it the duty of the superior to attend to spiritual things, but he must also extend his care to temporal affairs. For, as those whom he directs are composed of body and soul, he must, consequently, provide for the wants of both the one and the other. And he should do this in example of God, Who, though occupied from all eternity in begetting His only Son, and the Father and Son in producing the Holy Ghost, yet, besides these operations within Himself, has created the world outside of Himself, and is constantly occupied in preserving it and its dependencies, producing every year new grain on the earth, new fruit on the trees, and such like. And this care of His Adorable Providence extends so far as not to allow a leaf to fall without His order; He counts the hairs on our heads, and feeds the smallest worm, even the flesh worm. This consideration seems to me well calculated to show you that one ought not only to apply himself to what is elevated, as are the functions that regard spiritual things, but also that a superior, who, in some measure, repre-presents the reach of the power of God, should devote his care to the least of temporal affairs, and not imagine such care unworthy his position. Give yourself, then, to God to procure the spiritual good of the house to which you go.

"The Son of God recommended to His disciples, when first He sent them out, to possess no money; but afterwards, when the number of His disciples increased, He directed that one of them should have charge of the purse, whose duty it would be not only to assist the poor, but also to provide for the wants of His family. Still more, He suffered pious women to follow in His company for the same purpose, *who ministered unto Him*. If in the Gospel He ordains that we be not troubled about the morrow, it should be understood as cautioning us against too much anxiety and solicitude for the goods of this world, and not as meaning that we absolutely neglect the means to procure sustenance and raiment; otherwise the earth should not be tilled.

"With this I finish; this is enough for to-day. I repeat anew that you are about to undertake a very great work, *a grand work*. I pray Our Lord to impart His blessing to your management, and do you, in return, pray Him, with me, to forgive all the faults I have committed in the position I hold."

END OF VIRTUES.

LETTERS

AND

UNPUBLISHED FRAGMENTS

OF

MADEMOISELLE LE GRAS.

I

LOVE OF GOD.

On the word of Our Lord: "*And I, if I be lifted from the earth, will draw all things to myself.*" (John, xii.32.)

"This word of our dear Master and lover teaches us that we can and ought to aim at the perfection of true love. It is His clearly expressed intention to draw us to Him, and He speaks with power to effect his promises. Is there need of anything else, Dearest Beloved, to cause Thee to be loved above all? How is it that vanity has prevailed, and still prevails, against truth? Let us have more courage, dearest sisters, and accomplish, as far as possible, the word of God. Or, rather, pray Him to fulfill in us the promise He has made of drawing all to Himself; this will give the universal domination to the Author of all. Is it not just, is it not glorious, to co-operate with God in the execution of His designs? Let us, then, bow to the will of our dearest Love, that His word may be verified in us. What would it be, if, seeing Him raised above the earth for the purpose of drawing us to Him, we should remain so bound that the ties of our earthly affections would resist all the power and charm of His pure love? Draw us, then, O Lord! We will run, and the odor of Thy ointments will hold us so firmly that nothing will ever separate us from Thy charity. Thou, Thyself, dost wish to draw us; grant that we be strongly impressed with this word. If we belong to Thee, we will no longer be our own, for it would be a theft to withdraw ourselves, ever so little, from the possession of Thy love. Thou desirest to draw us to Thyself: I, too, wish it, my dear Spouse; I desire it; and in proof I follow Thee to the foot of the cross, which I select as my cloister. There I wish to abandon to earth all the affections of earth, being invited thereto by Thy voice telling my heart to incline my ear, and forget my people and the house of my father, that I may be filled with the greatness of Thy love. At the foot, then, of this sacred and holy cross, never expecting any joy save subject to Thy good pleasure, I sacrifice all that can alter the purity of the love Thou desirest of me.

"Be not frightened, my dear sisters. The Spouse of the Canticles, who has preceded us in this holy love and whom we should regard as our abbess, has said that the well-beloved was white and ruddy. Let not the thorns of these two roses prevent us from wearing the bouquet; but rather, since the property of love is to form a resemblance with the object loved, imitate His purity and His charity, the one represented by the white, and the other by the crimson of the rose: purity of God in Himself as indicated by His simplicity, in His favors and graces by His disinterestedness; charity of God in Himself shown in the unity of His essence and the distinction of the Divine Persons, love of God for men proved by His having willed that His Divine Son should become man, because His delight is to be with the children of men, and in order, by accommodating Himself to the manner of men, to show in all His human life that God has loved them from all eternity. Then, let us love this Love, and hold fast to it since the retaining of it depends on us. Let the actions of our Beloved be often present to our memory; He is not content with the love of all whom He calls in general; He desires, moreover, some who will be very dear to Him, who will be elevated to a singular love, a love more pure and perfect. Admire in this the goodness of our Beloved; and, in the simplicity of the dove, ask Him if He desires that we be of these privileged souls. Oh, my Lord, I have had a certain inexpressible suggestion of a love not common which Thou desirest of chosen creatures that they may exhibit on earth the purity of Thy love. See, we are here a little group; may we aspire to this love? It seems to me all our hearts have the desire. But the knowledge of our weakness, derived from our past infidelities, gives rise to the fear that Thou mayest refuse us. Yet, the recollection that Thou hast not limited the number of times we are to pardon our enemies leads us to believe that Thou wilt do the like in our regard. This being so, we believe that Thou lovest us. Thou truly lovest us because Thou art but one with Thy Father, and Thy Father has wished to testify His love by giving us Thee, His only Son. We are convinced that Thou wishest we should love Thee, since both Thy ancient and Thy new law command it, and because Thou, Thyself, has promised that, if we love Thee, we will be loved by the Father, and that He, with Thee, will come and dwell with us. Oh, the power of love! Oh, the wonderful treasure hidden in the inmost recess of the soul! Oh, pure love, how I love thee! As thou art strong as death, oh, take from me all that is opposed to thee! Behold us, then, oh, my Lord, at the foot of Thy cross, ready to be drawn to Thee, as Thou hast promised! Were it not that Thy word is all powerful, I would dread the weight of earthly affections; but Thou well knowest all, since Thou requirest neither our consent nor our effort. Act, then, mightily, and unite our love to Thy love, our life to Thy life, and our death to Thy death."

II

LITTLE PRACTICES OF DEVOTION.

"First, our interior converse with God ought to consist, it seems to me, in the thought of His holy presence, in adoring Him at all hours, and in eliciting acts of love towards His divine goodness, recalling to mind as much as we can the motives that most impressed us in prayer, and especially the affections and resolutions we made, in order thus to correct our faults and advance in

His holy love. Second, on all occasions painful to nature we should consider the paternal bounty of God, Who, like a good father, permits us to feel His divine justice; sometimes it is for the purpose of testifying greater love for us by giving us a share in suffering in order, to apply to us the merit of the sufferings of His Son, and to excite us to acts of gratitude. Third, when we meet with what pleases us, and when things succeed as we desire, we should, before entertaining the proffered joy, turn interiorly to God and express our gratitude for His mercy, which, through pure love, gives us this consolation, and, accepting it in this view, elicit an act of love. Fourth, we should do all that depends on us to make every object that presents itself to our senses an occasion to elevate our hearts to God; at times, regarding them as created by the all-powerful hand of God; then, again, reflecting on the design of God in their creation, remembering that all has been created for the use of man that man might show himself grateful. Fifth, think, again, on the excellence of the being God has given us, and, then, let us lift ourselves above the baseness to which corrupt nature inclines us in engaging our affections in numberless vanities that are not worthy to occupy our mind, and let us protest that we desire nothing on earth but God alone. Sixth, when borne down, as it seems to us, with great difficulties, we desire or hope for aid from creatures, and this aid does not come, either through a dispensation of Divine Providence, or through the fault of others, we should immediately think of the Divine Will, and, accepting it in this privation, elevate our heart and have recourse to God alone. From all eternity He has been, and now is, self-sufficing and, consequently, we should reflect that He can and ought to suffice for us. Since we are so blessed as to be in a state wherein we should love Him as our only consolation, we ought to form an act of this love by accepting cheerfully the privation of what is wanting to us, though the object may seem very reasonable and very necessary. Let each of us remain in peace with God without a murmur against creatures, for, not all united could give us the slightest cause of annoyance did not God permit it. But to place our hearts at the disposition of the divine pleasure in all the above-mentioned occasions, we must often produce acts of desire to know God and to know ourselves, and, hence, acts of love for God and of hatred for ourselves, in order to give to God what we owe Him and refuse ourselves whatever is displeasing to Him. We must frequently make an act of abandonment and show Him our hearts overflowing with love and gratitude."

III

WHILE ON A PILGRIMAGE.

"The design of God in creating souls is to send them on this earth as pilgrims, for their bodies are their companions only for a time. Hence the majority of our forefathers did not have a lasting habitation, but often went on pilgrimages through devotion, perhaps, in order to keep before their eyes the fact that their true home was not on earth. And, to confirm them in this truth, God has been pleased to often accompany them with His holy angels. This should induce me to cheerfully accept all changes of place when it will please His Providence to permit it, and I should interiorly join company with my angel guardian.

"Our first father, having contravened the designs of God, by wishing to become immortal in eating the forbidden fruit, in place of life grasped death, and to remedy this the Son of God came Himself to be a pilgrim; for his life, which should be our example, was a constant pilgrimage."

IV

WHEN OBEDIENCE CALLS TO ANOTHER HOUSE

"We should go to the new place with the intention of honoring the Divine Providence that conducts us thither, and be disposed to then do whatever this Providence will permit to be our duty. We should honor in this change that of Jesus and Mary from Bethlehem to Egypt and other places, and desire, no more than they, any fixed abode on earth."

V

SOME ADVICES AND SOME STRENGTH.

First: Fidelity to the rule of rising and morning meditation: "God be praised, my dear Sister, for it is the manna that God gives to those who rise early. Oh, if you knew the joy I feel when I hear you coming to the chapel in the morning! Oh! the sweetness there tasted well recompenses the difficulty experienced in overcoming self. We ought to rise promptly, without bargaining with the pillow, and then kneel, &c."

Second: In beginning a conference: "God be blessed, my dear Sister, because we have reason to hope that our Lord is with us, since He has said: '*When two or three are gathered in My name there am I in the midst of them.*' (Matt. xviii., 20). What do you think He does, my dear Sister? He darts forth His beams, as a Divine Sun, to enlighten and warm our hearts. We, then, should meet here to honor the assemblies that have gathered in the presence of our Lord, and with the desire to perfect ourselves and correct the faults of which we accuse ourselves."

Third: "If you only knew, my dear Sister, how consoled I was the other day when I learned that a poor person had beaten a sister, and she, by the grace of God, did not defend herself! Oh, well! He was a master somewhat rough; but it was necessary to suffer correction from him, for we are the servants of the poor and must endure everything from them."

Fourth: When giving "the simple and poor habit of the Daughters of Charity," she recommended love, purity of intention, and interior as well as exterior divesting of self; and, on putting on the cornette, she said: "Let us have our ears closed to worldly discourse and open to the eternal truths. Let this white head-dress be the symbol of purity. It is given last because the last thing we give up is our own judgment which has its seat in the head."

VI

ADVICE IN REGARD TO RECREATION.

First: "Let us keep in view the presence of God and the thought of the equality of all rational creatures in their creation; the least before men being oftentimes the most beloved by God."

Second: "Let us look upon this time as given us by the Goodness of God, that we may become united by a sincere interchange of thoughts, of words, and of actions, and thus honor the unity and distinction of the divine persons, and imitate the union of the saints in Heaven."

Third: "Let our conversation be, withal, truly cheerful and cordial, making no distinction between those who please and those whom we think disagreeable; let our answers be kind, and let us, without contention or taking anything in ill part, bear in mind the meekness of Jesus Christ in His words and actions, when, as frequently occurred, He was blamed. We ought not to belittle those who speak less correctly, unless we be assured they will not be displeased, and always without any thought against charity."

Fourth: "Receive in good part all little pleasantries, looking upon our sisters as better and more beloved in the sight of God than we, and let us consider it a happiness to serve them."

Fifth: "Let us elevate our hearts to God, reflecting that it is a time of relaxation given us that we may be the better able to serve God. Let us think of the joy of Heaven, and reflect that the bond of love is the blood poured out from the heart of Jesus Christ."

Sixth: "Let the example of Jesus Christ and the spirit of charity regulate our discourse, seeking the interests of others, without curiosity in regard to motives and actions, and flying all particular friendships.

Seventh: "Let us be kind to all; honor the superioress, who, in our regard, represents Jesus Christ on earth, blaming neither her action nor her regulations, for it is rather the spirit of God than her own that governs."

Eighth: "We ought to defend the absent, thinking of ourselves in their place, and of our own faults."

Ninth: "The subjects of our conversation should be such as are calculated to foster a love for the observance of the rule, for every other devotion, without this, is more prejudicial than profitable, as all our words should give edification."

VII

TO THE SISTERS IN POLAND ON THE OCCASION OF SENDING OTHER SISTERS.

"At last the moment has come which Divine Providence has chosen for the departure of our sisters, and it is with grief we endure this, because we thus become separated, but, again, it is with joy because of the assurance we have that they go to do the will of God and to unite with you in the accomplishment of his designs in the kingdom of Poland. Oh, my dear sister, of what great importance these are! I pray the goodness of God to grant you the grace to know it, because I am sure this knowledge will give rise within you to a great humility and confusion when you reflect that you are chosen for such a work, and will also inspire you with the desire to become less unworthy. And how will you do this, my very dear sisters, and I with you? We must, by the mortification of the senses, cause our passions and inclination to die within us; and also, empty our hearts of everything in order, by the grace of God, to have them filled with love, that thus His Divine Bounty may accept the sacrifice of yourselves, which you will often offer to His Majesty, and the services which, under the direction of the queen, you will render to the poor. Our Sister Margaret will tell you in regard to this all that our most honored father will have instructed her.

"My dear sisters, you have always informed me that you were, in the name and honor of the Most Holy Trinity, but one heart in your three persons. Now, I beg you to enlarge this heart and let our three other sisters enter this cordial union so that there will be no distinction between the first three and the last three. I assure you they go to you in the pure disposition of always trying to please God, and are not attached to their own interests, nor even their own satisfaction. Not that nature does not, at times, furnish even the most perfect with occasions for struggling; but you know that it is the test of the fidelity of souls that desire to belong to God. Do not, my dear sisters, be astonished at them; it is then our hearts should be all the more generous and, notwithstanding nature, practise virtue in the exercise of humility, thus proving that we wish to be really Christian, and to honor Jesus Christ in the practice of the virtues His sacred humility has taught us.

"Would you like, my dear sisters, that I draw your attention to a point that seems to me essential? It is that you, when together, never make use of the Polish language without explaining your conversation to our sisters. This, besides being a means for them the sooner to learn the language, will obviate many inconveniences that otherwise might arise.

"It appears to me that I will be unable to sufficiently rejoice at the union which I believe will exist among you in word and in action. Its manifestation will be a source of edification both for yourselves and for those outside who may be witnesses of it. Let there be among you six no secrets, but guard religiously from all externs whatever transpires in the house. In this case what good may we not expect? I supplicate our Lord in His bounty to bestow on you abundant graces for all that He requires of you, and I remain in His love, etc."

VIII

ON CHRISTMAS.

"It is not sufficient to have our intelligence enlightened by the knowledge of our fault; we must, moreover, have our will purified so that we may reject them. The first serves to cleanse our soul in preparation for the birth of Christ in us, and the other to adorn and beautify it for His reception. The purification is effected by a good confession of all our sins, and the embellishment by the exercise of virtue, and especially by prayer, by fasting and almsgiving. These will, in some sort, for persons in the world, take the place of the three vows of religion, namely, almsgiving will represent poverty, fasting chastity, and prayer obedience; we may also lay them at the crib, in union with the gifts of the three Kings: alms with the gold, fasting with the myrrh, and prayer with the frankincense; or again present the three to the Blessed Trinity: prayer to the Father, fasting to the Son, and almsgiving to the Holy Ghost;

in this way we will adore the Incarnate God in prayer with the angels, in alms with the Kings, in fasting with the shepherds, and God, in turn, will bless us."

IX

MUTUAL AFFECTION.

"I see you both, it seems to me, in great peace and animated with the desire of exciting one another to union and cordiality which consist in being open with each other, telling each other what each has done when alone, and informing one another whither you go when you leave the house, one through submission and the other through kindness and condescension. Act thus in all your little exercises, as, for instance, when one happens to be sad and melancholy let her overcome herself that she may contribute to the recreation of the other, and let her that is cheerful moderate her joy in order that, humoring the other for the love of God, she may, little by little, chase away her melancholy. You should do this that you may not listen to the temptation of seeking comfort elsewhere, and discharging the burden of your poor heart on strangers, a thing that would be the total ruin of the holy friendship that should exist between two sisters.

X

AGAINST DIVISION BETWEEN SUPERIOR AND INFERIOR.

"How is it, my Sister Barbe, that, by the little cordiality you manifest towards the sister God has given you, by your little disdains and the wants of kindness to her in her weaknesses, you have come to forget that, when you were appointed her superior, you assumed the obligations of spiritual mother which are far greater than those of a natural mother, for you, more than she, are bound to care for the salvation and perfection of those under your charge? This, too, obliged you to exercise great meekness and charity such as the Son of God recommended while on earth. Did you not, when accepting this charge, immediately perceive what humility it required on your part, since you have so much reason to know your own incapacity? Ought you not always have before your eyes, when you give any command, that it is because obedience requires it, and not that you, of yourself, have any right to command? But now, I trust the evil is not beyond remedy. Resolutely place your faults before you without trying to excuse them in any way; for, of the evil we do there is, in truth, no other cause than ourselves. Acknowledge this truth before God. Excite in your heart a great love for our Sister Louise; and, in view of the merciful justice of our good God, throw yourself at her feet and ask her pardon for all your coldness and all the pain you have occasioned her, promising that, with God's help, you will love her as Jesus Christ wishes. Show her all the consideration which you should have for her, and, with this feeling really in your heart, embrace her.

"And you, my dear Sister Louise, see how you are fallen again into your bad little ways! What do you think your condition is? Is it a life of liberty? Far from it. It ought to be a constant submission and obedience. Is it possible you never reflect on this? Or, if you do, have you so little love of God and so little fear of your salvation that you neglect to do what you are obliged? My daughter, use a little violence with yourself . . . . Do you not remember that you should do nothing nor go anywhere without the permission of my Sister Barbe, whom, before leaving, you accepted as your superior and whom you ought to love as much or more than your own mother?

"In noticing your faults my own rise up before me, and this impels me, my daughter, to express what is now uppermost in my mind. It is the bad example I have given you in the practice of the virtues I have recommended. I beg of you, my good sisters, to forget it and ask pardon for me, and the grace that I may correct myself." (Oct. 28th, 1639).

XI

DISUNION AMONG SISTERS, AND DISCOURAGEMENT IN CONTRADICTIONS.

"The principal object of this letter is to testify the displeasure I feel in seeing the evil disposition of our sisters and the want of union that appears among you. I am also very much astonished that by reason of some little contradictions some have listened to the desire of coming to Paris before obedience calls. Oh, my dear sisters, there is great reason to say that they do not know what they demand. Oh, well, you are a little hurt when these gentlemen, our fathers, (the poor) mortify you in the presence of the poor, who are your masters. Give them no cause, and do your duty so well that they can have no fault to find. When sometimes you think you have done something wrong, or when any of these gentlemen criticise you too harshly, according to your idea, and you imagine that that will injure you with the sick, humble yourselves by patiently enduring it, and then, afterwards, go and quietly tell them your reasons, begging them to quietly admonish you of your faults. . . . I pray you, my dear sister, to first give the example of the virtue you desire to see in all. I have noticed the little aversion that you mention, on the part of one of our sisters. Oh, my God, your charity must have great compassion and patience with her. Do you not know that, ordinarily, this is in our natural feelings, and that we are not always masters of it? But it is the duty of those in charge to try, without being perceived, to help them in banishing this antipathy. We must not be so tender as to worry if some neglect to speak to us, or if all do not meet us with a pleasant face, but should endeavor to win all hearts by patience and cordiality. Finally, my dear sister, those who have the care of others should look to their own satisfaction no more than if they were insensible . . . . . I know, my dear sister, there is a great deal of difficulty in properly discharging the duties of our office; but God Who has imposed them will not refuse us His grace. To obtain it, let us humble ourselves very much by a holy diffidence in ourselves and a great confidence in His mercy, a confidence that will make us ask of Him in all simplicity whatever He wishes we should give our dear sisters whom we will regard as His dear creatures and servants." (To Sister Turgis, Angers, Aug. 24th. 1643).

XII

SAME SUBJECT, TO THE SISTERS AT NANTES.

"How have the tares, which appear desirous of choking the good grain, succeeded in being introduced among you? Oh my dear sisters, I fear very much that my bad example has given rise to these dangerous impressions in your minds. If it be so, do me the charity to ask pardon of God for me, and do you yourself pardon me by doing better than you have seen me do, in order no longer to sadden our good God by giving His enemy what belongs to Him, and also that you may not lose the recompense His bounty promises those, who, being in His grace, perform works of mercy; for He rejects the greatest presents of those whom He sees filled with their own will . . . . Finally, my dear sisters, we must belong to God, and entirely to God; and to become so properly we must tear ourselves away from our own selves. And, believe me, if we, without any self flattery, probe our troubles and difficulties we will find that self-love alone is our greatest enemy and is the cause of our finding so much fault with others, and the reason why we so desire to gratify ourselves in everything."

XIII

TO THE SAME

"At last it has pleased our good God to give some relief to the pains you all have, for so long, endured, and especially you, my dear sister, whom our Lord has chosen to bear this heavy yoke. But as it was His own I am confident, dear sister, His mercy has aided you very much. Blessed forever be His holy name! I trust, too, that His grace will inspire you with strength and courage until He, in His goodness, will perfect this work . . . . You know that our happiness consists in entirely abandoning ourselves to His guidance.

"I have been wonderfully consoled with the hope that our Lord would have diffused great blessings, general as well as particular, on your family. I desire it with all my heart, and I pray you not to be uneasy if you do not obtain, as soon as you would like, by a firmly established tranquility, entire repose and consolation. You know that good is done only little by little. The evil one tries his hand, but he will not win, provided you gather yourselves together and become closely united at the foot of the cross, as the little chickens under the mother's wing when the cat is on the watch."

XIV

TO THE SAME, ON MUTUAL SUPPORT.

"Alas, my dear sisters, from whom will we suffer if not from those with whom we live? Will it be from persons at a distance, from those whom we have never seen, and probably never will see? From what does a member of the body suffer if not from the evil caused it by another member? From whom and through whom has our Lord suffered if not through His Apostles, His Disciples, and the people among whom He lived, who were the people of God? This is to show you, my dear sisters, that our daily crosses come from those only with whom we constantly are." (April 24th, 1649.)

XV

TO THE SAME IN SENDING THEM A LETTER OF St. VINCENT

I must, my dear sisters, tell you, in all simplicity, the thoughts that came to my mind whilst reading this letter. Oh, my dear sisters, the sweetness of his style, his remarks on the graces God has bestowed on you, and on us too, and the instructions his charity so gently gives you, all have inspired me with such a dread that I cannot express it. For I recall how often, through him, God has warned us of our obligations, how often he knew and kindly overlooked our faults and shortcomings, never wearying in inciting and encouraging us, taking all fatherly care of us, and giving himself as much trouble for us as if we were persons of merit. What return have we made him, unfruitful soil that we are? Nothing but displeasure and annoyance, by reason of our infidelities towards God for whom he wishes to gain us. At times it was grief over the departure of some member of the community, or some grievous fault committed against her vocation; at others it was the decline of the entire body that worried him. We are all stupid. It seems that all the admonitions God has caused to be given us have proved only so many useless words given to the wind; and, what is worse, I greatly fear that, having been pronounced in the presence of God and His angels, they will, to our great confusion, reappear at our judgment. Is it not with reason that my heart was seized with fear and just apprehension? Do not imagine that I say all this to frighten you, nor to you alone; I refer to myself and to all who, like me, have not made good use of their vocation. I beseech you all, for the love of the death of our Master, to renew yourselves in His resurrection, and receive the peace He has so often given us in the persons of His apostles. But, remark, He does not give it to them while idle, but while laboring and in memory of the wounds He has suffered for us, thereby teaching us that it is impossible for us to have peace with God, with our neighbor and ourselves, unless Jesus Christ gives it, and, moreover, that He will not grant it but through the merits of his wounds and sufferings. Now, these merits will never be applied to us save by the mortification of ourselves, and this we will acquire by imitating Him in doing the most holy will of God. How

y you are in comparison, not only with other young persons like you, but even with ladies of rank, who seek to be employed in the service of God and His poor, and who have such an ardent desire to do the will of God to be assisted therein! Yet they cannot obtain this consolation. To you nothing is wanting; still you seem dissatisfied, and, instead of making use of the means God gives you for your perfection, you spurn them. Forgive me, my dear sisters, if my affection for you employ such language; for I, myself, have often been guilty of faults, similar to those of which I suspect you. But, once for all, I wish to be faithful to God and I will for this often ask His grace. Do likewise; esteem and read, with affection, your rules and instructions desiring to put them in practice, and labor in all earnestness to do so for the love of God; especially, profit by the advice, the last, perhaps, that God gives you concerning what He desires of you. I have no thought, my dear sisters, of menacing you with the judgment of God; but let you and me fear His indignation if we neglect to accomplish His will."

XVI

PATIENCE IN TRIALS.

In the name of God, my dear sisters, do not grow tired o your troubles nor become disconsolate in seeing yourself deprived of all consolation save in God. Oh, did we know the secrets of God in placing us in this condition, we would perceive that it should be the occasion of our greatest consolation. Eh, well, you see a number of poor whom you cannot succor! God also sees them and He does not relieve them. Bear their burden with them; do your best to give them some little aid, and then remain in peace. Perhaps you share in the distress. If so that is a consolation for you; for, had you plenty, your hearts would be pained in enjoying it whilst seeing our lords and masters suffer much. Besides, God chastises His people for our sins. Is it not reasonable that we should suffer with others? Who are we that we imagine we ought to be exempted from the public miseries? If the mercy of God do not permit us to experience the most severe distress let us be heartily grateful, and believe that it is solely through His goodness and not from any merit on our part. . . . The majority of our sisters in the environs of Paris have been obliged to seek shelter elsewhere;

but, thanks be to God, up to the present they have suffered no
injury or vexation. You know the beautiful ceremony that
takes place to-day at the exposing of the shrine of St. Genevieve.
Oh, how good it is to be faithful to God, Who, as a mark of His
eternal affection, causes such honor to be rendered His faithful servants." (To Sister Barbe, Angiboa, Brienne. 1652.)

XVII

SAME SUBJECT—DANGER OF OFFICE.

"I have learned that Our Lord still continues you His grace
by permitting your infirmities to keep you constant company,
and that, at times, as I believe at present, they cause you great
suffering. You see clearly the way that God wishes you to go
to Him is His royal road of the cross. I am sure you will
cheerfully and willingly allow yourself to be conducted in this
road in order to do His holy will, as I also hope you have done
when His Providence imposed upon you the care of your little
family...... It is only our ignorance that causes us to believe
this to be an honor and a pleasure. Did we but understand
what it is to be a sister servant,—oh, how we, in receiving the
office, would be humbled, knowing what a burden we are to the
house, and what need we have to be supported by all; and also,
when we reflected that thus we become obliged to attend by
our care to all the duties of the house, and to give good
example in everything; and, too, that, if we do our duty well,
we must see that the others are first attended to, and our heart
must include them all. Let us try, my dear sister, to put all
this in practice. Let us prefer to our own wishes those of our
sisters when they are not contrary to the most Holy will of
God." (To Sister Charlotte. Richelieu.)

XVIII

SOME EXTRACTS OF LETTERS.

—"Those who are in office should be the mules of the
Community."

—"I believe you have the pleasure of the Queen's presence at Fontainbleau. If her Majesty should desire to speak with you do not raise any difficulty, though the respect you owe give you a fear to approach her. Her kindness and charity inspire the most humble with confidence to represent to her their wants. Do not forget to truly present those of the poor. I need not recommend modesty and reserve with those high personages. I know you have a singular esteem for those virtues; but do all you can for your poor, particularly in regard to the spiritual service you owe them."

—"I think you do all you can to comfort our Sister N., and that you look upon her as a young plant from which you may, one day, hope good fruit to present on the eternal table of our good God."

XIX

ADVICES TO SISTERS SUGGESTED BY THEIR NAMES.

My good Sister, are you very brave? Do you do, as the good shepherd, who risks his life for the welfare and security of the flock entrusted to his care? Yes, I believe so; for, if we have not always the opportunity of exposing our lives we have those in which we are required to give up our own will in order to accord with others, to overcome our habits and inclinations that we may give example to our sisters, and to conquer our passions so as not to excite those of others. This is what we are obliged to do, my dear sister, in order to maintain cordiality, to exercise patience, and to be in the close union of the charity of Jesus crucified, which I implore God to give us. Please say to Sister Mary Martha that I trust that she will be Mary Martha in effect as well as in name, that the name Mary obliges her to great purity, meekness and modesty, and requires her to be ever ready to do a favor for others; that her name Martha calls for great exactitude to the rule in all its points. As for Sister Cecilia, oh, what calm and tranquility she should possess that, after the example of her patron saint, she may sweetly sing the praises of God! And our Sister Bridget should love the duration of suffering in the continuance and accomplishment of the designs of God upon her. I hope God will grant Sister Frances that her strength of mind may supply for the weakness and smallness of her body, but, for this, tell her, my sister, she has need of great courage. I sincerely hope that her sickness is entirely gone and that she is thoroughly cured. What is good Sister Catherine doing? Do the exertions of great labor terrify her? Has she sufficient love for God, like her dear patroness, to resist all? Tell her that it all depends on herself, and that the same dear Spouse has as much grace and love to give her, provided she be faithful, as He gave the great St. Catherine. I say the same to Sister Barbe, to whom I wish perseverance and an increase in perfection, as also to you all, dear sisters. Be always mindful of the wants of the community, for it has need of your prayers and especially of the merit God gives to actions done for the service of the poor."

XX

TO A SICK SISTER.

"My dearly loved sister, I adore, with all my heart, the order of Divine Providence in the disposition He seems to wish to make of your life. If it be His holy will to call to Himself your soul, blessed be His Holy Name! He knows the regret I feel in being unable to assist you in this last act of love which I know you will make in very willingly returning your soul to the eternal Father in the desire to honor the death of His Son. Our good Sister Elizabeth will give you the assurance of the affection of all our Sisters, and their hope that you will remember them in heaven when God will show you that mercy; and particularly of our Sister Anne Marie, who says she is very sorry she cannot be with you at the last moment. Remember, dearest sister, the needs of the poor community to which God has called you. Be its advocate with His Goodness that it may please Him to accomplish His designs in regard to it. And, if His bounty permits, beg our good angels to help us. Good evening, my very dear sister, I pray with all my heart that Jesus crucified may bless you with all the virtues He has practised on the Cross."

XXI

PETITION FOR THE APOSTOLIC BENEDICTION, 1652.

Louise de Marillac, twenty-seven years a widow, servant of Jesus Christ, and in will, if not in reality, of His members, the poor, most attached by obedience to the Holy Father, in quality of Roman Catholic, and on account of the desire, long cherished, wished to receive, at least once in her life-time, the Apostolic Benediction. She, therefore, humbly asks M. Berthe, a Priest of the Mission, to present her in spirit at the feet of the Most Holy Father, true vice-gerent of Jesus Christ, on account of the zeal which His Holiness displays for the faith of the Church. She begs this in order that she may obtain the grace from our good God of doing, in all things, for the rest of her days, His holy will. In return for this charity, she will consider herself obliged to pray to God for His Holiness.

XXII

WILL OF MADEMOISELLE LE GRAS.

"In the Name of God the Father, Son, and Holy Ghost.

Prostrate in all humility, in the belief that God is everywhere, sole being and Creator of all immortal souls, with the true knowledge of my own nothingness and inability, without His grace, I very humbly implore His mercy on my miseries which have made me culpable of such ingratitude towards His goodness. And, though I have so often offended this goodness by my wretched sins that I am become unworthy to participate in the merits of Jesus crucified, yet in these I confidingly place all my hope. I beseech the Blessed Virgin to be to me a true mother and protectress, and to obtain for me, at the moment of my death, pardon for the abuse I have made of the graces of God. I, likewise, subject to the good pleasure of God, implore my holy angel guardian, St. Louis, and all the saints, to help me, by their intercession in this so important a passage. And, even were I not obliged, yet would I, for the love of God, submit in honor of the moment of the separation of the Divine soul of my Savior, Who desires the salvation of mine, that I may eternally glorify Him, with His Father, and the Holy Ghost.

"I protest before God, and before all creatures, that I wish to live and die in the bosom of the Holy, Roman Catholic, and Apostolic Church, and I command my son, as far as I can, to do the same, for I believe it to be the only path to paradise, for which we have been created. In the hope that God will grant him this grace I beseech His bounty to take full and entire possession of all that he is, to do in him and with him His most holy will. I likewise pray Him to water, with His efficacious grace, for time and for eternity, the blessing, which, as mother, He has empowered me to give, and which I now give him, in the Name of the Father, and of the Son, and of the Holy Ghost. Amen. I implore the sacred humanity of our Savior to have pity on our sinful souls at the hour of our death.

"I very humbly ask pardon of my guardian angel and of my most honored father and director, by whom it has pleased the mercy of God to hold me, willing, attached to the accomplishment of His most holy will, for the little correspondence and fidelity I have shown for the charitable care with which they have honored me in regard to my salvation. I acknowledge that, without this care, I would often have wretchedly turned away from God.

"I, also, very humbly demand forgiveness of all my dear neighbors whom, by my sins, I have disedified and scandalized; of those whom I have displeased or offended in any manner whatsoever, and of all creatures of which, contrary to the holy will of God, I have made bad use. I abandon myself to God to make such restitution, in this world or the next, as it will please His merciful justice to ordain.

"The obligation of mother, together with the strong natural affection I always had for my son, urges me to recommend to him to remember the care which, for his salvation, the goodness of God had of his education, and to be grateful to Him all his life, and strive never to do anything contrary to His most holy will. To aid you in this, my son, take counsel in all your affairs of persons who are capable and of good life. And that the advice you will receive may be of greater use to you, always ask it before you take any decision; otherwise, you will not freely give your reasons for and against the thing you propose, and then you will only deceive yourself. I rely so much on the generosity of M. Vincent that I am certain he will never refuse you his assistance in your wants, whether temporal or spiritual.

"You well know the obligation under which both you and I are to him, and hence I entreat you, should you ever be so happy as to have the opportunity of serving his community, to do so with all your heart, remembering that you are particularly obliged, not only by gratitude for the benefit we both have received, but also by reason of the service he renders the Church, our mother . . . . .

"I beseech my son to often remember to pray to God for the repose of the soul of his father, and to recall to mind his good life, how he greatly feared God, and was scrupulous in keeping himself irreproachable; especially should he remember his patience in the great sufferings that fell upon him in his last years, and during which he practised very great virtue . . . "

Here follow the different legacies: First, to the Priests of the Mission for masses and good works for the benefit of her and hers, on the anniversary of her death, "and this to honor the moment of the death of Our Lord on the Cross, that the merit of this perpetual divine sacrifice may be applied to those in the agonies of death, and to those persevering in mortal sin, in order, thereby, to obtain for them, from the mercy of God, efficacious grace to withdraw them." Second, to her confessor,

Third, to her god-daughter. Fourth, to the confraternities of which she was a member, "asking pardon of God for having so often failed in the devotions they recommend, and this makes me believe that it is better to enroll ourselves in few and be more faithful to their obligations." Fifth, to the Sisters of Charity, "as a help towards preparing the remedies they use for the sick poor who come to their house, whilst I affirm that I am obliged to do far more for them had God given me the means. Hence I implore my son to be grateful to them for the charity they have shown me, and to look upon it as a very great blessing if God should give him any opportunity to do them a kindness. I exhort him most earnestly not to fail in this." Sixth, to the poor, that some charitable priest will preach a sermon to them, ' begging him, in the name of Our Lord, to speak only for their instruction, teaching them their obligation to know God, the difference between good and bad poor, and how beneficial to their eternal welfare is poverty if they only know how to use it; moreover, what they should do before seeking alms; in what humility they should request it; their obligations of serving God and hearing mass on Sundays and festivals; and strive to induce them to say their night and morning prayers; and all for the glory of God and the salvation of souls who so often are lost through ignorance of their state and of their obligations." Seventh, to her son: "My son, as my sole heir, will at my death enjoy my property after my debts and legacies shall have been paid; at his death all I leave him will pass to the poor whom I substitute my heirs after him. In case he marries and has children, he and his children will enjoy it according to the law regulating substituted successions; but I intend and will that, should he have no legitimate offspring, the poor inherit the little God has given me. And, for this purpose, I humbly beg M. Vincent, founder and general of the Priests of the Mission, and, after him, his successors, to attend to this disposition; so that, should the substitution take place, they may collect the revenue and make an annual distribution; for I know that their principal function is to labor for the salvation of the poor, for which purpose I would, were it possible, willingly give up my life. But in case God gives a firm establishment to the Community of the Sisters of Charity of the parishes, or if it can subsist, as it has done for several years, remaining under the direction of the above named gentlemen of the Mission, my intention and last wish is that, with the exception of a yearly rent of a hundred francs which these same Gentlemen of the Mission will enjoy, the Sisters of Charity inherit, for the ends and on the conditions aforesaid, the little that I leave, that thus that may have more means wherewith to assist the sick poor in those country places where they may find less aid. I pray the goodness of God, should He please to give any merit to this disposition, to apply it as a means to bring down His mercy, of which we have great need for our salvation, on the soul of my son, and on my own, at the moment of death

"I very humbly pray M. Vincent, by the charity God has given him for his neighbor, and by the love he bears the Sacred Humanity of Our Redeemer, to pardon me all neglect of gratitude for the honor he has done me in exercising so much charity towards my son and myself. I now thank him from the bottom of my heart, and I beg him to continue his holy affection for my son and be to him a father, giving him good counsel and aid in all his needs. I also ask him to grant the prayer which, for the love of God, I make him, and his successor, should God call him away before me, of being, with my son, to whom I have proposed the substitution, the executor of this, my will. In return for the charity they will exercise in this point I promise, should God be pleased to show me mercy and permit me to enter His Paradise, to do for them all that a soul can do.

"I remit, and willingly abandon, my soul into the hands of God, its creator and last end: I freely leave my body to earth to await its resurrection. As to the place of my sepulture, I leave it entirely, under the disposition of Divine Providence, to the direction of M. Vincent, simply begging him to remember the great desire I have testified to be buried alongside the wall at the foot of the Church of St. Lazarus, in the little court, which, from the bones found there, appears to have once been a cemetery. I still greatly desire to be interred there, and I ask it of his charity, for the love of God. I also request that there be placed, as soon as possible, against the wall, a large wooden Cross with crucifix attached, and an inscription at its foot bearing the title: "*Only Hope*," the entire to be at the expense of the little I leave, and of which God has given me to dispose in this my testament.

"For my funeral, I declare that I do not wish any greater expense to be incurred than what is usual in the interments of our deceased Sisters; and that, should any desire to have it otherwise. I believe, even now, that he never had any regard for me. Because it is but reasonable that my miserable body, which so often offended God and has occasioned offense, should be held in no consideration. Moreover, though I am unworthy, that would be to pronounce me undeserving to appear as having died as a true Sister of Charity.

"Behold, oh, My God, Thy poor creature prostrate at the feet of Thy Grandeur and Majesty, acknowledging herself a criminal and meriting hell, to which Thy strict justice would have condemned me, were it not for the immense love that has made Thy Son become man to deliver me. May it please Thy Divine Goodness that I, with my son, be of the number of those who, through Him, will eternally glorify Thee! and deign to kindly look upon the acts, desires, and dispositions made in this testament, drawn up in the belief that, such is Thy divine will, which has always directed mine, and without which, I protest, with all my strength, never to will anything, and in which I affirm I wish to terminate my life as I have this writing, which I have done and signed with my hand, this Friday, the 15th day of December, 1645. Louise de Marillac, being by the Grace of God, sound of body and mind."

The 28th of December, 1653, Mademoiselle Le Gras added to this will a codicil, necessitated by the marriage of her son. She terminated thus: "Thou knowest, oh, my God, that I am all Thine, and that Thy Providence, through Thy mercy, has been the guide of my entire life. I thank Thee, my God, for this and humbly ask anew, and from the bottom of my heart, pardon for all my neglect and ingratitude. Moved by Thy will, and renouncing every other consideration, I offer Thee this little disposition; I implore Thee, for the love of Jesus crucified, to give me, my son, and his family, Thy blessing that we may glorify Thee eternally."

Finally, on the 11th of May, 1656, a little daughter having been born to her son, she revoked before a notary the substitution which she had confirmed in the codicil of 1653: "Having every reason to be satisfied with the conduct of Michael Le Gras, esquire, her only son, bailiff of St. Lazarus and advocate of the mint, and of Gabrielle Le Clerc, his wife, in token of the respect and proof of friendship she has received since their marriage, being assured that her above named son, dying without children, will have care to assist the poor with the goods he has, and will have, of the above named lady, his mother," she added a special legacy of eighteen livres a year, in favor of her grand-daughter, "to use in giving a little dinner to the poor of her parish, at which she will serve them."

GETHSEMANI ABBEY,
GETHSEMANI, P. O. KY.

THE END.

www.ingramcontent.com/pod-product-compliance
Lightning Source LLC
Chambersburg PA
CBHW030558300426
44111CB00009B/1026